# IMAGES OF FAIT                    RE
## 700–1500

LONGMAN MEDIEVAL AND RENAISSANCE LIBRARY

General Editors:
CHARLOTTE BREWER, Hertford College, Oxford
N. H. KEEBLE, University of Stirling

Published Titles:

Dee Dyas

# IMAGES OF FAITH IN ENGLISH LITERATURE 700–1500:
## An Introduction

LONGMAN
LONDON AND NEW YORK

**Addison Wesley Longman**
Edinburgh Gate
Harlow
Essex CM20 2JE
England
*and Associated Companies throughout the world.*

*Published in the United States of America*
*by Addison Wesley Longman Inc., New York.*

First published 1997

ISBN 0 582 30192 0 CSD
ISBN 0 582 30191 2 PPR

**British Library Cataloguing-in-Publication Data**

A catalogue record of this book is available
from the British Library

**Library of Congress Cataloging-in-Publication Data**

A catalog entry for this title is available from the
Library of Congress

Set by 7 in 10.5/12 Bembo
Produced by Longman Singapore Publishers (Pte) Ltd.
Printed in Singapore

# Contents

# Preface

To open many medieval English texts is to step into an intriguing but curiously alien world – where not only the language but the landscape may prove unfamiliar. On the horizon can be seen the gleaming ramparts of the Heavenly City and the ever-open gates of Hell. The roads are thronged with pilgrims, the exiled descendants of Adam and Eve, making their way to their eternal destination. Sinners jostle saints; virtues joust with vices. The whole material world is infused with the dimension of eternity and round every corner lies a symbol to be interpreted or a revelation to be received. To the modern reader the scene can appear both confused and confusing – yet the medieval universe has a logic all its own which, once understood, will enormously enhance our appreciation of all that we read and see. Glossaries and translations are available to help us comprehend the words; the object of this book is to offer a guide to the Christian world-view which so profoundly influenced the way those words were put together. Like a medieval tapestry or illuminated manuscript each story is packed with images and, if we can interpret them aright, every image will tell us yet another story.

As the title of this book makes clear, it claims only to be an introduction to a vast and fascinating area. The outline dates are inevitably somewhat imprecise, since so much Old English literature in particular is impossible to date with any certainty. What cannot be denied is that following the arrival of St Augustine in Kent, exactly fourteen hundred years ago, and the parallel mission of the Celtic Church in northern England, Christianity gradually became the dominant cultural influence in these islands and remained so for centuries. The aim of this book is therefore to provide insights into the influence of Christian thought and Church history on medieval literature and to make the process as painless as possible. I have not sought to offer a comprehensive literary survey of the period since there are already many excellent histories available. My approach has been instead to focus on frequently-read texts which require some understanding of their Christian dimension if they are to be properly appreciated, and to set such texts against the events and doctrines which are commonly held to have influenced them. The early chapters therefore sketch the spread of the Christian faith through Anglo-Saxon England and trace the subsequent tensions between Christian and pagan thought, the influence of the Celtic Church, the achievements of Anglo-Saxon culture and learning, and the fresh impetus subsequently given to learning and literature by Alfred the Great.

The five chapters on Middle English literature are obviously closely inter-related and should be viewed in parallel. It is, for example, vital to recognise the tensions in the relationship between the medieval Church and the everyday world, made apparent in the works of Chaucer and Langland, if we are to comprehend the motivation of the anchorites and mystics who felt it necessary to retreat into solitude in order to cultivate an inner life with God. Similarly, the strange blend of homeliness, passion and theological insight which characterised the lyrics can also be observed in the writings of the mystics and again in the religious plays which developed during the period. Passionate spiritual longing, blunt recognition of the Church's faults, sophisticated storytelling and heartfelt cries for reformation all surface time and again, sometimes in surprising combinations.

Even an introduction to such a rich and fascinating area of study has of necessity to be selective. It has not been my purpose to attempt to cover every area of critical debate but rather to offer a frame-work to assist in the appreciation and evaluation of ongoing dis-cussion. I have also sought, as far as space has allowed, to point the reader to the many valuable detailed studies of individual texts which are available. The Reference Section provides a short history of the early Church, together with brief biographies of key figures, an introduction to the teachings, worship and organisation of the medieval Church, a glossary and bibliography. Subjects covered in the Reference Section are highlighted in bold type in the text.

A book of this kind, spanning more than one discipline, inevitably draws widely upon the expert knowledge of many people. Many of these debts are acknowledged in the notes, but a number of people have been extraordinarily kind in sharing their time and scholarship. The late Alun Davies was the first to urge me to attempt this project and Rosalind Field and Helen Phillips have been tireless in providing support and feedback. Any attempt to make such a wide range of ideas accessible without falling into the trap of over-simplification is fraught with perils, and Professor Derek Brewer, Professor Christopher Brooke, Professor James Cross, Professor Christine Fell, Dr Lynne Grundy, Professor Bernard Hamilton, Professor Robert Markus, Professor Peter Meredith, Dr Diane Speed and Professor Thorlac Turville-Petre have all been generous with wise advice and encouragement. I am also grateful to Charlotte Brewer and the staff of Longman for their enthusiasm, helpfulness and guidance. The shortcomings which remain are of course my own. Finally, I would like to acknowledge the support of all my friends and family, especially that of my parents and my husband, who has encouraged and sustained me through the long years of research and writing. This book is therefore dedicated to Stuart and our sons Luke and Ben, without whose presence in my life it might well have been completed much sooner, but without whose love it might never have been finished at all.

Dee Dyas
Nottingham
March 1997

Now I preye to hem alle that herkne this litel tretys or rede, that if ther be any thyng in it that liketh hem, that therof they thanken oure Lord Jhesu Crist, of whom procedeth al wit and al goodnesse. And if ther be any thyng that displese hem, I preye hem also that they arrette it to the defaute of myn unkonnynge and nat to my wyl, that wolde ful fayn have seyd bettre.

(*Canterbury Tales*, X. 1081–2)

# Acknowledgements

We are grateful to the following for permission to reproduce copyright material:

Faber & Faber Ltd for extracts from *A Choice of Anglo-Saxon Verse*, selected and translated by Richard Hamer (1970); Penguin Books Ltd for extracts from *A History of The English Church and People* by Bede, translated by Leo Sherley-Price, (Penguin Classics 1955, Revised edition 1986), copyright © Leo Sherley-Price, 1955, 1986, and *Alfred the Great: Asser's Life of King Alfred and Other Contemporary Sources*, translated by Simon Keynes and Michael Lapidge (Penguin Classics 1983) Translation copyright © Simon Keynes and Michael Lapidge, 1983, and an extract from *Consolation of Philosophy* by Boethius, translated by V E Watts (Penguin Classics, 1969) copyright © V E Watts, 1969.

# Chapter 1

# *Beowulf* and a World Made New

metod hie ne cuþon,
dæda demend,   ne wiston hie drihten god,
ne hie huru heofena helm   herian ne cuþon,
wuldres waldend.

they knew not the Lord,
the Judge of our deeds,   were ignorant of God,
knew not how to worship   our Protector above,
the King of Glory.

(*Beowulf*, 180–3)

PROLOGUE

In the summer of AD 596 a party of apprehensive Christian **monks** waited in the island monastery of Lerins off the coast of Provence. They had sailed from Rome on the instructions of **Pope Gregory** to bring the faith to the pagan English who had conquered the remote islands to the north of Gaul, driving many of the Christian Britons into the mountains of Wales and the far West. Ahead of them still lay the turbulent land of Gaul and beyond that terrors which they could only imagine. Sworn to obedience as they were, their courage failed at the prospect. The Anglo-Saxon historian **Bede** (c. 673–735),[1] writing of the founding of the English Church from his **monastery** a century later, pictured them as 'appalled at the idea of going to a barbarous, fierce and pagan nation of whose very language they were ignorant' (Bede, *HE*, I:23). The alarmed monks sent their leader **Augustine** back to Rome to beg the **Pope** to release them from this perilous mission. Gregory, however, remained firm. Augustine was sent back to his task, his authority enhanced and his resolve strengthened. The mission went on.

Bede's dramatic preamble to the story of the conversion of the English was no doubt intended to emphasise the importance of the Roman mission for the future of his people. In fact, according to

Bede's own narrative, the prospects were not as bleak as Augustine and his companions may have imagined; the ruler of Kent, the kingdom in which they eventually landed, already had a Christian wife who was allowed to pray in an old church 'built in honour of St Martin during the Roman occupation of Britain' (Bede, *HE*, I:26). Nor were the Pope's emissaries the only bearers of the Christian message. On an island off the west coast of Scotland the Irish **monk Columba** (d. 597) had founded a monastery in the Celtic tradition which would play a vital role in the evangelisation of northern Britain. Yet Bede's account is important because it provides evidence of an ongoing sense of polarisation between the Christian faith and aspects of the culture which it encountered, and of the extraordinary way in which the supposed barbarians availed themselves of the great wealth of learning which Christianity brought in its wake. Bede the monk was acutely aware of the spiritual limitations of his pagan forbears; Bede the scholar, later described as *candela ecclesiae*,[2] was only one of many Anglo-Saxon men and women whose work as scribes, scholars, craftsmen and missionaries would illuminate western Europe.

With the missionaries came the Latin alphabet and a strong emphasis on literacy; those educated by the Church studied Latin grammar and literature, memorised the Latin **Psalter** and worshipped daily, using the Latin **liturgy**. Equipped with the universal language of Christianity, Anglo-Saxon scholars and poets were exposed to a wide range of knowledge and literary forms which inevitably influenced the literature produced in England in the centuries between **Augustine**'s arrival and the Norman Conquest. The world of the Anglo-Saxons, chiefly centred on the cold grey waters of the North Sea, expanded to encompass Rome, the Mediterranean and even the Holy Land. Augustine's mission had implications far beyond his immediate brief: the conversion of the English was to result in the development of a literature which would absorb and ultimately overshadow the ancient glories of Greece and Rome. Much of the fascination (and many of the difficulties) of Old English literature spring from the interplay of cultures which the process of conversion brought into being. Defining the beliefs and attitudes of the society which the missionaries encountered is not easy: surviving manuscripts are the work of monastic scribes and editors and accounts of pre-Christian customs may therefore be ill-informed or deliberately amended. It is clear, however, that Christianity brought a world-view which set the lives of men and women within a clearly-defined pattern of

**creation**, **sin**, **salvation** and **judgement** and which emphasised the presence and power of a benevolent Creator in a fallen world. The cosmic struggle between good and evil, evidenced in the stories of the **Bible** and the **legends** of Christian **saints**, offered a framework within which heroism, loyalty and sacrifice took on new significance.

The process of assimilating new beliefs and behaviour was long and often unsteady. The conversion of a people is never an instantaneous or orderly occurrence, a factor which needs to be kept in mind in the discussion of Old English poetry and prose. Kings and courts made formal decisions to adopt the new religion but it took many years for changes in social and moral codes to permeate everyday life. There was also, inevitably, a significant degree of interaction and synthesis. Anglo-Saxon Christianity owed much to Roman and Celtic traditions but it was also the faith of a Germanic people who interpreted it in the light of their own concerns and affinities. The poets who produced *Beowulf*, the *Seafarer* and the *Dream of the Rood* stand distanced from the present age not only by their way of life but by their beliefs and imaginative preoccupations. The greater our understanding of the way in which they perceived their world and of the way in which the teaching of the Church influenced those perceptions, the greater will be our appreciation of their legacy.

THE ANGLO-SAXONS

Much of our knowledge of the Germanic peoples who came to Britain during the fifth and sixth centuries is derived from the surviving poetry and the growing evidence supplied by archaeological discoveries. Their roots lay in the coastlands of northern Europe which they had left in such numbers that **Bede**, writing in the early eighth century, described one area, the homeland of the Angles, as being depopulated to his day. Bede offers a somewhat simplified version of the settlement, based on the kingdoms of his day:

> These newcomers were from the three most formidable races of Germany, the Saxons, Angles and Jutes. From the Jutes are descended the people of Kent and the Isle of Wight, and those in the province of the West Saxons opposite the Isle of Wight who are called Jutes to this day. From the Saxons . . . came the East, South and West Saxons. And from the Angles . . . are descended the East and Middle Angles, the Mercians, all the Northumbrian stock . . . and the other English peoples.
>
> (Bede, *HE*, I:15)

Around the time of **Augustine**'s arrival the kingdoms described by Bede were gradually taking shape. These were in essence confederations of tribes which had settled in the same areas. Leaders were chosen for their ancestry and their prowess in war. Shifts of power were frequent and it seems to have been common for certain kings to exercise overlordship over kingdoms other than their own. These overlords, or *bretwaldas*, were to play a key role in the spread of Christianity from kingdom to kingdom. For its stability, Anglo-Saxon society depended heavily on two fundamental principles: loyalty to one's lord and loyalty to one's kin. As early as 98 AD, the Roman historian Tacitus described the existence among the Germanic tribes of the *comitatus* principle, the close bond between a leader and his retainers. 'The chiefs fight for victory, the companions for their chief' (*Tacitus Germania*, XIV). Such companions counted it a disgrace to leave the field of battle alive after their leader had fallen. As the centuries passed and Anglo-Saxon literature developed, this ideal (though sometimes honoured in the breach rather than the observance) remained a recurring theme. It is seen clearly in the heroic poetry, as in the faithfulness shown by Wiglaf, Beowulf's young thane and kinsman, when confronted by the seemingly invincible dragon:

> Ne þynceð me gerysne   þæt we rondas beren
> eft to earde,   nemne we æror mægen
> fane gefyllan,   feorh ealgian
> Wedra ðeodnes.

> It is hardly right   that we should bear shields
> back to our homes   unless we can first
> kill off this monster,   save the life
> of the king of the Weders.

(Beowulf, 2653–6)

The *Battle of Maldon*, composed towards the end of the Anglo-Saxon period to commemorate the battle fought in 991, still articulates the same ideal, as Byrhtnoth's companions stand their ground, loyalty and courage undiminished though all hope is gone:

> frام ic ne wille,
> ac ic me be healfe   minum hlaforde,
> be swa leofan men,   licgan þence.

> Hence I will not,
> But I intend to die beside my lord,
> Give up my life beside so dear a chief.

(Battle of Maldon, 317–19)

From their own early conquests until the final defeat at the hands of the Normans, no Anglo-Saxon leader could expect more than brief interludes of peace. External threats from neighbouring kingdoms, or in later centuries from marauding Norsemen, were often coupled with danger from rivals within. Few Anglo-Saxon kings died peacefully in their beds. Loyalty, therefore, was not so much a romantic ideal as a practical necessity. No leader could long survive its waning. Nor was such commitment a one-sided affair. To attract and retain warriors, a king was expected to pay and pay generously. Not for nothing are kings described in the poetry as 'ring-givers', 'gold-friends', and 'treasure-guardians'. The status of a loyal companion was much enhanced by the gift of an ornamented sword or skilfully-crafted helmet.[3] The desirability of such rewards and the honour that they bestowed on the recipient are brought to life by the Sutton Hoo treasure: the grave goods of a seventh-century king now on display in the British Museum.[4] There was, however, a reverse side to this gleaming coin. James Campbell comments: 'To keep giving, [the king] must keep taking.'[5] Hence loyalty at home was purchased at the cost of conflict with neighbours and the ultimate risk of defeat. Loyalty to one's kin could also be as potent a force for discord as for harmony. Kinsmen inherited not only obligations of friendship but also the responsibility to pursue family feuds. It is therefore not surprising that the world reflected in *Beowulf* is also far from stable: as Barbara Raw comments, 'One striking feature of royal power in *Beowulf* is its fragility.'[6] References to splendid gifts are often linked with intimations of future treachery and violent death. While the grateful Hrothgar heaps gifts upon the victorious Beowulf, the bard's songs foreshadow the doom of his own house. Beowulf's final triumph, the slaying of the dragon and the acquisition of its treasure hoard, is achieved only at the cost of his own life.

With the advent of the invaders, the Roman towns had been largely left to decay. The *Ruin* describes the remains of one such town:

brosnade burgsteall.   Betend crungon
hergas to hrusan.   Forþon þas hofu dreorgiað.

The city crumbled, its repairers fell,
Its armies to the ground. And so these halls
Are empty.

(*Ruin*, 28–9)

England was a land of small settlements: pinpricks of light surrounded by a vast impenetrable darkness. The warmth and security of the great halls (such as Edwin of Northumbria's hall at Yeavering) must have contrasted sharply with the great tracts of forest and fenland, inhabited by the nameless terrors which stalked the dark places of the popular imagination. Our somewhat meagre understanding of pre-Christian Anglo-Saxon beliefs[7] does not seem to indicate that they offered a great measure of comfort in such an uncertain world. The study of place-names has indicated the existence of shrines, often associated with hills and groves, where gods such as Woden, Tiw, Thunor and Frig were worshipped. These deities were invoked by those seeking victory in war and good luck in everyday life. Trees and wells too were associated with spiritual forces, and charms and incantations would have been used to ward off evil influences. Many charms survived to be written down in the eleventh century, thinly covered by a Christian veneer which may have made them acceptable to the **monastic** scribes.[8] Burial customs may have been intended not only to provide comforts for the afterlife but also to prevent the dead from troubling the living. Fears of malevolent forces and monsters persisted well beyond the Conversion: Christians too believed in the existence of evil powers opposed to the welfare of mankind. Beowulf was not the only heroic figure to confront the likes of Grendel, the walker in the night, who came gliding through the shadows and haunted fell and fen. St Guthlac, the hero of two Old English poems found in the Exeter Book, is described by his eighth-century biographer Felix engaging in spiritual warfare against demons in his fenland retreat, a place where ordinary men could not live on account of 'the unknown portents', the 'terrors of various shapes' and 'the phantoms of demons which haunted it' (*Felix's Life of Saint Guthlac*, XXV).

## THE CONVERSION BEGINS

**Bede**'s account of the early stages of the Roman mission was based, according to the Preface to his *Ecclesiastical History*, on records and traditions preserved by the church in Canterbury and copies of papal letters, obtained from Rome. The narrative reveals not only Bede's own obvious sympathies with **Augustine**'s cause but the delicate balance which needed to be struck between the demands of the new religion and the existing loyalties of the English. According to Bede, Augustine's mission began well. Upon landing, he sent interpreters to Aethelbert, King of Kent, announcing that 'they came from Rome bearing very glad news, which infallibly assured all who would receive it of eternal joy in heaven and an everlasting kingdom' (Bede, *HE*, I:25). It is likely that highly pragmatic political considerations prompted the powerful Aethelbert, whose *imperium* (overlordship) stretched as far as the Humber, to give these messengers an audience. Some nine years earlier he had brought home a Christian bride, the daughter of the Frankish king of Paris, and he was presumably not averse to further links with influential states across the Channel. He was, we are told, impressed by Augustine's words and character but reluctant to abandon deep-rooted traditional loyalties (Bede, *HE*, I:25). The **monks** were granted a dwelling in Canterbury and permission to preach freely. By 601, Aethelbert himself had been baptised and Augustine had despatched messages to Rome asking for reinforcements and advice on the establishment of the English Church. Additional help eventually arrived in the persons of Mellitus, Justus and Paulinus, who were to become the first **bishops** of London, Rochester and York respectively. They brought from Rome everything considered 'necessary for the worship and service of the church, including sacred vessels, altar coverings, church ornaments, **vestments** for **priests** and **clergy**, **relics** of the holy **Apostles** and **martyrs** and many books' (Bede, *HE*, I:29). These priorities were significant. The Church which Augustine was to establish would be enriched by liturgical splendour, focus heavily on the relics and shrines of the **saints** and give high priority to scholarship. The seeds of the rich complexity of medieval English literature were being sown. Equally significant were **Gregory**'s instructions on managing the transition from the old to the new religion. Writing to King Aethelbert, Gregory urged him to 'suppress the worship of idols, and destroy their shrines' (Bede, *HE*, I:32), yet a letter which he sent to Mellitus some three weeks later shows a change of approach: 'We have been giving careful thought to the affairs of the English, and have come to the conclusion that the temples of the idols among that people should on no account be destroyed' (Bede, *HE*, I:30). Pagan temples were not to be torn down but sprinkled with holy water and rededicated to the worship of the true God. Festivals likewise were to be given a new meaning and the religious instincts of the people a new orientation:

> In this way we hope that the people, seeing that their temples are not destroyed, may abandon their error and, flocking more readily to their

accustomed resorts, may come to know and adore the true God. And since they have a custom of sacrificing many oxen to demons, let some other solemnity be substituted in its place, such as a day of Dedication or the Festivals of the holy martyrs whose relics are enshrined there . . . If the people are allowed some worldly pleasures in this way, they will more readily come to desire the joys of the spirit. For it is certainly impossible to eradicate all errors from obstinate minds at one stroke, and whoever wishes to climb to a mountain top climbs step by step and not in one leap.

(Bede, *HE*, I:30)

**Gregory**'s recognition that the majority of the population would need to be wooed into acceptance of the new faith, and that their present 'pleasures' needed to be re-directed rather than forbidden, had implications for the use which the Church was to make of vernacular poetry as a significant means of communicating Christian truth. Such guarded tolerance had also been sanctioned in the highly influential writings of **Augustine of Hippo** (354–420), who had recognised in some classical pagan literature and forms a genuine (albeit secondary) value:

If those who are called philosophers . . . have said things which are indeed true and are well accommodated to our faith, they should not be feared; rather, what they have said should be taken from them as from unjust possessors and converted to our use. Just as the Egyptians had not only idols and grave burdens which the people of Israel detested and avoided, so they also had vases and ornaments of gold and silver and clothing which the Israelites took with them secretly when they fled, as if to put them to a better use . . . In the same way all the teachings of the pagans contain not only simulated and superstitious imaginings . . . but also liberal doctrines more suited to the uses of truth, and some most useful precepts concerning morals . . . When the Christian separates himself in spirit from their miserable society, he should take this treasure with him for the just use of teaching the gospel.

(*On Christian Doctrine*, Bk II, Ch. XL)

In its turn the English Church sought to observe the morals to be drawn from pagan epics and to use poetry to touch the hearts of literate and illiterate alike. Thus **Bede** could say of **Caedmon**, the first recorded composer of poems in English: 'These verses of his have stirred the hearts of many folk to despise the world and to aspire to heavenly things. Others after him tried to compose religious poems in English' (Bede, *HE*, IV:24). Caedmon's purpose, adds Bede, was 'to turn his hearers from delight in wickedness and to inspire them to love and to do good.' Poetry turned to the service of Christ would urge men and women not only to heroism but to holiness.

## EXPANSION AND REVERSES

In 602 **Augustine** made his first recorded contacts with the Celtic Churches. Christianity came as a new religion to the Anglo-Saxons but not to the country which they inhabited. During the centuries of Roman rule the Christian faith had flourished among the British. They in turn had exercised a profound influence upon the people of Ireland when St Patrick (himself kidnapped as a young man from the shores of Britain) helped to establish a Church noted for its learning and missionary zeal. The influence of the Irish Celtic missionaries would prove crucial in the conversion of Northumbria, but Augustine's contacts with the British **bishops** from Wales and the West were less happy. The British clergy, nursing resentment towards the invaders and suspicion of the Romans, were not predisposed to consider unity. Augustine, less than conciliatory towards their traditions, failed to win their allegiance and their support for his work among the English. There were other problems for the Roman missionaries to face. In several kingdoms an initial response to the new faith was subsequently overwhelmed by a fierce pagan reaction. Other converts were less than wholehearted. Raedwald, King of East Anglia, baptised in Kent under the patronage of his *bretwalda* (overlord) Aethelbert, decided on his return home that it was politic to maintain both Christian and pagan altars in his temple. In 616, twenty years after the mission began, crises broke in Essex and Kent. Christian kings were now succeeded by sons strongly opposed to the new faith. The **bishops** of Rochester and London decided to abandon the ungrateful English and retreat to Gaul. According to **Bede**, Laurentius, **Archbishop** of Canterbury, was prevented from joining the rout by a dream of **St Peter**, whose verbal and physical chastisement changed his mind. In the morning the chastened bishop showed his scars to the king who, we are told, promptly renounced heathenism and requested **baptism** (*HE*, II:6).

The church in Kent was now poised for its most significant advance. Edwin of Northumbria, wishing to marry the sister of King Eadbald of Kent, promised her freedom of worship and expressed willingness to accept the new faith himself, if his advisers so recommended. The elements of Edwin's conversion, as described by **Bede**, shed light on the priorities of kings and the close-knit society which they ruled. There were, firstly, political advantages in adopting the new faith. Edwin himself had suffered exile and danger and was only too aware of the uncertain future of kings. Close links with a powerful ally, such as Eadbald, would have been highly desirable. He received flatteringly friendly messages from the **Pope** in Rome, another connection not to be despised. In addition the Christian God seemed to serve his followers well in battle; and the shadow of war always lay across the minds of kings. Edwin, we are told, listened carefully to the teaching of Paulinus, the queen's chaplain and **bishop**-elect. Eventually Edwin was convinced, but his *witan* (council) had to be consulted before he took a step so significant for his kingdom. The discussions attributed to these Northumbrian nobles suggest the factors, practical and philosophical, which may have opened minds to consider the new religion. Coifi, the high priest, is said to have been dissatisfied with the rewards of the established pagan religion, while to another counsellor Bede attributes a speech indicating a longing for certainties in an unpredictable world:

> Your majesty, when we compare the present life of man on earth with that time of which we have no knowledge, it seems to me like the swift flight of a lone sparrow through the banqueting-hall where you are sitting at dinner on a winter's day with your thanes and counsellors. In the midst there is a comforting fire to warm the room; outside, the storms of winter rain or snow are raging. This sparrow flies swiftly in through one door of the hall, and out through another. While he is inside, he is safe from the winter storms; but after a few moments of comfort, he vanishes from sight into the wintry world from which he came. Even so, man appears on earth for a little while; but of what went before this life or of what follows, we know nothing. Therefore if this new teaching has brought any more certain knowledge, it seems only right that we should follow it.
>
> (*HE*, II:13)

The 'new teaching' contained in the Christian faith claimed that it could indeed supply those missing elements: 'what went before this life', and (of even greater practical interest) 'what follows'. Christian **doctrine**, founded on the **Bible**, offered a complete account of the history and the purpose of the world from its **creation** by an all-powerful God to its predicted dissolution on the Day of Judgement. Mankind, it taught, had become alienated from God through Adam's rebellion in the Garden of Eden; hence the problems of **sin** and the evil which all could sense, whether in the lives of men and women or the dark shapes of lurking monsters. All was not lost however. God had acted to rescue men, sending his Son, Jesus **Christ**, to live on earth, die to win forgiveness for their **sin** and rise again from death. Christ even stormed **hell** itself to rescue those who had been languishing there, a theme which strongly appealed both to Anglo-Saxon and later medieval writers. After this brief life, then, there was the prospect of eternal joy with God, for those who chose allegiance to this new lord, declared themselves his followers through **baptism** and sought to follow his commandments. This was the message which had spread outwards from Jerusalem, which had transformed the Roman Empire and was now gradually taking root amongst the Anglo-Saxons. Edwin, 'with all the nobility of his kingdom and a large number of humbler folk', accepted the new faith and was baptised on Easter Day 627 at York. There followed six years of intensive evangelism during a period of peace, to which **Bede**, writing a century later, looked back with a touch of nostalgia: 'The proverb still runs that a woman could carry her newly-born babe across the island from sea to sea without any fear of harm' (*HE*, II:16). Inevitably, the brief idyll did not last. In 632 Edwin was defeated by the combined forces of Penda, the heathen king of Mercia and Cadwalla, the Christian king of Gwynnedd, North Wales. The Welshman, more conscious of hatred for the usurping English than affinity with their beliefs, was ruthless in victory. Paulinus and the widowed queen fled back to the safety of Kent and the future of the Northern Church hung in the balance. Such setbacks were mirrored elsewhere. Not all kings were single-minded in their new allegiance and their successors might well revert to paganism, especially in times of crisis. The establishment of the Christian faith was a long process:

> The question is sometimes put why the Anglo-Saxons were converted to Christianity so quickly. The truth is that they were not converted at all quickly. In spite of there being good political and cultural reasons for the conversion of kings to Christianity, in spite of an extraordinary galaxy of able and saintly missionaries, it took nearly 90 years to convert just the kings and the greater part of their aristocracy, not to speak of the countryside which was a matter of centuries ... The old religious instincts died hard.[9]

The resentful seventh-century Northumbrian peasants described by

**Bede** cannot have been alone in their complaints that the **monks** 'have done away with the old ways of worship and now nobody knows what to do' (Bede, *Life of Cuthbert*, Ch. 3). Life was also far from easy for those kings whose profession of faith was genuine. Sigebert of East Anglia, having become a Christian in exile in Gaul, eventually abdicated, entering a **monastery** where Bede records that 'he devoted his energies to winning an everlasting kingdom' (*HE*, 3:18). When his former kingdom was attacked by the marauding Penda, Sigebert was dragged protesting from the **cloister** to encourage the troops. Refusing to defend himself, he died in the ensuing battle. Some years later, his namesake Sigebert of the East Saxons was murdered by two of his kinsmen, allegedly 'because he was too lenient towards his enemies, and too readily forgave injuries when the offenders asked pardon' (*HE*, III:22). The Anglo-Saxon code required satisfaction for death or injury. A king who preferred to forgive seems to have been regarded as suspiciously weak. Where **Gospel** ethics met pagan practices head-on, the victory was not always decisive. Successive legal codes show that the Church's efforts to encourage the payment of *wergild* (the 'man-price' used to assess compensation according to rank) as a substitute for vengeance proved an uphill struggle throughout the period. Where payment of *wergild* was impossible or withheld, then many still felt themselves duty-bound to exact retribution. Dorothy Whitelock cites a family feud which was still being vigorously pursued in the eleventh century.[10]

In other areas too, difficulties remained to trouble spiritual and temporal leaders alike. Between 670 and 690 **Archbishop** Theodore was compelled to issue decrees against the provision of grave-goods for the afterlife (not thought necessary for those bound for the Christian **heaven**) and to appoint **penances** for those who persisted in sacrificing 'to devils' (i.e. the old gods) and other pre-Christian practices. Kings too threw their authority behind the enforcement of the standards required by the new faith. The laws of Wihtred, King of Kent, issued in 695, show areas where tensions persisted:

6. If a priest permits an illicit union, or neglects the baptism of a sick person, or is so drunk that he cannot [perform it], he is to abstain from his ministration until the bishop's sentence.

12. If a husband sacrifice to devils without his wife's knowledge, he is to be liable to pay all his goods and healsfang (apparently a proportion of the *wergild*); if they both sacrifice to devils, they are to be liable to pay healsfang and all their goods.

(*EHD*, Vol. 1, No. 31)

A century after Augustine's arrival, therefore, at a time when the whole country (except Sussex) had formally accepted the faith, old practices were still very much alive. The English kingdoms might be Christian in name but the new beliefs had yet to win the hearts and minds of many of their people.

'PAGAN' AND 'CHRISTIAN' ELEMENTS IN *BEOWULF*

It is against this background – the gradual cultural shift brought about by the coming of Christianity and the persistence of pre-Christian traditions and practices – that the achievement of the *Beowulf*-poet must be set and the problems posed by the poem considered. *Beowulf*, as we have it, is a poem which looks back to the heroes of Scandinavian tradition from a point somewhere in the Christian centuries. The only surviving manuscript was copied around 1000 AD but suggested dates for the poem's original composition range from the eighth to the eleventh centuries.[11] It has been argued[12] that the poem's references to the **Old Testament** Book of **Genesis** rule out an early date, since new converts would have been grounded first in the teachings of Christ and only later have moved on to less crucial doctrines. There are however theological, practical, cultural and intellectual arguments which indicate that the content of the early chapters of Genesis, dealing with the **Creation** and the **Fall of Mankind**, would have been included in basic Christian instruction of the period. The message brought by the missionaries concerned mankind's need of redemption. The means of **salvation** was described in the **New Testament**; the reason why it was necessary, mankind's estrangement from God, could only be explained by the dramatic story of the Temptation and **Fall** of Adam and Eve. It is clear from the surviving religious poetry that there was also considerable interest in the story of **Satan**'s rebellion and expulsion from heaven and his subsequent success in enticing man into sin. Moreover, faced with the animistic beliefs and practices of the pagan Anglo-Saxons, the missionaries would have found it essential to introduce a new concept of the world in which they lived and to explain that the world was not simply a dark, mysterious place, peopled by malignant spirits against whom human beings strove bravely but in vain. No sensible person would cease to offer sacrifices to pagan deities or the spirits of hill and spring unless convinced that these forces were superseded by a benevolent Creator who could be relied upon to protect His adherents and overcome evil. The early chapters of Genesis provided the key to this view of God and it is significant that even as he introduces Grendel, the *Beowulf*-poet reminds the audience of the fate of the giants who dared to oppose Him. That teaching concerning the **Creation** was offered at an early stage by Anglo-Saxon missionaries at work in Germany is evidenced by a letter (722–32) from Bishop Daniel of Winchester to Boniface in which he suggests arguments by which pagans might be convinced:

> When they have perforce learnt that the gods had a beginning, seeing that some were begotten by others, they should then be asked whether they think this world had a beginning, or has always existed without a beginning. If it had a beginning, who created it? . . . If they contend that the world always existed without beginning, strive to refute and overcome this with many proofs and arguments.
>
> (*EHD*, Vol. 1, No. 167)

Culturally, the **Old Testament** clearly appealed to the Anglo-Saxons, as the surviving poetry demonstrates. A tribal people themselves, they felt an affinity with the Israelites and were hardly likely to be offended by tales of bloody battle and God-given victory. The Anglo-Saxon poems *Genesis, Exodus, Daniel* and *Judith* all demonstrate the appeal of narratives which offered considerable scope for both entertainment and spiritual teaching. Intellectually, the **early Church** placed great emphasis upon the importance of the Old Testament, particularly as it foreshadowed the events of the New. **Gregory**'s great work of exegesis (highly influential in the Anglo-Saxon Church) was his commentary on Job, while **Augustine**, seeking a model for his teaching on pagan literature, turned to the story of the Israelites in Exodus. The Psalms too were a vital part of the church's life, dominating the pattern of worship and memorised by many. Whatever other reasons there may be, therefore, for seeking to set *Beowulf* in a particular time or place, it is unlikely that the Old Testament allusions in themselves can be used to exclude an early date.

Scholars have expended much energy on deciding whether the Christian references in the poem are integral to it and thus part of the world-view of its creator(s), or the work of a monastic scribe who found the original tone unacceptable. Was it the creation of a traditional *scop* (poet), bidden like Hrothgar's bard to entertain at the feast (*Beowulf*, 1065–70), or of a cleric, deliberately using the tales of the past to point a moral for the present? Should the poem be understood as pure entertainment or as a complex Christian allegory designed for edification?[13] It is essential to establish such historical background as we can before attempting to form a judgement on these issues. *Beowulf* must have been written down (whether by its composer or by a later scribe) by a man who owed his literacy to a clerical teacher. All learning derived from the Church and it is unlikely that anyone not destined to play some role in the Christian community would have been taught the precious skills of reading and writing. There is also the question of the poem's survival. It is not surprising, given the mixed atmosphere of Anglo-Saxon society, that a poem commemorating heathen forbears should have been composed even as late as the eighth or early ninth century. Kings continued to trace their lineage from Woden, Bede himself took pride in the identity of the Anglo-Saxon race, and the continuing sense of kinship with Continental Saxons inspired considerable missionary activity. The preservation and transmission in writing of such a poem is, however, another matter. Well-organised as the monasteries were to become, copyists' time remained precious and parchment expensive. *Beowulf* (longer than the Gospel of Mark) must have been considered of sufficient value to have been allotted a share of costly writing materials and scribal time. Probably a number of tales dealing with the pagan past did in fact fail the test of clerical censorship. It was no part of the church's duty to relay the customs which it sought to root out. Bede in *De Temporum Ratione* outlines his own knowledge of the pagan festivals, but adds firmly: 'Thanks be to you, good Jesus, for turning us from these vanities and granting us to offer you the sacrifice of praise' (XV). It is noticeable in this connection that *Beowulf* itself contains no references to pagan deities by name nor any detailed descriptions of pagan practices, save for a condemnation of the Danes' panic-stricken sacrifices, which the poet (or a later scribe) felt it necessary to include:

> Hwilum hie geheton æt hærgtrafum
> wigweorþunga, wordum bædon
> þæt him gastbona geoce gefremede
> wið þeodþreaum. Swylc wæs þeaw hyra,
> hæþenra hyht.

> At times they prepared sacrifice in temples
> war-idol offerings, said old words aloud,
> that the great soul-slayer might bring some comfort
> in their country's disaster. Such was their custom,
> the hope of the heathen.

(Beowulf, 175–9)

Fred C. Robinson comments:

> The poem does not describe [the Germanic characters] addressing
> prayers to Woden and the thunder-god or performing other pagan rites
> . . . Rather [the poet] puts into their speeches allusions to 'the almighty'
> (*se ælmihtiga*), 'the ancient creator' (*ealdmetod*) or 'the ruler' (*wealdend*).
> At times they use the word 'god', but we have to remember that this
> word, then as now, was a generic term for any deity as well as a term
> which, in a specialized sense, could be used to refer to the Christian
> God.[14]

The precise religious status afforded to the Danes within the
context of the poem is difficult to establish: are they seen as truly
pagan, worshipping what Christianity would regard as false gods, or
simply pre-Christian, similar in status to the people of the **Old
Testament** in that they knew nothing of Christ but had some
understanding of the true God? If they were considered to be in
the latter category then their sacrifices to idols might have been
regarded as equivalent to the occasional lapses seen amongst the
ancient Israelites when their trust in God also waned (see for
example Exodus 32). Such examples were of relevance to the
Anglo-Saxon Church. Bede noted two similar (though short-lived)
incidents of apostasy, both in response to outbreaks of plague: one
in Northumbria (*Life of Cuthbert*, Ch. 9), the other in the kingdom
of the East Saxons (665), when 'Sighere and his people abandoned
the mysteries of the Christian faith and relapsed into paganism . . .
Hoping for protection by this means, they therefore began to
rebuild the ruined temples and restore the worship of idols' (*HE*,
III:30). Some critics regard lines 178b–188 of *Beowulf* as a general
comment on paganism rather than a specific comment on the
Danes themselves. It is also conceivable that the poet is deliberately
vague, both about Danish customs and the eternal destiny of Scyld
and Beowulf himself. Attempting to maintain Christian doctrine
while praising noble if unenlightened ancestors would require no
small measure of tact. Whatever the attitude of the poem's audience
to their forebears, the warning note sounded by these lines would
not have gone unnoticed. Whether Hrothgar's people are to be
pitied for their lack of understanding or condemned for apostasising
in a time of crisis the moral of the story remains the same. Reliance
on the old gods was not only ineffectual but wrong.

*Beowulf*, then, did not glorify pagan practices but it certainly
praised pre-Christian heroes. Could such a poem be regarded as
acceptable in a Christian court? Not only at court but even, it

would appear, in **monasteries**. The ecclesiastical Council of Clovesho meeting in 747 found it necessary to forbid performances by poets and musicians in religious houses. The popularity of such songs within monastic circles is not surprising given the close connections and overlap of interests between court and cloister. At least thirty kings and queens abandoned secular power for a life of monastic discipline between 613 and 829. Their followers were equally drawn to the contemplation of eternity. Guthlac had been a renowned warrior before he confronted the spiritual foes of the fenlands and **Benedict Biscop**, founder of the monasteries of Jarrow and Wearmouth, was a thane of King Oswy and of 'noble Angle lineage' (Bede, *Lives*, Ch. 1). Anglo-Saxon monasteries, then, contained many who were of high birth and well versed in the theory and practice of the heroic code. Although official ecclesiastical policy was to eradicate such entertainment, at least from clerical circles, it was clearly an uphill struggle. Fifty years after Clovesho, **Alcuin** wrote in rebuke to the **monastery** of Lindisfarne: 'When priests dine together let the words of God be read. At such a time it is fitting to listen to the reader, not to the harpist. What has Ingeld to do with Christ ... The king of heaven will have no dealings with so-called kings who are heathen and damned'.[15] The Anglo-Saxons were not the first to grapple with the problem of a proper Christian attitude to pagan literature. As Peter Hunter Blair points out, **Alcuin**'s words seem to echo those of **St Jerome** writing four hundred years earlier about classical pagan authors: 'What has Horace to do with the Psalter, Virgil with the Gospel and Cicero with Paul?' (*Letters*, 22). What then was the value of *Beowulf* that it should have been considered worthy of preservation? The answer probably lies in the proposition advanced by **Augustine of Hippo** that it was possible for Christians to take much that was useful from pagan works while rejecting all pagan superstition. Thus the *Beowulf* poet could well have seen in his heroic material much that was worthy of imitation: courage, loyalty, steadfastness in the face of an evil enemy. There remained the difficult feat of presenting the heroic past in a form acceptable to the Christian present. How then was this accomplished? The answer lies both in the choice of material and in the perspective of the poet. The painting is of pagan heroes, but it is set in a Christian frame. Within the action of the poem, explicit Christian references are few. The *dramatis personae* are noble of their kind but their spiritual understanding is at best limited. They live in middle-earth, water above and below. It is the poet whose world is bounded by

the knowledge of the Creator. The dark figures of personified evil
now have a place within the scheme of things. Hrothgar may not
know Grendel's origins but the poet does:

fifelcynnes eard
wonsæli wer   weardode hwile,
siþðan him scyppend   forscrifan hæfde
in Caines cynne. Þone cwealm gewræc
ece drihten,   þæs þe he Abel slog;
ne gefeah he þære fæhðe,   ac he hine feor forwræc,
metod for þy mane,   mancynne fram.
Þanon untydras   ealle onwocon,
eotenas ond ylfe   ond orcneas,
swylce gi[ga]ntas,   þa wið gode wunnon
lange þrage;   he him ðæs lean forgeald.

unblessed, unhappy,
he dwelt for a time   in the lair of the monsters
after the Creator   had outlawed, condemned them
as kinsmen of Cain   – for that murder God
the Eternal took vengeance,   when Cain killed Abel.
No joy that kin-slaughter:   the Lord drove him out,
far from mankind,   for that unclean killing.
From him sprang every   misbegotten thing,
monsters and elves   and the walking dead,
and also those giants   who fought against God
time and again;   He paid them back in full.

(*Beowulf*, 104–14)

These references to the early chapters of **Genesis** would have been
charged with significance for a Christian audience. Adam and Eve
had rebelled against God, refusing to live within the boundaries
which He had set. The ongoing consequences of their **sin** emerged
in the relationship of their sons. Cain, having failed to win God's
approval, murdered Abel in a jealous rage (Genesis 4), thus
condemning himself to exile. The curse laid upon one who had
murdered his own kin would have seemed highly appropriate to a
society which regarded such a betrayal of loyalty with particular
horror. The giants of Genesis 6 were mighty men born of the
liaisons between the sons of God (believed to be spiritual beings)
and the daughters of men. Their existence was seen as the
crowning factor in the increase of wickedness which caused God to
send the Flood to cleanse the earth. Grendel then is set against a
background of rebellion, jealous hatred, murder and growing evil.

Like Cain he is an outcast and his enmity towards God overflows into a hatred of all human happiness. The song of Creation, with its account of God's authority over the earth, would have been particularly galling to Grendel:

> Ða se ellengæst    earfoðlice
> þrage geþolode,    se þe in þystrum bad,
> þæt he dogora gehwam    dream gehyrde
> hludne in healle;    þær wæs hearpan sweg,
> swutol sang scopes.    Sægde se þe cuþe
> frumsceaft fira    feorran reccan,
> cwæð þæt se ælmihtiga    eorðan worh[te].

> Then the great monster    in the outer darkness
> suffered fierce pain,    for each new day
> he heard happy laughter    loud in the hall,
> the thrum of the harp,    melodious chant,
> clear song of the scop.    He spoke, who could tell
> the beginning of men,    knew our ancient origins,
> told how the Almighty    had made the earth.

(Beowulf, 86–92)

By setting the monster within the cosmic struggle between good and evil which Christians believed to lie behind life on earth, the poet enhances both Grendel's stature and the horror of his deeds: 'The monsters do not depart whether the gods go or come. A Christian was (and is) still like his forefathers a mortal hemmed in by a hostile world. The monsters remained the enemy of mankind . . . and became inevitably the enemies of the one God'.[16] Grendel's resentment and malice place him alongside **Lucifer** in *Genesis B*, consigned to **hell** after his rebellion against God and resolved that mankind should not enjoy what he was denied:

> Uton oðwendan hit nu monna bearnum,
> þæt heofonrice, nu we hit habban ne moton, gedon þæt
> hie his hyldo forlæten.

> Since we may not regain it
> Let us wrest heaven's realm from the sons of men.

(Genesis, 403–4)

Hatred of God and envy of mankind drive Grendel to an orgy of destruction. Set against the horror of the unseen adversary, cloaked by darkness, is the concept of the Creator as Light-giver. Grendel, who prowls by night, is at his most terrible when men, deprived of natural light, are at their most vulnerable and fearful. The dragon too is a creature of darkness, a barrow-dweller who ventures forth, like Grendel, to destroy by night and returns to its lair at dawn. In contrast, the *scop* in Heorot tells how God:

> gesette sigehreþig   sunnan ond monan
> leoman to leohte   landbuendum.

> victory-creative,   set out the brightness
> of the sun and moon   as lamps for earth-dwellers.

(*Beowulf*, 94–5)

Light is the gift of the Creator; the sun *beorht beacen godes*, 'God's bright beacon' (570) and *rodores candel* 'heaven's candle' (1572). Just as darkness is associated with evil, so light is charged with spiritual significance. When Beowulf, having ventured into the depths of the cave in pursuit of Grendel's mother, finally overcomes his evil adversary, the whole scene is flooded with radiance (1570–2).

In seeking to disentangle pagan and Christian elements in *Beowulf*, it is necessary to remember that no culture, however deeply influenced by a set of religious beliefs, is ever totally penetrated by those beliefs. Old ideas die hard; new concepts are transmuted even as they are absorbed. Culture and language constantly undergo a process of assimilation and change. It is possible that references in *Beowulf* to *wyrd*, which seem to sit uneasily beside belief in a sovereign Christian God, illustrate this fact and should be understood in this context. *Wyrd* has been variously translated as 'fate', 'fortune', 'destiny' (and thus understood as an essentially pagan concept) or as the far less specific 'what will happen', which could be a synonym for Christian Providence. It may be that *wyrd* rapidly lost any specifically pagan connotations and became a relatively neutral word;[17] yet there remain moments in the poem when it is seen as a malign force against which God's protection is needed. Thus when Hrothgar arranges payment of compensation for the thane murdered by Grendel, it is said that more lives would have been lost:

> nefne him witig god   wyrd forstode
> ond ðæs mannes mod.   Metod eallum weold
> gumena cynnes,   swa he nu git deð.

> had not wise God   and Beowulf's [lit. that man's] courage
> changed that fate.   The Lord then ruled
> all the race of men,   as He still does now.

(*Beowulf*, 1056–8)

Perhaps the problem is less that of the Anglo-Saxon poet, who may well have been happy to employ different shades of meaning and allow them to co-exist within a flexible world-view, than of the modern reader who might prefer a neater scheme of reference. The poet's comments do, however, provide a significant link between his consciousness of dark forces at work in the world and the sense of transience which permeated Anglo-Saxon thought. *Wyrd*, whatever its origin, is viewed in *Beowulf* as subject to God's intervention, yet its influence on the lives of men helps to make the world an uncertain and frequently an unhappy place. The coming of Christianity did not remove from the Anglo-Saxon mind the consciousness that life was brief and its pleasures transitory; indeed biblical teaching reinforced it.[18] Death remained an ever-present reality for which men and women had to be prepared; all too often it came swiftly and unannounced, if not through a ravaging monster, then through illness or battle. Even Beowulf had to die; courage and strength could postpone but not avert the final journey.

## BEOWULF – A CHRISTIAN HERO?

It may be generally accepted that the poem is written by 'a Christian whose intellectual horizons have been expanded to include not only Christian learning but the wider world of Christian-Latin learning in general',[19] but what is the spiritual standing of his hero? Some critics have suggested that Beowulf is presented as a type of Christian Saviour, delivering his people from the oppression of demonic foes, at the eventual cost of his own life. Parallels have been traced[20] between the death of **Christ**, betrayed by one follower, and deserted by ten of the remaining eleven, and that of Beowulf, drawn into danger by the wretched slave and abandoned by all but Wiglaf. Others regard Beowulf as heroic in his achievements but flawed in his moral character and guilty of reckless pride in undertaking his final foray against the dragon. Beowulf's own companions declare that of all kings he was:

> manna mildust   ond mon[ðw]ærust,
> leodum liðost   ond lofgeornost.

> the kindest to his men,   the most courteous man,
> the best to his people,   and most eager for fame.

(Beowulf, 3181–2)

It is the last word of this epitaph which has attracted the greatest attention. Does the use of *lofgeornost* indicate approval or suggest spiritual reservations? What kind of fame or glory was Beowulf striving for, earthly or heavenly? He has fulfilled Hrothgar's ideal of a ruler but has he achieved entry to heaven? Wisely perhaps, the poet seems to leave these questions unresolved. Beowulf, for all his virtues, belonged to an era which had not, in Christian eyes, received the full revelation of God. When Beowulf is contrasted not with the men of his own time but with the new heroes of the Christian age, his flaws become apparent. His courage may be praiseworthy but his motivation is secular and his chief concern is for his own reputation rather than the glory of God. This becomes clear when he is set alongside a fully-fledged Christian hero, St Guthlac, commemorated in a Latin life and in two Old English poems. Guthlac, a warrior of the Mercian royal family, turned from a life of battle and plunder to enter a monastery. After two years he took up his stand on the remote fen island of Crowland, the haunt of fearful demons. Single-handed, Guthlac battled against fiends who assumed the shapes of monsters and hideous humans:

> Hwilum wedende   swa wilde deor
> cirmdon on corðre,   hwilum cyrdon eft
> minne mansceaþan   on mennisc hiw
> breahtma mæste,   hwilum brugdon eft
> awyrgde wærlogan   on wyrmes bleo,
> earme adloman   attre spiowdon.

> Sometimes raging like wild beasts they would clamour in chorus, sometimes the evil and wicked ravagers would turn back into human form with the utmost din, sometimes the damned faithbreakers would be transformed again into the shape of a dragon.
>
> (*Guthlac*, B, 907–12)

There are strong similarities between these enemies, described by Guthlac in Felix's *Life* as the seed of Cain, and those faced by Beowulf: Grendel, his formidable mother, and the dragon. All are outcasts inhabiting waste places and all appear to combine elements of both popular superstition and Christian belief. Owen[21] cites place-names which reflect belief in the monsters listed in *Beowulf*, and the entry in the *Anglo-Saxon Chronicle* for 793 records the sighting of 'fiery dragons flying in the air' as an omen of imminent Viking raids. The Book of Revelation also portrayed Satan as a dragon (Rev. 12). Moreover, most of Guthlac's contests, like those of Beowulf, occur at night when the forces of evil were believed to be most powerful. Guthlac, however, is a hero of a quite different type. He has renounced the use of earthly weapons and fends off his assailants with a quiet confidence to which Beowulf never aspires. Beowulf is proud of his courage and strength yet cannot predict the outcome of his encounter with Grendel. He lacks the inner certainty of God's protection which characterises Guthlac throughout:

> Þeah þe ge me deað gehaten,
> mec wile wið þam niþum genergan   se þe eowrum nydum wealdeð.
> An is ælmihtig god,   se mec mæg eaðe gescyldan;
> he min feorg freoþað.

> Though you vow death to me, he will preserve me against those acts of spite, who wields the constraints upon you. God alone is almighty; he can shield me with ease and he will protect my life.

(*Guthlac*, A, 240–3)

As Beowulf awaits death (a man's preparation for dying was a significant test of character in Anglo-Saxon thought), he once more fails to attain to a fully Christian perspective on life. Rejoicing that he has remained true to his code, he declares:

> Ic ðas leode heold
> fiftig wintra . . .
>                     heold min tela,
> ne sohte searoniðas,   ne me swor fela
> aða on unriht.   Ic ðæs ealles mæg
> feorhbennum seoc   gefean habban;
> for ðam me witan ne ðearf   waldend fira
> morðorbealo maga.

> I ruled this people
> for fifty winters . . .
>                     held my own well,
> sought no intrigue, not often I swore
> deceitful oaths.   Sick with my death-wound
> I can take joy in all these things;
> the Ruler of men   need not blame me
> for murder of kin.

(*Beowulf*, 2732–3, 2737–42)

Such standards of conduct were laudable and important for the stability of society, but from a Christian viewpoint there was still something lacking. Beowulf's virtues are largely negative and decidedly earthbound. It is useful to compare Beowulf's philosophy, summarised in his exhortation to Hrothgar:

> wyrce se þe mote
> domes ær deaþe;   þæt bið drihtguman
> unlifgendum   æfter selest.

>                         let him who may
> win fame before death.   That is the best
> memorial for a man   after he is gone.

(Beowulf, 1387–9)

with that expressed in the *Seafarer*, a poem strongly coloured by biblical thought:[22]

> Forþon þæt bið eorla gehwam   æftercweþendra
> lof ligendra   lastworda betst,
> þæt he gewyrce,   ær he on weg scyle,
> fremum on foldan   wið feonda niþ,
> deorum dædum   deofle togeanes,
> þæet hine ælda bearn   æfter hergen,
> ond his lof siþþan   lifge mid englum
> awa to ealdre,   ecan lifes blæd,
> dream mid dugeþum.

> Therefore for every warrior the best
> Memorial is the praise of living men
> After his death, that ere he must depart
> He shall have done good deeds on earth against
> The malice of his foes, and noble works
> Against the devil, that the sons of men
> May after praise him, and his glory live
> For ever with the angels in the splendour
> Of lasting life, in bliss among those hosts.

(Seafarer, 72–80)

For Beowulf immortality consists of living in his people's praises, though the poet intimates that after his death their hard-won security will be short-lived. The Seafarer seeks praise from men *together with* glory among the angels. Like Guthlac his goal is eternity spent in the presence of God (*Seafarer*, 119–122). Beowulf may be confident that 'the ruler of men' will not charge him with the murder of kinsfolk but his comfort at the last comes not from a prospect of eternity but from the sight of the treasure he has won

(2747–51). Ironically the gold, on which he looked with so much pride, is buried with him, of use neither to the dead nor to the living (3166–9). The *Seafarer* has an apposite comment on the provision of burial goods which, like the practice of cremation, was regarded with disapproval by the Church:

Þeah þe græf wille    golde stregan
broþor his geborenum,    byrgan be deadum,
maþmum mislicum    þæt hine mid wille,
ne mæg þære sawle    þe biþ synna ful
gold to geoce    for godes egsan.

> though a brother
> May strew with gold his brother's grave, and bury
> His corpse among the dead with heaps of treasure,
> Wishing them to go with him, yet can gold
> Bring no help to a soul that's full of sins,
> Against God's wrath.

*(Seafarer, 97–102)*

Despite the fact that Beowulf may in the end have to be cast as a noble pagan rather than a Christian hero, the poem as it has survived is strongly influenced by Christian teaching. Christian references are scattered throughout and more than one character occasionally slips into Christian thought patterns, as if such allusions are too natural to the poet for him to maintain a strict demarcation. Familiarity with concepts of **sin** and **judgement** is apparently taken for granted and although explicit biblical references are limited to the **Old Testament**, there are passages which may contain echoes of the **New Testament** and the writings of the **Fathers of the Church**. Hrothgar's assertion that Beowulf's mother might well claim that '*hyre ealdmetod este wære*' (that Eternal God was gracious to her) in her child-bearing (945–6) has been seen as an oblique reference to the praise heaped upon the **Virgin Mary** as the mother of Jesus (Luke 11:27). Later, addressing the victorious Beowulf, Hrothgar delivers a **homily**-like speech warning that growing arrogance and a slumbering conscience can lay even heroes open to spiritual attack: the *biteran stræle* (sharp arrow) of the slayer of souls (1725–68). This passage draws on images which would probably have been familiar themes in sermons and religious writings of the time. Hrothgar seems to be warning against three of the **Deadly Sins**, as defined by **Gregory**: Pride, Sloth and Avarice.[23] Pride was recognised as a particular temptation of the great, and the Old Testament revealed that even men used by God, such as Samson and David, could still fall victim to complacency. The picture of the adversary with a bow derives originally from Ephesians 6:10, where **St Paul** urges Christians to don the spiritual armour which will protect them against 'all the fiery darts of the most wicked one'. These passages in *Beowulf*, together with other moral reflections, have been dismissed as interpolations by critics who have considered them inappropriate in a poem of this type. In this as in other questions of propriety of taste, we must accept that attitudes which appear inconsistent to us may have seemed perfectly proper to Anglo-Saxon Christians. That a poet, engaged in recording heroic deeds and the quest for glory, should pause to draw a moral from his story may seem strange to a modern reader; to a poet of his day it would have appeared not only natural but essential. How else could a reworking of the pagan past be justified unless it offered some measure of edification? Nor would this have seemed an artificial exercise. The Church regarded the whole of creation and history as a book set out for the wise to read and interpret. If human life provided material from which to learn, then why not also the history and traditions of the Germanic peoples? In its treatment of this material, *Beowulf* offered its audience not only entertainment but insight into the world in which they lived, holding up for emulation qualities which would equip them to face the physical and spiritual dangers which that world contained.

NOTES

1. Bede's *Ecclesiastical History*, written originally in Latin, completed c.731, inevitably reflects his own beliefs and preoccupations but remains a vital source for the period. The translation used is *History of the English Church* (*HE*) which is easily available; see also Colgrave and Mynors edition.

2. 'That most skilful investigator of the scriptures, the monk Bede, who . . . has lately shone in the house of God among you with knowledge of the Scriptures like *a candle of the church*.' (Letter of Boniface to Hwaetberht, Abbot of Wearmouth 746–7, *EHD*, I, 180.)

3. For the importance of gold and treasure to the Anglo-Saxons see Dodwell (1982).

4. See Bruce-Mitford (1975–83); Evans (1986).

5. Campbell (1982, 53ff). See also Yorke (1990, Ch. 1).

6. Raw (1992, 173).

7. See Owen (1981); Wilson (1992).

8. For example: 'Erce! Mother of earth! May the Ruler of all, the everlasting Lord, grant you fields sprouting and shooting' (*Anglo-Saxon Poetry*, 547).

9.  Mayr-Harting (1991, 29).
10. Whitelock (1972, 44).
11. See Jacobs (1977); Chase (1981); Newton (1993).
12. See Whitelock (1951).
13. See Nicholson (1963); Short (1980); Parker (1987); Clark (1990); Fulk (1991).
14. Robinson (1991, 150–1).
15. Hunter Blair (1970, 282), citing *MGH Ep. Car.* 124.
16. Tolkien (1936, 264). See also Orchard (1995, Ch. 2).
17. See Trahern (1991).
18. See Fell (1991).
19. Robinson (1991, 142).
20. Critics who suggest varying degrees of Christian parallels and allegory in *Beowulf* include Klaeber (*Beowulf and the Fight at Finnsburg*); McNamee (1960); Cabaniss (1955); Whallon (1962); Donahue (1965); Goldsmith (1970). See also Hill (1994).
21. Owen (1981, 64–5).
22. See Chapter 2.
23. See Parker (1987, 141–3).

# A New Perspective on Life –
# Pilgrimage, Transience and the Elegies

Uton we hycgan   hwær we ham agen,
ond þonne geþencan   hu we þider cumen,
ond we þonne eac tilien,   þæt we to moten
in þa ecan   eadignesse.

Let us think where we have our home
And then consider how we may come thither
And let us labour also, so that we
May pass into eternal blessedness.

*(Seafarer*, 117–20)

## THE CONTRIBUTION OF THE CELTIC CHURCH

In the event, the death of Edwin of Northumbria in 633 proved only a temporary setback in the advance of the Church. Indeed, the unheroic exit of the Roman **bishop** Paulinus provided an opportunity for another player to emerge from the wings. On recapturing the kingdom, Edwin's nephew Oswald turned not to Rome but to the Irish monks of Iona, a small island off Scotland, where **St Columba** (d. 597) had founded a **monastery**. According to **Bede**: 'Oswald greatly wished that all the people whom he ruled should be imbued with the grace of the Christian Faith, of which he had received such signal proof in his victory over the heathen. So he sent to the Scottish elders among whom he and his companions had received the sacrament of Baptism when in exile, asking them to send him a bishop' (Bede, *HE,* III:3). It seems that the first missionary was not a success. Bede relates that he returned to Iona in disgust, complaining that the Northumbrians were 'an ungovernable people of an obstinate and barbarous temperament,' whom it was impossible to teach (Bede, *HE,* III:5). In his place came **Aidan**, who established a base not at York, the choice of his Roman predecessor, but on the windswept island of Lindisfarne.

There he set up a school whose pupils included two influential English brothers, Cedd and Chad.

**Aidan**'s priorities, the selection of an isolated (though strategic) base and his emphasis on education, were characteristic of the Celtic[1] tradition which he represented. The Irish were renowned scholars. In their **monasteries** piety and learning went hand in hand. Although communications with England and Europe had been disrupted by the Germanic invasions, Irish monasteries had maintained a rich and varied intellectual life. Scholars from the troubled Continent had fled to Ireland during the fifth and sixth centuries. The manuscripts they brought were faithfully copied and their knowledge transmitted to succeeding generations. Irish scholars knew Virgil and Horace, understood Ptolemy's concept of geography, read **Ambrose** and **Augustine**, together with the works of the Greek **Fathers** in Latin translation. The Celtic monks, therefore, brought with them a vigorous tradition of classical learning. Nor was this important influence confined to Northumbria. Celtic missionaries were involved in the conversion of East Anglia, Mercia and Essex and founded Malmesbury Abbey, where the noted scholar **Aldhelm** (d.709/10) was to be both pupil and abbot. English students flocked to the schools of Ireland: 'There were many English nobles and lesser folk in Ireland who had left their own land . . . either to pursue religious studies or to lead a life of stricter discipline' (Bede, *HE,* III:27).

PILGRIMS AND STRANGERS

The Irish were not only scholars; they also made ideal pioneers. Their spiritual quest frequently took the form of **pilgrimage**, 'one of the great driving forces in Irish Christianity.'[2] A number of scholars have discerned in the tradition of *peregrinatio pro amore dei* (pilgrimage for the love of God) and the attitudes which undergirded it a significant key to the interpretation of two of the Old English 'elegies' found in the Exeter Book: the *Wanderer* and the *Seafarer*. These, more reflective and intensely personal than the heroic poetry, still present some problems for the modern reader. The depiction of personal emotion and suffering is coupled with a moralising strain in a way which may initially appear incongruous and has led to speculation about the existence of different voices within the poems.[3] The *Seafarer* appears to be composed of two sections, the first dealing with dangers and sufferings experienced at sea and the second providing a series of homiletic reflections. The relationship between these different elements has generated much controversy but the majority of scholars now conclude that the poem is a monologue and that its tone is deeply influenced by Christian thought. The speaker begins with an account of his own lonely exile:

> Mæg ic be me sylfum    soðgied wrecan,
> siþas secgan,    hu ic geswincdagum
> earfoðhwile    oft þrowade,
> bitre breostceare    gebiden hæbbe.

> I sing my own true story, tell my travels,
> How I have often suffered times of hardship
> In days of toil, and have experienced
> Bitter anxiety.

(*Seafarer*, 1–4)

His sufferings, he claims, are beyond the experience of those who know only the relative security of dry land. Yet, within a few lines, comes a declaration that despite the rigours of such a life, his heart longs to venture forth once more across the sea. This puzzling transition takes place, as Ida Gordon has noted in her edition of the poem, within a sentence and without a break in the metre:

> For þon him gelyfeð lyt,    se þe ah lifes wyn
> gebiden in burgum    bealosiþa hwon,
> wlonc ond wingal,    hu ic werig oft
> im brimlade    bidan sceolde.
> Nap nihtscua    norþan sniwde,
> hrim hrusan bond,    hœgl feol on eorþan,
> corna caldest.    For þon cnyssað nu
> heortan geþohtas    þaet ic hean streamas,
> sealtyþa gelac    sylf cunnige –
> monað modes lust    mæla gehwylce
> ferð to feran,    þaet ic feor heonan
> elþeodigra    eard gesece.

> He can little know
> Who, proud and flushed with wine, has spent his time
> With all the joys of life among the cities,
> Safe from such fearful venturings, how I
> Have often suffered weary on the seas.
> Night shadows darkened, snow came from the north,
> Frost bound the earth and hail fell on the ground,

Coldest of corns. And yet the heart's desires
Incite me now that I myself should go
On towering seas, among the salt waves' play;
And constantly the heartfelt wishes urge
The spirit to venture, that I should go forth
To see the lands of strangers far away.

(*Seafarer*, 27–38)

It was Dorothy Whitelock[4] who suggested that the problem of the Seafarer's apparently contradictory impulses could be resolved if he were to be understood as a *peregrinus*, a pilgrim-hermit, willing to leave home and family and to endure earthly perils and discomfort in pursuit of heavenly security. The conviction that life on earth should be viewed in terms of a journey or pilgrimage to heaven was one of the most profound and influential concepts inherited by the Anglo-Saxons from the **early Church**, and undergirds much of their spirituality. It was believed that the disobedience of Adam and Eve resulted not only in their own expulsion from the Garden of Eden but also in the imposition of a permanent sentence of exile upon their descendants. All men and women were therefore viewed as wanderers on earth, cut off from their true home in heaven. In the Old English poem *Genesis*, God's speech sentencing the unhappy pair to 'oðerne eðel secean . . . and on wræc hweorfan (seek another homeland and wander in exile)' (927–8) is followed by the poet's comment that this explains the present misfortunes of mankind:

we nu gehyrað   hwær us hearmstafas
wraðe onwocan   and woruldyrmðo

now we have learned
How our many sorrows, our mortal woe,
Befell us all.

(*Genesis*, 939–40)

Restoration of an individual's relationship with God meant exchanging the aimless wanderings of a doomed exile for the purposeful journey of a citizen to his homeland: the transformation of involuntary exile into voluntary pilgrimage. Since banishment stemmed from rebellion, returning to God meant adopting a life of obedience and clear allegiance to his kingdom, sacrificing such short-term security as this world offered, and living instead as temporary residents, en route to their true home. God's call to Abraham to: 'Go forth out of thy country, and from thy kindred . . . and come into the land which I shall shew thee' (Genesis 12: 1), and the later journey of the Israelites through the desert to the

Promised Land were seen as symbolic of this need for mankind to sacrifice ties with the material world in order to regain citizenship of heaven. All were heirs to Adam's punishment; some were willing to choose Abraham's route to redemption. Thus the writer of the *Letter to the Hebrews* urged his readers to imitate the faith of the great figures of the Old Testament: 'All these died according to faith . . . confessing that they are strangers and pilgrims (**Vulgate**: *peregrini et hospites*) on the earth . . . they desire a better, that is to say, a heavenly country. Therefore God is not ashamed to be called their God: for He hath prepared for them a city' (Hebrews 11:13–16). **St Peter** also counselled: 'I beseech you *as strangers and pilgrims*, to refrain yourselves from carnal desires which war against the soul' (I Peter 2:11).

These twin ideas, that Christians should not regard this world as their true home and that close contact with its temptations could impede their spiritual progress, were constantly reiterated in the writings of the **Fathers**. **Augustine of Hippo**, seeking to clarify the relationship of Christians to the world around them, developed the concept of two cities: 'Now Cain was the first son born to those two parents of mankind, and he belonged to the city of man; the later son, Abel, belonged to the City of God . . . Scripture tells us that Cain founded a city, whereas Abel, as a pilgrim, did not found one. For the City of the saints is up above, although it produces citizens here below, and in their persons the City is on pilgrimage until the time of its kingdom comes' (*City of God*, XV, 1). This formula, like so much of Augustine's teaching, was reiterated in the preaching of **Caesarius of Arles**, bishop in Gaul 502–542: 'There are two cities, dearest brothers: one is the city of the world, the other is the city of paradise. In the city of the world the good Christian is always a pilgrim; in the city of paradise he is an acknowledged citizen' (*Sermo* 151.2 in *Sources and Analogues*).

The understanding of life as a pilgrimage features significantly in the thought of **Gregory the Great** (c. 540–604), whose writings were held in great esteem by the English Church. In his commentary on the Song of Songs, Gregory wrote of the exile endured by the human race since it was 'expelled from the joys of paradise and came into the pilgrimage of this present life' (*PL* 79), and in his *Cura Pastoralis* (Pastoral Care), he exhorted his readers not to let earthly prosperity divert them from their heavenly goal, 'lest they love their pilgrimage instead of their country; lest they turn the supplies for their journey into hindrances to their arrival at its end' (*Pastoral Care*, Ch. XXVI).

This concept of life as a pilgrimage to the heavenly homeland found three chief forms of practical expression during the Anglo-Saxon period, each of which involved a degree of detachment from home and kindred. Firstly, there was a desire to visit holy places, sites associated with biblical events or containing the shrines of **saints**, where particular spiritual benefits were to be expected. Men and women alike journeyed to Rome and even the Holy Land, travels made possible by the legacy of Roman roads. Some travelled to Rome to die near the tombs of **St Peter** and **St Paul**, others to learn. Among the earliest recorded Anglo-Saxon pilgrims were the young Northumbrians **Wilfrid** (d. 709) and **Benedict Biscop** (628–689). According to Eddius Stephanus, Wilfrid's biographer, 'the youthful Wilfrid, prompted by the Holy Ghost, conceived a great desire to visit the See of St Peter, Prince of the Apostles . . . believing that he would wash away every trace of sin thereby and receive a great blessing' (*Life of Wilfrid,* Ch. 3 in *Age of Bede*). When offered incentives to abandon his journey to Rome, Wilfrid is said to have cited Abraham as his model in the decision to leave 'my kinsfolk and my father's house' and to learn 'the laws of ecclesiastical discipline so that our nation may grow in the service of God' (Ch. 4). **Wilfrid** and **Benedict Biscop** were profoundly influenced by their experiences in Rome and Gaul and returned to share their new-found knowledge with the English Church. Both were destined to play major roles in the future of that church, Wilfrid as **bishop**, Benedict Biscop as founder of the twin **monasteries** of Wearmouth and Jarrow. Both would make further journeys to Rome.

Secondly, the **monastic** life was seen as a form of **pilgrimage** in which men and women renounced home and family in order to fix their thoughts and desires on **heaven**. There was, throughout this period, an underlying conviction that serious religious commitment meant becoming a **monk** or a **nun**. Thus kings and queens, noblemen and noblewomen, together with those of lesser rank, entered the **cloister** to seek eternal life. An entrant to a monastic community left behind not only the right to personal possessions and the other trappings of society but also the right to self-determination. Readiness to renounce self-will and place oneself under the will of a superior was fundamental to the monastic vows. In his enormously influential *Rule*, **St Benedict** (c. 420–c. 550) emphasised the crucial role of obedience in repairing the damage done by Adam's rebellion: 'Hear O son, the precepts of the master; so that by the labour of obedience you may return to Him from whom by the sloth of disobedience you fell away' (*Rule of St Benedict, Prol.*). **Monks** usually lived in community, but a significant number desired to take their detachment from the world a stage further. Within the **monasteries** of the Celtic tradition, a calling to the solitary life of **hermit** or anchorite was regarded as a high honour, only bestowed on those who had already mastered the earlier stages of spiritual development. **St Cuthbert** (634–687) was delighted when he was thought worthy 'to ascend to the stillness of divine contemplation' (Bede, *Life of Cuthbert*, Ch. 17). The Church had long recognised the existence of two spheres within Christian devotion: the '**active**' and '**contemplative**' lives. **Augustine** and others compared the respective roles of **Martha** who was busy serving Jesus and **Mary** who preferred to sit at his feet and listen to his teaching (Luke 10:38–42). Both were necessary and, as **Bede** wrote in one of his homilies, they were not unconnected. The **mystical** experience at which he hints would flower again in England during the thirteenth and fourteenth centuries:

> The active life is Christ's servant devoting himself to righteous labors: first to keeping himself unspotted by this world . . . then also to coming to the aid of his neighbour in need . . . The contemplative life . . . is when one who has been taught by the long practice of good actions . . . learns to be free of all affairs of the world and to direct the eye of his mind towards love alone; and he begins, even in the present life, to gain a foretaste of the joy of the perpetual blessedness which he is to attain in the future, by ardently desiring it, and even sometimes, insofar as is permitted to mortals, by contemplating it sublimely in mental ecstasy.
>
> (*Homilies*, I:9)

The third and most radical category of pilgrims chose to leave both home and homeland without hope of return, literally making themselves exiles for the sake of God. Some went into exile as **penance**; others were missionaries desiring to preach the **Gospel** in far countries. **St Boniface** (d. 754), who became **archbishop** to the Germans, described himself as an exile in Germany, 'exulem Germanicum' (Letter 30) and gave 'timor Christi' and 'amor peregrinationis' (the fear of Christ and love of pilgrimage) (Letter 94) as the cause of his separation from friends in England. Such journeys carried very real risks. Boniface himself was eventually murdered and both he and and his successor, Bishop Lul, mention the perils of sea-travel frequently in their correspondence. The Celtic Churches developed this particular concept of pilgrimage into a highly specialised spiritual activity. Through contacts with the monasteries of Gaul, they had learned of the **Desert Fathers**, commemorated in the writings of **John Cassian** (d. c. 432) and others. From the third century onwards these pioneers of the monastic life had retreated from the materialism and corruption of society and moved into the deserts of Egypt, Palestine and Syria, settling in small cells carved out of rock, where they prayed, studied, meditated upon the scriptures, and led a life of extreme **asceticism**. This was the pattern which the Irish **monks** adopted and adapted to their own environment. Ireland denied them the deserts to which the **hermits** of Egypt had retreated, so they launched forth in small boats to seek 'deserts in the ocean' (*Adomnan's Life of Columba*, I:6). The remains of their tiny beehive huts can still be seen clinging precariously to rocky islands off the Irish coast. Not for Irish monks the cautious planning of the Roman-trained **Augustine** and his successors. Placing themselves in the hands of God, they were carried by the ocean currents as far as Iceland. They were not necessarily motivated by the desire to establish missionary outreach, they simply wished to express a total obedience to and dependence upon God. The *Anglo-Saxon Chronicle* records that in 891, 'Three Irishmen came to King Alfred in a boat without any oars, from Ireland whence they had stolen away because they wished for the love of God to be on pilgrimage (*hi woldon for Godes lufan on elþiodignesse beon*), they cared not where. The boat in which they set out was made of two and a half hides, and they had taken with them provisions for a week' (*Anglo-Saxon Chronicle*, 891). This was 'perfect pilgrimage' as explained by a tenth-century Irish writer, departure without hope of return:

> The Lord Himself gave this friendly counsel . . . unto Abraham . . . that he should leave his own country . . . and that he should go for his pilgrimage into the land which God would show him, to wit, the Land of Promise . . . Now the good counsel which God enjoined here on the father of the faithful is incumbent . . . on all the faithful; that is to leave their country and their land, their wealth and their worldly delight for the sake of the Lord of the Elements, and to go into perfect pilgrimage in imitation of him.[5]

Pilgrimage, therefore, in the minds of Anglo-Saxon Christians, was a concept capable of a wide range of interpretations, from the fundamental understanding of the Christian life as a journey to heaven to the literal abandonment of all earthly security in order to seek God's kingdom. Establishing which of these meanings is closest to the voyage contemplated by the Seafarer has prompted considerable debate. Not all scholars accept Dorothy Whitelock's view that the *Seafarer* describes a literal *peregrinus* in the Celtic tradition, and a number of allegorical interpretations of the poem have been offered.[6] Somewhat overlooked in these discussions has been the emphasis in the *Seafarer* on the spiritual distinction between life on land and life at sea.[7] In the clearest statement of motivation in the poem, the speaker asserts:

> gielleð anfloga,
> hweteð on hwælweg   hreþer unwearnum
> ofer holma gelagu.   Forþon me hatran sind
> drytnes dreamas   þonne þis deade lif,
> læne on londe.

> The cuckoo [lone flier] cries, incites the eager breast
> On to the whale's roads irresistably,
> Over the wide expanses of the sea,
> Because the joys of God mean more to me
> Than this dead transitory life on land.

(*Seafarer*, 62–66a)

Here the paradoxical phrase *deade lif* recalls the reminder given by **St Paul** to the church at Ephesus: 'And you, when you were dead in your offences and sins, wherein in time past you walked according to the course of this world' (Ephes. 2:1, 2). A useful parallel to this apparent use of life on land and life at sea to signal spiritual commitment occurs in the Old English *Exodus*. As Peter Lucas observes in his edition of the poem,[8] the Egyptians, the enemies of God, are referred to as *landmenn* (179), whereas the Israelites, on their way through the desert to the promised land, are called *saemen* (105). Indeed the central section of the poem is dominated by what Irving calls an 'extraordinary extended metaphor,'[9] which portrays the Israelites 'sailing' across the desert. A key to the interpretation of this unlikely image is provided by the parallel use of *ingefolc* ('native people') (142) to describe the Egyptians and *wraecmon* ('exile') (137) for the people of Israel. Thus the Egyptians are depicted as remaining in their native land while the Israelites become wanderers in search of a new homeland promised by God. The contrast, comments Lucas, 'implies that the Egyptians will never embark on the voyage to the heavenly home but will be confined in hell.'[10] The use not only of *wraecmon* but also of *saemen* in the description of the Israelites argues a strong link in the mind of the *Exodus*-poet between the concept of being God's obedient people on the move and sea-travel. This connection may have been a logical development of the broader concept of pilgrimage expressed in the Letter to the Hebrews. The Old Testament patriarchs, Abraham, Isaac and Jacob, states the writer, sojourned in tents in order to inherit an eternal city whose solid foundations and design speak of security and permanence (Hebrews 11: 9,10). St John Chrystostom (c. 347–407) commented on this passage: 'The whole of virtue, is to be a stranger to this world, and a sojourner, and to have nothing in common with things here but to hang loose from them, as from things strange to us ... [Abraham] built no splendid houses, he enjoyed no luxuries, he had no care about dress, which are all things of this world; but lived in all respects as belonging to this city yonder' (*Homilies on Hebrews*, No. XXIV). This teaching, that those who have given their allegiance to this world dwell in cities, symbols of earthly security, enjoying all that earth has to offer, whereas those who follow God live in tents, symbols of impermanence, and suffer deprivation, may lie behind the description of the land-dweller in *Seafarer* 27–9:

> se þe ah lifes wyn
> *gebiden in burgum*,   bealosiþa hwon,
> wlonc ond wingal

> Who, proud and flushed with wine, has spent his time
> With all the joys of life among the cities.

The other two allusions in the *Seafarer* to those who live on land (12–15, 55–7) are also concerned with ease and comfort. On each occasion the reference establishes the inability of the land-dweller, secure and comfortable, to understand the life endured by the Seafarer, the one identified within the poem as possessing spiritual motivation. The land and the city, therefore, appear to represent worldly security, comfort and enjoyment; the sea, that most unpredictable of elements, symbolises commitment to travel and abandonment to the will of God. This contrast is further reinforced by the description of the land-dweller as *wlonc and wingal* (29). Anne Klinck, in her edition of *The Old English Elegies*, points out that

> the word *wingal*, 'flushed with wine', occurs also in *Daniel* 116 (þa onwoc wulfheort [Nebuchadnezzar], *se ær wingal swæf*), where it is clearly pejorative ... The second element, *gal*, 'wanton, lascivious' certainly has a bad connotation. Cf. *symbelgal* (*Judgement Day I* 79), *medugal* (*Daniel* 702 and *Judith* 26), *meodugal*, *-gales* (*Fortunes of Men* 52 and 57). In all these examples the *-gal* words indicate wanton

self-indulgence ... In *Seafarer*, the word *wingal* suggests a heedless delight in earthly pleasures.[11]

The use of *wlonc*, 'proud, splendid', also probably carries negative connotations, since pride has never been considered a Christian virtue. Lines 106–7 present twin concepts (their message reinforced by the parallelism of form) which summarise the contrast between believer and unbeliever:

Dol biþ se þe him his dryhten ne ondrædeþ; cymeð him se deað
  unþinged.
Eadig bið se þe eaþmod leofaþ; cymeð him seo ar of heofonum

Foolish is he who does not fear his Lord,
For death will come upon him unprepared.
Blessed is he who humble lives; for grace
Shall come to him from heaven.

(*Seafarer*, 106–7)

Viewed from the perspective of biblical and **patristic** writings, therefore, the land-dweller, in his comfortable ignorance, is not a neutral figure, but one who risks eternal condemnation. The Seafarer, on the other hand, is the one who is willing to cut free from earthly ties and sacrifice all for the sake of the heavenly kingdom. In allegorical terms it seems that the Christian *viator* ('traveller') may have become, in Anglo-Saxon thought, a Christian seafarer. Such an interpretation does not necessarily exclude the possibility that this particular pilgrim through life may also have been a literal *peregrinus* in the Irish tradition, who chose to live out the metaphor by placing himself literally at the disposal of God and the currents of the sea. In view of the various overlapping understandings of pilgrimage in the Anglo-Saxon period, it may be that the modern distinction between literal and allegorical interpretations of the poem is artificial and hence unnecessary. Whether the Seafarer's voyage is to be understood figuratively or literally, however, the essential spiritual motivation of the speaker remains: true security is to be found not on earth but in heaven.

The second part of the poem shows the influence of Christian Latin elegies in its rejection of earthly wealth (66–7) and in its commentary on the decline of the world (80–90). The influence of the **Bible**, particularly the Psalms, is also apparent. Lines 97–102, which stress the inability of earthly treasure to protect the soul from God's judgement, recall the warning in Psalm 48: 8 that 'No brother can redeem, nor shall man redeem: he shall not give to God his ransom', together with the injunction in the Sermon on the Mount, 'Lay not up to yourselves treasures on earth . . . But lay up to yourselves treasures in heaven' (Matt. 6:19, 20). Many other echoes of the Psalms can be detected and it is possible that the whole structure of the poem reflects the substantial group of Psalms[12] in which the speaker outlines his suffering (often commenting on the fact that those who do not fear God appear to be prospering), reminds himself of God's goodness, and comes to the point of reaffirming a spiritual perspective which he then encourages himself and others to follow. Thus in Psalm 101, the writer covers very similar themes to those expressed in the *Seafarer*, beginning with his own sufferings and ending with a confident assertion of the security to be found in God:

> My days are vanished like smoke: and my bones are grown dry like
>     fuel for the fire . . .
> I am become like to a pelican of the wilderness: I am like a
>     night-raven in the house . . .
> My days have declined like a shadow, and I am withered like grass.
> But thou, O Lord, endurest for ever: and thy memorial to all
>     generations . . .
> In the beginning, O Lord, thou foundedst the earth: and the
>     heavens are the works of thy hands.
> They shall perish but thou remainest: and all of them shall grow old
>     like a garment . . .
> But thou art always the self-same, and thy years shall not fail.
> The children of thy servants shall continue: and their seed shall be
>     directed for ever.

The *Seafarer* concludes with an exhortation to seek admission to the heavenly homeland, couched in terms akin to those used in several Old English **homilies**:

> Uton we hycgan    hwær we ham agen
> ond þonne geþencan    hu we þider cumen,
> ond we þonne eac tilien,    þæt we to moten
> in þa ecan    eadignesse
>
> Let us think where we have our home,
> And then consider how we may come thither;
> And let us labour also, so that we
> May pass into eternal blessedness.

(Seafarer, 117–20)

A tenth-century homily contained in the *Vercelli* manuscript follows a description of mankind's pilgrim condition with a very similar injunction:

> Utan we nu forð tilian þæt we becuman moton gesæglice to þam ecan 7 to þam ealdorlican eðle.

> Let us now, henceforth, strive in order that we may deserve that which we may happily meet with in that eternal and in that princely homeland.

> (*Vercelli Homily*, XI, 55–7)

Surviving accounts of the Anglo-Saxon Church suggest that such exhortations did not fall on deaf ears. Longing for **heaven** and fear of hell together made a powerful motivating force. **St Cuthbert**, still the favourite **saint** of Northumbria, is said to have entered the **monastery** of Melrose after seeing a vision of Bishop **Aidan**'s entry into **heaven**: 'Spurred on by his heavenly vision of the joys of eternal bliss, he was ready to suffer hunger and thirst in this life in order to enjoy the banquets of the next' (Bede, *Life of Cuthbert*, Ch. 6). Like many others Cuthbert practised severe self-discipline in order to detach his spirit from the demands of the flesh. Bede also notes the example of Drycthelm, another Melrose **monk**, who used to stand in the river with blocks of ice swirling around him, reciting psalms and prayers. He was said to have been motivated by a vision of souls who had postponed repentance till the hour of their death: 'When the wretches could no longer endure the blast of the terrible heat, they leaped into the heart of the terrible cold; and finding no refuge there, they leaped back again to be burned in the middle of the unquenchable flames' (Bede, *HE*, V:12). When questioned about his endurance he would reply simply, 'I have known it colder.' Physical trials, isolation and hardship were all welcomed as a means of preparing the soul for eternity and thus avoiding the far harsher torments of **hell**. Bede considers this story an edifying example of a man 'inspired by an insatiable longing for the blessings of **heaven**'. If the protagonist of the *Seafarer* was a man of similar convictions, then the danger and loneliness of a bitter sea-voyage could have been welcome as a means of future blessings. Had he perished alone on his ocean voyage, as many Irish **monks** must have done, it would not have mattered. God would have seen his sacrifice.

THE WORLD'S DECLINE

The teaching of the Church made it clear that the material world, for all its occasional flashes of splendour, was doomed. The Anglo-Saxons were acutely aware of the transient nature of human achievement,[13] a message reinforced by the crumbling remnants of the great empire which had once dominated the land:

> brosnade burgsteall.   Betend crungon
> hergas to hrusan.   Forþon þas hofu dreorgiað,
> ond þæs teaforgeapa   tigelum sceadeð
> hrostbeages hrof.   Hryre wong gecrong
> gebrocen to beorgum,   þær iu beorn monig
> glædmod ond goldbeorht   gleoma gefrætwed,
> wlonc ond wingal   wighyrstum scan;
> seah on sinc, on sylfor,   on searogimmas,
> on ead, on æht,   on eorcanstan,
> on þas beorhtan burg   bradan rices.

> The city crumbled, its repairers fell,
> Its armies to the earth. And so these halls
> Are empty, and this red roof now sheds
> Its tiles, decay has brought it to the ground,
> Smashed it to piles of rubble, where long since
> A host of heroes, glorious, gold-adorned,
> Gleaming in splendour, proud and flushed with wine,
> Shone in their armour, gazed on gems and treasure,
> On silver, riches, wealth and jewellery,
> On this bright city with its wide domains.

> (*Ruin*, 27–37)

Here in the description of a city which may well have been Bath, the memory of past glories only serves to heighten the sense of melancholy, since all the skills of the builders could not withstand the forces of death and decay. A similar sense of creeping decline lies behind the Seafarer's view of his world. Ever since Adam was expelled from the Garden of Eden, the might of men, it was believed, had been steadily waning.

> Dagas sind gewitene,
> ealle onmedlan   eorþan rices;
> næron nu cyningas   ne caseras
> ne goldgiefan   swylce iu wæron.

> The great old days have gone, and all the grandeur
> of earth; there are not Caesars now or kings
> Or patrons such as once there used to be.

> (*Seafarer*, 80–4)

Mankind's gradual decay was mirrored in the world around. According to the teaching of **St Paul** (Romans 8:19–22), the whole of creation had been caught up in the effects of man's fall from grace and now it waited, 'groaning' as if enduring the pains of childbirth, for man's restoration. Thus the speaker in the *Wanderer* finds little to assuage his melancholy as he surveys history:

> Forþon ic geþencan ne mæg   geond þas woruld
> for hwan modsefa   min ne gesweorce,
> þonne ic eorla lif   eal geondþence,
> hu hi færlice   flet ofgeafon,
> modge maguþegnas.   Swa þes middangeard
> ealra dogra gehwam   dreoseð ond falleþ.

> Therefore I see no reason in the world
> Why my heart grows not dark, when I consider
> The lives of warriors, how they suddenly
> Have left their hall, the bold and noble thanes,
> Just as this earth and everything thereon
> Declines and weakens each and every day.

(Wanderer, 58–63)

He looks at the evidence of decay, which many contemporaries thought would accelerate as the millennium approached, and with it the prospect of the world's dissolution. Of the seven ages of the world since its Creation, five, it was believed, had already passed and the sixth was drawing to a close.

> Ongietan sceal gleaw hæle   hu gæstlic bið,
> þonne ealre þisse worulde wela   weste stondeð,
> swa nu missenlice   geond þisne middangeard
> winde biwaune   weallas stondaþ,
> hrime bihrorene,   hryðge þa ederas.

> The wise must know how awesome it will be
> When all the wealth of earth stands desolate,
> As now in various parts throughout the world
> Stand wind-blown walls, frost-covered, ruined buildings.

(Wanderer, 73–7)

Lines 85–7 recall that God has already acted in judgement once, in sending the flood recorded in Genesis 6 and judgement, as the 'wise' know, will come again. This view of history, a commonplace of Christian thought, is also seen in *Guthlac A*:

> Woruld is onhrered,
> colaþ Cristes lufu,   sindan costinga

geond middangeard   monge arisene,
swa þæt geara iu   godes spelbodan
wordum sægdon   ond þurh witedom
eal anemdon,   swa hit nu gongeð.
Ealdað eorþan blæd   æþela gehwylcre.

The world is embroiled; love for Christ cools; many are the tribulations
arisen throughout the world, just as God's spokesmen declared in their
sayings long ago and spelt out in prophecy everything just as it is now
happening. Earth's vitality is aging in each of its noble qualities.

(Guthlac A, 37–43)

The transience of this world's glories was not merely a matter for
regret but a cause for soul-searching. The Church taught that with
the world's end would come the **Last Judgement** for which all
men must prepare. Gold and treasure, as the *Seafarer* made clear,
would be valueless then (100-1). Life therefore was no longer
simply a matter of maintaining a good name for loyalty and
courage, but of preparing to render an account to God. This new
perspective had profound implications for poetry. An important
function of the heroic poetry was to commemorate and immortalise
the heroes of the past that listeners might admire and emulate them.
Widsith, the archetypal *scop*, commends the generous patron who
understands the fame which poets can confer:

se þe fore duguþe wile   dom aræran
               ... lof se gewyrceð,
hafað under heofonum   heahfæstne dom.

Who would not have his fame fail among the guard
             ... Lasting honour shall be his
A name that shall never die beneath the heavens.

(Widsith, 140, 142–3)

But Bede, his mind shaped by both Roman and Celtic spirituality,
wrote,

Fore them neidfæræ   nænig uuiurthit
thoncsnottura,   than him tharf sie
to ymbhycggannae   aer his hiniongæ
huæt his gastæ   godæs æththa yflæs
æfter deothdæge   doemid uueorthæ.

Before the journey that awaits us all

No man becomes so wise that he has not
Need to think out, before his going hence
What judgement will be given to his soul
After his death, of evil or of good.

(*Bede's Death-Song*)

**Bede** too was interested in immortality, but from a different standpoint. He also wrote of great men but his purpose was to stir his readers to consider their eternal fate; and other writers of **saints'** lives, such as the poet Cynewulf, shared his motivation. In poetry, as in life, hardship and sacrifice were to be willingly accepted in the hope of eternal reward. Thus the homiletic sections of poems such as the *Wanderer* and the *Seafarer* are not to be regarded as empty moralising but are integral to the poet's concept. Experience viewed aright could lead to wisdom, that is an understanding of the ways of God to man, and such wisdom should obviously be passed on. If life, as the Anglo-Saxon Church believed, was to be viewed from an eternal standpoint, then what could be more important than reminding oneself (and others) of these truths? Some critics seeking to reconcile these elements have suggested that the poem is a dialogue, between the wanderer (*eardstapa*) and the wise man (*snottor on mode*).[14] But as Shippey points out,[15] this approach does not give sufficient weight to the Anglo-Saxon view of how wisdom is achieved and there is general agreement among modern critics that the poem is a monologue in which the poet's experience is placed in a wider context and the speaker is seen to achieve wisdom through careful reflection on his solitary existence. The *Wanderer* begins with a statement which combines a bleak view of the world with the seeds of a Christian perspective:

Oft him anhaga    are gebideð
metudes miltse,    þeah þe he modcearig
geond lagulade    longe sceolde
hreran mid hondum    hrimcealde sæ,
wadan wræclastas;    Wyrd bið ful aræd!

Often the solitary man enjoys [awaits/experiences]
The grace and mercy of the Lord, though he
Careworn has long been forced to stir by hand
The ice-cold sea on many waterways,
Travel the exile's path; fate is relentless.

(*Wanderer*, 1-5)

The Wanderer is a man without companionship, lacking the security of kinsmen or a lord to protect him. Unlike the Seafarer he has not sought exile voluntarily, and his meditations are not so much about choosing hardship in this world as about learning to endure those hardships which inevitably afflict all mankind. In line 58 he moves from personal sorrow to a wider view of the world. His experience is but one instance of the greater truth that the whole world is steadily declining. Such experience is valuable because it leads to an understanding both of the world and of oneself. In lines 58-111, the Wanderer proceeds to cast doubt on the reliability of the earthly consolation which he seeks. He has stated his hope of finding a new lord to serve (26-9) but his reflections on the ruins of the past seem to undermine any hope of a stable future:

> Se þonne þisne wealsteal   wise geþohte
> ond þis deorce lif   deope geondþenceð,
> frod in ferðe,   feor oft gemon
> wælsleahta worn,   ond as word acwið:
> 'Hwær cwom mearg?   Hwær cwom mago?   Hwær cwom
>    maþþumgyfa?
> Hwær cwom symbla gesetu?   Hwær sindon seledreamas? . . .
> Her bið feoh læne,   her bið freond læne,
> her bið mon læne,   her bið mæg læne,
> eal þis eorþan gesteal   idel weorþeð!'

>                   He who has wisely thought
> And carefully considered this creation
> And this dark life, experienced in spirit
> Has often pondered many massacres
> In far off ages, and might say these words:
> 'Where is the horse now, where the hero gone?
> Where is the bounteous lord, and where the benches
> For feasting? Where are all the joys of hall? . . .
> Here property and friendship pass away,
> Here man himself and kinsmen pass away,
> And all this earthly structure comes to nought.'

>                    (*Wanderer* 88–93, 108–110)

The objects of his quest, a generous lord, the joys of the mead-hall, the companionship of kinsmen, are seen in the light of history as tragically vulnerable to forces beyond man's control. The repeated question 'Where are they now?' probably derives from the *Ubi sunt* passages which were common in sermons reminding Christians of the transience of life.[16] J. E. Cross suggests that the *Wanderer* should be understood in relationship to the Latin *consolatio* which was employed by both classical and Christian writers.[17] The most famous example of this genre, the *Consolation of Philosophy* by Boethius, was translated into Old English during Alfred's reign. An important question remains: since the poet more than once praises the ability to bear sorrows in silence, why does he reveal his own sufferings with such honesty? The answer comes near the end of the poem. A man should not reveal his cares unless he also knows the remedy (112–14). The apostle **James** suggested that Christians should be slow to speak in anger or complaint (James 1:19) and the Psalmist refused to express his anger at the unfairness of life until he understood God's purposes (Psalm 72). Similarly the Wanderer regards it as unwise for a man to broadcast his doubts and questionings until he has reached a position of understanding. He is now free to reveal the extent of his trials precisely because he has become *snottor on mode* and found the answer he sought.

> Til biþ se þe his treowe gehealdeþ . . .
>                                    Wel bið þam þe him are seceð,
> frofre to fæder on heofonum,   þær us eal seo fæstnung stondeð.

> Blessed is he who keeps his faith . . .
> Well shall it be for him who looks for grace
> And comfort from our father in the heavens,
> Where is ordained all our security.

> (*Wanderer*, 112, 114–5)

Although the Wanderer is not, like the Seafarer, a deliberate exile, the consolation he finds is that of the Christian who views this world as a temporary home and can therefore remain steadfast in the face of bitter loss. True security is to be found not in the hall of an earthly lord, but in allegiance to the Lord of Heaven. The conviction which motivates the Seafarer is also the hope which sustains the *anhaga*, the solitary man, in his wanderings.

THE CELTIC LEGACY

By the middle of the seventh century it must have been clear that the Christian faith would eventually unite all the kingdoms of the English. Roman missionaries had been hard at work in the southern kingdoms and the island was now a patchwork of different Christian traditions introduced from Rome, Ireland and Gaul.

Given the inter-relationships of the various kingdoms and the increasing travels of men such as **Wilfrid**, questions were bound to arise. To whom would the emerging Church in England owe allegiance? How were the different strands of Christian observance to be reconciled? The uncertainty finally came to a head in 664 at the Synod of Whitby.[18] Oswy of Northumbria, Oswald's successor and *bretwalda* at the time, was married to a Kentish wife. When he (following the Irish calculations) was celebrating **Easter**, his wife and her household (following the Roman custom) were still observing **Lent**. Oswy summoned a council of **bishops** and clergy to meet at the double **monastery** of Streoneshalch (Whitby) which was ruled by Hild, herself a member of the Northumbrian royal family. Whilst debate at the Synod undoubtedly reflected underlying questions of dominance and allegiance, it is also true that during this period Easter was the chief festival of the Christian year and its observance a matter of real concern to the devout. Oswy made it clear that he wanted a unified rule of life for all Christians to follow. In the sometimes acrimonious discussion which followed, Colman, Bishop of Lindisfarne, pleaded the authority of **St John**, Polycarp and **St Columba**. **Wilfrid**, on the other hand, speaking for the Roman party, argued that their custom was now followed universally and carried the weight of the great **Apostle Peter** to whom **Christ** had given 'the keys of the kingdom of heaven'. Oswy announced that he could not risk offending the doorkeeper of **heaven** and decided for Rome.

There followed a period of re-adjustment. Colman and his **monks** refused to conform to the new order and left Lindisfarne for Iona. Others, however, agreed to accept this new custom which **Bede** would later defend with considerable zeal. This positive outcome was no doubt made easier by the fact that the differences between Rome and the Celtic Churches were largely those of temperament rather than teaching. The Celtic Churches were orthodox in doctrine but had fallen out of step with Rome through isolation and separate development rather than through opposition to Roman authority. The future now belonged to Rome. But Celtic **monks** had left their stamp on the Church which emerged. The pages of Bede's *History* are full of the achievements of men whom he held up as examples for his own day. **Aidan**, **Cuthbert** and their successors were not just individual practitioners of piety; they infused their spirit into the Church. An important Celtic contribution to the life of the English Church was the practice of **penance**.[19] In the **early Church**, penance had been a public ritual presided over by a **bishop**. The Irish developed a private form in which spiritual conflict and failures were articulated, with the help of a **priest**, and an appropriate **penance** devised, through which repentance could be expressed. Penitents could confess their temptations as well as their wrong thoughts and actions. Penances, which could vary from prayer and **fasting** to enforced **pilgrimage**, were regarded as medicine for the soul. Thus it was that Saint Columba's 'soul-friend', Saint Laisren, heard the confession of his war-making and prescribed as penance his voyage into exile. This approach emphasised the individual's responsibility for his own spiritual well-being. Not only monks but devout lay-people, both those living near **monasteries** and further afield, came to **confessors** to have penances assigned to them. By making amends for their **sins** now, they hoped to avert the terrors of future punishment. Archbishop Theodore later adopted and developed the Irish system, prescribing appropriate penances for specific offences. Eventually the whole practice became open to abuse as weaker penalties, including the payment of money, were substituted. In the early days of the Anglo-Saxon Church, however, its purpose was serious and its practice apparently widespread. **Bede** describes the impact of the preaching of **St Cuthbert**: 'Such was his skill in teaching . . . that none dared keep back from him even the closest secrets of their hearts. They confessed every sin openly – indeed they thought he would know if they held anything back – and made amends by "fruits worthy of repentance", as he commanded' (*Life of Cuthbert*, Ch. 9).

Another Celtic characteristic was the self-denial and simplicity of lifestyle warmly commended by Bede in his account of Bishop **Aidan**: 'The highest recommendation of his teaching to all was that he and his followers lived as they taught. He never sought or cared for any worldly possessions and loved to give away to the poor who chanced to meet him whatever he received from kings or wealthy folk' (Bede, *HE*, III:5). Celtic **asceticism** could become extreme, yet their outlook on life was neither barren nor dreary. Their **monasteries** were centres of beauty and creativity, where classical learning and artistic skill flourished. Men delved into the buried treasures of the scriptures and the learning of the past and produced jewel-bright manuscripts, such as the Lindisfarne **Gospels** and the Codex Amiatinus. They preserved ancient and contemporary literature. Scribes toiled in spartan conditions to meet the demand for copies of popular works, especially those of **Bede**, whose wide-ranging interests and scholarship made him famous on the Continent. Abbot Cuthbert, of Wearmouth and Jarrow, indicated some of the pressures on his own scriptorium in a letter to Lul, Bishop of Mainz, in 764.

> I have sent in accordance with your wishes the books about the man of God, Cuthbert, composed in verse and prose. And if I could do more I would gladly have done so. For the conditions of the past winter oppressed the island of our race very horribly with cold and ice and long and widespread storms of wind and rain, so that the hand of the scribe was hindered from producing a great number of books.
>
> (*EHD*, Vol. I, No. 185)

Fortunately the life of a scribe was not always so gruelling, as a ninth-century Irish scribe recorded in the margin of his manuscript:

> The clear cuckoo sings to me, lovely discourse,
> in its grey cloak from the crest of the bushes;
> truly – may the Lord protect me!–
> well do I write under the forest wood.[20]

That the creators of the Lindisfarne **Gospels** were equally aware of their surroundings is demonstrated by the incorporation into their art of birds reminiscent of the shags and kittiwakes which still frequent the coast of Northumbria. Stories about birds and animals occur frequently in the *Lives* of the **saints**, whose closeness to God was seen as conferring on them a particular affinity with nature. In one such incident, **St Cuthbert** is described slipping silently out of the **monastery** by night to pray in the bitter-cold waters of the North Sea:

> One night one of the monks watched him creep out, then followed him stealthily to see where he was going and what he was about. Down he went towards the beach beneath the monastery and out into the sea until he was up to his arms and neck in deep water. The splash of the waves accompanied his vigil throughout the dark hours of the night. At daybreak, he came out, knelt down on the sand and prayed. Then two otters bounded out of the water, stretched themselves out before him, warmed his feet with their breath and tried to dry him on their fur. They finished, received his blessing, and slipped back to their watery home.
>
> (*Life of Cuthbert*, Ch. 10)

The decision at Whitby then was not all gain, but neither was it all loss. The English would benefit from the organisation of the Roman Church and Continental links would be strengthened. Books, paintings, skilled masons and glaziers would be imported to enrich the as yet simple worship of the English Church. Yet the legacy of the Celtic missionaries, revered even by those who rejected their ecclesiastical idiosyncrasies, was a potent one. Their spiritual devotion, adventurous spirit, love of beauty and passion for scholarship, all bore fruit in that flowering of scholarship and spirituality known as the Golden Age of Northumbria.

NOTES

1. On the extent of differences between the Roman and Celtic branches of the Church see Hughes (1987).
2. Mayr-Harting (1991, 90).
3. For critical approaches to these poems see *Seafarer*, ed. Gordon; *Wanderer*, eds Dunning and Bliss; Green (1983); Mandel (1987), and *Old English Elegies*, ed. Klinck.
4. Whitelock (1950).
5. Old Irish *Life of St Columba* in the *Book of Lismore*. Cited Henry (1966, 30).
6. Anderson (1937); Smithers (1959; 1958); Holton (1982); Vickrey (1982).
7. For a fuller treatment of this subject see my forthcoming article 'Land and sea in the pilgrim life', *English Language Notes*, (Autumn, 1997).
8. *Exodus*, 104, note on lines 178b–799.
9. *Old English Exodus*, 74.
10. *Exodus*, 104.
11. *Old English Elegies*, 131.
12. For example Psalms 3, 5, 6, 12, 21, 24, 27, 30, 31, 37, 38, 41, 42, 50, 54, 55, 58, 60, 61, 62, 63, 68, 69, 70, 72, 76, 85, 101, 108, 115, 129.
13. See Fell (1991).
14. See Pope (1965).
15. Shippey (1972, 59).
16. See for example *Blickling Homily X*.
17. Cross (1961).
18. See Mayr-Harting (1991, Ch. 7).
19. See Frantzen (1983).
20. Jackson (1935, 3).

# Chapter 3

# Saints, Scholars and the Scriptures

Nu scylun hergan    hefænricæs uard,
metudæs mæcti    end his modgidanc,
uerc uuldurfadur,    sue he uundra gihuæs,
eci dryctin,    or astelidæ.

Now must we praise the Guardian of heaven,
The power and conception of the Lord,
And all His works, as He, eternal Lord,
Father of glory, started every wonder.

(Caedmon's Hymn, 1–4)

The story of the Northumbrian poet **Caedmon** (c. 680), as told by **Bede**, offers a glimpse of literary history in the making. Here we find not only clues to the development of the Christian poetry which dominates the surviving manuscripts, but also the earliest extant biography of an English writer. To Bede, looking back over half a century, the unlettered cowherd was still unequalled as a composer of religious poems in English. The reason for his supremacy: Caedmon, like the writers of the Holy Scriptures before him, was considered to have been directly inspired by God. Bede's account is well known, but worth repeating for the insights it gives into contemporary attitudes. Caedmon lived within the orbit of **Abbess** Hild's double **monastery** at Whitby:

> He had followed a secular occupation until well advanced in years without ever learning anything about poetry . . . when he saw the harp coming his way, he would get up from the table and go home. On one such occasion he had left the house in which the entertainment was being held and went out to the stable . . . in a dream he saw a man standing beside him who called him by name. 'Caedmon,' he said, 'sing me a song.' 'I don't know how to sing,' he replied, 'It is because I cannot sing that I left the feast and came here.' The man . . . then said,

'But you shall sing to me.' 'What should I sing about?' he replied. 'Sing about the Creation of all things,' the other answered. And Caedmon began to sing verses in praise of God the Creator which he had never heard before ... When Caedmon awoke, he remembered everything that he had sung in his dream, and soon added more verses in the same style to a song truly worthy of God.

(Bede, *HE,* IV:24)

The significance of Caedmon's poetry was that it represented the fusion of the vernacular poetry of everyday entertainment with the new treasury of learning of which the Church was custodian. Hild (d. 680) was evidently quick to recognise the potential of this new form. She admitted Caedmon into the **monastic** community and had him instructed in 'the events of sacred history'. His renderings of the scriptures were, **Bede** says, so melodious that they 'turned his instructors into his audience'. Monastic scholars, Bede himself included, were not impervious to the charms of poetry, but scholars were only a fraction of the population. Caedmon's verses could make the teachings of the Church attractive and memorable to unlettered men and women like himself: 'So skilful was he in composing religious and devotional songs that when any passage of Scripture was explained to him by interpreters, he could quickly turn it into delightful and moving poetry in his own English tongue' (Bede, *HE*, IV:24). Caedmon himself seems to have remained illiterate but his poetry was composed within a context of considerable erudition. Before her death in 680, Hild made her **abbey** at Whitby an educational centre of some importance. No less than five future English **bishops** were trained there. Caedmon's ability might be God-given but monastic scholarship was required to ensure that he had a sound grasp of doctrine. A considerable degree of theological sophistication has been detected in Caedmon's hymn[1] and the poetry of his successors would be shaped by both **liturgical** influences and the knowledge of Latin literature for which English schools became justly famous. Inspiration and scholarship proved a fruitful partnership.

A NEW TREASURY OF LEARNING

Whitby was not unique as a centre of learning in late seventh-century Northumbria. Fifty miles up the coast the twin **monasteries** of Wearmouth and Jarrow were to nurture **Bede**, the finest writer of the age. **Benedict Biscop**, returning to Northumbria c. 672, had shown the king his collection of books and **relics** gathered during visits to Gaul and Rome. Deeply impressed, the king granted him land, and the monasteries which were eventually built reaped the benefits of Benedict's cosmopolitan background. In all, he made six journeys to Rome, bringing back 'a great mass of books of every sort' and paintings for the church at Jarrow: 'Thus all who entered the church, even those who could not read, were able whichever way they looked to contemplate the dear face of Christ and His saints . . . to put themselves more firmly in mind of the Lord's Incarnation (Bede, *Lives*, Ch. 6). Benedict was determined that in their scholarship, worship and architecture, his **monasteries** should reflect all that he had seen in Rome and Gaul. The monastic **rule** which he introduced for his **monks** was a compilation 'of all I found best in the life of the seventeen monasteries I visited during my long and frequent pilgrimages' (Bede, *Lives*, Ch. 11). Unable to find the requisite skills amongst his own people, he imported stone masons and glaziers from France. He even persuaded the **Pope** to allow John, chief cantor at St Peter's in Rome, to teach the monks of Wearmouth-Jarrow 'the order of chanting and singing the psalms and conducting the **liturgy** according to the practice in force at Rome' (Bede, *Lives*, Ch. 6). It was in this atmosphere that the young **Bede** (b. c. 673) grew up:

> On reaching seven years of age, I was entrusted by my family first to the most reverend Abbot Benedict and later to Abbot Ceolfrid for my education. I have spent all the remainder of my life in this monastery and devoted myself entirely to the study of the scriptures. And while I have observed the regular discipline and sung the choir offices daily in church, my chief delight has always been in study, teaching, and writing.
>
> (Bede, *HE*, V:24)

That an obscure Northumbrian **monk**, born less than a century after **Augustine**'s arrival in Kent, should be a scholar at all is a matter for wonder; that he should shine like a candle in the darkness of his age and influence students for seven centuries to come is truly astonishing.[2] The list of **Bede**'s writings, given at the end of his *Ecclesiastical History*, reveals an extraordinarily wide-ranging mind. His delight in scholarship overflowed into many areas, scientific and literary. A student of time and cosmology, he was also eager for information on geography and natural history and wrote a book on poetry. He researched and recorded the actions of rulers and church leaders: 'for if history records good things of good

men, the thoughtful hearer is encouraged to imitate what is good
(*HE, Preface*). Though Bede wrote almost exclusively in Latin he
was described by his pupil Cuthbert as 'familiar with English
poetry'[3] and translated the **Lord's Prayer** and **Creed** into
Anglo-Saxon for the less learned. The primary focus of his studies,
however, remained the **Bible**. Bede described himself as living on
the 'uttermost edge of the world' (*PL*, XCI, 1077) yet thanks to
**Benedict Biscop** he had access to an unusually well-equipped
library. Examination of Bede's works[4] has shown that he was well
versed in the writings of **Augustine of Hippo**, **Jerome**, **Ambrose**
and **Gregory the Great**. With the possible exception of Virgil, his
acquaintance with writers of the classical period was apparently
through collections made by others. He knew the Christian Latin
poets such as Juvencus, Prudentius and Paulinus of Nola; he made
extensive use of Pliny's *Natural History* and had some knowledge of
the historians Josephus, Eusebius, Orosius, Isidore of Seville, and
Gregory of Tours.

In the Preface to his *Ecclesiastical History*, Bede cites **Abbot**
Albinus of Canterbury as his 'principal authority and adviser' and
the man who persuaded him to embark on his greatest work. Links
between Canterbury and Northumbria were strong and Bede had
great respect for the Canterbury school, founded in 669 by
**Archbishop** Theodore and **Abbot** Hadrian. Theodore, a Greek
**monk** from the Orthodox Church of the East, and the
African-born Hadrian had been sent to England by the **Pope** after
plague had decimated the leadership of the English Church.
Together they imparted to eager students a wealth of knowledge
gathered in Rome, Athens, and Byzantium:

> In addition to instructing them in the holy Scriptures, they also taught
> their pupils poetry, astronomy, and the calculation of the church
> calendar. In proof of this, some of their students still alive today are as
> proficient in Latin and Greek as in their native tongue.
>
> (Bede, *HE*, IV:2)

Irish influence on scholarship remained strong. The great
Anglo-Saxon scholar **Aldhelm** (d.c. 709), mentioned briefly by
**Bede** (*HE*, V:18), owed much to his Irish mentors at the **Abbey**
of Malmesbury, though he too was drawn to Canterbury.
According to a twelfth-century account by William of Malmesbury
(*Gesta Pontificum*, Vol. 5), Aldhelm used to compose and perform
English songs in order to attract an audience for his preaching.

Unfortunately, none of Aldhelm's English poems have survived. His Latin writings show Celtic influence in their difficult, ornate style. More attractive are the riddles which he exchanged with, among others, his close friend Aldfrith, ruler of Northumbria (685-705), such as this description of the scholar's basic tool, a wax writing-tablet:

> Of honey bees I first was born;
> But in the forest grew my outer coat;
> My tough backs came from shoes. An iron point
> In artful windings cuts a fair design,
> And leaves long, twisted furrows like a plough.
> From heaven unto that field is borne the seed
> Or nourishment.
>
> (Aldhelm: *Riddles*, 32)

The Anglo-Saxons delighted in the intellectual stimulus and spiritual lessons to be gleaned from discovering hidden meanings, since for them all created things had symbolic significance. **Aldhelm**'s writings also illustrate the dilemma of the Christian scholar faced with the pagan writings of the classical era. The attitude of churchmen to such literature had always varied. Even the **Fathers of the Church** did not agree, **Gregory the Great** showing the greatest disapproval. Aldhelm's style and content are more heavily influenced by classical authors than those of the more cautious **Bede**, yet he still told a young friend embarking on studies in Ireland that he considered it absurd:

> to turn from the inextricable rule [of the Old and the New Testament] and undertake a journey through the slippery paths of a country full of brambles, that is to say, through the troublesome meanderings of the (worldly) philosophers . . . What pray . . . is the benefit to the sanctity of the orthodox faith to expend energy by reading and studying the foul pollution of base Proserpina?
>
> (Aldhelm, *Prose Works*, Letter III)

It was precisely because classical studies formed an indispensable framework for education in Anglo-Saxon England that the monastic student had to guard against being seduced by forbidden delights. The Church needed the writings of the ancients and continued to preserve and transmit them. Grammar, rhetoric and the study of literature: all these were tools necessary to achieve a full understanding of that most important of books, the **Bible**. The Bible in its turn was seen as shedding light on all other branches of study and its pre-eminence was never forgotten. In this, as in many other respects, the influence of **Augustine of Hippo** can be discerned:

> But just as poor as the store of gold and silver and garments which the people of Israel brought with them out of Egypt was in comparison with the riches which they afterwards obtained at Jerusalem . . . so poor is all the useful knowledge which is gathered from the books of the heathen when compared with the knowledge of Holy Scripture. For whatever a man may have learned from other sources, if it is hurtful, it is there condemned; if it is useful it is therein contained.
>
> (*On Christian Doctrine*, Book II, LII)

Another outstanding Anglo-Saxon scholar was **Alcuin**, born in the year of **Bede**'s death (735). Alcuin presided over the great cathedral school at York, which by the mid-eighth century boasted one of the finest libraries in the West, until his fame led to an invitation from Charlemagne to establish schools within the Frankish empire. He undertook this task with enthusiasm, but confessed in a letter to his royal patron that he still missed 'to some extent the rarer books of scholastic learning which I had in my own country' (*EHD*, Vol. 1, No. 20). Nor were women excluded from the joys of scholarship.[5] Aldhelm wrote letters to a community of **nuns** at Barking, indicating that in addition to studying the scriptures, they were expected to be familiar with the writings of the **Fathers**, history, allegory, grammar and metre. **Boniface**, the Apostle of Germany, relied heavily on the support of Anglo-Saxon nuns, as is shown by the letters which he exchanged with women such as Leoba, who joined him in the German mission, and Abbess Bucge (*EHD*, Vol. 1, Nos 168, 172, 173). Leoba, who is described by her biographer as having been 'educated from early infancy in grammar and the study of the other liberal arts' (*EHD*, Vol. 1, No. 159), even sent for his criticism some lines of poetry, an art which she had learned from Eadburgh, Abbess of Minster in Thanet (*EHD*, Vol. 1, No. 169).

SCRIPTURE IN SONG

It was to Eadburgh that **Boniface** wrote, asking her to copy for him in letters of gold, 'the epistles of my Lord, **St Peter** the **Apostle**, to secure honour and reverence for the Holy Scriptures when they are preached from before the eyes of the heathen' (*EHD,* Vol. 1, No. 172). Boniface wanted the scriptures written in a manner worthy of the reverence with which he and his Christian contemporaries regarded the very text of the Word of God. A riddle found in the Exeter Book describes the painstaking labour involved in the production of such a volume.

Mec feonda sum    feore besnyþede,
woruldstrenga binom,    wætte siþþan,
dyfde on wætre,    dyde eft þonan,
sette on sunnan,    þær ic swiþe beleas
herum þam þe ic hæfde.    Heard mec siþþan
snað seaxses ecg,    sindrum begrunden;
fingras feoldan,    ond mec fugles wyn
geond speddropan    spyrede geneahhe,
ofer brunne brerd  . . .
                              Mec siþþan wrah
hæleð hleobordum,    hyde beþenede,
gierede mec mid golde.

An enemy ended my life, deprived me
of my physical strength; then he dipped me
in water and drew me out again,
and put me in the sun where I soon shed
all my hair. After that, the knife's sharp edge
bit into me and all my blemishes were scraped away;
fingers folded me and the bird's feather
often moved over my brown surface,
sprinkling meaningful marks  . . .
                              Then a man bound me,
he stretched skin over me and adorned me
with gold.

(*Riddle 26*, 1–9, 11–13 in *Anglo-Saxon World*)

The same care that went into the reproduction of the text was also employed in its interpretation. Anglo-Saxon Christians did not come to the scriptures in a vacuum. Their understanding was coloured by centuries of commentary and interpretation which had overlaid the text with complex levels of meaning. The early centuries of Christianity had produced two main schools of biblical interpretation: one chiefly associated with Antioch, the other with Alexandria. The Antiochian approach made use of history, geography and natural science to expound the literal sense of the text. The chief exponent of this method in England was **Archbishop** Theodore of Canterbury, himself a native of Asia Minor and thus uniquely equipped to bring the world of the **Bible** alive for his Anglo-Saxon audience. Reports of his teaching reached **Bede** who passed on the information in his turn:

> The same apostle [Paul] said, 'a day and a night I was in the depth of the sea' (II Cor. 11:25). I have heard certain men assert that Theodore of blessed memory, a very learned man and once archbishop of the English people, expounded the saying thus: that there was in Cyzicus (Asia Minor) a certain very deep pit, dug for the punishment of criminals, which on account of its immense depth was called *the depth of the sea*. It was the filth and darkness of this which Paul bore, amongst other things, for Christ.
>
> (*PL* 93, cols 456D–457A)

It was, however, the allegorical approach of the Alexandrian school which exercised the greatest influence on Western theology and literature. Through the **Fall**, it was maintained, humankind had lost the ability to perceive the truth directly. However, for those who were prepared to develop their spiritual perceptions there was hope: just as in the person of Jesus **Christ**, the presence of God was concealed by human form, so, contained within the words of the **Bible** (the 'letter'), lay the Word of God ('the spirit'). Bede, in his work *On Tropes and Figures*, recognises four levels of allegory: 'the historical, allegorical or typological, tropological or moral, and the anagogical (or spiritual).' He goes on to illustrate his point from Psalm 147:12–13: '"Praise the lord, O Jerusalem. Because . . . he has blessed your children within you". This trope can rightly be taken as referring literally to the citizens of the earthly Jerusalem, allegorically to the Church of Christ, tropologically to each saved soul, and anagogically to the celestial homeland' (*Art of Poetry*, Ch. 12). In this way large sections of the biblical narrative were invested with allegorical significance, an approach which was particularly useful with those parts of the **Old Testament** which might appear at first glance completely unedifying. Here too **Augustine of Hippo** had laid down guidelines: 'In all cases this is the method: whatever in Scripture cannot literally be related to purity of life or to the truth of faith, may be taken as figurative' (*On Christian Doctrine*, Bk III, Ch. X). Many of the interpretations which resulted from this approach may seem somewhat arbitrary and absurdly fanciful to the modern reader but this was a science with its own rules, chief among which was Augustine's insistence that 'What is read must be diligently turned over in the mind until an interpretation is found that promotes the rule of charity' (Bk II, Ch. XXV). This allegorical technique was applied by Anglo-Saxon poets to their own rendering of the scriptures. Thus in *Exodus*, the apparently straightforward story of the Israelites' escape from Egyptian tyranny is infused with allegorical significance drawn from long-established tradition. **St Paul**, in I Corinthians, had pointed to the Exodus narrative as full of significance for the young Church: 'For I would not have you ignorant, brethren, that our fathers were all under the cloud, and all passed through the sea, And all in Moses were baptized . . . Now these things were done in a figure for us' (I Cor. 10:1–6). The Exodus from Egypt marked the establishment of the nation of Israel; an event which in Christian thought prefigured the birth of the Church. God's action in saving his people from the Egyptians was seen not only as a historical event but as a foreshadowing of the greater redemption which would come through the death of Christ. There were other parallels to be drawn: 'Egypt was seen as the World, Pharaoh as the Devil, the crossing of the Red Sea as Baptism, the trek through the wilderness as the journey of exile through this life, the pillar of cloud and fire as the Holy Spirit which guides Christians eventually to the Promised Land of heaven.'[6] The poet interrupts the account of the crossing of the Red Sea to refer to Noah, whose deliverance from the flood was also seen as a figure of **baptism**, and cites Abraham as another example of faith. Abraham's willingness to obey God and sacrifice his only son Isaac was understood to prefigure God's eventual sacrifice of His Son to bring about mankind's deliverance from sin. Among the treasures which **Benedict Biscop** had imported from the Continent Bede noted:

> a set of pictures . . . very skilfully arranged to show how the Old Testament foreshadowed the new. In one set, for instance, the picture of Isaac carrying the wood on which he was to be burnt as a sacrifice was placed immediately below that of Christ carrying the cross on which he was about to suffer.
>
> (*Lives of the Abbots*, Ch. 9)

The twin themes of obedience and deliverance run through the poem. Pharaoh and his great army are doomed because they have dared to set themselves in opposition to God. And God (as the Anglo-Saxons never failed to note) could be relied upon to ensure victory even against overwhelming odds:

> He onfond hraðe,
> siððan grund gestah   godes andsaca,
> þæt wæs mihtigra   mereflodes weard.

God's adversary quickly found, when he sank into the abyss, that the Guardian Lord of the ocean was the greater in might.

(*Exodus*, 502–4)

The poem's audience are urged to interpret and apply the message themselves:

> gif onlucan wile    lifes wealhstod,
> beorht in breostum,    banhuses weard,
> ginfæsten god    gastes cægon.
> Run bið gerecenod,    ræd forð gæð,
> hafað wislicu    word on fæðme,
> wile meagollice    modum tæcan
> þæt we gesne ne syn    godes þeodscipes,
> metodes miltsa.

If the faculty which interprets life's meaning, the body's tenant, radiant within the breast, has the will to unlock the ample benefits with the keys of the spirit, the mystery will be explained and wisdom will issue forth. It has wise words in its keeping and earnestly desires to instruct our minds so that we may not be lacking in God's Law and the Lord's mercy.

(*Exodus*, 523–30)

This plainly is not simply poetry of entertainment. *Exodus*, together with the other poems found in the *Junius* manuscript (*Genesis, Daniel, Christ and Satan*), deals with the material upon which the Church reflected during the season of **Lent**. The poems may well have been collected and arranged in their present form to provide suitable reading for the monastic refectory. *Exodus* in particular appears to have been influenced by the **liturgy** for **Holy Saturday** (the day before **Easter Sunday**) when carefully-prepared candidates were baptised and the appointed readings included the biblical accounts of the Flood, the crossing of the Red Sea and the story of Abraham and Isaac. The selection of readings for church services contained in the **lectionaries** inevitably played a part in shaping popular understanding of the biblical message. Few would have enjoyed the privilege of seeing a complete copy of the **Bible**, so for most people the relationship between different portions of the scriptures would have been established by the **lectionary** readings. These had evolved during the early centuries of the Church, as the practice of reading the Bible straight through in a year was gradually modified by a growing emphasis on festivals associated with Easter and Christmas. The calendar of seasons and related biblical lessons which emerged was known as the *temporale*. In addition to readings from the canonical scriptures there were extracts from the **Apocrypha** and increasingly from saints' *Lives*. Gradually this extra-biblical material became part of the **Daily Office**. The Anglo-Saxon Church would not have been unduly disturbed by distinctions between **canonical** and non-canonical writings and the poets draw on **apocryphal**, **patristic** and biblical material with apparent impartiality.

At one time, the *Junius* poems were thought to be the work of **Caedmon** himself, since they corresponded with the list of themes supplied by **Bede**:

> He sang of the creation of the world, the origin of the human race, and the whole story of Genesis . . . of Israel's departure from Egypt, the entry into the land of promise . . . He sang of the Lord's **Incarnation**, **Passion**, Redemption and **Ascension** into heaven, the coming of the **Holy Spirit**, and the teaching of the **Apostles**. He also made many poems on the terrors of the **Last Judgement**, the horrible pains of **Hell** and the joys of the Kingdom of **Heaven**.
>
> (*HE*, IV: 24)

It is now agreed that only the hymn recorded by Bede can be safely attributed to Caedmon and that the *Junius* poems are of varying authorship and date. By the time Bede wrote his account, Caedmon already had imitators, though not, in Bede's opinion, of equal stature. Caedmon's poetry, however, set an impressive agenda for the poets who followed him, covering as it did the whole sweep of Christian history from the **Creation** to the **Day of Judgement**. In Christian thought, history was regarded as having both direction and purpose: as linear rather than cyclical. The **Old Testament** foreshadowed the New, the **New Testament** provided the key to interpret the Old. The story of the **Fall of Man** in Genesis was of prime importance in the history of the world but could not be fully appreciated without reference to the parallels contained in **Christ**'s redemption of the world. Adam was tempted in the Garden of Eden and succumbed, Christ was tempted in the wilderness but resisted. Eve was the cause of humanity's downfall; Mary, as mother of Jesus, the instrument of redemption. The *Genesis* text in the *Junius* manuscript is now recognised as being the work of at least two poets. *Genesis A* (lines 1–234 and 852–2936) opens with an exhortation reminiscent of *Caedmon's Hymn* and of the Preface to the **Mass**:

Us is riht micel   ðæt we rodera weard,
wereda wuldorcining,   wordum herigen,
modum lufien!

It is proper and right   that we praise with our lips
And love with our hearts   the Warden of heaven
The Lord of hosts.

(Genesis, 1–3)

The account of the angels' rebellion and God's subsequent decision to create human beings to take their place in heaven owes its inspiration not to the biblical account but to the mass of material which had grown up around the Creation story, in particular the interpretation of **Gregory the Great**. Other notable authors of commentaries on the Hexameron (Six Days of Creation) included St Basil of Caesarea, **Ambrose** and **Bede**. The *Genesis A* poet's familarity with these traditions coupled with his faithfulness to the Vulgate text have led to the conclusion that he must have been a cleric. Lines 235–851, usually referred to as the *Later Genesis* or *Genesis B*, are an interpolation, translated from Old Saxon, and usually assigned to the ninth century. They provide a second version of **Lucifer**'s expulsion from heaven and chart his vengeful campaign to contrive a similar downfall for Adam and Eve:

Uton oðwendan hit nu monna bearnum,
þæt heofonrice, nu we hit habban ne moton.

Since we may not regain it
Let us wrest heaven's realm from the sons of men.

(Genesis, 403–4)

The power of this poem owes much to its forceful characterisation of **Satan** as a rebellious thane who yet requires loyalty from his own followers and is capable of a kind of malignant greatness even in defeat. *Genesis B* is far more than a careful paraphrase of the *Vulgate* account. The unknown poet treats the original story with great freedom. His Eve does not **sin** knowingly but is deceived by Satan's emissary disguised not as a serpent but as an angelic messenger. Adam, when first approached, refuses the bait but eventually succumbs to Eve's pleadings to take the fruit, pleas which the poet insists sprang from good intentions (708). When the terrible truth is revealed, the pair turn not only to recriminations but to repentance. Adam's notion of **penance** seems to owe something to the concept of *peregrinatio*:

Gif ic waldendes   willan cuðe,
hwæt ic his to hearmsceare   habban sceolde,
ne gesawe þu no sniomor,   þeah me on sæ wadan
hete heofones god   heonone nu þa,
on flod faran.

If I but knew

The will of God,   the penance I must pay
You would see no one more swift   though the Lord of heaven
Should bid me fare   through the ocean-flood.

(Genesis, 828–32)

When the Genesis A narrative resumes, it is made clear that exile is
indeed the sentence; not just for them but for the whole human
race:

þu scealt oðerne   eðel secean,
wynleasran wic,   and on wræc hweorfan
nacod niedwædla,   neorxnawanges
dugeðum bedæled.

To another home,   an unhappier dwelling
You shall wander in exile   naked and needy
Deprived of the blessings   of Paradise.

(Genesis, 927–30)

In medieval thought, the conflict between God and **Satan** was a
continuing saga of which the Genesis narrative was only the first
instalment. The Junius manuscript includes not only Daniel which
portrays righteous men standing firm against the onslaught of evil,
but Christ and Satan which describes Satan's enduring enmity
towards humankind (144–8) and temptation of **Christ** in the
wilderness (665–88). **Hell** is revealed as a harsh place of exile where
the joys of the heavenly home are seen all the more clearly by
those who, through disobedience, have lost them for ever. The
stark contrast accentuates the choice facing each human soul: to
succumb to temptation and share Satan's bleak exile or renounce
evil and enter **Christ**'s glorious kingdom.

HEROES OF GOD

Hwæt! We gefrunan   on fyrndagum
twelfe under tunglum   tireadige hæleð,
þeodnes þegnas . . .
Wæs hira Matheus sum.

> Lo, we have heard   of twelve mighty heroes
> Honoured under heaven   in days of old,
> Thanes of God  . . .
> > One was Matthew.
> > > > *(Andreas,* 1–3, 11)

That Anglo-Saxon poets should be happy to dress characters from biblical times in their own customs and battle-gear is hardly surprising; what other garb could they have envisaged? There is, however, a deeper significance to this continual interweaving of Germanic and biblical idioms than obliviousness to anachronism. The missionaries brought with them a particular sense of history and continuity. The Germanic invaders who had conquered the land of the Britons were now linked by ties of allegiance and affection to the **Pope** in Rome and through him to the venerable Apostles **Peter** and **Paul**. More than that, they had become kin to all the people of God through the ages. They felt a strong sense of spiritual affinity with the biblical characters of whom they learned. They identified with their struggles, sought to learn from their adventures and, where appropriate, to enlist their prayers. This attitude was extended to the many **saints** and **martyrs** whose piety was commemorated day by day in the worship of the Church. Such stories had proliferated; their function both liturgical and psychological:

> Eventually the number of saints who found a place of honour in the *sanctorale* (calendar of saints) became so great that it was necessary to rank liturgical commemorations as a means of resolving the problem of conflicting memorials. These rankings are often indicated in medieval calendars by colors (usually red, blue and gold), so that one could tell at a glance, for example, which were the 'red-letter days' . . . the continuous line of martyrs and confessors of the Name which extended from New Testament times helped to enhance the eternal relevance of the scriptures in the minds and hearts of later worshippers.[7]

**Saints'** lives provided Anglo-Saxon audiences with a 'heroic spiritual past'[8] which offered both excitement and edification. For scholars and clerics there were Latin prose lives of favourite saints, such as **Cuthbert**, **Wilfrid** and Guthlac (d. 714). These owed much to forms inherited from the continent and reflect traditional accounts of figures such as St Anthony and St Martin of Tours. **Bede** also included vignettes of the lives of 'home-grown' saints such as Oswald in his *Ecclesiastical History* which help to explain why Bede, the biblical scholar, felt it worthwhile to devote so much precious time and resources to a history of his church and land. Bede saw the story of the church in his own day as, in effect, a continuation of the Book of Acts. His accounts of miracles and visions, seemingly out of place in a historical work, are included as signs that God was still authenticating the ministry of his saints even in the far-off islands of Britain. Such occurrences were to be expected and, if properly vouched for (Bede is always careful to give his sources), accepted with humility and reverence. He cites a letter sent by **Gregory** to **Augustine of Canterbury** in the early days of the English mission:

> I hear that Almighty God has worked great wonders through you for the nation which He has chosen. Therefore let your feeling be one of fearful joy . . . that the souls of the English are being drawn through outward miracles to inward grace.
>
> (*HE*, 1:31)

Gregory knew that, if the Anglo-Saxon church was to confront paganism with any degree of success, it had to demonstrate power superior to that which it challenged. Saints' lives had their part to play in reinforcing this message. **Saints** shared not only in God's holiness but in his authority. Thus even the gentle **Cuthbert** exerts influence over the forces of nature and Guthlac (like St Anthony before him) challenges the forces of evil in their lonely strongholds. Guthlac, a warrior who in many respects simply exchanges one form of warfare for another, apparently appealed to the Anglo-Saxon temperament. In addition to the Latin *Life* by Felix, two Old English poetic accounts have survived in the Exeter Book: *Guthlac A* and *Guthlac B*. These are thought to date from the eighth century and to originate from Mercia since Guthlac himself was a member of the Mercian royal house. These *Lives* serve as a reminder that scholarship in seventh- and eighth-century England was not confined to Northumbria. It was to Mercia that Alfred the Great was to look for scholars in the ninth century, long after the glories of Northumbrian learning had been reduced to ashes by the ravages of the Viking raiders. Northumbria produced **Caedmon**, the originator of scriptural poetry in the language of the people; Mercia, it seems, was responsible for the next major development in English poetry: the composition of saints' lives. There was at this time no developed tradition of narrative prose in Old English, so verse was the only vernacular medium available. That these poems should be a later development is understandable. The first objective of the Church was to teach the essentials of the faith together with the necessary biblical framework. It was left to a later generation to explore the wider resources of Christian Latin literature: the histories of **saints, martyrs** and **confessors**.

The author of three **saints'** lives of this period, *Juliana*, *Elene*, and *The Fates of the Apostles*, left his name, *Cynewulf*, encoded in runes within each poem. It is probable that Cynewulf was a **monk**, since all his signed poems are linked with occasions in the Church's calendar. The *Fates of the Apostles* is presented as a work of consolation in which the poet reviews the 'triumphs' of the martyred **apostles** in an attempt to solace his own fear of death:

> Hwæt! Ic þysne sang  siðgeomor fand
> on seocum sefan,  samnode wide
> hu þa æðelingas  ellen cyðdon,
> torhte and tireadige.

> Listen! morbid over dying, I devised this song in my sick spirit. I gleaned it abroad, how these noble men, illustrious and glorious, gave witness of their courage.

> *(Fates of the Apostles, 1–4)*

In this poem, as in the others, Cynewulf reveals his name because he desires the prayers of his audience for his own **salvation**. Characteristically he weaves in references to the transient nature of this world, man's mortality and the looming ordeal of Judgement Day: all recurring themes in his work.

> Her mæg findan  foreþances gleaw,
> se ðe hine lysteð  leoðgiddunga,
> hwa þas fitte fegde.  ᚠ· þær on ende standeþ,
> eorlas þæs on eorðan brucaþ;  ne moton hie awa ætsomne,
> woruldwunigende; ·ᚹ· sceal gedreosan,
> ·ᚢ· on eðle,  æfter tohweorfan,
> læne lices frætewa,  efne swa ·ᛚ· toglideð.
> Þonne ·ᚻ· ond ·ᚾ·  cræftes neotað
> nihtes nearowe,  on him ·ᛏ· ligeð,
> cyninges þeodom.

Here the person clever at deduction, and who takes pleasure in the
recitation of lays, can find out who composed this poem: Wealth (F)
shall be at its end there. Men enjoy this on earth, but not for ever will
they be allowed to remain together abiding in the world. The pleasure
which (W) is ours (U) in this native place will fail and then the body's
borrowed fineries will crumble away, even as the sea (L) will vanish
away when fire (C) and trumpet (Y) exercise their strength in the straits
of the night; coercion (N) will lie upon them – their thraldom to the
King.

(*Fates*, 96–105)

In *Juliana* we see the customary ingredients of the **saint**'s life. It was
a popular legend, other versions appearing in Latin, Middle English,
Middle High German, Old French and Middle Irish, but the
reasons for its popularity may not be immediately apparent to the
modern reader. Juliana, whose **feast** day was February 16, was
believed to have lived during the reign of Emperor Maximilian, a
period of severe persecution for Christians. In the poem she refuses
to marry a wealthy pagan senator and her infuriated father delivers
her to her rejected suitor to be tortured until she yields. At stake
are her Christian integrity – she will not sacrifice to pagan gods –
and her purity – she has dedicated her virginity to **Christ**. Calmly
the saint submits to being flogged, hung from a gallows by her hair,
cast into prison and placed in a cauldron of boiling lead, until at
last, still serene and apparently unscathed, she is beheaded and her
soul dispatched to heaven. This grisly saga and its kind had a
particular role in popular spirituality. Like **Bede**'s carefully-
researched biographies of **Cuthbert** and the **Abbots** of Wearmouth-
Jarrow, they were indebted to conventional forms,[9] yet their
approach and tone are strikingly different. The primary emphasis of
*Juliana* and other similar saints' lives was not historical accuracy but
spiritual clarity. Rosemary Woolf warns that it would therefore be
inappropriate to judge them by the standards of modern biography:
'The garish, spectacular action of most saints' lives is designed to
reveal a kind of religious truth which would not stand out so
clearly from the confused appearances of everyday life.'[10] Central to
the narrative of *Juliana* is her confrontation with the **Devil**, who
visits her prison cell disguised as an angel from God. Forced to
reveal his true identity, he confesses his role as enemy of those who
wish to obey God:

>         Þus ic soðfæstum
> þurh mislic bleo   mod oncyrre.
> Þær ic hine finde   ferð staþelian

to godes willan,  ic beo gearo sona
þæt ic him monigfealde  modes gælsan
ongean bere  grimra geþonca,
dyrnra gedwilda,  þurh gedwolena rim.

Thus I in a shifting shape, pervert the mind of the man steadfast in truth. Where I find him buttressing up his spirit to the will of God I am instantly ready to induce in him multifarious lustings of the heart, savage thoughts and secret aberrations, by means of a series of delusions.

(*Juliana*, 362–8)

Behind the gods of the pagans lurks the *fyrnsynna fruman*, 'the author of sins' (347). Opposed to the heroes of God are massed the forces of the enemy of God. The message of the saint's life was plain: ordinary Christians too must remain steadfast and on their guard.

**Relics** of the **saints** were seen as a physical link with the unseen spiritual world; and holy places associated with God's chosen servants as points at which earth and heaven intersected. Hence relics were regarded as of great importance in the consecration of churches. David Rollason comments: 'The saint provided a means by which God was brought closer to men, an avenue of approach to the majesty of an all-powerful deity ... The saint continued after death to be an intercessor on behalf of the living, all the more as it was believed that his or her spirit enjoyed a simultaneous existence in heaven and in the tomb.'[11] Fierce rivalry sprang up for possession of relics which seemed to confer particular blessings and thus attracted more pilgrims. Some ecclesiastical foundations were not above pious thefts of the bodies of saints to whom they felt a justifiable claim and the subsequent rounds of substitutions and repossessions led to considerable confusion. Where more than one **monastery** claimed, for example, to possess the arm of St Oswald, the truth of the matter could only be demonstrated by the resultant miracles. It was up to the saint to give judgement.

THE TREE OF GLORY

Alongside these strange and somewhat gruesome tales runs an important strand of popular spirituality which is seen at its best in poems such as *Elene* and the *Dream of the Rood*. Both were inspired by the growing devotion to the Cross which had originated in the Eastern Church. Two significant dates for the English would have been 701 when Pope Sergius I discovered a fragment of the 'True Cross' (Abbot Ceolfrith of Wearmouth-Jarrow was in Rome at the time and may have brought back the cult with him) and 885 when Alfred the Great was given a piece of the Cross. Cynewulf's *Elene* recounts the Emperor Constantine's vision of the Cross in 312, his subsequent conversion to Christianity, and his mother's journey to the Holy Land to discover the true Cross. Elene is ruthless in her treatment of the unfortunate Jews, particularly the recalcitrant Judas Cyricus who eventually leads her to the buried cross and is rewarded with the bishopric of Jerusalem. Despite the attention given to the three human protagonists, the true hero of the poem is the Cross itself. Having described the power of the Cross to convert emperors and convince the unbeliever, the poet includes himself amongst those who have received spiritual comfort (and poetic inspiration) through knowledge of the *wuldres treow* (the tree of glory) on which **Christ** died (1236–55). The *Dream of the Rood* is widely regarded as one of the most attractive and accomplished of all the surviving Old English poems. In the form in which it is preserved in the *Vercelli* manuscript it appears to have affinities with the Cynewulfian school and shares the emotional quality of the conclusion of *Elene*. Lines corresponding to early passages in the poem have been found carved on the Ruthwell Cross near the Scottish border, indicating the existence of an earlier version, dating from around 700 AD. No immediate source has been discovered for the *Dream of the Rood*, although echoes of Latin **liturgy** and hymns have been detected, and the Anglo-Saxon poet has been given full credit for the artistry with which he resolves the complex theological and literary problems presented by his theme. The dream-form, a mode of revelation familiar to the Anglo-Saxon Church from both **Bible** stories and **saints**' lives, was particularly appropriate in this case, since it recalled Constantine's vision of a cross of light. It also enabled the poet to draw his audience into a world of supernatural wonder and mystery, through a gradual process of illumination:

Þuhte me þæt ic gesawe   syllicre treow
on lyft lædan,   leohte bewunden,
beama beorhtost.   Eall þæt beacen wæs
begoten mid golde.   Gimmas stodon
fægere æt foldan sceatum,   swylce þær fife wæron
uppe on þam eaxlegespanne.

It was as though I saw a wondrous tree
Towering in the sky suffused with light
Brightest of beams; and all that beacon was

Covered with gold. The corners of the earth
Gleamed with fair jewels, just as there were five
Upon the cross-beam.

(*Dream of the Rood*, 4–9)

At once the *syllicre treow* is identified as a symbol of cosmic
importance. The poet is able to draw on a wealth of Christian
iconography:[12] the tree towers in the sky, signifying Christ's
universal dominion, the five jewels on the cross-beam may
represent the **Five Wounds** inflicted during his **Passion**. It is a
symbol of eternity and of judgement to come; yet also a sign of
hope for mankind and all creation. Just as Adam, Eve, and all
creation with them, had fallen through disobediently plucking the
fruit of the tree of knowledge, now God offered the prospect of
rescue through his son's obedient death on another tree. This
parallel, a common theme in Christian hymns, had also been used
by Venantius Fortunatus, bishop of Poitiers (d. c. 600): 'The Maker,
grieving over the deception of our first-created parent when he
tumbled into death at the bite of a fatal apple, then chose a tree
Himself to redeem the injuries caused by a tree' (*Pange, Lingua* in
*Sources and Analogues*). Confronted with the splendour of the
jewelled tree, the dreamer, like the prophet Isaiah in the Temple
(Isaiah 6), is overwhelmed by the sense of his own unworthiness:

> Syllic wæs se sigebeam,   ond ic synnum fah,
> forwunded mid wommum.

> Wonderful was that tree of victory and I with sins was stained,
> wounded with guilt.

(13–14)

His awe deepens as marks of suffering are revealed amidst the glory.

> Geseah ic þat fuse beacen
> wenden wædum ond bleom;   hwilum hit wæs mid wætan
> bestemed,
> beswyled mid swates gange,   hwilum mid since gegyrwed.

> I saw that lively beacon
> Changing its clothes and hues; sometimes it was
> Bedewed with blood and drenched with flowing gore,
> At other times it was bedecked with treasure.

(21–3)

The changing clothes of the Cross may reflect the practice of
draping crosses as part of the Passiontide ritual or may even go back

to the Roman practice of carrying trophy crosses, draped with the imperial cloak.[13] The variations in colour probably represent the different aspects of the Cross which the poet wishes to communicate. An eighth-century prayer for the blessing of a cross includes these words: 'Let the splendour of the divinity of thine only-begotten Son shine forth in the gold, the glory of his passion shine in the wood, our redemption from death glow in the crimson, the purification of our life in the brightness of the crystal.'[14] The effect of the vision is profound:

> Hwæðre ic þær licgende   lange hwile
> beheold hreowcearig   hælendes treow.

> So I lay there watching the Saviour's tree.
> Grieving in spirit for a long while.

> (*Dream of the Rood*, 24–5)

Here in embryo we see the process of *compunction*: the awakening of **contrition**, sorrow for sins and a willingness to repent. In the later medieval period the contemplation of the **Passion** of **Christ**, as a means of stimulating such a response, would come to dominate popular spirituality, inspire many of the religious lyrics and characterise the experience of **mystics** such as **Richard Rolle** and **Julian of Norwich**. The tree itself takes up the narrative of the **crucifixion** drama, a literary device reflecting a tradition stretching back to the **apocryphal** *Gospel of Peter*, where the cross is shown preaching to those who died before the time of Christ: 'They saw again three men coming out of the sepulchre, and two of them sustaining the other and a cross following after them . . . And they heard a voice out of the heavens saying: Hast Thou preached unto them that sleep? And an answer was heard from the cross saying: Yea' (*Apocryphal New Testament*, 92–3). The poet's skill is seen at its height as he tackles the intricate series of paradoxes inherent in any description of the Crucifixion. God is apparently overpowered by man, the eternal put to death. The death in question is technically that of a criminal, yet this is 'no felon's gallows'; the cross itself, an instrument of hideous torture, becomes *wuldres treow*, a tree of glory. In the poet's mind, these paradoxes, deep-rooted in the theology of the **New Testament**, in fact make sense of one another. An event which seemed to have been instigated by the malicious cruelty of man was in reality planned by God and purposefully undertaken by the apparent 'victim'.

Ongyrede hine þa geong hæleð,   (þæt wæs god ælmihtig),
strang ond stiðmod.   Gestah he on gealgan heanne,
modig on manigra gesyhðe,   þa he wolde mancyn lysan.

The young hero (who was God Almighty)
Got ready, resolute and strong in heart.
He climbed onto the lofty gallows-tree
Bold in the sight of many watching men
When he intended to redeem mankind.

(39–41)

**Christ**, who is 'God Almighty', willingly submits to an ignominious death in order to save those who cannot save themselves. The **New Testament** made it clear that since death was the ordained punishment for **sin** (Romans 6:23), only Christ, being free from sin, could voluntarily suffer the penalty on behalf of others (I Peter 2:24: 'Who his ownself bore our sins in his body upon the tree'). The cross, the instrument of his suffering, was therefore translated into a symbol in which Christians could glory (Galatians 6:14). In order to maintain both the narrative tension and theological orthodoxy, the poet had to take care to balance the elements of divinity and humanity within the person of Christ. To over-emphasise either aspect of Christ's nature was to stray in the direction of heresy. The *Dream*-poet treads this theological tight-rope with consummate skill: 'The most remarkable achievement of the poem is its balance between the effects of triumph and suffering, and their paradoxical fusion in the Crucifixion is suggested first by the alternation between the jewelled radiant cross and the plain and blood-covered cross in the prelude, and secondly and much more subtly and powerfully by the two figures of the heroic victorious warrior and the passive enduring cross'.[15] The doctrine of the day also allowed for the co-existence of two separate theories about the 'mechanics' of the redemption of mankind. In the first, the **Devil**, who was said to have claimed 'rights' to mankind because of Adam's **sin**, was outwitted and defeated by the Son of God; here the stress was laid on Christ's divinity and his heroic triumph. In the second, the focus was on the need for Christ to offer himself as a sacrifice on behalf of sinners; the emphasis was accordingly placed on his humanity and sufferings. In the *Dream*, the poet contrives to exploit the emotional power inherent in each tradition, without apparent contradiction. This not inconsiderable feat is achieved through the partial identification of the Cross with Christ himself. Thus the saviour, the 'young hero', approaches the scene with swift determination: in the biblical account (Matthew 27:31) Christ was stripped by his tormentors but here the poet states that he stripped himself, implying deliberate preparation for the trial ahead. The element of human apprehension and suffering is transferred to the tree which, ironically, can only show its loyalty by becoming the reluctant agent of its lord's death. The biblical narrative (John 19:17-34) has been pared down to the bare minimum; no secondary character, not even the **Virgin Mary**, is allowed to deflect attention from Christ, his enemies and his cross:

Rod wæs ic aræred. Ahof ic ricne cyning,
heofona hlaford, hyldan me ne dorste.
Þurhdrifan hi me mid deorcan næglum. On me syndon þa dolg
gesiene,
opene inwidhlemmas. Ne dorste ic hira nænigum sceððan.
Bysmeredon hie unc butu ætgædere. Eall ic wæs mid blode
bestemed,
begoten of þæs guman sidan, siððan he hæfde his gast onsended.

A rood I was raised up; and I held high
The noble King, the Lord of heaven above.
I dared not stoop. They pierced me with dark nails;
The scars can still be clearly seen on me,
The open wounds of malice. Yet might I
Not harm them. They reviled us both together.
I was made wet all over with the blood
Which poured out from His side, after He had
Sent forth His spirit.

(44–9)

This vision of a suffering tree rather than a suffering Saviour reflects the reluctance of the Church to countenance any realistic portrayal of the crucified Christ. It was not until well into the tenth century that the graphic depictions of a pain-racked figure, so beloved of the later medieval Church, began to appear. The climax is a masterpiece of restrained emotion and theological sophistication, the sense of personal grief heightened by the cosmic significance of the event:

Geseah ic weruda god
þearle þenian. Þystro hæfdon
bewrigen mid wolcnum wealdendes hræw,
scirne sciman, sceadu forðeode,
wann under wolcnum. Weop eal gesceaft,
cwiððon cyninges fyll. Crist wæs on rode.

I saw the God of hosts stretched grimly out
Darkness covered the Ruler's corpse with clouds,
His shining beauty; shadows passed across,
Black in the darkness. All creation wept,
Bewailed the King's death; Christ was on the cross.

(51–6)

The poet is too wise to dwell long on the paradox of a dead God. Christ 'rests', until his power is again revealed in the **Harrowing of Hell** and the **Resurrection**. The cross becomes the focus of attention – and devotion:

> Is nu sæl cumen
> þæt me weorðiað   wide ond side
> menn ofer moldan,   ond eall þeos mære gesceaft,
> gebiddaþ him to þyssum beacne.   On me bearn godes
> þrowode hwile.

> Now the time has come
> That far and wide on earth men honour me,
> And all this great and glorious creation,
> And to this beacon offer prayers.

(80–4)

Just as Christ through willing submission to a humiliating death attains greater honour (Philippians 2:8, 9), so the cross by association is transformed from a symbol of death to a sign of life and shares in the glory of the Saviour. In words which echo the **Creeds** (95–119), the Dreamer is exhorted to share his new-found insight with others. The urgency of this commission is underlined by the link, constantly reiterated in the teaching and **liturgy** of the Church, between the death of Christ on the Cross and the forthcoming **Last Judgement**. According to **patristic** tradition derived from Matthew 24:30, the cross would appear again in the sky on Judgement Day. Then too it would cause grief; not the repentant sorrow shown by the Dreamer, but the grief of those who have perceived the truth too late. The *Blickling Homily for Easter Sunday* makes the same point: 'Now we hear, dearly beloved, how many things the Lord suffered for us when he bought us with his blood from the captivity of hell. Let us therefore consider what recompense we are able to offer him, when he recounts and tells all this, at this same time when he sits on his judgement seat' (*Anglo-Saxon Prose*, 67). The Cross in the *Dream of the Rood*, therefore, stands in eternity, pointing back to the Crucifixion and forward to the Judgement Day when all men will need its help. The Dreamer completes his testimony by affirming his own confidence in the ability of the Cross to carry him to the joys of **heaven**. He concludes with an appropriately-tailored message of hope, calculated to inspire and reassure penitent sinners. Biblical tradition (Ephesians 4:8, I Peter 3:18–20) claimed that the first great demonstration of Christ's power to save sinners came immediately after the **Crucifixion**. According to additional details supplied by the **apocryphal Gospels** of Nicodemus and Peter, Christ stormed the gates of **hell**, accompanied by the Cross, the symbol of His triumph, and rescued Adam, Eve and the patriarchs, who had long languished in the clutches of **Satan**. The Anglo-Saxon church drew comfort from this story of the **Harrowing of Hell** and the subsequent vision of **Christ** leading the newly-liberated souls into **heaven**. Here in essence was the message which inspired the *Dream of the Rood*: 'And then the glorious Lord stretched out his right hand and said. 'All you my saints . . . come to me; and you who were condemned by the fruit of the tree, you now see that through the tree of my cross on which I was hung you shall vanquish death and the Devil as well' (*Anglo-Saxon Prose*, 154–5).

The deep devotion to the cross within the Anglo-Saxon church is attested by numerous stone crosses, such as that at Ruthwell. They were erected as memorials and as focal points for preaching and prayer, for those without access to a church: 'On the estates of the nobles and good men of the Saxon race it is a custom to have a cross, which is dedicated to Our Lord and held in great reverence, erected on some prominent spot for the convenience of those who wish to pray daily before it' (*Life of St Willibald* in *Anglo-Saxon Missionaries in Germany*, 155). Some still stand; enduring symbols of the faith which claimed the allegiance of kings and shaped the imaginations of poets. Many other glories of the eighth century were to vanish, consumed in the holocaust which descended on the Anglo-Saxons with the force of a judgement from God. The age of Bede had been a period of relative peace and stability; Angles, Jutes and Saxons were slowly becoming one nation, bound together by a common faith and a developing culture. The final years of the eighth century saw a fresh onslaught from the sea. Population growth amongst the Scandinavian peoples pushed out groups of raiders looking first for plunder and later for new settlements. The coastal **monasteries** of Northumbria, vulnerable and well-endowed, offered easy pickings. In 793, the island monastery of Lindisfarne was attacked from the sea. Defenceless **monks** were butchered, their treasures looted. **Alcuin**, grief-stricken at this attack and fearful of further horrors to come, besieged his brethren with letters of consolation and exhortation:

> It is nearly 350 years that we and our fathers have inhabited this lovely land, and never before has such terror appeared in Britain as we have now suffered from a pagan race ... Behold the church of St Cuthbert spattered with the blood of the priests of God, despoiled of all its ornaments ... Behold judgement has begun, with great terror, at the house of God ... Would that their correction would be the amendment of others.
>
> (*EHD*, Vol. 1, p. 193)

**Alcuin**'s worst forebodings were to be fulfilled. Other **monasteries**, including Wearmouth-Jarrow, suffered similar onslaughts and, although monks returned to Lindisfarne, they found no lasting security there. Sporadic Viking raids eventually evolved into a determined attempt at Danish settlement. Wessex, Kent, East Anglia and Mercia all suffered. In 866 a Danish army struck northwards and occupied York. It was probably at this point that the famous library, of which Alcuin wrote, perished. There followed 'a process of virtual annihilation of churches and monasteries in Deira (the southern kingdom of Northumbria)'.[16] In 875 the monks of Lindisfarne gathered such treasures as they had left, and wandered, accompanied by the sacred relics of **St Cuthbert** and St Oswald, until they came to rest eight years later at Chester-le-Street. The inexorable advance of the Norsemen had a catastrophic impact upon the cultural achievements of the Christian centuries.[17] While it is known that some scholars remained active in Mercia, and that there were illuminators busily occupied in Canterbury, there can be no doubt that many scholars perished with their monasteries and cherished manuscripts. The coming of the Vikings jeopardised not only the sovereignty of individual kingdoms but the intellectual heritage of the Anglo-Saxon peoples. Both hung in the balance until the emergence of a prince of Wessex on whom the double task of repelling the Danes and reconstructing literacy would devolve.

NOTES

1.  Huppé (1959, Ch. 4).
2.  See Laistner (1957, 93–116); also Ward (1990).
3.  *Epistola de Obitu Bedae* in *Eccles. Hist.*, 581.

4. See Laistner (1957, 117–49); also Ogilvy (1967).

5. For a fuller account of the role of women in religious and intellectual life, see Fell (1984); Damico and Olsen (1990); Thompson (1991).

6. Lucas, *Exodus*, 56; see also Cross and Tucker (1960).

7. Fowler (1976, 16).

8. Woolf (1966, 37).

9. Farrar (1973).

10. Woolf (1966, 40).

11. Rollason (1989). For the use of relics in consecrations see Binns (1989, 13); Brooke and Brooke (1984, 33–5).

12. See Raw (1970; 1990). Also Dodwell (1982, 210–13) on crucifixes.

13. See Smith (1975); *Sources and Analogues*, 54; Raw (1970, 245).

14. *Pontifical of Egbert*, 112.

15. Woolf (1958, 29). See also Garde (1991).

16. Godfrey (1962, 278).

17. Recent scholarship has questioned the extent of Viking ravages. For an assessment of the arguments see Campbell (1982, 144–9); Jones (1984).

# Chapter 4

# Alfred and the Development of English Prose

> I would have it known that very often it has come to my mind what men of learning there were formerly throughout England, both in religious and secular orders ... and how people from abroad sought wisdom and instruction in this country; and how nowadays, if we wished to acquire these things, we would have to seek them outside. Learning had declined so thoroughly in England that there were very few men on this side of the Humber who could understand their divine services in English or even translate a single letter from Latin into English, and I suppose that there were not many beyond the Humber either. There were so few of them I cannot even recollect a single one south of the Thames when I succeeded to the kingdom.
>
> (*Preface to Gregory's Pastoral Care* in *Alfred the Great*, 124)

Alfred had succeeded to the West Saxon kingdom in 871, at a time when the tide of Viking invasions seemed set to sweep away the last vestiges of Anglo-Saxon resistance. The uneasy peace of the early years of the century had been steadily eroded by the increasingly serious incursions recorded in the *Anglo-Saxon Chronicle*. Ironically, the sea-borne raiders were motivated by the same social patterns which governed their Anglo-Saxon kin, with leaders reliant upon treasure-giving to retain a loyal following. Pushed out from their homelands by a combination of factors including population growth, they were essentially opportunists, acting by turns as pirates, traders and colonists. The descendants of the fifth-century adventurers Hengist and Horsa now found the tables turned on them with a vengeance. By 851, a Danish army was over-wintering in Kent, and London, Rochester, and Canterbury all came under attack. In 865 another Viking force, 'a great heathen army', began a relentless progress through East Anglia, Northumbria and Mercia:

> 867 (866). In this year the [heathen] host went from East Anglia over the mouth of the Humber to York in Northumbria ... and immense

slaughter was made of the Northumbrians there . . . and both the kings were slain, and the remnant made peace with the host.

868 [867]. In this year the same host went into Mercia to Nottingham . . . And Burhred, king of Mercia, and his councillors begged Æthelred, king of Wessex, and his brother Alfred to help them fight against the host . . .

870 [869]. In this year the host went across Mercia into East Anglia . . . and the same winter St Edmund the king fought against them and the Danes won the victory, and they slew the king and overran the entire kingdom and destroyed all the monasteries to which they came.

(*Anglo-Saxon Chronicle*)

That Alfred's Wessex did not succumb to the fate of its neighbours is remarkable. For seven difficult years the outcome hung in the balance as Alfred rallied his beleaguered forces against the invaders. Eventually in 878, Alfred secured a major victory and a significant peace settlement. Guthrum, the Danish king, submitted to **baptism** and agreed to withdraw into the territory which became known as the Danelaw, leaving the lands south of the Thames, together with south-west Mercia, under English rule. This did not end the Danish threat, which would form a continuous backcloth to Anglo-Saxon life and literature well into the eleventh century. It did, however, herald a period of relative peace and security during which Alfred could rebuild English defences and turn his mind to the restoration of a Christian culture.

THE WESSEX RENAISSANCE

To Alfred[1] the revitalisation of learning was not a luxury. From a purely pragmatic standpoint there was a need for educated men who could be employed in the re-organisation of his battered kingdom. It is also apparent from his writings that he was possessed by both a passion for knowledge and the conviction that the preservation and transmission of knowledge was a Christian duty, which rulers neglected at their peril. Addressing his bishops, key figures in his educational programme, he lamented the decline of learning in the early years of the ninth century and intimated that the Danish invasions might well be seen as a judgement on those so careless of God's gifts:

Remember what punishments befell us in this world, when we

ourselves did not cherish learning nor transmit it to other men. We were Christians in name alone, and very few possessed Christian virtues. When I reflected on all this, I recollected how, before everything was ransacked and burnt, the churches throughout England stood filled with treasures and books. Similarly, there was a great multitude of those serving God. And they derived very little benefit from those books, because they could understand nothing of them, since they were not written in their own language.

(*Alfred the Great*, 125)

Alfred's assessment of the state of contemporary learning has been challenged in recent times and he has been accused of exaggerating the needs in the interests of promoting his own reforms.[2] It is evident, however, from warnings issued by **Bede** (*EHD*, 180) and **Alcuin** (*EHD*, 193), that they had anticipated some such decline in monastic life and devotion to scholarship. It is also probable that the enthusiasm with which Anglo-Saxon teachers joined **Boniface**'s mission to Germany had left the English schools sadly depleted. Some of the remaining scholars may have been affected by outbreaks of plague, to which monastic communities were particularly vulnerable; others undoubtedly suffered violence at the hands of the Danes. The great minsters offered treasure and there was no reason for the 'heathen host' to treat them with forbearance. Canterbury, Rochester, Wimborne and Malmesbury had been burned and plundered; the famous schools of Lindisfarne, Jarrow and York were gone and the kingdoms of the North and the Midlands occupied by the Vikings. It was small wonder that Alfred looked back with nostalgia.

Tackling the situation with what seems to have been characteristic determination and vigour, Alfred firstly recruited scholars from those areas which had escaped the worst of the tribulations. From western Mercia came Aethelstan, Werwulf, Plegmund (later Archbishop of Canterbury), and Waerferth, Bishop of Worcester. Asser (later Bishop of Sherborne) was persuaded to leave his native Wales for six months of each year, John of Saxony became abbot of Athelney and the Archbishop of Rheims was coaxed into granting the services of Grimbald, a monk from Flanders. These seven scholars were indispensable for the king's second line of strategy, outlined in his Preface to the *Pastoral Care*:

that we too should turn into the language that we can all understand certain books, which are the most necessary for all men to know . . . so that all the free-born young men now in England, who have the means to apply themselves to it, may be set to learning (as long as they are not useful for some other employment) until the time that they can read English writings properly. Thereafter one may instruct in Latin those whom one wishes to teach further and wishes to advance to holy orders. When I recalled how knowledge of Latin had previously decayed throughout England, and yet how many could still read things written in English, I then began, amidst the various and multifarious afflictions of this kingdom, to translate into English the book which in Latin is called *Pastoralis*, in English 'Shepherd-book', sometimes word for word, sometimes sense for sense, as I learnt it from Plegmund my archbishop, and from Asser my bishop, and from Grimbald my mass-priest and from John my mass-priest. After I had mastered it I translated it into English as best I understood it and as I could most meaningfully render it; I intend to send a copy to each bishopric in my kingdom.

Much as Alfred might have wished it, he could not turn the clock back. Latin scholars could not be produced overnight so the essentials of Latin literature must be made available in a form which literate Englishmen could absorb. This was not the beginning of English prose. Ever since the days of Aethelbert of Kent (Bede, *HE*, II:5), laws had been written down in the language of the people and in later years charters, wills and other legal transactions had been recorded in the vernacular. There were a number of inter-linear glosses on manuscripts of the **Psalter** and the **Canticles** and we know that Bede himself rendered the **Lord's Prayer**, the **Creed** and part of the Gospel of John into English. There may also have been a Mercian prose tradition of which only hints survive. Those 'things written in English' with which Alfred's contemporaries were familiar were adequate for their purpose[3] but remained limited in their scope. The development of prose within a society always lags behind that of poetry and whilst the prose writings which Alfred inherited provided a useful basis for his programme of translation, they could not compare with the rich poetic tradition which had flowered during the previous three centuries. Alfred's role was not confined to that of royal patron of the arts. With the help of the scholars he had gathered, he embarked on the task of translation, producing in the process some lively original prose. Determining which of the works belonging to this period can be attributed to Alfred himself is not easy. In the first place it is unlikely that the king actually wrote down anything himself. We know that he travelled constantly, supervising the defence and well-being of his kingdom, and that he was accompanied by scholars and clerks with whom he held discussions and to whom, no doubt, he dictated his translations.[4] Alfred acknowledged the help of these scholars in the Prefaces to the *Pastoral Care* and Augustine's *Soliloquies*, and when Alfred's responsibilities, his persistent ill-health, and the range of literature from which he drew are taken into account, it is clear that their contribution must have been substantial. It has been shown[5] that Alfred can be credited with five texts: the *Pastoral Care*, the translations of Boethius and Augustine, the prose psalms found in the *Paris Psalter* and a collection of laws. In addition he requested Bishop Waerferth to translate Gregory's *Dialogues*. There remain a number of works which have been associated with Alfred and may well have been translated or initiated as part of his educational programme. Under this heading we can place the *Universal History of Orosius*, Bede's *Ecclesiastical History*, the *Old English Martyrology*, a book of medical remedies and the *Anglo-Saxon Chronicle*. Some of these contain references to Alfred but variations in style and dialect make it clear that a number of translators and scribes were involved. In examining all the works of this period, therefore, it is important to bear in mind Frantzen's caution that: 'Alfred must be considered an author in a special sense . . . the literary works attributed to him are best regarded as a collective achievement, supervised by Alfred and guided by his spirit.'[6]

The works which Alfred and his advisers apparently regarded as 'most necessary for all men to know' may seem at first sight a somewhat motley collection: a book of miracle stories, a treatise on church government, part of the Book of Psalms, a sixth-century philosophical dialogue, **Augustine**'s *Soliloquies* and two books of history, one English, one Roman in origin. It may be that their choices were strictly limited by the Latin texts available at the time, yet it would appear on closer examination that these books would in fact have had considerable relevance for Alfred and his beleaguered countrymen. It is not, for example, hard to see why the writings of **Gregory the Great** should have been considered of value. The English Church held Gregory in special affection, since it was he who had dispatched Augustine on his mission to England and had been responsible for guiding the infant church in its early years. It seems probable that Alfred requested a translation of Gregory's *Dialogues* largely for his own encouragement, though at least one copy was circulated. To a king facing the constant need to protect his territory and deeply conscious of his earthly responsibilities, Gregory's accounts of heroes of the church and reflections on immortality would have had an understandable appeal. The preface, which bears Alfred's name, speaks of 'the most urgent necessity occasionally to calm our minds amidst these earthly anxieties and direct them to divine and spiritual law' (*Alfred the Great*, 123). Faced with the 'earthly anxieties' of kingship, earlier Anglo-Saxon kings had renounced their thrones and entered the **cloister**. During the Viking wars, the king of neighbouring Mercia left his kingdom and went on **pilgrimage** to pray for God's aid. That option was not for Alfred. Whether through conviction or necessity, he could not abandon the task of defending and restoring his kingdom. His undoubtedly sincere spiritual devotion was coupled with a highly practical desire to see his country soundly organised and well protected. Hence Alfred built and fortified towns and cities, re-organised his army, designed warships and reformed the structures of government. It is not surprising therefore that the writings with which he was most intimately involved demonstrate a preoccupation with the proper exercise of power and the Christian reponsibilities of both ruler and subjects. In the introduction to his law code he laid great emphasis on the Christian duty of a man to remain loyal to his lord, reminding his subjects that even the **Councils of the Church** had regarded treachery as particularly abhorrent:

> for almost every misdeed at the first offence secular lords might with their permission receive without sin the monetary compensation, which they then fixed; only for treachery to a lord did they dare not declare any mercy, since Almighty God adjudged none for those who despised Him, nor did Christ, the Son of God, adjudge any for the one who betrayed Him to death; and He commanded everyone to love his lord as Himself.
>
> (*Alfred the Great*, 163–4)

The bond of loyalty, so important to the stability of Anglo-Saxon society, was thus given divine endorsement.

**Gregory**'s *Book of Pastoral Rule* (often called the *Pastoral Care*) was particularly well-suited to Alfred's needs. Designed as a manual for church leaders, it also had much to say to those who wielded secular power. It was already regarded as a classic in the English church and Pope Honorius had exhorted another Anglo-Saxon king, Edwin of Northumbria, to read it frequently (Bede, *HE*, II: 17). One of the problems of assessing Alfred's treatment of his sources is the difficulty of identifying the texts which he used. Popular texts could become corrupted in transmission, and changes may have been due to scribal error rather than deliberate policy. It is generally held, however, that the translation of the *Pastoral Care* was closer to the original than some of Alfred's later works, possibly due to the widespread respect in which Gregory was held. In a detailed examination[7] of the Old English version, Richard Clements concludes that those changes which do appear were made in the interests of greater clarity, of softening Gregory's severity towards sinners and reflecting Alfred's personal preoccupations. Alfred's *Preface to the Pastoral Care*, the most famous of his works, reflects his concern with the proper foundation and responsibilities of government. The golden age was, in Alfred's view, a time when kings 'obeyed God and his messengers', 'not only maintained their peace, morality and authority at home but also extended their territory outside' and succeeded 'both in warfare and wisdom'. His analysis of the progressive decline of the nation[8] was matched by a determination to restore the ideal as he perceived it. Gregory's treatise provided an opportunity to explore the Christian understanding of authority and the exercise of power.[9] Of equal importance to Alfred may have been Gregory's emphasis on the **bishop**'s role as teacher. Alfred's educational programme could not succeed unless the bishops and clergy shared his vision. The Church would remain the only channel of learning, both sacred and secular, for centuries to come.

The third chapter of the *Pastoral Care* could have served as an introduction to Alfred's translation of another seminal work of the Middle Ages:

> In prosperity a man is often puffed up with pride, whereas tribulations chasten and humble him through suffering and sorrow. In the midst of prosperity the mind is elated, and in prosperity a man forgets himself; in hardship he is forced to reflect upon himself, even though he may be unwilling . . . Very often a man is responsive to the lessons of adversity.
>
> (*Alfred the Great*, 127–8)

The *Consolation of Philosophy*, written in the early sixth century while its author, **Boethius**, lay in prison, was hugely influential throughout the medieval period and beyond. Translations were subsequently made by Chaucer and Elizabeth I amongst others, and Dante would place **Boethius** next to **Bede** in Paradise. The complaint of an eminent Roman statesman and philosopher, suddenly deprived of high rank and faced with the prospect of execution, established that favourite medieval theme: the sudden reversal of fortune:

First fickle fortune gave me wealth short-lived,
Then in a moment all but ruined me
Since Fortune changed her trustless countenance
Small welcome to the days prolonging life.
Foolish the friends who called me happy then
Whose fall shows how my foothold was unsure.

(*Boethius*, 35)

His subsequent reflections, embodied in the form of a dialogue with Lady Philosophy, offered consolation to all suffering adversity in an uncertain world. The Preface to Alfred's version of the *Consolation* begins: 'King Alfred was the translator of this book: he turned it from Latin into English, as it now stands before you. Sometimes he translated word for word, sometimes sense for sense, so as to render it as clearly and intelligibly as he could' (*Alfred the Great*, 131). In fact he 'translates' the work with considerable freedom, omitting sections of the original and adding reflections and illustrations of his own. Katherine Proppé has highlighted the characteristically Anglo-Saxon preoccupation with 'chance, exile, mutability, despair, and melancholy',[10] familiar from the poetry, citing Alfred's description of Boethius: 'Then it happened that the wise man became very anxious . . . dejected and despairing.' This is still the world of the *Wanderer* and *Seafarer*, in which a man must search for understanding and consolation. Later, Boethius is supplied with an expanded speech,[11] born of the experience of an Anglo-Saxon ruler rather than that of a consul of ancient Rome:

Wisdom, you know that desire for and possession of earthly power never pleased me overmuch, and that I did not unduly desire this earthly rule, but that nevertheless I wished for tools and resources for the task that I was commanded to accomplish . . . In the case of the king, the resources and tools with which to rule are that he have his land fully manned: he must have *praying men, fighting men and working men*.

(*Alfred the Great*, 132)

The twelfth-century historian, William of Malmesbury claimed that **Bishop** Asser helped Alfred in his task of translation by explaining the text to him in simpler terms. Alfred might well have been grateful for assistance as he tackled a work which drew on the riches of Graeco-Roman philosophy in expounding the mysterious ways of Providence and Fate. Whether through the influence of Asser or his own inclination, Alfred's version is more explicitly Christian than the original.[12] Though 'undoubtedly a Christian and even a theologian',[13] Boethius chose to utilise arguments based on reason and natural law, rather than on the Judaeo-Christian revelation, and the biblical references which he did employ were not clearly signalled in the text. Alfred's rendering 'baptises Boethius' Platonic conceptions':[14] Lady Philosophy is converted into the biblical figure of Wisdom and the Good becomes God. In Alfred's remaining major work of translation, the *Soliloquies of Augustine*, he also treats the text with considerable freedom, adding a third book of his own which draws on a number of **Augustine**'s other works and reveals a wide knowledge of **patristic** writings. The Preface contains an extended metaphor outlining Alfred's labours in gathering wisdom for his stay on earth and the final book concludes with a plea that others might follow his example: 'A man strikes me as very foolish and very ill-advised who does not seek to increase his understanding while he is in this world, and at the same time does not wish and desire that he may come to that eternal life where nothing shall be concealed from us' (*Alfred the Great*, 152).

Alfred's quest for eternal life found natural expression in his translations of the Psalms. The prose versions of the first fifty psalms in the *Paris Psalter* are believed to be his work and William of Malmesbury claimed that the king was still engaged in this task at the time of his death. Alfred frequently paraphrases the original, occasionally adding heartfelt comments of his own: 'The Lord is our protection and strength and our support in our trials *which have befallen us exceedingly*' (Ps. 45:1). Alfred may well have decided to translate the Psalms not only as a stimulus to popular spirituality, but out of a sense of identification with another God-fearing king, besieged by enemies and the cares of the world.[15] This sense of identification is reflected in the introductions, which were based on a work mistakenly attributed to Bede. Thus from the thirteenth psalm is elicited a message very close to Alfred's heart:

> When David sang this thirteenth psalm, he lamented to the Lord in the psalm that in his time there should be so little faith, and so little wisdom should be found in the world. And so does every just man who sings it now: he laments the same thing in his own time. And so did Christ with respect to the Jews, and Hezekiah with respect to Rabsaces, king of the Assyrians.
>
> (*Alfred the Great*, 158)

For thoughtful Christians of the period, the lessons of history, particularly their own history, were not to be ignored. Two translations of historical works survive from Alfred's reign. Orosius wrote his *Historiae adversus Paganos* (Histories against the Pagans) in the early fifth century to refute the suggestion that the rise of Christianity had brought about the decline and fall of Rome. In the process he provided a history of the world to his own day, which was adapted and augmented by the unknown West Saxon translator. The importance of **Bede**'s *Ecclesiastical History* is obvious. The careful translation, possibly by one of Alfred's Mercian scholars, is selective in its approach to the original, omitting details of papal documents and the controversy over Easter. Bede's history would have been important to Alfred and his contemporaries, not only as a symbol of the great age of scholarship but also as a statement of the comforting thesis that God was actively involved in the affairs of the English nation. While there is no evidence that Alfred himself was involved in the compilation of the *Anglo-Saxon Chronicle*, there are clear links with his court. The *Chronicle* (which was subsequently copied and continued in various **monastic** centres well into the twelfth century) was based on annals which evolved from tables used by the church for calculating the date of Easter in any given year. Brief records of significant events were added to identify particular years for posterity. The compilers of the *Anglo-Saxon Chronicle* apparently drew on earlier annals, together with Bede's eighth-century *Ecclesiastical History* in producing a record of their nation's history. They incorporated events (historical and mythical) from the story of the Christian Church, together with traditions concerning their Germanic ancestors:

444. In this year St Martin passed away.
448. In this year John the Baptist showed his head to two monks who came from the east to worship in Jerusalem . . . at that time came the Angles to this land, invited by king Vortigern, to help him overcome their enemies. They came to this land with three warships, and their leaders were Hengist and Horsa . . . afterwards they turned against the king and against the Britons, and destroyed them by fire and by the edge of the sword.

Such warlike enterprise, commendable in ancestors, was naturally less acceptable in those contemporary invaders, the Vikings. When Alfred died in 899, the Danish threat was far from over and the future of his kingdom far from secure. In the years to come the balance of power would ebb and flow between the royal house of Wessex and the inhabitants of the Danelaw. Yet Alfred had done all that could be asked of an Anglo-Saxon king: he had secured the kingdom for his lifetime, and provided a system of laws and administration on which others could build. He had done more. Not content with defending a kingdom, he had sought to recreate a civilisation. He took the utilitarian prose of the past and transformed it into an educational medium capable of expressing profound philosophical and spiritual concepts. For those who shared his passion for learning he provided a wide-ranging selection of books which were still being copied in Norman England:

> By the end of his reign, a man who could read English could have had access to a standard work on ancient history and to another on the history of the English Church; from both he could have drawn the moral that the course of history reveals the working out of the divine purpose. He could have read of the history of his own people in the *Anglo-Saxon Chronicle*. From the *Cura Pastoralis* he could have learnt much of ethics and religious morality and have acquired insight into human personality. The discussion of deep matters of theology, concerning God's mysterious rule, divine foreknowledge and human free-will, and the destiny of the soul, would have been within his reach in the *Boethius* and the *Soliloquies* and in the last book of *Gregory's Dialogues*. He could have derived edification and pleasure from the stories of saints in the *Dialogues* and in the *Martyrology* . . . To make all this knowledge available to many was surely a great conception.[16]

Perhaps the tribute which Alfred himself would have liked best is that contained in the *Chronicle* of Aethelweard, ealdorman of the western shires and himself a patron of the great prose stylist **Aelfric**. Writing nearly a century after Alfred's death, Aethelweard's comments bear witness that Alfred's ideals had indeed lived on:

> Finally in the same year [899], the magnanimous Alfred passed from the world, king of the Saxons, unshakeable pillar of the western people, a man replete with justice, vigorous in warfare, learned in speech, above all instructed in divine learning. For he had translated unknown numbers of books from rhetorical Latin speech into his own language – so variously and so richly, that [his] book of Boethius would arouse tearful emotions not only in those familiar with it but even in those hearing it [for the first time] . . . Now, reader, say 'O Christ our Redeemer, save his soul'.

> (*Alfred the Great*, 191)

THE BENEDICTINE REVIVAL

In his *Preface to the Soliloquies*, Alfred made it plain that his task was unfinished and appealed for others to share and complete his vision:

I gathered for myself staves and posts and tie-beams, and handles for each of the tools I knew how to work with, and cross-bars and beams, and, for each of the structures I knew how to build, the finest timbers I could carry. I never came away with a single load without wishing to bring home the whole forest ... Accordingly I would advise everyone who is strong and has many waggons to direct his steps to the same forest ... and to fetch more for himself.

(Alfred the Great, 138)

Had he been able to observe the actions of his immediate successors, it is likely that Alfred would have felt some disappointment. Whether through force of circumstances or personal inclination, Alfred's descendants seem to have concentrated on military rather than cultural priorities. Edward the Elder, assisted by his formidable sister Aethelflaed, Lady of the Mercians, united the kingdom as far north as the Humber; and Edward's son Aethelstan won a famous victory at Brunanburh, which was duly celebrated in the *Anglo-Saxon Chronicle*. Not until the reign of Alfred's great-grandson Edgar (959–975) were conditions ripe for a further cultural and spiritual revival. For twenty years the country enjoyed a respite from the threat of invasion and the king was wholehearted in his support of a movement for religious reform, led by Dunstan, **Archbishop** of Canterbury, Aethelwold, **Bishop** of Winchester, and Oswald, Bishop of Worcester. These men, inspired by the achievements of the great **Benedictine monasteries** of the Continent, set about the reformation and reconstruction of the religious communities of southern England. Aethelwold's vigorous approach was recorded in the *Chronicle*:

963. In this year St Aethelwold was chosen by king Edgar to be bishop of Winchester ... In the year after he was consecrated he established many monasteries, and drove out the secular clergy from the cathedral because they would not observe any monastic rule, and replaced them with monks. He established two abbeys, one of monks and the other of nuns, both at Winchester. Then he came to king Edgar and asked him to give him all the monasteries which the heathen had destroyed, because he wished to restore them: and the king cheerfully granted it.

(Anglo-Saxon Chronicle)

In a bid to unify the spreading movement, the king, together with a council of **bishops**, **abbots**, and representatives of Continental monasteries, issued the *Regularis Concordia* (c. 970), a book of monastic customs designed to supplement the sixth-century **Rule** of **St Benedict**. Its preamble states that the council, having summoned **monks** from Fleury-sur-Loire and Ghent:

gathered from their praiseworthy customs much that was good and thus, even as honey is gathered by bees from all manner of wild flowers and collected into one hive, so also the said monastic customs, tempered by great and subtle judgement of reason, were by the grace of Christ the Saviour of the world, embodied in this small book.

(*Regularis Concordia*, 3)

A notable feature was the introduction from the Continent of a more elaborate daily ritual than **St Benedict** had originally intended for his monks. Greater emphasis on the *opus dei* (work of prayer) replaced the more evenly-balanced programme of worship and manual labour which Benedict had encouraged. Monks, as Alfred had stated in his *Boethius*, were the king's 'praying men' and as such had a vital role in the welfare of the nation. The *Regularis Concordia* also contains the first surviving text of the *Quem Quaeritis* **trope**, an early forerunner of the medieval mystery plays.[17] This simple dramatic elaboration of the **Gospel** text was designed for the benefit of less learned members of the congregation. The **Easter** observance began with the laying of the Cross in the 'sepulchre' where it was to be watched over by monks until Easter morning. This practice and the subsequent encounter at the sepulchre were borrowed from elsewhere, being described as worthy of imitation 'for the strengthening of the faith of unlearned common persons and neophytes':

> While the third lesson is being read, four of the brethren shall vest, one of whom, wearing an alb as though for some different purpose, shall enter and go stealthily to the place of the 'sepulchre' and sit there quietly, holding a palm in his hand. Then, while the third response is being sung, the other three brethren, vested in copes and holding thuribles in their hands, shall enter in their turn and go to the place of the 'sepulchre', step by step, as though searching for something. Now these things are done in imitation of the angel seated on the tomb and of the women coming with perfumes to anoint the body of Jesus. When, therefore, he that is seated shall see these three draw nigh, wandering about as it were and seeking something, he shall begin to sing softly and sweetly, *Quem quaeritis* [Whom do you seek?]. As soon as this has been sung right through, the three shall answer together, *Ihesum Nazarenum* [Jesus of Nazareth]. Then he that is seated shall say *Non est hic. Surrexit sicut praedixerat. Ite, nuntiate quia surrexit a mortuis* [He is not here. He has risen as he foretold. Go! Proclaim that he has risen from the dead]. At this command the three shall turn to the choir saying *Alleluia. Resurrexit Dominus* [The Lord has risen]. When this has been sung he that is seated, as though calling them back, shall say the antiphon *Venite et videte locum* [Come and see the place], and then rising

and lifting up the veil, he shall show them the place void of the Cross and with only the linen in which the Cross had been wrapped. Seeing this the three shall lay down their thuribles in that same 'sepulchre' and taking the linen shall hold it up before the clergy; and, as though showing that the Lord was risen and was no longer wrapped in it, they shall sing this antiphon: *Surrexit Dominus de sepulchro* [The Lord has risen from the grave]. They shall then lay the linen on the altar.

(*Regularis Concordia*, 49–50)

The **Benedictine** Revival, which continued into the eleventh century, was an age of considerable literary and cultural importance. To this period belong the *Vercelli*, *Junius*, *Exeter* and *Cotton* codices, which contain almost all the surviving Old English poetry; the anonymous **homilies** of the *Blickling* and *Vercelli* manuscripts, and the writings of **Aelfric** and **Wulfstan**. The creativity and love of beauty so characteristic of the Anglo-Saxons were given free rein. Dunstan and Aethelwold were not only clerics but skilled craftsmen and both English metalwork and English embroidery were renowned for their splendour. Book production was resumed in earnest and manuscripts of a beauty rivalling those of the Northumbrian renaissance emerged from the 'Winchester' school of illumination. Among Aethelwold's pupils in Winchester was Aelfric, generally acknowledged as the greatest writer of Old English prose.[18] Between 989 and 1002, he produced three series of sermons which included a mixture of **homilies** and **saints**' lives. In the *Preface* to the first volume of his *Catholic Homilies* Aelfric outlined the need for such works in English:

It entered my mind, by the grace of God, I trust, to turn this book from the Latin language into the English tongue, not from confidence of great learning, but because I saw and heard much error in many English books, which unlearned men in their simplicity accounted great wisdom; and I was sorry that they did not possess the evangelical teaching among their books, except for those men alone who knew Latin, and except for the books which King Alfred wisely translated from Latin into English.

(*EHD*, 850)

The 'error' to which Aelfric refers may incude some of the more sensational accounts included in the *Vercelli* and *Blickling* homilies, such as the **apocryphal** *Vision of St Paul*, a work which has been linked with the description of Grendel's mere in *Beowulf* (1357–79, 1408–17):[19]

As St. Paul was gazing towards the northern part of this world . . . he also saw there above the water a certain grey stone . . . and there were dark mists; and beneath the stone was the dwelling place of water-monsters and evil spirits. And he saw that on that cliff many black souls bound by their hands were hanging in the icy groves; and the devils in the shape of water-monsters were clutching at them, just like ravenous wolves. And the water under the cliff below was black; and between the cliff and the water was about twelve miles. And when the twigs broke, the souls which hung on the twigs dropped below and the water-monsters seized them. These were the souls of those who had sinned wickedly here in the world, and would not turn from it before their life's end. But let us now earnestly beseech St. Michael to lead our souls into bliss, where they may rejoice in eternity without end. Amen.

(*Anglo-Saxon Prose*, 75)

**Aelfric** was more discerning in his own selection of sources[20] as he sought to provide collections of sermons garnered from the writings of the **Fathers of the Church** such as **Augustine of Hippo**, **Gregory** and **Bede**, for each of the seasons of the Church's year. Together these offered a complete history of the world from the **Creation** to the **Last Judgement**. These could be read during the service of the **Mass** in explanation of the *pericope* (**Gospel** reading) set for the day. Aelfric was pre-eminently a teacher, concerned that his instruction should be easily intelligible and unquestionably orthodox. His prose is 'clear, gentle and civil'.[21] In his homily *On the Epiphany of the Lord* (*Catholic Homilies* I, 7) Aelfric states that the wise men signified 'all heathen men' and explains the meaning of the gifts they brought to the infant Christ: 'The gold signified that he is a true king, the frankincense that he is the true God, the myrrh that he was then mortal; but that he remains immortal in eternity' (*Anglo-Saxon Prose*, 81). In his conclusion he returns to the perennial theme of man as exile and pilgrim:

The astrologers pointed out something important when they returned to their country by another way. For our country is Paradise to which we cannot return by the way we came. The first-created man and all his offspring were driven from the delight of Paradise through disobedience and for eating the forbidden food, and through pride when he wanted to be greater than the Almighty Creator had created him. But it is very necessary for us that we should by another way avoid the treacherous Devil, so that we may come happily to our homeland, for which we were created.

(*Anglo-Saxon Prose*, 82)

These **homilies** included many passages from the **Vulgate** which Aelfric had endeavoured to translate 'sense for sense' and in his *Tract on the Old and New Testament*, he listed a number of passages which he had 'turned into English'. Although Aelfric has been described as 'the most important figure in the history of the **Bible** in the English vernacular before **Wyclif**',[22] his work of translation was restricted by a question which exercised the minds of theologians and rulers through the medieval period: was it really advisable to allow unlearned lay people access to the scriptures? In the *Preface* to his rendering of *Genesis*, he warned his patron Aethelweard: 'I fear, if an ignorant man reads this book or hears it read, that he will think that he can live now under the new law as the old fathers lived in the time before the old law was established or as men lived under the law of Moses', adding, 'I dare not and will not translate any book of the Bible after this book' (*Heptateuch*, 76). **Saints**' lives, fortunately, posed no such problem. The English were proud of their saints and Aelfric's account of the *Passion of St Edmund*, the East Anglian king killed by the Danes, was very popular. To Aelfric and his contemporaries the presence and merits of the English **saints** were a token of God's favour on their land:

> The English nation is not deprived of the Lord's saints, since in England lie such saints as this saintly king [i.e. Edmund], and the blessed Cuthbert, and in Ely Æthelthryth and her sister also, incorrupt in body, for the confirmation of the faith. There are also many other saints among the English who work many miracles – as is widely known – to the praise of the Almighty in whom they believed.
>
> (*Anglo-Saxon Prose*, 102)

His labours were inspired in part by the conviction, shared by many of his contemporaries, that with the approaching millennium would come Judgement Day: 'men particularly require good teaching in this age which is the end of the world' (*EHD*, 850). God's judgement is also a constant theme in the sermons of **Wulfstan**, Bishop of Worcester and Archbishop of York (1002–23), a man fired by 'an acute awareness of sin and the consequences of sin, a passion for order and a burning zeal for reform.'[23] His famous *Sermo Lupi ad Anglos* combines a thunderous denunciation of the social wrongs of the age with an impassioned plea to the English to repent of their misdeeds and return to God's laws. Plagues, crop failures, excessive taxes and humiliating defeats at the hands of the Danes are all seen as God's interim judgements upon the **sins** of the people:

Alas for the misery and alas for the public disgrace which the English now bear, all because of the wrath of God! Often two pirates, or sometimes three will drive herds of Christian men out through this people from sea to sea, huddled together as a public shame to us all . . . They ravage and they burn, plunder and rob and carry away on board; and indeed what else is there in all these events but the wrath of God clear and visible towards this nation.

*(Anglo-Saxon Prose,* 120)

This king presiding over this catalogue of disasters has gone down in English history as the most ineffectual of monarchs. Aethelraed, whose name meant 'Noble Counsel', was rechristened *Unraed* (No counsel) by later generations. His policy of attempting to buy off invading armies of Danes not unnaturally turned them into frequent visitors. (The fate of the more resolute men of Essex was commemorated in the *Battle of Maldon.*) After years of struggle the unthinkable finally happened and in 1016 a Dane became king of England. Ironically, in Cnut the English acquired not only an able leader but a Christian king whose conversion made him anxious to atone for his heathen youth and the deeds of his pagan forebears. A generous benefactor to the Church, Cnut, like many of his Anglo-Saxon predecessors, made a **pilgrimage** to Rome. Wulfstan remained archbishop under the new regime, involved in law-making, reforming the Church and endeavouring to eliminate the remnants of Scandinavian paganism. Cnut's sons did not long survive him and in 1043 the throne was again occupied by an Englishman: Aethelraed's son, Edward the Confessor.

SONGS OF BATTLE AND GLORY

The advances made by Old English prose under Alfred, **Aelfric** and **Wulfstan** did not completely eclipse the older skills of the poets. A love of English poems seems to have characterised several generations of Alfred's family and strongly influenced life at Alfred's court. It is possible that one of the major poems of the later period was in fact inspired by Alfred's daughter Aethelflaed. *Judith*, a rousing drama based on an **apocryphal** book of the **Old Testament** (Chapters 12-15), shows its redoubtable heroine inspiring her people to victory by disposing of an enemy general single-handed. It is not difficult to see possible parallels between this saga and the achievements of the valiant 'Lady of the Mercians.' Widowed in 912, Aethelflaed led her embattled people against the marauding Danes with remarkable success. The account in the

*Anglo-Saxon Chronicle* consistently attributes her victories to the 'help of God' and describes her as Mercia's 'rightful lord' (918). Whether or not *Judith* can be linked directly with Aethelflaed, the story would have provided much-needed inspiration to a Christian population which saw itself threatened on all sides by heathen hordes. In the apocryphal account, the Assyrian commander, Holofernes, is sent by Nebuchadnezzar to destroy the Israelite city of Bethulia. The inhabitants are overcome by terror; only Judith, a beautiful and resourceful widow, has the faith (and initiative) to devise a plan of attack. Seductively dressed, she infiltrates the enemy camp by pretending to betray her countrymen. Waiting until the drunken Holofernes is at her mercy, she decapitates him, carrying his head home to her people who are thus emboldened to rout the enemy. The original narrative presents certain moral problems, since despite the purity of her motives, Judith does not hesitate to lie and to make use of her feminine charms. The Anglo-Saxon poet does his best to overcome these difficulties: Judith's widowed state is not mentioned; instead the poet treats her as if she were one of the virgin saints so beloved of the Anglo-Saxon church, describing her as 'blessed maid', 'holy woman' and 'the hand-maiden of the Lord' (a term used of the **Virgin Mary** at the **Annunciation**). Like *Juliana* she is beautiful; unlike Juliana or St Agatha,[24] however, she is not passive in the face of danger and suffering. Anglo-Saxon women[25] were capable of considerable energy and initiative and Judith is a worthy model. Like the *Exodus*-poet before him, the creator of *Judith* selects carefully from a much longer narrative, focusing on the confrontation between the lecherous Holofernes and the chaste Judith:

> Þa wearð se brema on mode
> bliðe, burga ealdor,   þohte ða beorhtan idese
> mid widle ond mid womme besmitan.   Ne wolde þæt wuldres
>                                                                 dema
> geðafian, þrymmes hyrde,   ac he him þæs ðinges gestyrde,
> dryhten, dugeða waldend.

> The famous prince
> Of cities then exulted in his heart
> Planned to pollute that lady fair with sin
> And foulness; but the Guardian of might,
> The Judge of glory would not let it be,
> The King of hosts restrained him from the deed.

(Judith, 57–61)

The poet's anxiety to stress the sovereign power of God removes any hint of suspense and the outcome is never in doubt. All the peripheral elements in the original are stripped away; we are left with only the two protagonists, Judith's maidservant, and the ever-watchful presence of God. Just before striking the fatal blow, Judith invokes God's help in a prayer to the **Trinity** which seems quite deliberately anachronistic:

> Ic ðe, frymða god    ond frofre gæst,
> bearn alwaldan,    biddan wylle
> miltse þinre    me þearfendre,
> ðrynesse ðrym.

> To you, God of creation, joyous Spirit,
> And Son of the Almighty, will I pray:
> Show me your mercy in my need, O Might
> Of Trinity.

(*Judith*, 83–6)

This, after all, was the God to whom the poet's readers would pray in their time of need. Holofernes is despatched with an extraordinary matter-of-factness and Judith returns to her townsfolk to urge them to attack the leaderless enemy. The scenes which follow demonstrate that Anglo-Saxon battle poetry had lost none of its power during the Christian era – indeed the desire to wipe away shameful tyranny is undergirded by the concept of the justice of war against those who deny the true God.

Two 'secular' war poems commemorating tenth-century battles against invaders are the *Battle of Brunanburh* and the *Battle of Maldon*. *Brunanburh* forms the entry for 937 in several manuscripts of the *Anglo-Saxon Chronicle* and commemorates the victory of Alfred's grandsons, Aethelstan and Edmund, over a combined army of Norsemen from Ireland. The final lines of *Brunanburh* show not only that Alfred's heirs were capable of distinguishing themselves in battle, but that one poet at least had acquired an Alfredian regard for history:

> Ne wearð wæl mare
> on þis eiglande    æfre gieta
> folces gefylled    beforan þissum
> sweordes ecgum,    þæs þe us secgœð bec,
> ealde uðwitan,    siþþan eastan hider
> Engle and Seaxe    up becoman,
> ofer brad brimu    Brytene sohtan.

> Nor has there on this island
> Been ever yet a greater number slain,
> Killed by the edges of the sword before
> This time, as books make known to us, and old
> And learned scholars, after hither came
> The Angles and the Saxons from the east,
> Over the broad sea sought the land of Britain.

(Brunanburh 65–71)

In contrast, the *Maldon*-poet has no glorious victory to commemorate; his is a story of heroic loyalty in the face of defeat. The end of an era was now in sight. The threat from the Danes was growing steadily and it was after the Battle of Maldon (991) that Aethelraed began the ineffectual policy of attempting to buy off the invaders with *Danegeld*. The action of the poem hinges on the character of the English leader, Earl Byrthnoth of Essex. As a hero he can be placed somewhere between the brave but unenlightened Beowulf and the saintly Edmund, whose response to arrogant Danish demands had been a Christ-like submission to a violent death: 'When Ivar came, King Edmund stood within his hall, mindful of the Saviour and threw aside his weapons; he would imitate the example of Christ, who forbade **St Peter** to fight against the savage Jews with weapons' (*Aelfric: Passion of St Edmund* in *Anglo-Saxon Prose*, 99). There is nothing submissive about Byrhtnoth. A resolute leader of men, loyal to his unsatisfactory king, he refuses to pay tribute to the Viking invaders. Like the Israelite warriors of the **Old Testament** he has no difficulty reconciling piety with prowess in battle, and rejoices as he slays an attacking Viking:

> Se eorl wæs þe bliþra,
> hloh þa, modi man,  sæde metode þanc
> ðæs dægweorces  þe him drihten forgeaf.

> This made the earl more glad;
> the bold man laughed, and said thanks to the Lord
> for the day's work that God had granted him.

(Battle of Maldon, 146–8)

Byrhtnoth decision to give up his strategic advantage and face the Danes on equal terms is attributed to *ofermod*, variously translated as 'pride' and 'overconfidence'.[26] This all-too-human flaw is apparently atoned for by the manner of his death. Christian warriors had two battles to face, one earthly, one spiritual; and the latter was the more crucial. Recognising his end is near, Byrhtnoth prays

Nu ic ah, milde metod,   mæste þearfe
þæt þu minum gaste   godes geunne,
þæt min sawul to ðe   siðian mote
on þin geweald,   þeoden engla,
mid friþe ferian.   Ic eom frymdi to þe
þæt hi helsceaðan   hynan ne moton.

Now gracious Lord, as never before,
I need your grace, that my soul may set out
on its journey to you, O Prince of Angels,
that my soul may depart into Your power in peace.
I pray that the devils may never destroy it.

(*Battle of Maldon*, 175–80)

Though not a **saint**, Byrhtnoth could perhaps be viewed as a **martyr**[27] who died defending king, country and people from 'the heathen'. For his loyal followers, revenge is not only a human instinct but a sacred duty:

                    and god bædon
þæt hi moston gewrecan   hyra winedrihten
and on hyra feondum   fyl gewyrcan.

                    and they prayed to God
That they might take revenge for their loved lord,
Achieve the slaughter of their enemies.

(*Battle of Maldon*, 262–4)

In some ways the Anglo-Saxon period drew to a close much as it had opened, with songs of courage, loyalty and glory in battle. But there had been changes. By the time of the Norman Conquest, poets had also explored the use of allegory in poems such as the *Phoenix* and the *Physiologus*, and developed a lyrical voice of considerable beauty. In the *Phoenix*, based by the Old English poet on the fourth-century Latin *Carmen de Ave Phoenice*, the ancient pagan myth is transformed into a sophisticated Christian allegory of death and resurrection. The poet first describes the serene loveliness of the paradisal setting, the beauty of the Phoenix and his exquisite song, before recounting how every thousand years the ageing bird flies westwards to Syria. There, in a sweet-scented nest of his own building, he is consumed by fire and, after a space, reborn. His renewed beauty attracts flocks of followers, until in a passage which recalls Christ's **ascension** into heaven (Acts 1) he soars beyond their reach and returns to his home. Leaving his first source, the poet draws on a commentary by **St Ambrose** to elicit the full meaning of his tale:

Swa fenix beacnað,
geong in geardum,   godbearnes meaht,
þonne he of ascan   eft onwæcneð
in lifes lif,   leomum geþungen.
Swa se hælend us   helpe gefremede
þurh his lices gedal,   lif butan ende.


So the Phoenix fowl   with youth refashioned
When out of the ashes   he wakes again
To the life of life   perfected in form,
Is a symbol of the power   of the Son of God;
Just so our Saviour   granted us grace,
Enduring life,   through his body's death.

(*Phoenix*, 646–54)


THE ANGLO-SAXON LEGACY

The splendours of Old English poetry and prose were among the many casualties of the brutal period of repression which followed the Norman Conquest. Newly-created Norman nobles replaced the older Saxon families; Norman **bishops** and **abbots** assumed the direction of the Church and Anglo-Norman French became the language of the ruling class. Yet there was continuity; many of the themes and preoccupations of Anglo-Saxon literature would re-emerge when English flowered once more as a language of culture and creativity. The Northmen (now transmuted into Normans)[28] had finally conquered; yet, like all their predecessors, they would eventually be absorbed into the life and literature of what would remain the English nation. The achievements of Alfred and Aelfric were not entirely lost. Old English manuscripts continued to be copied; homilies were still written and preached in English; and scholars have traced links between Anglo-Saxon prose and the spiritual writers who emerged in the thirteenth century. A tradition of alliterative poetry survived, to surface new-minted in the fourteenth century. The familiar themes of **judgement** and **salvation**; the impulse to go on **pilgrimage**; passionate devotion to the **saints** and their **relics**: all these recur time and time again in the literature of the Middle Ages and beyond. Yet perhaps the most potent legacy of the Anglo-Saxon era was simply an attitude to life – and death. The coming of Christianity had brought with it a new perception of the world as a stage on which a conflict between good and evil was played out, with the destiny of every human soul at stake. That drama would continue to dominate the minds and imaginations of poets, writers of prose, and makers of plays, for centuries to come.

NOTES

1. See *Alfred the Great* for extracts from Alfred's writings and contemporary documents. See also Smyth (1995), who challenges many assumptions of Alfredian scholarship, especially the authenticity of Asser's *Life*.

2. Morrish (1986) claims that Alfred's account is greatly exaggerated; Gneuss (1986) argues the credibility of Alfred's assessment.

3. See Gordon (1966).

4. See Clements (1986, 139).

5. See Bately (1982).

6. Frantzen (1986, 1).

7. Clements (1986).

8. See Shippey (1979).

9. Frantzen (1986, 25–6).

10. Proppé (1973).

11. The original reads: 'Then I spoke to her and said that she was well aware of how little I had been governed by worldly ambition. I had sought the means of engaging in politics so that virtue should not grow old unpraised.' *Boethius*, 72.

12. See Whitelock (1966, 82–3); also Bolton (1986).

13. Lewis (1964, 76).

14. Alexander (1983, 188).

15. Frantzen (1986, 105) suggests that Alfred identifies with King David 'as a teacher, leader, king and man of prayer.'

16. Whitelock (1966, 98).

17. See Woolf (1972, 5–10); Harris (1992); and Ch. 9 below.

18. See Clemoes (1966); Szarmach and Huppé (1978); Gatch (1977); Grundy (1989).

19. See Orchard (1995, 39–42).

20. See Gatch (1977, 14–15).

21. Alexander (1983, 188).

22. Shepherd (1969, 374).

23. Bately (1991, 81). See also Bethurum (1966).

24. Compare Aelfric's *Life of St. Agatha* (*Anglo-Saxon Prose*, 103)

25. See Fell (1984).

26. See *Battle of Maldon*, 148, 203.

27. See Bloomfield (1963); also Cross (1965).

28. 'Normandy was, so to say, the French Danelaw, the one great French principality which owed its origin to Viking leaders alone.' Brooke (1961, 94).

# Chapter 5

# The Church in the World – Piers Plowman and The Canterbury Tales

| | |
|---|---|
| As I biheeld into the eest an heigh to the sonne | *east; high* |
| I seigh a tour on a toft trieliche ymaked | *tower, knoll; choicely* |
| A deep dale bynethe, a dongeon therinne, | *valley; dungeon* |
| With depe diches and derke and dredfulle of sight. | *dark* |
| A fair feeld ful of folk fond I ther bitwene – | *field; found* |
| Of alle manere of men, the meene and the riche. | *kinds; humble* |
| Werchynge and wandrynge as the world asketh. | *working; requires* |

(*Piers Plowman*, Prol. 13–19)[1]

'A FAIR FEELD FUL OF FOLK

The *Vision of Piers Plowman* opens with the universe depicted in the stark imagery of the medieval stage: heaven is imagined on high, reserved for the redeemed; hell's mouth gapes hungrily below, ready for those whose sins weigh heavy upon them. In between lies the world of human experience: a mixed place, full of difficult choices, where frail mortals must prove themselves saints or sinners. The *Piers Plowman* poet, usually identified from clues in the text as one William Langland,[2] could be said to have had a foot in each camp. He seems to have been a cleric in **minor orders**, living, not in **monastic** seclusion, but in London, that hive of bustling medieval activity and haunt of sinners. He was not even celibate – long considered a sure path to sanctity – but married with a child. He earned his living singing other people's souls out of **purgatory**:

| | |
|---|---|
| The lomes that I labore with and lyflode deserve | *tools; livelihood; win* |
| Ys *Pater-noster* and my prymer, *Placebo* and *Dirige*, | **Lord's Prayer**; **Primer**; |
| | *prayers (for the dead)* |
| And my sauter som tyme and my sevene psalmes. | *salter; (penitential)* |
| | *psalms* |
| This I segge for here soules of suche as me helpeth. | *say* |

(C-Text, V, 45–8)

Small wonder then that his Dreamer asks with such intensity the burning question of the age: 'How may I save my soule?' Langland, Chaucer and their contemporaries faced a formidable dilemma. By the fourteenth century, almost all those living in Western Europe, irrespective of their personal degree of spiritual fervour, shared a world-view shaped by the teachings of the Church. Man's eternal destiny would be determined by his behaviour on earth; and who could be sure that they had met God's exacting standards? It was all very well for **saints** whose **martyrdom** or extraordinary sanctity had won them eternal bliss; but what of ordinary folk all too susceptible to the deadly enticements of sloth, gluttony, lechery and avarice?

> 'Allas,' quod Haukyn the Actif Man tho, 'that after my cristendom,
> *baptism*
>
> I ne hadde be deed and dolven for Dowelis sake!    *buried; Do-Well's*
> 'So hard it is,' quod Haukyn, 'to lyve and to do synne.    *miserable*
> Synne seweth us evere,' quod he.    *follows*
> (XIV, 320–3)

Haukyn's lament expresses the spiritual quandary of those he represents: **baptism** was held to wash away **original sin**, the inherited consequence of Adam's **Fall** from grace, but what of **sins** committed thereafter? How could men and women live amid the myriad allurements of the world without endangering their immortal souls? For the world had much to offer. Illuminated manuscripts glowing with colour, carvings executed with delicacy and frequently with considerable wit, soaring churches finished with loving attention to detail even in corners the human eye could never reach: all bear witness to the abundant vitality, the joyous creativity of the age. Human creativity was matched by human curiosity. Men journeyed to exotic lands (or said they did), and there was a ready audience for tales of the marvellous. Poets plundered the legends of Greece and Rome and borrowed from the story-tellers of Italy and France to produce tales of romance, high drama and sudden falls from Fortune's favour. Even preachers illustrated their sermons with stirring anecdotes of uncertain authenticity, highly-coloured accounts of miracles, and travellers' tales of the kind told by Sir John Mandeville.

The later Middle Ages also witnessed the development of intense intellectual speculation and controversy. The eleventh century had seen a renewal of interest in logic amongst theologians such as Lanfranc and **Anselm**, his successor as **Archbishop** of Canterbury. By the twelfth century scholars of the calibre of **Peter Abelard** were emerging: stimulating, argumentative, delighting in debate for its own sake. The newly-acquired tool of dialectic prompted the examination of traditional beliefs in the light of human reason and the increasing application of systematic study to the science of theology. The twelfth-century 'Renaissance' saw the recovery of knowledge lost since antiquity, the assimilation of the heritage of **patristic** writings, and the organisation of each field for systematic study. Universities were born: in Paris, Oxford and Cambridge. No longer were the privileges of scholarship confined to the **cloister**; armed with a knowledge of Latin, the common language of learning, scholars rich and poor could sit at the feet of English and European masters, bringing away treasures which were dispersed far and wide. No longer was the Church the only profession for able young men, though many combined membership of the lower ranks of the clergy with lay careers. The world of trade was opening up; the craft guilds growing in pride and status. A new breed of writer was emerging. Langland may have been a cleric; Chaucer combined the roles of poet, courtier and diplomat.

So much was new; yet so much stayed the same. The old questions still required an answer. Interwoven with the gorgeous colours of the tapestry of medieval life were the darker threads of war, famine and plague. Life for the poor, as Langland knew (C-Text, X, 71ff), could be infinitely cruel; life for the rich was equally uncertain. The Anglo-Saxons had acknowledged the transience of human security, and the centuries which followed Harold's defeat at Hastings did little to disprove that view. The calculated brutality of the Norman Conquest, the barren years of conflict between Stephen and Maud, 'when God and His saints slept,' the long-running French wars: all took their toll of rich and poor alike. Death and disease were no respecters of persons. Langland and Chaucer both lived through the first terrible visitation of the Black Death which reached England in 1348. Raging through crowded, insanitary towns, decimating isolated villages, it carried off one-third of the population. Lords and ladies, burgesses and labourers, **priests** and their parishioners died faster than men could bury them. Recurring outbreaks cast a shadow over the remainder of the fourteenth century and contributed to the morbid preoccupation with death and decay which pervades much fifteenth-century art and sculpture.[3] Examples include the tombs of Archbishop Chichele (Canterbury Cathedral), Bishop Fleming (Lincoln) and Alice, Duchess of Suffolk (Chaucer's granddaughter), all of which show two effigies: the upper splendidly robed, the lower a decomposing skeleton. John Myrc's *Instructions for Parish Priests* recommend meditation upon death as a cure for pride:

> ded mennus bonus ofte to se,                         *bones*
> And þenke þat he schal syche be.                    *such*
>
> (1670–2)

The horrors of the plague and its inexplicable, remorseless advance through populations helpless to resist were interpreted by the English, in common with other Europeans, as signs of God's judgement. The Bishop of Winchester warned his flock: 'it is much to be feared that man's sensuality . . . has now fallen into deeper malice and justly provoked the Divine wrath by a multitude of sins to this chastisement.'[4] The **bishop** ordered penitential processions but his fears were justified: the suffering in his **diocese** was considerable and almost half his clergy died. Penalties for **sin** were apparently not confined to the next life; they could strike at any moment. When Langland had Reason declare that 'thise pestilences was for pure synne' (V, 13), he was echoing not only the official verdict of the Church but the apprehensive guilt of the common man. And if these were but God's interim judgements, how would sinners fare at the great Judgement Day? Images of the **Last Judgement** were all around, painted on the chancel arches of village churches or carved over the doors of the great cathedrals. St Michael could be seen weighing souls in his balance: angels escorted those judged worthy to **heaven**; grotesque demons dragged the damned to **hell**. The Dreamer's question to Holy Church demanded an answer: how indeed could a man save his soul? Traditionally, the Church had offered two solutions; neither without problems. Men and women could withdraw into the **cloister**, renouncing the temptations of this world in favour of the promises of the next. Or, more hazardous by far, they could live the **active life**, playing their part in society, availing themselves of the **Sacraments** of the Church and endeavouring to keep their spiritual accounts in credit. The traditional contrast between the 'active' and the 'contemplative' lives was based on a passage in the **Gospel** of Luke:

> [Martha] had a sister called Mary, who sitting also at the Lord's feet, heard his word. But Martha was busy about much serving. Who stood and said: Lord, hast thou no care that my sister hath left me alone to serve? . . . And the Lord answering said to her, Martha, Martha, thou art . . . troubled about many things. But one thing is necessary. Mary hath chosen the best part, which shall not be taken away from her.
>
> (Luke 10:38–42)

*Monasticism*

From the early centuries of the Church there had been a strong conviction that the **monastic**[5] life was the only sure route to heaven. This view is vividly attested in the poignant testimony of the English-born historian Orderic Vitalis (d. 1143), who told how his father, 'weeping, gave me a weeping child' into the care of a Norman **monastery**, in the belief that 'if I became a monk I should taste of the joys of heaven with the Innocents after my death' (Orderic Vitalis, *Ecclesiastical History*, Bk XIII). The movement began with those who fled the materialism of Rome to seek a life of spiritual discipline in the Egyptian desert. The first **monks** (*monos*, alone) were indeed solitaries, but communities soon sprang up, developing traditions and patterns of worship. Monks took vows of poverty, chastity and obedience, thus renouncing possessions, marriage and self-will. Their motivation was encapsulated in the early sixth-century *Rule of St Benedict*, which combined ambitious spiritual aims with refreshing common sense: 'If we would escape the pains of hell and reach eternal life, then must we – while there is still time, while we are in this body . . . hasten to do now what may profit us for eternity' (*Rule of St Benedict*, Prologue). Communal life was built around the *opus dei* or work of God. In the *Rule* **Benedict** explained the origins of this pattern of worship which remained central to the monastic life throughout the Middle Ages:

> The prophet saith: *Seven times a day have I given praise to thee* [Psalm 119: 164]. We shall observe this sacred number of seven if we fulfil the duties of our service in the Hours of Lauds, Prime, Terce, Sext, None, Vespers, and Compline; for it was of these Day Hours that he said: *Seven times a day have I given praise to thee*. But of the Night Office the same prophet saith: *At midnight I rose to give praise to thee* [Ps. 119: 62]. At these times therefore let us render praise to our Creator.
>
> (*Rule*, Ch. 16)

Benedict recognised two types of good **monks**: the **anchorites** (or **hermits**) and the **coenobites**; and two types of bad monks: the worldly and the wanderers. The latter continued to plague the monastic movement, giving ammunition to satirists and reformers alike. All too often monks withdrew from the world only to find that it had pursued them into the **cloister**. Material possessions were not easy to leave behind. Gifts, including grants of land, came from those desirous of the monks' prayers for their spiritual welfare or anxious to place their children suitably. As large landowners, **abbots** were inevitably drawn into the political sphere, often called upon to entertain important visitors to the **abbey** and spending long periods away in the service of king or **pope**. Senior monks also had to lay aside the contemplation of eternity to manage the earthly affairs of the **monastery**. Chaucer's monk was reckoned

> A manly man, to been an abbot able
>
> (*C. Tales*, Gen. Prol., 167)[6]

less for his holiness than his prowess in hunting. Jocelin of Brakelond's *Chronicle* of the great Benedictine Abbey of Bury St Edmunds, written some two centuries before Chaucer's *Canterbury Tales*, shows that acrimonious disputes could break out over the handling of abbey finances and that monks were inclined to accumulate possessions in defiance of the *Rule*. Forms of worship became increasingly elaborate, leaving little time for the manual labour which **Benedict** had advocated; well-born novices were not always inclined to endure austerity and discipline became lax. In the twelfth and thirteenth centuries, new orders sprang up, born of a longing to recapture the purity of the **monastic** vision. The intellectual revival of the eleventh century had led monks back to a study of the 'apostolic life' as exemplified in the Book of Acts. They looked afresh at the three patterns which had shaped monastic tradition – the **Rule** *of St Benedict*, the lives of the **Desert Fathers** as recorded by **Cassian** and others, and the less rigorous communal life practised by groups of **canons** – and in different ways sought to revive all three. The **Cistercians** ('white monks') founded houses (including Rievaulx and Fountains) in remote areas, claiming that their simple lifestyle, rather than that of the **Benedictines** ('black monks'), embodied the spirit of **St Benedict**. The **Carthusian** order emulated the austere spirituality of the early **hermits**, building clusters of small stone cells around a central **cloister**. There they combined the barest framework of community life with ample opportunity for private prayer. Each cell also served as a scriptorium, dedicated to the production of books as a service to the wider church (hence this intriguing request from the great abbey of Cluny: 'Send us, if you please, the larger volume of St Augustine's Letters, for a large part of ours has been accidentally eaten by a bear').[7] The growth of the **canons regular** was stimulated by the revival of the 'Rule of St Augustine' at the end of the eleventh century. This 'Rule', a letter by **Augustine of Hippo** on the virtues of chastity, charity and concord together with some instructions on community life, was adopted by several groups including the **Premonstratensians** and the **Dominican friars**. Chaucer's Monk, whose precise allegiance is left unclear (possibly to make him a more universal figure), was certainly aware of it, if not inclined to submit to its teachings:

> What sholde he studie and make hymselven wood,        *mad*
> Upon a book in cloystre alwey to poure,        *pore over*
> Or swynken with his handes, and laboure,        *work*
> As Austyn bit? How shal the world be served?        *directs*
>
> (Gen. Prol, 184–7)

Chaucer's **Prioress**, in her turn, highlights the somewhat problematical role of women within the later phase of the monastic movement. The Anglo-Saxons had established a number of double **monasteries** where extremely capable **abbesses**, often with royal connections, held sway. The success of the **Gilbertines**, a double order founded in the mid-twelfth century by Gilbert of Sempringham, indicates that women were no less desirous of entering the religious life in the later period, but double monasteries were regarded with suspicion because of the risk of scandal, and lay patrons were reluctant to endow nunneries, since women could not offer **masses** for the souls of benefactors. There remained one powerful motive for endowing a community of women: the provision of a suitable environment for the unmarried daughters or widows of the upper classes. This must have been the social *milieu* of the Prioress who is commended for the elegance of her manners rather than her piety. Even where women entered convents from motives of devotion rather than convenience, their progress was dogged by prejudice and suspicion. The Gilbertine **nuns**, living as they did alongside small communities of **canons regular** and served by both lay brothers and sisters, soon met controversy. Despite Gilbert's careful organisation, indiscretions occurred. Hints of scandal circulated of a type reflected in Wrath's malicious account of life in a nunnery, under the direction of a lady not unlike Chaucer's Prioress.

> 'I have an aunte to nonne and an abbesse:        *who is a nun; abbess*
> Hir were levere swowe or swelte than suffre any peyne . . .        *she'd rather*
>         *faint; die; pain*
> I was the prioresse potager and other povere ladies,        *prioress's stew-maker;*
>         *poor*
> And maad hem joutes of janglyng – that Dame Johane was a bastard . . .
>         *stews of squabbling*

And Dame Pernele a preestes fyle – Prioress worth she nevere,    *priest's concubine; will be*

For she hadde child in chirie-tyme, al oure Chapitre it wiste!'    *cherry-time; Chapter; knew*

(*Piers Plowman*, V, 151ff)

By the mid-fourteenth century the process of decline within the **monastic** movement had begun. In 1348 there had been perhaps 10,000 **monks** and **regular canons** and 3,000 **nuns** in England and Wales out of a total population in the region of 3,700,000.[8] These numbers were severely reduced by recurring outbreaks of the Black Death, never reaching the same level again. Limited resources kept recruitment low, since orders did not wish to see their standard of living reduced. Resentment brewed among labourers and poor tenants on abbey lands, finding violent expression during the Peasants' Revolt of 1381, when clerics were prime targets. Langland denounced acquisitive, uncaring, monastic landlords:

Of the povere have thei no pite – and that is hir pure charite,    *poor, entire*

Ac thei leten hem as lordes, hir lond lith so brode.    *consider themselves, extensive*

(X, 314–5)

yet this attack is prefaced by a powerful statement of the monastic ideal:

For if hevene be on this erthe, and ese to any soule,    *peace, tranquillity*
It is in cloistre or in schole, by manye skiles I fynde.    *arguments; note*
For in cloistre cometh no man to [querele] ne to fighte,    *quarrel*
But al is buxomnesse there and bokes, to rede and to lerne.

*cooperativeness; books*
(X, 299–302)

### The Search for Salvation

This vision of the cloistered life was firmly stamped upon people's minds. The disappointment which followed upon disillusionment was correspondingly great, explaining the sometimes bitter criticism voiced by Langland and Chaucer; their models of spiritual perfection had let them down. Those who remained in the world needed inspiration. Their path to **heaven** was less clearly charted and full of obstacles. Yet lay-people of the fourteenth century could be more hopeful of **salvation** than their counterparts before the

Conquest. The teaching of the church had been steadily clarified and systematised so that even the illiterate might remember the essentials. The **scholastic theologians** of the twelfth and thirteenth centuries had defined seven **Sacraments** through which God's grace could be received: **Baptism**, Confirmation, the **Eucharist**, **Penance**, Marriage, Ordination and Unction (the anointing of the sick in preparation for death). There were **Seven Virtues** for which to aim – love, hope and faith (the 'Theological' virtues implanted by God); prudence, temperance, courage and justice (the 'Cardinal' virtues). There were likewise **Seven Deadly Sins**[9] to avoid: Pride, Envy, Anger, Sloth, Avarice, Gluttony and Lechery. As encouragement, **parish** churches were adorned with wall paintings,[10] graphically portraying the heroic (if gruesome) struggles of **saints** such as St Catherine or St Edmund, who had been willing to die for the sake of **Christ**. St George could be seen slaying the Dragon or St Christopher carrying the Christ Child. There were also sharp reminders of Judgement Day, yet here too theologians could offer some comfort. Everyone agreed that God demanded reparation for **sin**. Men and women must repent, make their **confessions** and perform appropriate **penances** as evidence of their desire to make amends. No one, however, could be sure that adequate recompense had been made, especially for those who left repentance till their death-beds. **Scholastic theologians** therefore developed the concept of **Purgatory**: an 'antechamber to heaven'[11] where **penance** could be completed and the soul purified ready for admission to **heaven**. Purgatory, though still a fearful prospect, did offer a measure of hope, fending off the yet more dreadful vision, graphically portrayed in a Winchester psalter of the mid-twelfth century, of an angel locking the door of **hell** (and presumably throwing away the key). Those who had led a reasonably good life, confessed their sins and received **absolution** before death, might, after an appropriate period of purgatorial suffering, look forward to admission to **heaven**. Inevitably, the evolution of this doctrine significantly strengthened the power of the Church, which came to be valued supremely for its role of interceding for the dead. A vision of **Purgatory**, told by a Norman **priest** and recorded by Orderic Vitalis, stressed that the salvation of those trapped there rested on the prayers and **masses** of their friends on earth. The horrified priest recognised his brother, a knight, among those suffering torments and was informed:

> The arms which we bear are red-hot . . . burning with everlasting fire. Up to now I have suffered unspeakable torture from these punishments,

but when you . . . sang your first Mass for the faithful departed, your father Ralph escaped from his torments and my shield, which caused me great pain, fell from me . . . Remember me, I beg: help me with your prayers and compassionate alms.

*(Ecclesiastical History*, Vol. 4)

How could any earnest soul refuse such a plea; or fail to make provision for their own eternal well-being? If extra **masses** would shorten the period spent in **purgatory**, then all those with the means to do so naturally left money in their wills to provide for this vital service. In 1415 Thomas Walwyn of Herefordshire asked that 10,000 masses should be said for his soul 'in all hast' (*Fifty Earliest English Wills*, 23). In the early thirteenth century it was decreed that **parish priests** should not celebrate more than one mass in a day. The rising numbers of requests for extra masses, particularly after the Black Death, led to the appointment of **chantry** priests, paid by the patrons whose spiritual welfare they promoted. Both Langland and Chaucer criticised those who preferred the easy option of singing masses in large towns to the care of country parishes impoverished by the the Black Death:

Persons and parisshe preestes pleyned hem to the bisshop    *Rectors; vicars;*
                                                             *complained*
That hire parisshes weren povere sith the pestilence tyme,    *poor; plague*
To have a licence and leve at London to dwelle.    *official permission*
And syngen ther for symonie, for silver is swete.    *sing (masses) for payment*
(*Piers Plowman*, Prol. 83–6)

The building of **chantry** chapels, where such **masses** could be said, was the growth industry of the fourteenth century. Elaborate chantries can still be seen in English **cathedrals**; that of William of Wykeham, Bishop of Winchester, boasting three carved **monks** praying in perpetuity for the repose of his soul. The granting of **indulgences** offered a further gleam of hope to the apprehensive sinner. When Pope Urban preached the First **Crusade** in 1095, he declared that participation would count as a substitute for all other **penance** and win the crusader immediate entry into **heaven**. William of Malmesbury gives this account of Urban's speech:

Let such as are going to fight for Christianity, put the form of the cross upon their garments . . . enjoying *by the gift of God, and the privilege of St. Peter, absolution from all their crimes*: let this in the meantime soothe the labour of their journey; satisfied that they shall obtain after death, the advantages of a blessed martyrdom.

(*Gesta Regum*, Book IV, Ch. 2)

Eventually the practice was widened and it became possible to buy plenary **indulgences** to be granted at the point of death. Indulgences were also offered to those who visited Rome and other holy places on special occasions, and to those who gave alms to worthy causes. In 1343 Pope Clement VI justified his authority to issue indulgences thus:

> One drop of Christ's blood would have sufficed for the redemption of the whole human race. Out of the abundant superfluity of Christ's sacrifice there has come a treasure which is . . . to be used. This treasure has been committed by God to his vicars on earth, to St Peter and his successors, to be used for the full or partial remission of the temporal punishments of the sins of the faithful who have repented and confessed.[12]

This 'treasury of merit', made up of the abundant goodness of **Christ**, the **Virgin Mary** and the **saints** and from which the debts of ordinary sinners could be paid, was useful to **priests** whose parishioners were reluctant to carry out severe **penances**. The system was, however, wide open to abuse by those licensed to grant **indulgences** in exchange for gifts for the work of the church. This **Pardoner**'s Licence was issued in 1400 by the Archbishop of York:

> to the proctors or messengers of the hospital or chapel of the most blessed Virgin Mary of Roncesvalles near Charing Cross in the city of London *to publish indulgences and privileges conceded to the benefactors of the same hospital or chapel and to collect and receive alms given or to be given by any of the faithful of Christ to the said hospital or chapel* throughout the archdeaconries of York, Cleveland and Nottingham.[13]

Here was wide scope for exploiting the ignorant and undermining the need for true **contrition**. Langland and Chaucer, whose Pardoner was also 'of Rouncivale' (*Gen. Prol.* 669), had scant respect for these travelling salesmen:

| | |
|---|---|
| Ther preched a pardoner as he a preest were: | *as if he were a priest* |
| Broughte forth a bulle with bisshopes seles, | *bull; seals* |
| And seide that hymself myghte assoilen hem alle | *absolve* |
| Of falshede of fastynge, of avowes ybroken. | *deceit; broken vows* |
| Lewed men leved hym wel and liked hise wordes. | *uneducated; believed* |

(*Piers Plowman*, Prol. 68–72)

*The Friars*

The development of lay spirituality received a considerable stimulus with the arrival in England in the early 1220s of the **mendicant friars**. The **Franciscans** and the **Dominicans**, founded separately yet influencing one other, were dedicated to the service of the poor, particularly in the towns, and to proclaiming a radical Christianity, based on the commandments of Christ in the **Gospels**. The Franciscans ('grey friars') had landed in England in 1224, establishing themselves rapidly in Canterbury, London and Oxford. The vision of their founder, **Francis of Assisi**, son of a wealthy merchant, was the literal fulfilling of the commandment of Christ (Matt. 10:7-10): 'Preach, saying: "The kingdom of heaven is at hand." Heal the sick, raise the dead, cleanse the lepers, cast out devils . . . Do not possess gold, nor silver, nor money in your purses: nor scrip [wallet, bag] for your journey, nor two coats, nor shoes nor a staff.' The **Dominican** Order of Preachers ('black friars') sprang from the conviction of their founder **Dominic**, a Spanish **canon regular**, that if orthodox preachers were to overcome the Catharist heretics of France, they must outdo them in austerity and self-denial. From the beginning the Dominicans, who reached England in 1221, concentrated on study, winning converts in the universities and providing training in preaching and the hearing of confessions. The friars led a revival of popular preaching, an aspect of pastoral care neglected by many ill-educated **parish** clergy. Their lively, well-delivered sermons were directed not to encouraging withdrawal from the world but to the application of Christian principles within it, offering a welcome vision of practical spirituality for lay-people.

For a time the **mendicants**' sacrificial lifestyle and effective preaching won them general acclaim. They recruited able young men from the universities and produced some of the greatest scholars of the age. The **Dominicans** in particular provided careful training, not only in the art of preaching but also in that of hearing confessions. Their aim was to supplement the shortcomings of the **parish** system but (not surprisingly) their efforts were not always welcomed by the parish clergy. The enthusiasm with which men and women of all classes flocked to the **friars**, taking their fees and offerings with them, threatened to undermine the established order. Moreover, as the **monastic** orders had discovered, popularity and prosperity are not always conducive to spiritual growth. Faced with gifts from devout patrons and sorely in need of churches and study centres, even the **Franciscans** relaxed their rules to admit the ownership of property. Naturally those established clergy who saw the friars as a threat were quick to exploit hints of scandal or corruption. Friars, it began to seem, could (with some fine exceptions) be as venal as the next man. By the period in which Chaucer and Langland wrote, the four orders (the **Carmelities**, **Augustinians**, **Dominicans** or Jacobins, and **Franciscans** or Minorites) were derisely nicknamed CAIM (Cain). This perceived betrayal of lay ideals may account for the particular venom with which Langland attacked the friars. Of **monks** he has little to say and that mostly good. It was left to the sophisticated satire of Chaucer to expose the inconsistencies and petty vanities of the **cloister**. Yet, despite their failings, the mission of the friars was better suited to the age than the counsel of withdrawal from worldly perils. An increasingly vocal and literate laity welcomed the idea of a full-blooded Christianity to be lived out in the everyday world. For even had the monastic movement lived up to its ideals, it could never have been an option for the majority. As King Alfred had pointed out in his translation of Boethius, a king needed men who could fight and work as well as those who prayed. Medieval society required soldiers, administrators, butchers, bakers – and ploughmen. Langland's model therefore was not a monk nor any kind of cleric but a man on whose labour the structure of society depended. Like Chaucer's Parson, he set forth a piety which combined profundity with a dazzling simplicity – and practised it. Lords and ladies, clerics **regular** and **secular**, might well learn from such an example.

THE QUEST FOR TRUTH

The *Vision of Piers Plowman* opens in easy-going style with a poet, eager for new experiences, setting off in the sunshine to see the world. Gradually this light-hearted search for 'wondres' is transmuted into an earnest quest for **salvation**, for both the Dreamer and the society he represents. Within the poem, dream sequences are used to introduce the narrator (and his audience) to ever-deepening levels of reality and revelation. Like the Dreamer in *Pearl* and many biblical figures before him, 'Will' is taught truths through this means which he could not have discerned unaided:

> Slepynge, hadde y grace
> To wyte what Dowel is ac wakynge neuere!

(C-text, XIII, 215–16)

The Prologue demonstrates this technique well. A kaleidoscopic survey of church and state brings the audience face-to-face with the nub of Langland's disquiet: the anomaly of a 'Christian' society which patently fails to live up to Christian ideals. Wherever he turns the spotlight, contradictions and confusion are revealed: many religious fail to keep their vows; most of those who live in the world are ensnared by **sin**. There are of course exceptions:

> In preieres and penaunce putten hem manye *prayers*
> Al for the love of Oure Lord lyveden ful streyte *strictly, ascetically*
> In hope to have heveneriche blisse *blessed happiness of the kingdom of heaven*
> (Prol. 25–7)

but, in the main, hypocrisy appears to be the order of the day:

> Pilgrymes and palmeres plighten hem togidere *vowed, pledged themselves*
> To seken Seint Jame and seintes in Rome; *seek St James*
> Wenten forth in hire wey with many wise tales, *way; speeches*
> And hadden leve to lyen al hire lif after . . . *leave; tell lies; life*
> Grete lobies and longe that lothe were to swynke . . . *lubbers; tall; reluctant; work*
> . . . shopen hem heremytes hire ese to have. *turned themselves into; comfort*
> I fond there freres, alle the foure ordres, *friars; four orders*
> Prechynge the peple for profit of [the] womb[e]: *belly*
> (Prol. 46–9, 55, 57–9)

It is not only the **mendicant** orders and the pseudo-religious who catch Langland's satirical eye. Gaps left in the ranks of the **parish** clergy by the ravages of the Black Death had frequently been filled by those whose education and commitment left much to be desired. **Bishops** who should have regulated their clergy were all too often to be found at court assisting in affairs of state. Even the papacy, which in theory should have provided stability and direction for the church, had become a cause of unease. The costly lifestyle of the **pope** and his **cardinals** (XIX, 415) was financed in part by dues and rents from English parishes. These payments were deeply resented by the English, Edward III remarking pointedly to Pope Clement VI (1342–52) that 'the successor of the Apostles was commissioned to lead the Lord's sheep to the pasture, not to fleece them.'[14] English anger was intensified by the 'Babylonian captivity' (1309–77) when the popes lived in Avignon on close terms with England's enemy, France. The Great Schism of 1378, when rival popes were elected, one Italian, one French, caused much confusion and distress. The Church was on its guard against the appearance of the **Anti–Christ**, deceiver of the faithful. Could one of the 'popes' be he; and if so which? Langland's was one among many voices raised in complaint. Orthodox preachers of the period, such as Thomas Brinton, Bishop of Rochester, who has been identified as the angel of the Prologue,[15] denounced abuses within the church: 'In the matter of title and honours, so ambitious are the ecclesiastics that, if they possess a fat living, it is not enough for them unless they have a prebend . . . If they have several, they affect to be a bishop; and then a bishop at court.'[16]

At the beginning of Passus I the poet signals that the first level of meaning of his tale is about to be unveiled. Holy Church descends from the castle and challenges the Dreamer to perceive the spiritual realities behind the bustle of fourteenth-century life (I, 5–9). Her warnings of the threat posed by the World, the Flesh and the Devil (I, 36–69) stimulate the Dreamer to ask with real urgency: 'Tel me . . . How I may save my soule' (I, 83–4). Here is the heart of the Dreamer's quest. Holy Church has shown him that his own position (like that of Haukyn) is somewhat equivocal: bound to the Church by his **baptism**, he has lost the **grace** which that baptism conferred. The teaching given by Holy Church at this point is crucial to an understanding of the poem as a whole. The poet has been disillusioned by the sordid self-centredness of much church life yet continues to hold fast to a vision of the eternal Church, pure and untainted by **sin**. This ideal Church is the guardian of truth and her teaching is all that the pilgrim requires, even though her earthly representatives may not always live it out (XV, 92–5). Langland is neither a heretic nor a revolutionary. His view of the Church seems to accord with his complaint against society: he does not disagree with the principles on which they are founded; he would just like to see them put into practice. Holy Church makes it clear that Truth is not merely a set of doctrines requiring intellectual assent. Understanding of truth only benefits those who are willing to obey what they are taught. **Lucifer** knew truth from beholding God in heaven, yet chose disobedience and lies in **hell**. At points in the poem, therefore, the Dreamer is chided for idle curiosity and warned of the dangers of theological speculation as an end in itself. Truth and Love are, moreover, dynamic forces, aspects of the character of God himself. Love, for **Christ**, meant action: involvement with mankind:

> For hevene myghte nat holden it, so was it hevy of hymselve,
> Til it hadde of the erthe eten his fille.                    *eaten*

| | |
|---|---|
| And whan it hadde of this fold flessh and blood taken, | *earth* |
| Was nevere leef upon lynde lighter therafter, | *leaf; linden tree* |
| And portatif and persaunt as the point of a nedle, | *portable; piercing* |
| That myghte noon armure it lette ne none heighe walles. | |
| | *(So) that; armour; stop* |
| | (I, 153–8) |

Love, for Christ's followers, must also be demonstrated in deeds. An arid, loveless piety is of use neither to God nor man. Holy Church offers a pithy, down-to-earth re-working of I Corinthians 13:

| | |
|---|---|
| For though ye be trewe of youre tonge and trewliche wynne, | *honestly* |
| | *earn (profit)* |
| And as chaste as a child that in chirche wepeth, | |
| But if ye loven leelly and lene the povere | *Unless; faithfully; give to* |
| Of swich good as God yow sent goodliche parteth, | *sends; liberally share* |
| Ye ne have na moore merite in masse ne in houres | *the Divine Office* |
| Than Malkyn of hire maydenhede, that no man desireth. | *virginity* |
| | (I, 179–84) |

Thus early in the poem the Dreamer catches a vision which moves him to begin his spiritual pilgrimage. The words of Holy Church contrast sharply with the deceit and self-interest which apparently govern so much human activity:

| | |
|---|---|
| Love is leche of lif and next Oure Lord selve, | *physician; closest; himself* |
| And also the graithe gate that goth into hevene . . . | *direct way* |
| When alle tresors ben tried, Treuthe is the beste. | *treasures* |
| | (I, 204–5, 7) |

As yet his understanding is minimal; it is enough for him to know that such things exist and to set out in search of them. In a world distorted by **sin**, however, truth is not always easy to see, as the story of Mede demonstrates. The Dreamer asks to be taught to discern good from evil; the answer, in essence, is that Falsehood, especially as represented by his daughter Mede (reward, payment), is all around him, permeating Church and state. The Dreamer, though forewarned, is still dazzled by his first glimpse of Mede (II, 17); small wonder then that the king finds it hard to discover the rights and wrongs of her case. Strictly speaking, Mede should be regarded as a neutral force, since the **Bible** stated not that money was intrinsically evil but that the devoted pursuit of it would lead to wrong-doing (I Tim. 5:9–10). This point is made initially by theology, but it soon becomes clear that no one can tangle with Mede without risking moral and spiritual decline. Her very presence at court is a signal for corruption to spread. This too was a favourite topic of the preachers.[17] Owst cites the Dominican Bromyard's denunciation of avarice: 'As among the clergy, so among the religious, Money or *Meed* is lord of the sciences and the churches. Moreover, everywhere it opens the gates of lands and palaces, and the doors of inner chambers', together with the acid comments of a Malmesbury chronicler about a papal appointment to Canterbury: 'But the Lady *Pecunia* decides every matter in that court!'[18] The Dreamer and the reader have learned their first lesson: life is not simple and choices are not always straightforward. Langland's world is complex and therefore his Dreamer will not always see clearly, understand fully or act correctly. Just as the Church over the centuries had seen the ebb and flow of spiritual vision and vigour, so too the Dreamer's spiritual pilgrimage will combine flashes of illumination and insight with periods of doubt, confusion and even inertia. That the poet devotes so much space to the story of Mede indicates its importance in his thinking. Not only did he believe that the **salvation** of individuals and the well-being of society depended on the proper use of power and possessions; he was also painfully aware of how many religious orders had foundered on the question of handling money. The episode in which a **friar** acts as '**confessor**' to Mede lays bare the hypocrisy and venality which Langland saw disfiguring the Church:

> Thanne Mede for hire mysdedes to that man kneled,          *kneeled*
>         *(in confession)*
> And shrof hire of hire sherewednesse – shamelees I trowe;
>         *confessed; wickedness*
> Tolde hym a tale and took hym a noble          *gave; noble (coin)*
> For to ben hire bedeman and hire brocour alse. *beadsman (one who prays);*
>         *go-between too*
> Thanne he assoiled hire soone and sithen he seide,   *absolved; at once; next*
> 'We have a wyndow a-werchynge, wole stonden us ful hye;   *a-building;*
>         *cost us a great deal*
> Woldestow glaze that gable and grave there thy name,   *If you would;*
>         *engrave*
> Sykir sholde thi soule be hevene to have.'          *certain*
> (III, 43–50)

It is clear from surviving manuals of instruction for **priests** that the **friar** is breaking all the rules of the confessional, completely failing to bring Mede to recognise her guilt or to indicate any desire for reform. Moreover he commits the offence against Church law of which friars were most often accused,[19] that of offering easy **absolution** in return for payment, an accusation also implied by Chaucer of his friar (Prol. 223). By the fourteenth century criticism of the friars was widespread. Their early ideals of poverty and service had been undermined; their practice of living by gifts now looked uncomfortably like extortion. A carved **misericord** seat in Beverley Minster, showing a fox friar preaching to a crowd of silly geese while his ape assistant takes the pickings, is far from unique as a satire on the friars' fondness for money. Mede's response shows that she has the friar's measure. If he will excuse the deadly sin of Lechery, then,

> I shal covere youre kirk, youre cloistre do maken . . .   *roof (vb); have built*
> That every segge shall see I am suster of youre house.     *man; sister*
> (III, 60, 63)

The practice of granting letters of fraternity to lay people who wished to be associate members of an order was a further fruit of the admiration felt for the **mendicants**. Such lay brothers or sisters were granted the right of burial in a friar's habit and assured of the community's prayers for their souls. Those who hoped to gain admittance to **heaven** by clinging to the friars' spiritual coat-tails were willing to pay handsomely for such privileges. Whether, in Langland's estimation, the friars will draw Mede to heaven or she them to **hell** seems a moot point.

In Passus V 'Will' faces the need for personal repentance. Reason, like **John the Baptist** before him (Luke 3:2–14), reminds the people of coming Judgement and calls upon them to reform their way of life. His instructions are specific and his preaching ranges across the social spectrum, without fear or favour. Tom Stowe is ordered to discipline his shrewish wife and the King to take better care of his subjects. The Church too must put its house in order:

> If ye leven as ye leren us, we shul leve yow the bettre.   *live; teach;*
> *believe*
> (V, 44)

Will's tearful identification with sinful humankind paves the way for the entry of the **Seven Deadly Sins**. To modern readers the Sins may seem comic in their grotesqueness; for a fourteenth-century audience they would also have been charged with spiritual significance. Langland's clerical audience would have known these stereotypes as tools of their trade; to laymen they may have been uncomfortable reminders of the probing of a conscientious **confessor**:

> 'Hast þou I-synget in glotonye?               *sinned; gluttony*
> 'Hast þou synged in lechery?'                        *sinned*
>                          (Mirk: *Instructions*, 1313, 1347)

Langland was clearly acquainted with at least one of the manuals of confession and **penance** which had multiplied in the previous century. Since the edict of 1216, which decreed that every Christian should go to confession at least once a year in preparation for receiving the **sacrament** at **Easter**, there had been greater emphasis on the classification of **sin** and the thorough examination of the human conscience. **Scholastic theologians** such as **Peter Abelard** and **Thomas Aquinas** had become interested in the psychology of the sinner and begun to explore aspects of motive and intention in **sin**. The time, place and manner of sinning were also regarded as important in assessing the degree of culpability. John Mirk's *Instructions for Parish Priests* provides illuminating examples of the type of questioning a penitent might expect. Langland's Sins are well aware of the appropriate responses:[20]

MIRK:
> Hast þow ete wyth syche mayn,
> þat þow hast cast hyt vp a-gayn?                      (1315–6)

GLUTTONY:
> [I have] overseyen me at my soper and som tyme at nones,
>                          *forgotten myself; supper; midday*
> That I, Gloton, girte it up er I hadde gon a myle.       *vomited*
>                                              (V, 372–3)

MIRK:
> Hast þou be slowe and take non hede,
> To teche þy godchyldre pater noster and crede?
>                                **Lord's Prayer**; **Creed**
> Hast þow be slowe for to here,
> Goddes serues when tyme were?                        *services*
> Hast þou come to chyrche late
> And spoken of synne by þe gate?                       (1161–7)

SLOTH:
> I kan noght parfitly my *Paternoster* as the preest hit syngeth . . .
>                                *do not know properly*
> I am ocupied ech a day, halyday and oother

With ydel tales at the ale and outherwhile in chirches . . .

*idle gossip; other times*

And vigilies and fastyng dayes – alle thise I late,    *let*

And ligge abedde in Lenten and my lemman in myne armes

*lie; Lent; lover*

Til matyns and masse be do.

(V, 395, 403–4, 410–2)

Repentance proves himself a good **confessor** according to the manuals: probing, refusing to accept inadequate confession, yet willing to lighten the allotted **penance** when Avarice seems on the point of despair. The characterisation of the Sins is also indebted to the vivid denunciations which thundered from the pulpits of the day. Sloth's confession:

I have be preest and person passynge thritty wynter,    *more than*

Yet kan I neyther solve ne synge ne seintes lyves rede,    *'sol-fa'; sing by*

*note; read saints' lives*

But I kan fynden in a feld or in a furlang an hare    *find; ten-acre area*

Better than in *Beatus vir* or *Beati omnes*    *the Psalms*

Construe clausemele and kenne it to my parisshens.

*clause by clause; teach;, parishioners*

(V, 416–20)

would not have surprised the Berkshire vicar, William de Pagula who wrote:

Many are the priests, in these days, who neither know the law of God nor teach others. But *giving themselves up to sloth*, they spend their time on banquetings and carousals . . . constantly in the streets, rarely in the church, slow to investigate the faults of their parishioners, ready to track the footprints of hares or some other wild beast.[21]

To recognise that Langland has drawn heavily on penitential and homiletic material in personifying the **Seven Deadly Sins** is in no way to undervalue his achievement. Beneath the comedy he evokes a sense of the evil which has warped his world, exposing the roots of greed, dissension and exploitation.

Their confessions complete and their **penances** allotted, the Sins fade from view. They will of course reappear, for **sin** is not so easily eradicated from society, but at least the Dreamer will be better equipped to recognise them. The general mood of penitence prompts a mass **pilgrimage** in search of Truth but the pilgrims are hampered by their own ignorance. Wandering aimlessly, they meet a professional pilgrim, whose ignorance of Truth's whereabouts reveals him and his brethren as shams (V, 535). This disappointment is the cue for the entrance of Piers Plowman. He knows Truth and the way to his home. His instructions are orthodox: they must move via humility and listening to Conscience, to the observance of God's commandments. The castle of Truth is, in an image made familiar through sermons, the human heart. There are clear parallels between the instructions of Piers and the admonitions of Holy Church in Passus I. Both insist on the necessity of obedience and putting faith into practice. Postponing participation in the **pilgrimage** until his ploughing is done, Piers sets the company to work according to their skills and degree. Here is medieval society as the Church, and Langland, would like to see it: the knight acting justly, guarding the church and defending the poor; the hard-working rewarded; wastrels punished. The Utopian dream is short-lived; **sin** begins to rear its head again and Piers has to call upon Hunger to discipline his unruly companions. Once again, natural disasters are interpreted as chastisement from God, intended to bring mankind to their senses. At this point Truth intervenes to stop the pilgrimage. Genuine repentance and reformation can and should be expressed at home. The Pardon with its lengthy gloss (interpretation) is not a cheap **indulgence** but a restating of the law. God's **grace** is only for the true penitent who desires to mend his ways. Piers, presumably with his recent experiences in mind, is painfully aware of the difficulty of obeying God's will in the world. His abrupt tearing of the pardon through 'pure tene' (*sheer anger*) (VII, 115) has prompted much discussion.[22] Was the anger provoked by the intervention of the priest or the inadequacy of the pardon? He is not, it seems, angry with Truth since he goes on to reaffirm his own faith in the words of Psalm 23, announcing his determination to abandon the **active life**:

> 'I shal cessen of my sowyng,' quod Piers, 'and swynke noght so
>   harde,                                                  *leave off; labour*
> Ne aboute my bely joye so bisy be na moore;              *pleasure in food*
> Of preieres and of penaunce my plough shal ben herafter,'  *In; consist*
>                                                              (VII, 118–120)

The figure of Piers is plainly crucial to the narrative yet curiously hard to pin down. When first encountered he is apparently a simple labourer, whose instinctive piety is a rebuke to the hollow religion of his betters:

I knowe [Truth] as kyndely as clerc doth hise bokes.    *intimately; scholar*
(V, 538)

Here he is the ideal layman, spiritually perceptive, anxious to serve Truth. In later appearances he assumes a new authority and a deeper significance. He always represents the longed-for spiritual ideal and his teaching is received as true, yet his identity seems to shift. One moment he is identified with **St Peter**, the next with **Christ** – or is it the Good Samaritan? Is he the perfect Christian or is he the Church? These overlapping interpretations pose less of a problem in theological terms than they do within the literal level of the story. The Dreamer needs not only to understand Truth but to bridge the gulf which exists between sinful man and God's requirement of goodness. The evolving figure of Piers offers in turn a guide (V–VII), an instructor (XVI), an example (The Good Samaritan in XVII) and a saviour, as Jesus wins forgiveness for mankind (XVIII). Piers, like **St Peter**, like the Church, like **Christ** Himself, is a channel of God's progressive revelation to man.

The Dreamer's visions in Passus I–VII have not resolved his questions; they have instead inspired a further quest. He has examined the world and its failings in the perspective of eternity; he has acquired the ability to recognise evil and been convicted of his own sinfulness. Challenged by Holy Church and inspired by the example of Piers, he must now find a sure path to **salvation**. Though he accepts the value of **indulgences** and **masses**, they are not, he suspects, 'so siker [sure] for the soule, certes, as is Dowel' (VII, 181). Holy Church has told him that Love is 'the graithe [direct] gate that goth into hevene (I, 205)'. He therefore goes in search of love wherever it is to be found. An initial perusal of the Dreamer's search for Do-Well, Do-Bet and Do-Best may tempt the modern reader to conclude that Langland is guilty of piling contradiction upon confusion. The Dreamer wants to understand what Do-Well, Do-Bet and Do-Best 'doon among the peple' (VIII, 111). The answer apparently depends entirely upon whom you ask. Allegorical figures come and go, promoting interminable theological debate and philosophical speculation; the Dreamer disputes with the ubiquitous friars, is lectured by Intelligence and rebuked by Study, argues with Scripture and is led astray by Fortune. Caught up in a whirlwind succession of biblical characters and events he lives through the **Crucifixion**, the **Harrowing of Hell**, the birth of the Church and the coming of **Anti-Christ**. The poem concludes with the Church under siege and the beginning of yet another **pilgrimage**. Langland has been accused of lack of structure, endless unprofitable digressions, and an inability to discipline his writing in order to produce a coherent whole. Yet it would be hard to account for the popularity of his work if he were indeed wilfully obscure or out of touch with his contemporaries. Medieval men and women enjoyed argument for its own sake and found religion a subject of absorbing interest. They were unlikely to be put off by the exploration of intriguing byways on the road to truth. Nor was the teaching of the medieval Church a monolithic structure but a cluster of doctrines, many still in the process of formulation and subject to the speculations of theologians. Great weight was placed upon 'authorities', foremost among which were the **Old and New Testament** scriptures, followed by the **Apocrypha**; yet just as Jewish rabbis had augmented the Torah with detailed interpretations and rulings on everyday life, so for centuries Christian scholars had expounded and applied the words of scripture to the issues of their own day. These writings in turn acquired authority, particularly when associated with one of the **Doctors of the Church**. Inevitably this mass of teaching contained many contradictions and the material for endless controversy; occasional **Councils** were convened to seek unanimity on points of particular importance. The patchwork history of **monasticism** showed that while all agreed on the need for **salvation** there were varying views on how it could be achieved. One of the great tasks of the **scholastic theologians** of the twelfth century had been to set out differing views on major doctrines in order to attempt a resolution. The Dreamer, therefore, can be seen to be ranging far and wide over the ground covered by contemporary debate, seeking illumination through using his own faculties and the wisdom to be gleaned from the teaching of others. Large sections of his quest take the form of debate, since that was the method by which students were trained to examine propositions and reach conclusions. Sometimes he is humbled, sometimes argumentative, sometimes (the reader may sympathise) he is simply confused. It is not until he finds Piers again that the movement of the poem is resumed, for the answer to this particular puzzle lies not in propositions but in a person. In Passus XIII, neither Clergye (Learning) nor Conscience could provide definitive explanations of Do-Well; they could only point to Piers and indicate that meeting him would make all clear. Anima too, having explained the true nature of Charite (Love), asserts that only through Piers can Love be discerned (XV, 211–12).

In Passus XVI Piers is revealed as the guardian of the Tree of Charity. Here at least two, possibly more levels of meaning are operating simultaneously. Anima's explanation of the Tree[23] is straightforward and could easily have been turned into one of the diagrams beloved of medieval thought:

> Mercy is the more thereof; the myddul stok is ruthe;       *root; trunk; pity*
> The leves ben lele wordes, the lawe of Holy Chirche;       *leaves; faithful*
> The blosmes beth buxom speche and benigne lokynge. *willing; kind looks*
> (XVI, 5–7)

So far so good. But then the Dreamer falls into a deeper trance and the image begins to shift. The diagram comes to life as Piers is shown warding off the assaults made upon the Tree by the World, the Flesh and the **Devil** (against whom the Christian was pledged to fight at **baptism**), through the power of God the Father (Creator of the world), Jesus **Christ** (the Word made Flesh) and the **Holy Spirit**. The point of the drama is encouragement. Man's quest for holiness does not rely upon the exercise of Freewill alone; he can call upon the combined resources of the **Trinity** to come to his aid. Next Piers indicates three well-recognised[24] levels of spiritual development: Marriage, Continence (Widowhood) and Virginity. When he shakes the tree these fruits fall to the ground in recognisable form: Adam, Abraham, Isaiah, Samson, Samuel and the last of the prophets before **Christ**, **John the Baptist**. Despite their faith they are defenceless against the Devil and are carried off to **Limbo**. Here is a vital dramatic and theological link in the poem's development. An individual's search for **salvation** has suddenly expanded into a cosmic drama. Angered by the **Devil**'s depredations, Piers sets in motion the events which lead to Christ's **Incarnation**, his defeat of the **Devil** on the Cross and the final triumphant **Harrowing of Hell** by which the **Old Testament** patriarchs are to be rescued. The biblical time sequence breaks off briefly so that the Dreamer's theological understanding can catch up with his dream experiences. Abraham (Faith) and Moses (Hope) represent the faith and laws of the **Old Testament**. The Dreamer finds it hard to reconcile their differing emphases until he encounters the Good Samaritan (Love) who by his actions and his words points forwards to the climactic events in Jerusalem where Christ through love will satisfy the demands of the **Old Testament** law and thus bring hope to those in the grip of the devil. Now the Dreamer's waking life (in terms of the **liturgical** calendar),[25] his spiritual understanding, and his dream-experience of the biblical drama finally correspond. Roused by the Easter bells, the memory of Christ's victory fresh in his mind, he is ready to proclaim the message of the **Resurrection** (XVIII, 428–33).

Many poets might have been content to end the story here, on a high note. Not Langland; partly because the biblical narrative did not stop there and partly because that was not the whole picture of Christian experience. Christ, who we are told in Passus XIX exemplified Do-Well, Do-Bet and Do-Best, bequeathed his work on earth to the Church, giving the **Holy Spirit** as helper and guide. The battle however was not over. The Church remained in the world and therefore subject to attack. The Book of Revelation was written to encourage the **early Church** in its conflict with the world and to warn against the deceptions of the **Anti-Christ** who would seek to subvert the truth. Hence Langland portrays Holy Church resisting the headlong onslaught of Pride and Lechery but falling to the old insidious enemies: hypocrisy and venality. Once the **friars** enter, the case is desperate and only Piers can restore the Church to its true character and mission.

> 'The frere with his phisyk this folk hath enchaunted,      *bewitched*
> And plastred hem so esily [hii] drede no synne!'
> 'By Christ!', quod Conscience tho, 'I wole bicome a pilgrym,
> And walken as wide as the world lasteth,
> To seken Piers the Plowman, that Pride myghte destruye.'

(XX, 379–383)

So the poem ends, as it began, with a quest. There is, it would appear, no rest this side of heaven. The Dreamer has learned much, yet remains subject to the woes of this world. Similarly the Church, though holding the treasure of **salvation**, is always in danger of being undermined. Neither can afford to rest on their spiritual laurels, for it is incumbent upon every individual and generation to discover and follow Truth for themselves. The Church portrayed in *Piers Plowman* seems comfortably settled in the world; Langland wanted Christians to remember that their calling was to perpetual pilgrimage, en route to their true home in **heaven**.

### PILGRIMES WERE THEY ALLE

Medieval Christianity was by no means all fervent devotion and **asceticism**, nor were all medieval **pilgrimages**[26] occasions of great solemnity. Just as the observance of 'holy' days varied according to the piety of the individual concerned, so too the concept of pilgrimage was capable of a wide range of interpretations. All sorts and conditions of men and women could be found upon the roads of England, Europe and the Holy Land: the devout pilgrim seeking healing or remission of **sins** at the shrine of a favourite **saint**; the carefree tourist intent on exploring the world (with a little spiritual benefit thrown in); even the penitent criminal ordered to travel to a distant shrine in atonement for past crimes. In some fourteenth-century pilgrimages, the 'holiday' element seems to have almost completely superseded all other objectives. Contemporary critics alleged that pilgrimages were an excuse for the telling of 'idle tales' and the **Lollard** William Thorpe, a prominent campaigner for reform, complained that some pilgrims 'will ordain beforehand to have with them both men and women that can well sing wanton songs. And some other pilgrims will have with them bagpipes so that every town that they come through shall know of their coming, what with the noise of their singing and the noise of their piping, what with the jangling of their Canterbury bells and the barking of the dogs after them.'[27] Certainly the setting of the *Canterbury Tales*, with its well-dressed, mounted pilgrims ambling comfortably towards the shrine of **St Thomas Becket**, seems to signal that this is not an expedition to be taken too solemnly, since serious penitents and petitioners usually travelled on foot. The Miller's bagpipes, the Host's occasionally offensive exuberance and the questionable morality of some of the stories told, would seem to confirm this suspicion. Langland saw life as a spiritual pilgrimage. Chaucer, a more urbane and courtly poet, turns the image on its head: his 'pilgrimage' offers a slice of life. 'Saints' keep company with unabashed sinners, exchanging tales in which piety and bawdiness sit oddly together, tales[28] which reveal the strange mixture of spirituality and earthiness which characterised fourteenth-century society. Chaucer's pilgrims are a microcosm of the Church and hence, in medieval understanding, of the society in which he lived. Everyone in Chaucer's world belonged to the Church by virtue of their **baptism**; all were Christians in name if not in practice. That was the nub of the problem which occupied both Langland and Chaucer. The Church in the fourteenth century was not just the committed few, it embraced everyone – and their worldly ways. Everyday life was shaped by the festivals of the Church and permeated by its doctrines; even the immoral layman was caught up in the Church's year and ceremonies. At the same time the unholy cleric could find many opportunities to exploit the system, thus undermining its credibility. Concerned observers might well wonder whether the Church was redeeming the world or the world subverting the Church. Chaucer's vantage point on life was quite different from that of Langland, his characters more subtly drawn, his verse more sophisticated; yet both were deeply concerned about the Church's integrity. Langland's *Prologue* stripped bare the hypocrisy of Church and state; Chaucer's technique is more subtle yet he too constantly hints at a gulf between appearance and reality. Few of Chaucer's pilgrims emerge with their integrity untarnished.

The Church allowed several motivations for **pilgrimage**; some Chaucer includes, others are conspicuous by their absence. The concept of pilgrimage as **penance** had been encouraged by the Celtic Church and many had tramped to distant shrines appointed by **confessors**, some perishing on the way. With the growing availability of **indulgences** came a new impetus to pilgrimage. By visiting certain holy sites men and women could win remission from the torments of **purgatory**. Strictly speaking, such journeys did not of themselves remove guilt. A sermon from the *Liber Sancti Jacobi* warns that visiting the shrine of **St James** at Compostella will not automatically win pilgrims **salvation**. Their attitude must be right, their pilgrimage austere and they must be willing to undergo a total moral reformation: 'If he was previously a spoliator, he must become an almsgiver; if he was boastful he must be forever modest; if greedy, generous; if a fornicator or adulterer, chaste; if drunk, sober . . . from every sin which he committed before his pilgrimage, he must afterward abstain completely.'[29] Few of Chaucer's pilgrims seem inclined to comply with this advice. Though the Parson, in his *Tale*, advises his companions of the value of **penance**, the mood of their pilgrimage is hardly penitential. Sinners there are in plenty but repentance does not appear high upon their agenda.

The first conventional motive given for this pilgrimage is gratitude, born of answered prayers for healing:

> to Caunterbury they wende,  *go*
> The hooly blisful martir for to seke,  *blessed martyr*
> That hem hath holpen whan that they were seeke.  *helped; sick*
> (*Gen. Prol.* 16–18)

Given a high incidence of disease and the uncertain benefits of contemporary medical practice, it is not surprising that many resorted to prayer to **saints** and visits to their shrines.[30] In the case of pilgrims to the shrine of **Thomas Becket**, thankfulness was probably mingled with prudence. Medieval **saints** could become touchy if favours granted were not met with appropriate acknowledgement and St Thomas appears to have been particularly sensitive on this point. The thirteenth-century windows in the Trinity Chapel of Canterbury Cathedral were not purely decorative; they held a message. Depicted in still-glowing colours are accounts of the many miracles wrought by St Thomas and the retribution which befell those who failed to keep their vows. Even his friend, Sir Jordan Fitz-eisulf, was not immune from the **martyr**'s displeasure; failing to deliver a thank-offering of money after his son's recovery from the plague, he was brought to his senses by the death of a second son and hastily fulfilled his vow. Major shrines such as that of Becket were laden with splendid gifts (which served as capital for the church) and often displayed wax models representing the illness from which pilgrims had been, or still hoped to be, delivered.[31]

Despite the enormous popularity of his cult, **Becket** (d. 1170) was an unlikely **saint**. An able, ambitious lawyer, he had risen to become Chancellor and achieved a close friendship with the young Henry II. Reluctantly accepting the post of **Archbishop** of Canterbury, he underwent a radical transformation, exchanging the luxuries of court for a hair-shirt and his loyalty to Henry for a fierce determination to defend the rights and privileges of the Church. The King, who had hoped to benefit from a closer alliance between Church and state, was understandably annoyed. Years of struggle and acrimony culminated in Henry's frustrated demand to be rid of the 'turbulent priest'. Four of Henry's knights took up the challenge and murdered Thomas in his cathedral. Within days miracles were reported from the **archbishop's**'s resting place. Outrage at Thomas's death swept Europe, and Henry had to undergo a penitential scourging at the **martyr**'s tomb. Even the King of France came as suppliant to the saint and his prayers were answered. Small wonder that rich and poor alike should follow suit.

Behind the stated motive of Chaucer's pilgrims, however, lurk others, less spiritual in nature. All save the Parson lie open to the charge that their **pilgrimage** owes less to piety than to wanderlust. Inspired by the coming of spring, they long to be on the road, exploring the world. For some this is perfectly valid; for others such as the rotund **Monk** and the elegant **Prioress**, it hints at dereliction of duty. Both were supposed to have renounced the world they so obviously enjoy. **Monastic** vows included a commitment to stability and the *Regularis Concordia* stated that 'The brethren shall not *gad about* visiting the properties of the monastery unless either great necessity or reasonable discretion require it' (8). Neither the

**Monk** nor the **Prioress** demonstrates the simplicity and austerity of dress which their respective founders would have wished; neither is noted for their inner sanctity. The description of the Prioress strikes an ambivalent note. She has apparently achieved success and respect within a sphere which may not have been her own choice, yet her motivation is unclear: is her life devoted to *Amor* (human love) or *Caritas* (divine love)? Her tale, a sentimental, anti-semitic legend of a type specifically forbidden by successive **popes**,[32] is not remarkable for the charity it displays. Instances of her compassion are limited to tears shed over dead mice and the pet dogs which nuns were in fact forbidden to keep. This in an age when hundreds of thousands perished through plague, hunger and war. Perhaps there is no great harm in her but no evidence of any great good either. In his apparently straightforward presentation of the ecclesiastical figures, Chaucer in fact invites judgement by conjuring up a parallel image of what each *should* be. The Monk, by quoting his monastic forebears so dismissively, evokes the true monastic ideal as practised by **Benedict**, **Augustine**, **Bede** or **Aelred**; all greater men than he. Behind the **Friar** stands the infinitely more dynamic and attractive figure of **St Francis**. Francis, in love with life yet indifferent to wealth, revered all creatures and all men. His calling was to identify with the beggar and serve the leper, two classes which this friar is at pains to avoid:

> He knew the tavernes wel in every toun
> and everich hostiler and tappestere                 *every; innkeeper, bar-maid*
> Bet than a lazar or a beggestere;                    *leper; beggar-woman*
> For unto swich a worthy man as he                                   *such*
> Acorded nat, as by his facultee,
> To have with sike lazars aqueyntaunce.                              *sick*
> (*Gen. Prol.* 240–5)

Blatantly ignoring biblical commands to care for widows and orphans, this unchaste, uncharitable friar sees only targets for exploitation (*Gen. Prol.* 253–5). He embodies many of the failings for which the **mendicant** orders were criticised: he claimed greater authority in the hearing of confessions than the **parish** clergy and gave easy **absolution** in return for alms; he dressed luxuriously, 'lyk a maister or a pope'; like his counterpart in the *Summoner's Tale* he was open to the charge of preying on 'weak women'.

The **Summoner** and the **Pardoner**, introduced as a pair, are plainly opportunists. The former derived his authority from the **archdeacon** who was responsible for punishing immorality amongst clergy and people, and his power from the opportunities of blackmail and intimidation offered by the system. The Pardoner's activities illustrate both the popular craving for indulgences and popular credulity where **saints' relics** were involved:

| | |
|---|---|
| For in his male he hadde a pilwe-beer | *pillow case* |
| Which that he seyde was Oure Lady veyl . . . | *veil* |
| And in a glas he hadde pigges bones. | |

(Gen. Prol. 694–5, 700)

Veneration of **relics** dates back to at least the second century. Long before the fourteenth century relics had acquired such significance that they had become a marketable commodity. Even the finger bone of a well-known **saint** was valuable, though difficult to authenticate. The fall of Constantinople (1204) to the forces of the Fourth Crusade dispersed the vast collection of the emperors of Byzantium throughout Western Europe. Relics were useful as gifts for kings, as sources of revenue and as attractions for pilgrims. It is hardly surprising that there was a brisk trade in pious forgeries and not a little body snatching. Relics multiplied: there were phials of **Christ**'s blood, pieces of the Crown of Thorns, and enough splinters of the True Cross to construct a sizeable ship. Since the body of the **Virgin Mary** was believed to have been taken up to heaven there could be no physical remains to be venerated but more than one shrine claimed to possess samples of her clothing and milk. The body of **St James** was miraculously, not to say mysteriously, discovered in Spain at a moment when the morale of the Christian army was flagging. The resulting cult made Compostella a great **pilgrimage** centre. Chaucer's Pardoner, skilled in preaching but unattractive in person, is simply the everyday face of a hugely profitable (if ethically bankrupt) medieval industry.

As compensation for this rogues' gallery of ecclesiastical and lay hypocrites, we are given one praiseworthy cleric, one irreproachable layman and one sincere scholar. **Parish** clergy were not necessarily any more virtuous as a class than other clerics but Chaucer chooses to present a good example, described in terms which evoke Langland's criticisms of less worthy pastors:

| | |
|---|---|
| He sette nat his benefice to hyre | *did not farm out* |
| And leet his sheep encombred in the myre | *left; stuck* |
| And ran to Londoun unto Seinte Poules | *St Paul's Cathedral* |
| To seken hym a chaunterie for soules . . . | *appointment as* **chantry priest** |
| Cristes loore and his apostles twelve | *Christ's teaching* |
| He taughte; but first he folwed it hymselve. | *followed* |

(Gen. Prol. 507 ff)

The figure of his brother, the Plowman, may well be a tribute to the earlier poem. Together, the two illustrate a model relationship between clergy and people. The Parson is conscientious, compassionate, reluctant to exact his dues, and impervious to social rank. In an age when the Church's faults were attributed to its vast possessions, he stands as a shining example of pious contentment, immune to the corrupting lure of wealth. The Plowman too would have won Langland's approval: he may be a humble labourer but he lives out the two great Commandments and gives gladly to his neighbour and his church. This likeable pair represent integrity within the Church: a cleric who practises what he preaches and a layman who practises what he is taught. Here is the standard required by Holy Church in *Piers Plowman*: faith seen in action. The knight also seems[33] a worthy representative of his class. It was customary for those who had survived the dangers of the **crusades** to make a **pilgrimage** to give thanks for their safe return. By Chaucer's time crusading had lost the early idealism which had fired the First Crusade[34] in 1096, the expedition to liberate Jerusalem and succour the afflicted Eastern Church having degenerated into sordid squabbles between rival princes and the sacking of Christian cities. If the knight had remained a model of chivalry in the atmosphere of the later crusades then he was indeed worthy of praise.

The motives of the remaining pilgrims are fairly straighforward: adventure, travel, perhaps some profit, and an agreeable sense of piety pervading the whole enterprise. The much-discussed Wife of Bath is the eternal tourist, already well-travelled and keeping an eye open for husband number six. No stranger to *ferne halwes*, she has already completed the arduous trip to Jerusalem (three times), visited Rome, the shrine of the Three Kings at Cologne, the image of the **Virgin** at Boulogne and the shrine of **St James** at Compostella (Galice). Among these pilgrims, as in life, sinners seem to outnumber, or at least outweigh, saints. Chaucer's characters are far more lively and individual than Langland's, yet somewhere in their ancestry lurk the familiar characteristics of the **Seven Deadly Sins**. We can recognise Pride and Lechery in the Wife of Bath, as she elbows her way to the altar ahead of her neighbours and eyes a fine pair of legs at her fourth husband's funeral; Avarice in the Doctour of Physik; and Gluttony in the Franklin. This does not mean that Chaucer was introducing these qualities according to any elaborate scheme, simply that like others of the time he was accustomed to understand human psychology in the terms of the confessional.[35]

While Langland's fair field of folk offered a panoramic survey of medieval society, Chaucer's **pilgrimage** provides a selection of close-up shots, yet the underlying concerns are very similar. Langland was exercised by the hypocrisy of the Church and the inherent tensions facing Christians in everyday life, and though his technique differs, Chaucer's analysis of these problems is no less penetrating. The group he assembles are pilgrims in a dual sense, since, as the Parson reminds them (*Prol.* 50), all Christians were engaged in a journey through the world to their true homeland of **heaven**. The stories which they tell on their brief ride to Canterbury reveal, through their blend of humour, crudity and piety, the attitudes which direct that longer (and ultimately more significant) pilgrimage. They also present the key issues, practical and theological, which faced those seeking to live as Christians in the everyday world: sex, marriage, the place of women, the lure of earthly riches and the ever-present threat of death. The long-running marriage 'debate'[36] interacts with another recurring motif: the inevitability and purpose of suffering in a transient world. Marriage is not only a prime illustration of the difficulty of living a spiritual life in the world; it is also an arena in which human weakness is exposed and commitment to Christian values tested. Thus Constance in the *Man of Law's Tale* is a model of Christian endurance in adversity as well as a virtuous and loyal wife, and the *Clerk's Tale*, though set in the context of marriage, is primarily concerned not with wifely submission but with the patient endurance of God's will. Griselda, like Job, is an example to all:[37]

> This storie is seyd, nat for that wyves sholde
> Folwen Grisilde as in humylitee,
> For it were inportable, though they wolde,      *intolerable*
> But for that every wight in his degree,          *person*
> Sholde be constant in adversitee
> As was Grisilde.
>
> (*Clerk's Tale*, 1142–7)

Other tales tackle the vexed question of human sexuality more directly. For centuries the Church had wrestled with the problem of whether it was possible to achieve spiritual perfection within marriage. Writers such as **Augustine of Hippo** and Peter Damian (1007–72), saw the marital act as repulsive, justified only by the need to populate the world. They could not deny that marriage was affirmed in the **Bible**, but emphasised passages from the **Epistles** and **Gospels** which seemed to urge celibacy (I Cor. 7; Matt. 19:10–12). Since, however, **St Paul** had said that it was better to marry than 'to burn with vain desire' (I Cor 7:9), marriage could be allowed as a second-best, changing 'deedly [**mortal**] synne into **venial** synne betwixe hem that been ywedded' (*Parson's Tale*, 919). The married, however, could still expect to experience 'tribulation in the flesh' (I Cor 7:28). The marriage tales reflect this ambivalence as pilgrims and their characters make selective use of 'authorities' in order to support their own views and behaviour. Thus the *Wife of Bath's Prologue* ironically resembles a sermon,[38] with the Wife's own experience supplying both the required *auctoritee* and *exemplum*. Uninhibited, earthy, argumentative, she rejects both virginity and chaste widowhood; if that is perfection, it is not for her. Nor does she accept the Church's requirement of faithfulness set out in the Sarum marriage service (alluded to in the *Merchant's Tale*, 1704): 'May the yoke of peace and love be upon her, may she be a faithful and chaste wife in Christ . . . bound to thy faith and thy commandments may she remain united to one man; may she flee all unlawful unions' (*Sarum Missal*, 155). Instead she boasts of her disloyalty and infidelities. Her *Prologue* and *Tale* promote a 'religion' of her own making; not Christianity, nor even 'courtly love', but a self-centred creed of personal dominance and unashamed sensuality. Domineering and unchaste, she unconsciously illustrates to perfection the complaints of the anti-feminists whose writings she so abominates.[39] Anti-feminist literature was a curious mixture of cautionary tales concerning the wiles of women, taken from ancient Rome, and warnings against the snares of the adulteress, culled from Jewish wisdom literature, which had been endorsed and elaborated upon by **Jerome** and later **monastic** writers. Such works furnished Chaucer with the bare bones of his portrayal of the Wife of Bath but the use which he made of them is less easy to determine. Recent criticism has sought to establish a feminist perspective[40] on Chaucer's depiction of the Wife of Bath but both author and character have proved difficult to categorise. The Wife may be a victim of contemporary structures but she seems remarkably adept at appropriating the methods of her oppressors. We may agree that her Prologue shows women used as commodities[41] but it is also true that her unabashed exploitation of her sexuality hardly indicates moral superiority to the men in her life. When opportunity comes she, like January in the *Merchant's Tale*, 'buys' a young mate. A rebel she may be, but she is no reformer.

Over all the picture of marriage offered is not appealing: good women are oppressed, bad women betray their husbands with

servants, neighbours, even (in the *Shipman's Tale*), a monk. Men are
lecherous and predatory. Even the seemingly idyllic partnership of
Averagus and Dorigen is threatened by the illicit passion of
Aurelius. This is the sinful World, with the Flesh and the Devil in
close attendance. The most positive view of marriage, an
affirmation of the Christian ideal of mutual commitment, is offered
in the *Parson's Tale*: 'God made womman of the ryb of Adam, for
womman sholde be felawe [companion] unto man. Man sholde
bere hym [conduct himself] to his wyf in feith, in trouthe, and in
love . . . [a wife] sholde loven hire housbonde with al hire herte
and to hym be trewe of hir body. So sholde a housbonde eek be to
his wyf' (927). This often-overlooked tale frequently provides a
useful prose 'commentary' on the other tales, in the form of
balanced, orthodox statements. Thus January's attempts to justify his
lustful preoccupation with his young wife (*Merchant's Tale*,
1835–40) are countered by the Parson's sober comments on the
purpose of sex within marriage: 'For thre thynges a man and his
wyf flesshly mowen assemble. The first is in entente of engendrure
[procreation] of children to the service of God . . . Another cause is
to yelden everich of hem to oother the dette of hire bodies . . . The
thridde is to eschewe leccherye and vileynye' (938).

Sexual sin was but one of the dangers threatening the soul and
the shadows of death and judgement provide the backdrop to
several tales. In the *Pardoner's Tale* Death stalks the land like a
'privee [secret] theef' (675) and the three revellers meet their
sudden end through avarice, the **Pardoner**'s own besetting sin; in
the *Friar's Tale*, the corrupt **summoner** blindly delivers himself
into the **Devil**'s clutches and is carried off still unrepentant to **hell**;
in the *Miller's Tale* it is the threat of a flood like that which swept
away sinners in Noah's day (Genesis 6) which enables Nicholas to
dupe the unfortunate carpenter. Rarely is the broader spiritual
dimension totally absent. Even the tragi-comic story of Emily and
her hapless suitors is put into perspective by Egeus thus:

> This world nys but a thurghfare ful of wo,
> And we been pilgrymes, passynge to and fro.

> (*Knight's Tale*, 2847–8)

This is a view reiterated by the Parson who rounds off his
sermon-tale with an exhortation designed to point his companions
to the ultimate destination of all earthly **pilgrimage**; the heavenly
city pictured in Revelation 21. This, as his *Prologue* indicates, has
been his intention all along:

> To shewe yow the wey, in this viage,  *journey*
> Of thilke parfit glorious pilgrymage  *perfect*
> That highte Jerusalem celestial.  *is called*
> (49–51)

The motley band of pilgrims now becomes a congregation challenged to fix their sights on eternity. In Canterbury, they hope to find temporary respite from physical ailments and gaze on the splendid shrine of **Thomas Becket**; in **heaven**, all earthly trials will cease and they will look upon God himself: 'Ther as the body, that whilom was syk, freele and fieble, and mortal, is inmortal, and so strong and so hool that there may no thyng apeyren [injure] it; ther as ne is neither hunger, thurst, ne coold, but every soule replenyssed with the sighte of the parfit knowynge of God' (1078–80).

The tenor of the *Parson's Tale*, together with the 'Retraction' which follows it in most manuscripts, have puzzled many readers. Was the creator of the Wife of Bath really ready to jettison her and all her kind? Was the Retraction itself some final twist of irony, a last laugh on Chaucer's part? Or could this complex man, who also translated Boethius, genuinely have felt that in exposing evil he had fallen into the trap of making it too attractive? As the prospect of eternity loomed, Chaucer like any other medieval Christian could have felt impelled to set his spiritual house in order.[42] Nor are the sentiments of the *Parson's Tale* and the 'Retraction' new. To a large extent they simply restate the message with which Chaucer had concluded the story of *Troilus and Criseyde*:

> O yonge, fresshe folkes, he or she,
> In which that love up groweth with youre age
> Repeyreth hom fro worldy vanyte,  *return home; from*
> And of youre herte up casteth the visage
> To thilke God that after his ymage
> Yow made, and thynketh al nys but a faire  *fair (i.e. temporary amusement)*

> This world, that passeth soone as floures faire.  *flowers*
> And loveth hym, the which that right for love
> Upon a crois, oure soules for to beye  *cross; redeem*
> First starf, and roos, and sit in hevene above.  *died; rose; sits*
> (Bk V. 1835–44)

## HERETICS OR REFORMERS

Some commentators, inspired by Chaucer's criticism of ecclesiastical abuses and encouraged by his links with **Lollard** sympathisers, have claimed that he, like Langland, may be open to the charge of heresy. Certainly Chaucer's patron, John of Gaunt, showed considerable sympathy for the views of **John Wyclif** (c. 1330–84), leader of the Lollards and critic of much established teaching and practice. An eminent Oxford scholar, Wyclif had concluded that the doctrine of **transubstantiation** was philosophically unsound. Concerned by abuses in the Church, he fiercely attacked both the **papacy** and the **friars** and, despite earlier support from Gaunt and Chaucer's friend Sir Lewis Clifford, his opinions were eventually condemned in 1382. Many orthodox Christians of the day, however, were also troubled by the inconsistencies and abuses so manifest within the Church and unafraid to say so. Langland shows far more caution in voicing political comments than in venting his feelings about the Church, and preachers such as Bromyard and Brinton often outdid him in denouncing clerical wrongdoing. Far from being the monolithic structure sometimes imagined, the medieval Church experienced a constant process of reform, renewal and conflict. There was often a fine line between the inspired radicalism of a **Francis of Assisi**, approved by an imaginative **pope**, and the forbidden teachings of other equally sincere movements, rigorously suppressed by Church authorities. What Chaucer thought of Wyclif's desire to translate the **Bible** so that every ploughman might understand it, and attacks on **transubstantiation**, is not known. Despite his Lollard contacts, Chaucer gave no indication that his theological views were anything but orthodox. Though Chaucer's Parson would no doubt have agreed with the Lollard William Thorpe when he stated: 'I call them true pilgrims which travel towards the bliss of heaven . . . hating and fleeing all the deadly sins,'[43] he plainly did not endorse Lollard attacks on the cult of the **saints** and the contemporary practice of **pilgrimage**. The *Canterbury Tales* contains much criticism of individual pilgrims but never calls into question the validity of devout pilgrimage. Neither the Parson nor his creator, it would appear, despised the old, familiar, comforting ways of the Church.

NOTES

1. Quotations from Schmidt's edition of the B-text (1995) unless otherwise stated. See also his parallel edition of the A, B, C and Z versions.
2. See Kane (1965), Simpson (1990), Du Boulay (1991) and Schmidt's edition of the B-text.

3. See Boase (1972).

4. Cited Ziegler (1969, 149).

5. On monasticism, see Brooke (1974) and Lawrence (1984).

6. Chaucer, *Riverside Chaucer*, Ed. Benson (1988).

7. Lawrence (1984, 134).

8. Numbers taken from Knowles and Hadcock (1971).

9. See Bloomfield (1952) on the Sins and their role in Middle English literature.

10. Rouse (1980) gives a helpful introduction to the purpose, conventions and location of the many surviving medieval wall paintings.

11. See Hamilton (1986, 46) and Boase (1972, 46–7).

12. Cited Southern (1970, 138).

13. *Chaucer Sources and Backgrounds*. Ed. Miller (1988).

14. Cited Meade (1988, 157)

15. Owst (1966, 266).

16. Owst (1966, 247).

17. On the relationship between *Piers Plowman* and contemporary sermons see Wenzel (1988).

18. Owst (1966, 248; 285).

19. Lawrence (1984, 209) points out that the friars attempted a more complex examination of intention and circumstances in assessing guilt and assigning penance and thus were not restricted by the old tariff of fixed penalties.

20. I owe the idea of juxtaposing Mirk's *Instructions* and confessions made by Langland's Sins to Braswell (1983, 72–4), although I have used different examples. On Gluttony's confession see Gray (1986).

21. Cited Owst (1966, 278).

22. See Woolf (1969). Also compare the pardon given to Piers by Christ after the Crucifixion and Resurrection (XIX, 184ff).

23. Trees are a common biblical image e.g. Ps. 1; Rev. 22:2.

24. See Bloomfield (1958) and Robertson and Huppé (1951, 195). A window in Canterbury Cathedral groups Marriage, Continence and Virginity together.

25. On the relationship of the poem's structure to the liturgical year see Simpson (1990, 217–20).

26. For the biblical background to pilgrimage and Anglo-Saxon pilgrims see Ch. 2 above. See also Brooke and Brooke (1984) and Sumption (1975).

27. *Examination of William Thorpe* (*Fifteenth-Century Prose*, 138).

28. See Benson and Robertson (1990).

29. *Liber Sancti Jacobi*. Cited Sumption (1975, 125).

30. See Ward (1987) for accounts of miracles of healing, particularly at Canterbury.

31. In 1443 Margaret Paston wrote to her convalescent husband: 'My mother-in-law has promised another image of wax weighing as much as you for our lady of Walsingham . . . I have promised to go on pilgrimage to Walsingham . . . for you' (*The Pastons*, 18).

32. See Schoeck (1960).

33. Jones (1980) thinks the portrait ironical; Pratt (1987) defends the knight.

34. Riley-Smith (1977); Riley-Smith and Riley-Smith (1981).
35. On the characterisation of the pilgrims see Mann (1973).
36. See Kelly (1975); Aers (1986a, Ch. 4); Brooke (1989).
37. See Martin (1990, 144) and Mann (1991, Ch. 4).
38. See Dillon (1993a, 62–70).
39. For examples of anti-feminist writings see *Women Defamed*.
40. Mann (1991, 82); Delany (1990).
41. Aers (1986b, 69).
42. Dean (1989) argues from contemporary parallels that Chaucer's repentance is more likely than some critics have allowed. See also Cooper (1989, 410–11).
43. *Examination of William Thorpe* (*Fifteenth-Century Prose*, 129).

# Chapter 6

# The Contemplative Life – Anchorites and Mystics

It is made clear how good it is to be alone in both the old law and the new law; for in both it is found that God did not show his dearest friends his hidden counsels and heavenly secrets in a crowd of people, but did so when they were alone.

(Ancrene Wisse, III AS 105)[1]

This part of contemplation God gives wherever he wills . . . but it is a special gift and not a common one. Moreover, though a person in active life may have it by a special grace, I consider that no one can have the full use of it unless he is solitary and contemplative in life.

(Scale, Bk 1, Ch. 9)[2]

## THE CONTEMPLATIVE WAY

It would be easy to conclude from the works of Langland and Chaucer that the medieval Church was populated almost exclusively by corpulent time-serving clerics and woefully immoral layfolk, its spiritual aspirations hopelessly undermined by worldliness and compromise. Examples of abuse and hypocrisy there were in plenty, and all of them grist to the satirist's mill; yet even the *Prologue* to *Piers Plowman* acknowledged a group whose soberly-clad figures stood out in sharp contrast to the colourful, corrupt world around them:

| | |
|---|---|
| In preires and penaunce putten hem manye | *prayers* |
| Al for the love of Oure Lord lyveden ful streyte | *strictly, ascetically* |
| In hope to have hevenriche blisse - | *the joy of the heavenly kingdom* |
| As ancres and heremites that holden hem in hire selles | *anchorites; cells* |

(Prol. 125–9)

In the early Church the terms **anchorite** and **hermit** were virtually synonymous: to be an anchorite or hermit was to withdraw (*anachorein*) to the desert (*eremos*). In the later Middle Ages 'anchorite' came to mean one whose spiritual commitment was marked by enclosure, as they entered upon a solitary existence of self-denial and prayer, turning their backs upon the pleasures and temptations of the everyday world and closing the door firmly behind them. Given the common desire to avoid **hell** and win **heaven** and the difficulties apparent in following Christian teaching in a materialistic society, it is understandable that deeply religious souls should take this path of withdrawal, cutting loose from earthly ties in order to find space and quiet in which to foster their relationship with God. In the view of those who took such a step and in that of their contemporaries this was neither eccentricity to be condemned nor deprivation to be bewailed; their calling was a privilege, their life of **contemplation** the pinnacle of Christian spirituality. Ann Warren concludes: 'In the Middle Ages the anchorite was viewed as leading the sanest of lives, a life more perfect than any other. Far from being neurotics, solitaries led the most authentic life considered possible for the Christian.'[3] The presence of recluses was 'so taken for granted that the index of one of Henry II's Liberate Rolls [1240-5] lists them under "trades and occupations".'[4]

The great heroes and heroines of the solitary life were the fourth-century **hermits** of the Egyptian desert; their stories had been transmitted to the Western Church through the writings of **John Cassian** and many of their emphases were taken up and built into Western **monasticism** by **St Benedict** (d. c. 547) whose *Rule* acknowledged the special role of the **anchorite**. The Celtic church had brought the vision of the desert into Anglo-Saxon spirituality, producing a crop of **saints** such as **Cuthbert**, who chose a life of prayer in tiny remote oratories. By the twelfth century, this austere model had been adapted and modified, especially for the women who seem to have constituted the majority of recluses;[5] potentially easy prey in the wilderness, they were instead safely immured in anchorholds attached to churches, or within reach of benefactors. Theirs was a strange 'solitude', confined within a small enclosure yet often living in close proximity to the citizens of a bustling medieval town; the world they had renounced ever visible through their window. Nor was the 'world' minded to leave them alone. Their devotion to God made them much admired and, like the earlier hermits in Egypt, they attracted others to their seclusion in search of counsel and prayers, and possibly in the hope that a little of their sanctity might rub off.

The desire of both men and women to penetrate the external trappings of religion and encounter God in personal experience prompted a significant development in English prose. Formal worship in **parish** churches and **monasteries** was in Latin; how many of the **parish** clergy were really equipped to understand the services they conducted is hard to gauge; even in monasteries where **liturgy** dominated daily life, many would have been unable to participate fully. This was particularly true for women; **nuns** often could not understand Latin and the majority of those who chose the **contemplative** life would not have been able to read or pray intelligently in Latin or even French. In seeking to meet the needs of such women (and less literate men), the author of the widely-read *Ancrene Wisse* or *Ancrene Riwle* was followed by the great **mystical** writers of the fourteenth century: **Richard Rolle** (c. 1300–49), **Walter Hilton** (d. 1395) and the unknown author of the *Cloud of Unknowing* (wrote c. 1350–1400). Their purpose was to foster an intensely personal yet disciplined devotion to God; their attempts to articulate complex spiritual truths in a language intelligible to all, enriching and enlarging the medium they chose. The desire for encounter with God, which they sought to encourage, is reflected in the writings of two very different women: **Julian of Norwich** (c. 1342–1416) and **Margery Kempe** (c. 1373– c. 1438). In many respects the **anchorites** and **mystical** writers of the thirteenth and fourteenth centuries provide a mirror image of the Church as portrayed by Chaucer. His Prioress is countered by Julian, truly devout yet far from naive; his sensual **Monk** by the passionate **Rolle** who castigated the monasteries for their half-heartedness; even the Wife of Bath, earthy to the point of crudity, is matched by Margery Kempe, locked into a desperate struggle to achieve sanctity in the everyday world.

## THE ANCHORESSES' GUIDE

The life of the medieval **anchoress**, as depicted in the early thirteenth-century[6] *Ancrene Wisse*, is a curious blend of the dramatic and the mundane. True anchorites renounced the world for life, and entry into the anchorhold was often attended by ceremonies of awesome symbolism; the earliest surviving service[7] for the enclosure of anchorites dates from the twelfth century and includes prayers for the dead together with the Office of Extreme Unction. The *Ancrene Wisse* refers to the cell as 'God's prison' and asks, 'What is an anchorhouse but a grave?' (II AS 88). The author even recommends the sight of an open sepulchre within the cell, often used by the anchorite as a bed, as a (no doubt) highly effective antidote to sinful proclivities (II AS 92). There could be no doubt that the anchoress's purpose was solemn and the sacrifices involved real, yet after her symbolic 'death' the anchoress had still to live. The solitude she sought was of necessity spiritual rather than physical. Even an anchoress needed servants to supply food, clothing and protection. Her 'cell' may well have consisted of at least two rooms and a garden and (as in *Ancrene Wisse*) she may have had companions living nearby. Devoted to a life of prayer, she still could not entirely disregard the running of her small household. The *Ancrene Wisse* therefore combines high spiritual counsel – 'Think anchoress what you looked for when you forsook the world in your enclosure . . . to lose wholly all the joy of this life so as to embrace your joyful lover joyfully in the eternal life of heaven' (II AS 88) – with sturdy common sense. The **anchoress** may keep a cat (for company or for mice?) but not a cow: 'For then she has to think of the cow's food, of the herdsman's hire, to flatter the bailiff, curse him when he impounds it, and pay the damages anyway . . . *An anchoress ought not to have anything which draws her heart outward*' (VIII AS 201). The cow may damage her reputation; more seriously, it will draw her thoughts away from their proper focus and out into the world which lies so close at hand. Some contact with the outside community is unavoidable; even anchoresses have to eat and servants must go forth on their behalf, yet they must be at pains to guard against the insidious infection of the world, particularly the forbidden delights of gossip (II AS 81). The anchoress needed to be free of all responsibilities, even the Christian duty of hospitality. The writer is firm: 'Some anchoresses take their meals outside, with their guests; this is being too friendly . . . it is opposed to the anchoritic order, which is dead to all the world,' adding tartly, 'One hears often of the dead speaking with the living – but eating with the living? I have never heard of it' (VIII AS 200).

A number of suggestions have been made concerning the identity of the author of the *Ancrene Wisse* and the three sisters for whom he primarily wrote.[8] The former was clearly a man of eclectic reading and some independence of mind. While drawing on several traditions for the benefit of his protegées, his response to their request for a 'rule of life' is surprisingly radical. What matters, he contends, is not external regulations but inner attitudes. He therefore provides a minimal 'Outer Rule' (I and VIII) on the pattern of daily prayer and such practical issues as the anchoresses' dress and behaviour; and a much more extensive 'Inner Rule'

(III–VII) which covers the Custody of the Senses, Regulation of the Inward Feelings, Temptations, Confession, Penance, and Love. The Inner Rule is the lady of the house, the Outer Rule simply her handmaid (Intro. AS 48). Life in an anchorhold clearly needed some kind of structure. The anchoress may have entered full of high spiritual ideals but human nature required guidance and correction. For the everyday enemies of boredom, discouragement and the difficulty of focusing unruly thoughts on the task of prayer, the writer prescribes a rigid timetable of prayer and repeatedly exhorts them to avoid idleness at all costs. With regard to the disciplines of **fasting**, prayer and self-mortification, however, he shows both flexibility and gentleness. A long section on temptation, in which the author urges unceasing vigilance and self-discipline, includes an examination of the **Seven Deadly Sins**, the first such treatment of them in English, in which they are portrayed as dangerous animals, lurking in the 'wilderness' of the life of solitude: 'the lion of pride, the serpent of poisonous envy, the unicorn of anger, the bear of deadly sloth, the fox of covetousness, the sow of gluttony, the scorpion with the tail of stinging lechery, that is, Lust' (IV AS 86). This wide-ranging survey of the Sins has caused speculation that here a wider audience is in mind. Certainly the *Ancrene Wisse* was both widely read and extremely influential in the succeeding centuries. The portrait of the Glutton, for example, foreshadows Langland's satire written at least one hundred and fifty years later:

> The greedy glutton is the devil's manciple, but he always keeps close to the cellar or the kitchen. His heart is in the dishes, his thought all in the cups, his life in the barrel, his soul in the jug. He comes before his Lord besmutted and besmeared, a dish in his one hand, a bowl in his other. He says his words badly, totters like a dead drunk who is on the point of falling – see his huge belly! – and the devil laughs.
>
> (IV AS 127)

Though much of this may seem inappropriate for those so sheltered from the world, the author may well have been genuinely concerned for their prospects of **salvation**. This seeming lack of trust in their virtue stems from the long tradition which linked solitary prayer with the battle against evil. Christian teaching nowhere suggests that those who aim at perfection will thereby become immune from temptation; rather the reverse: 'the higher the hill, the stronger the wind on it. Since the hill of sublime and holy life is higher, the enemy's blasts, the winds of temptation, are greater and stronger on it' (IV AS 114). In particular, the **anchoress** must guard her reputation and chastity. She must be wary of male visitors, especially any who ask to see her face; even **bishops** are to be treated with circumspection (II AS 72). A mid-thirteenth century Norwich diocesan statute ruled:

> Since . . . chaplains are frequently chatting with anchorites in their own houses under the pretext of questioning them, their maids having been sent outside in scandal to the church of God and with not a little cost of souls, we enjoin each of our deans . . . that, wherever anchorites live serving churches they shall bind all chaplains with an oath; that they shall not speak with them [the anchorites] within the enclosure of their houses, but shall seek them out only at their windows that turn to the church.[9]

**Friars**, however, may be accepted as **confessors** (II AS 73), an exception which demonstrates the early date of the work; neither Langland nor Chaucer would have seconded this unqualified vote of confidence. This apparent obsession with the danger of sexual sin is echoed in similar works. An earlier rule, *De Institutione Inclusarum*, written by **Aelred of Rievaulx** (d. 1167) for his anchoress sister, urges 'Strecche out therfor al thy wille in kepynge this maydenhode' (Bodley Mss ix), and all but one of the five prose texts of the Katherine group (found in association with *Ancrene Wisse*) are devoted to the praise of virginity and the heroic struggles of the **saints** to resist the blandishments and threats of would-be suitors. The **Devil**'s assaults will not only be numerous ('Our enemy, the warrior from hell, shoots more bolts at one anchoress . . . than against seven and fifty ladies in the world': II AS 70) but also varied and subtle. If the **anchoress** cannot be seduced through her senses then she may be tempted through doing good. She may be induced to become a distributor of alms or a schoolmistress; actions worthy in themselves but not part of her vocation. There are frequent reminders of the crucial difference between the respective callings of **Mary** and **Martha**.

Many modern readers find the outer frame of the *Ancrene Wisse* the most intriguing part of the whole work, yet for a contemporary audience the chief value would have rested in its spiritual teaching: how to fix one's heart on God, how to deal with temptation, how to stir up love for God by meditating on the sufferings of **Christ**. Though writing primarily for those who have left ordinary human society, the writer does not hesitate to use everyday illustrations to drive home his spiritual message, some of his observations showing a surprisingly homely touch for a presumably celibate **priest**:

> Our Lord, when He allows us to be tempted, is playing with us as a mother with her young darling. She runs away from him and hides herself, and lets him sit alone and look eagerly about crying 'Mother! Mother!' and crying for a while; and then with open arms she jumps out laughing, and hugs and kisses him and wipes his eyes.
>
> (IV AS 132)

Many a lay reader would have identified with this cameo of family life or found themselves brought up short by an uncompromising statement of the value of illness as a cleanser of the soul: 'God knows it, dear sisters, all the woe of this world in comparison with the least pain of hell, all is mere ball-play' (IV S 80).

Particularly representative of a growing theological emphasis of the period is the section on Love, in which the significance of **Christ**'s death on the cross is examined. Here we move far beyond the accounting-book approach to religion, the perpetual balancing act between **sin** and **penance**, to a focus on God's love for man and the love which he may reasonably expect in return. At the time of the *Dream of the Rood*, one of the finest of all Anglo-Saxon poems, theologians had regarded Christ's death for man primarily in terms of a heroic conquest of the **Devil**: man through **sin** had fallen into the power of **Satan**; Christ 'the young hero' suffered to set him free. The *Ancrene Wisse* reflects a shift in theological emphasis[10] as the focus moved to the need for Christ to suffer in man's place in order to assuage God's justifiable wrath and thus bring pardon. This voluntary self-sacrifice for the sake of others was seen not only as a means of averting God's judgement but as a demonstration of the depth of Christ's love for those he sought to rescue. Poets, artists and theologians portrayed in increasingly graphic detail the sufferings inflicted on this willing victim. Meanwhile spiritual writers such as the author of the *Ancrene Wisse* reminded their readers of the response which such loving sacrifice should evoke: 'God has earned our love in every kind of way . . . He not only gave us of his own, but gave his whole self . . . "Christ," says St Paul, "so loved his beloved that he paid for her the price of himself"'' (VII AS 190). The image of Christ as a chivalrous knight prepared to give his life for an unresponsive and wholly undeserving lady was a favourite allegory of medieval preachers and writers. This curious synthesis of theological concept and medieval romance owed its ultimate inspiration to the biblical writers. In the

**Old Testament**, Israel was frequently presented as an ungrateful bride, who needed to be rescued from the perilous state into which her infidelity had led her. The Song of Songs, a favourite hunting-ground for medieval allegorists, was interpreted in devotional works as an allegory of the love-relationship between Christ and the individual soul, whose response (or lack of it) was analysed in great detail. The portrayal of Christ as the 'lover-knight' clearly evoked a considerable emotional response, yet the image contained an inherent flaw which has been pin-pointed by Rosemary Woolf:

> So long as art represented Christ on the Cross as a hero triumphant, the self-evident differences between the Crucifixion and a battle remained satisfactorarily unobtrusive. But once the moment of the Crucifixion chosen for representation was the time when Christ hung dead and blood-stained from the Cross, the latent but violent discrepancy became manifest ... The conceits in the Christ-knight literature depend upon an implicit question: if Christ on the Cross is likened to a knight in battle or tournament, in what manner then was He armed?[11]

The elaboration in the *Ancrene Wisse* VII, of the metaphors of the shield and Greek fire (one of the most powerful weapons of contemporary siege warfare, which has been compared in its effects to napalm,[12] represents the author's attempt to grapple with this problem. Christ's victory is achieved through submission and costly obedience; his only weapons are his body which is offered in sacrifice and his burning love which can only be quenched by urine (sin), sand (idleness) and vinegar ('a heart soured by spite or envy': AS 196). The **anchoresses** are apparently of gentle birth and the courtly tone of this theological romance demands that they should respond as befits their position, both social and spiritual. Would not any lady incapable of responding to such love be judged to possess an evil nature, asks the author in his parable. The final appeal combines strong emotion with an remorseless logic: 'Let everyone now choose one of these two, earthly comfort or heavenly, whichever she wants to keep – because she must let the other go ... Stretch out your love to Jesus Christ ... Is not God incomparably better than all that is in the world?' (VII AS 197).

With its basic thesis the desirability of withdrawal from the world and the constant repetition of the dangers of external contamination, *Ancrene Wisse* could be accused of propagating an overly self-absorbed, defensive, even negative form of spirituality; and, to a certain extent, the charge would be justified. In this sense the **anchorites** were the direct spiritual heirs of those who fled the dangerous pleasures of Rome for the seclusion of the desert or the Celtic *peregrini* who abandoned earthly security in order to win heaven. *Ancrene Wisse* also reveals a positive calling: the anchoress is seeking an intimate knowledge both of her own soul and of God. There is little direct teaching about contemplation, possibly because the author was too busy establishing the ground-rules of the solitary life, possibly because the works of the pseudo-**Dionysius**, which so influenced the *Cloud of Unknowing*, had not yet reached England. Yet he refers to the anchoress flying like the night-raven 'in contemplation', and all his instructions on self-examination and self-discipline are accepted stages of preparation for encounter with God. When heart and mind have been quietened and trivial cares set aside, when sin has been shed and all barriers removed, then God may visit the hungry soul with an experience of intimacy and love which will cast all hardships into oblivion: 'After the kiss of peace when the priest consecrates the **host**, forget all the world, be wholly out of your body, embrace in shining love your lover who has alighted into the bower of your heart from heaven, and hold him as tight as you can until he has granted all you ever ask'. (I AS 59)

THE ENGLISH MYSTICS

The experiences at which the author of the *Ancrene Wisse* hints were subsequently explored and charted by the English **mystical**[13] writers of the fourteenth century. In England as on the Continent, this period saw a flowering of mystical experience and teaching, a phenomenon which arose at least in part out of a growing disenchantment with communal **monasticism** and a desire to exchange formal theology for personal experience of God. What the mystics sought (and claimed to experience) was a direct encounter with God, experience of God rather than knowledge about him: in fact a foretaste of heaven itself.

> The goal of mystics, briefly put, is to be so carried out of the physical world in the *ecstasis* of contemplation that the soul enters into an inner and utter communion with God, an inexpressible 'foretaste of eternal sweetness' as Rolle says. The experience is profoundly emotional and interior: the degree of communion with God acquired by the mystic is determined by the intensity of his or her experience of love towards God. It is typical of mystics to proclaim what they aver cannot be described.[14]

Inexpressible such encounters may have been; vague or heretical they were not. **Rolle**, **Hilton** and the *Cloud*-author were all highly orthodox, their individual experience undergirded by a well-developed framework:

> The great psychic and moral readjustment which contemplative prayer necessarily demands is usually described in the time-honoured three stages of Purgation, Illumination and Perfection, a progressive purification beginning with the struggle to master the senses and root out sin and culminating in the final abegnation of all selfhood, when the soul is 'knit' to God by the 'gostely knot of burning love' in spiritual union and accordance of will.[15]

Thus their writings are at once intensely emotional and highly systematic, firmly founded on a tradition which stretched back to biblical times.[16] Despite this shared heritage each mystic was very much an individual and in their works we see mysticism interpreted through their own personalities and experience. **Richard Rolle** fed his soul by meditating on the sufferings of **Christ** and placed great stress on emotional, even physical, intimations of God's presence; the *Cloud*-author on the other hand insisted on the *via negativa*, the negative way, rejecting all that could be known or experienced through the mind or emotions in favour of piercing the Cloud of Unknowing and entering into an encounter beyond the power of human thought to conceive. These two approaches, the affirmative and the negative, were to some degree combined in the writings of **Walter Hilton**, who wrote not only for anchorites but for those seeking to attain perfection while still living in the world.

The audience for these writings was indeed surprisingly wide. Often the primary audience were recluses or **nuns**, yet there were a host of devout lay men and women who shared their spiritual aspirations. The **mystics** represented the longings of late medieval spirituality in a peculiarly intense and highly developed form: they had scaled the heights of contemplation but below them were plenty of lay men and women sturdily determined to climb at least the foothills. This interested but not especially learned audience needed instruction in the vernacular and the subsequent popularity of the resulting treatises is well established. The interest shown by the nobility in the works of the mystics is well documented in wills and bequests; nor were the middle classes far behind. The mystical writers, though theologically competent themselves, were at pains to insist that formal theological training was not a pre-requisite for contemplation, although they do pre-suppose a basic framework of doctrine and morality. **Rolle**'s *Prologue* to his Latin work the *Fire of Love* makes the point: 'I offer, therefore, this book for the attention, not of the philosophers and sages of this world, nor of great theologians . . . but of the simple and unlearned, who are seeking rather to love God than to amass knowledge' (46). Statements such as this indicate a partial reaction against the sometimes arid **scholastic theology** of the twelfth and thirteenth centuries. The great theme of the mystics is the need to experience and respond to the love of God. Any exclusivity demonstrated by these authors is therefore directed towards sifting the motivation rather than the qualifications of their readers. The *Cloud*-author was particularly concerned lest his work fall into the wrong hands: 'Fleschely ianglers . . . rouners [tale-bearers] & tutilers of tales [gossips], & alle maner of pinchers [cavillers]; kept [cared] I neuer þat þei sawe þis book. For myn entent was neuer to write soche þing unto hem' (*Cloud* 2/19).

### RICHARD ROLLE

Richard Rolle, the **hermit** of Hampole (b. c. 1300) who wrote in both Latin and English, was a passionate advocate of the solitary life. According to the *Office of St Richard*, compiled by **nuns** of Hampole in the hope of his canonisation, his own highly dramatic conversion involved abandoning his studies in Oxford and the security of his family home to pursue the vocation which he never ceased to urge upon others. Fearful of worldly contamination, he rejected the communal life of the **monastery** as dangerously half-hearted, opting instead for solitude in the wilds of Yorkshire. Whatever judgements may be drawn regarding Rolle's experiences and teaching, there can be no doubting the passionate sincerity of his message. Wholehearted in the pursuit of his own vision, he could not abide any vestige of hypocrisy in others. An early work in Latin asks those in monastic communities: 'Why do you live tepidly in a monastery? You might as well live that way in the world.'[17] He has an equally stinging rebuke, this time in English, for a nun who (like so many of her kind) had a weakness for finery: 'How may þou for schame, þat es bot servand, with many clathes and riche folow þi spowse and þi Lorde, þat yhede in a kyrtel, and þou trayles als mykel behynd þe as al þat he had on?' (*The Commandment*, *EW* 77). When it came to the vexed question of the relative merits of the **active** and **contemplative** lives, Rolle had no doubts: 'Actyve lyfe es mykel owteward, and in mare travel, and in mare peryle for þe temptacions þat er in þe worlde. Contemplatyfe lyfe es mykel inwarde; and forthi it es lastandar and sykerer, restfuller, delitabiler, luflyer, and mare medeful' (*Form of Living*, *EW* 117).

Rolle's writings betray his weaknesses: conviction verging on the self-opinionated, outspokenness at times hardly distinguishable from plain rudeness. Convinced as he was of the superiority of his own vocation (he frequently teeters on the brink of claiming that the solitary life is the *only* sure route to heaven), pride must always have been lurking around the corner. He was, he tells us, persecuted by those who, understandably, resented his wide-ranging denunciations of worldly clergy and wealthy landowners. His life was troubled by not only personal but communal suffering: civil war, famine and the Black Death. Yet his writings are shot through with joy; his headstrong pursuit of holiness brought him an experience of God so immediate, so intense, that his prose frequently erupts into poetry: the words hardly adequate for that which he has to communicate. His lyrics achieved widespread popularity and influence and poetry and song were at the very heart of the formative experience which he describes in the Latin work significantly called the *Incendium Amoris* or *Fire of Love*:

> I was sitting in a certain chapel, delighting in the sweetness of prayer or meditation, when I suddenly felt within myself an unusually pleasant heat . . . I realised that it was from none of his creatures but from the Creator himself . . . But it was just over nine months before a conscious and incredible sweet warmth kindled me, and I knew the infusion and understanding of heavenly, spiritual sounds, sounds which pertain to the song of everlasting praise . . . I began to sing what previously I had spoken; only I sang inwardly and that for my Creator.
>
> (*Fire of Love,* 93)

To Rolle this was the crowning reward of the **contemplative**; an undeserved gift of God yet an experience which required due preparation. In the *Form of Living*, written in English for a nun of Hampole subsequently enclosed as an anchoress, he made it clear that these heady experiences were not for beginners: 'swilk a grace may þou noght have in þe fyrst day bot with lang travell and grete bysiness' (*Form of Living*, *EW* 100). The true contemplative must be willing to relinquish all worldly desires and delights, to confess and renounce sinful thoughts and acts, and then pursue God with the single-minded intensity which Rolle himself demonstrated: 'For hym may na man fele in joy and swetenes, bot if þai be clene and fylled with his lufe; and þartill sal þou com with grete travaille in praier and thynkyng' (*Form of Living, EW* 103). The world at large might pity or deride; Rolle is full of encouragements to the faint-hearted to expect overwhelming (and lasting) rewards.

> þe thynk [now] peraventure hard to gife þi hert fra al erthly thynges, fra al ydel speche and vayne, and fra al fleschly lufe, and to be alane, to wake and pray and thynk of þe joy of heven and of þe passyon of Jhesu Criste . . . Als sone as þi hert es towched with þe swetnes of heven, þe wil lytel lyst þe myrth of þis worlde . . . For al melody and al riches and delites, þat al men in þis world can ordayne or thynk, sownes bot noy and anger til a man's hert þat verraly es byrnand in þe luf of God; for he hase myrth and joy and melody in aungels sang.
>
> (*Ego Dormio, EW* 62)

Rolle's characteristic[18] emphasis upon experiencing the 'fire' of God's love and the delights of celestial song surfaces constantly in his writings. In the *Form of Living* he urges his disciple to progress through the three stages of love until the goal is attained:

> He or scho þat es in þis degre, mai als wele fele þe fyre of lufe byrnand in þaire saule, als þou may fele þi finger byrn if þou put it in þe fyre. Bot þat fire, if it be hate, es swa delitabell and wondyrful þat I kan noght tell it. þan þi sawle es Jhesu lufand, Jhesu thynkand, Jhesu desirand, anly in þe covatyties of hym anedande [breathing], til hym syngand, of hym byrnand, in hym restand. Ðan þe sange of lovyng and of lufe es commen, þan þi thoght turnes intil sang and intil melody.
>
> (*Form of Living, EW* 105)

In order to achieve this ecstatic pitch of awareness of **Christ**, Rolle endorsed two devotional practices which became key strands of medieval religion: meditation on the **Passion** or physical sufferings of Christ and devotion to the Holy Name. In his *Meditations on the Passion*, Rolle illustrates the emotional intensity generated by contemporary preoccupation with the humanity of Christ:

> A, Lord, þi sorwe, why were it not my deth? . . . I se in my soule how reufully þou gost, þi body is so blody, so rowed and so bledderyd; þi crown is so kene þat sytteth on þi hed; þi heere mevyth with þe wynde, clemed with þe blood; þi lovely face so wan and so bolnyd with bofetynge and with betynge, with spyttynge, with spowtynge.
>
> (*Meditations, EW* 21)

Rolle's devotion to the Holy Name seems to stem from an incident during his early life as a **hermit**, when invoking the name of Jesus delivered him from an overwhelming temptation to **sin**. Certainly he did much to popularise the cult:

> [I]f þou wil be wele with God, and have grace to rewle þi lyf . . . þis name Jhesu, fest it swa fast in þi hert. . . If þou thynk Jhesu contynuly, and halde it stabely, it purges þi syn, and kyndels þi hert; it clarifies þi sawle, it removes anger and dose away slawnes; it woundes in lufe, and fulfilles of charite; it chaces þe devel and puttes oute drede; it opens heven, and makes a contemplatif man.
>
> (*Form of Living*, *EW* 108)

Assessments of Rolle's importance within the **mystical** tradition have varied considerably; his teaching, though orthodox, was predominantly the fruit of his own experience, a fact which both contributed to his considerable popular appeal and caused misgivings amongst later writers. Both the *Cloud* author and **Hilton** were wary of such a strong emphasis upon emotional, even tangible, intimations of God's presence, and felt it necessary to correct any dangerous misunderstandings which might have taken hold amongst Rolle's followers. Nevertheless he is credited with starting a new stream of religious life in England, and his commentary on the **Psalter** made him the most important figure before **Wyclif** in the field of biblical translation. Though believing fervently in the merits of the solitary life Rolle was not indifferent to the needs of those around him. He devoted much time to preaching and teaching, wrote a manual to help a **parish priest** in his pastoral work, and is said to have died tending the victims of the Black Death in 1349. His writings reveal a broader, more dynamic concept of love than that expressed in *Ancrene Wisse*; Rolle was a **hermit**, not an **anchorite**; he withdrew to experience God's love but remained free to minister to the world which that love encompassed: 'Luf es a lyf, copuland togedyr þe lufand and þe lufed . . . lufe makes us ane with God. Lufe es a st[i]ryng of þe saule, for to lufe God for hymself, and all other thyng for God' (*Form of Living*, *EW* 109).

## THE *CLOUD OF UNKNOWING*

The question of the identity of the author of the *Cloud of Unknowing*, who wrote c. 1350–1400, has never been satisfactorily resolved. Attempts to prove that the *Cloud* and related works[19] were written by **Hilton** have failed to command general support

and the only biographical details which can be offered with any
certainty are those deduced from the texts. A competent theologian,
careful to maintain orthodoxy, he was probably a **priest** and seems
to have had experience of the solitary life himself. Though sharing
**Rolle**'s preoccupation with the love of God, the *Cloud*-author was
rooted in a very different strand of **mystical** tradition. In the *Form
of Living*, Rolle had stated confidently that God reveals himself to
the solitary 'in swetnes and delyte, in byrnyng of luf, and in joy and
melody, and dwelles ay with þam in thaire saule, sa þat þe
comforth of hym departes never fra þam' (*EW* 90). To the
*Cloud*-author this statement would have indicated that Rolle was
merely a beginner in the mystical way; his dramatic experiences but
the early encouragements given to the **contemplative** before the
real struggle began. As the full title of the *Cloud* indicates, the
author's ultimate goal was the union or *onyng* of the soul with God.
It was for this that man was originally created: 'For þis is þe werk,
as þou schalt here after, in þe whiche man schuld haue contynowed
ȝif he neuer had synned, to þe whiche worching man was maad . .
. by þe whiche a man schal be reparailed aȝein' (*Cloud* 19/19). The
route to be taken, however, was quite different from that advocated
by Rolle. The *Cloud*-author favoured the *via negativa*, a tradition
which stretched back through the early centuries of the Church to
the Greek Platonists. The most influential statement of this
approach was contained in the works of the sixth-century writer
known as **Dionysius the Areopagite**, and was subsequently taken
up and interpreted for the medieval church in the west by John
Scotus Erigena in the ninth century and by scholars associated with
the Augustinian **monastery** of St Victor near Paris in the twelfth
and thirteenth centuries. In essence this tradition suggested that
since God is too great to be fully understood by the human mind,
the first stage of any quest for encounter with him must involve the
deliberate setting aside of all human understanding, as too limiting
and potentially misleading:

> For haue a man neuer so moche goostly [spiritual] vnderstondyng in
> knowyng of alle maad goostly þynges, ȝit may he neuer bi þe werk of
> his vnderstondyng com to þe knowyng of an vnmaad goostly þing, þe
> which is nouȝt bot God. Bot by þe failyng it may; for whi þat þing þat
> it failiþ in is noþing elles bot only God. & herfore it was þat Seynte
> Denis [**Dionysius**] seyde: 'Þe moste goodly knowyng of God is þat, þe
> whiche is knowyn bi vnknowyng.'

> (*Cloud* 125/5)

The *Cloud*-author therefore urges the would-be **contemplative** (after due preparation) to embark upon a series of exercises which may, after many struggles, culminate in a glimpse of the transcendent glory of God. In this he is to follow the example of Moses (Exodus 34) who, in order to receive the Ten Commandments, climbed Mount Sinai and there, surrounded by the clouds, encountered God and experienced His revelation. The contemplative must be motivated by a pure, intense desire for God:

> Lift up þin hert vnto God wiþ a meek steryng of loue; & mene him-self, & none of his goodes. & þerto loke þee loþe to þenk on ou3t bot on hym-self, so þat nou3t worche in þi witte ne in þi wille bot only him-self. & do þat in þee is to for3ete alle þe creat[u]res þat euer God maad . . . Þis is þe werk of þe soule þat moste plesiþ God.
>
> (*Cloud* 16/3)

The soul's impulse upward to God will initially be met not by revelation but by darkness, a 'cloude of vnknowyng'. This is, the *Cloud*-author maintains, an inevitable fact of the contemplative life: '3if euer schalt þou fele him or see him, as it may be here [i.e. in this life], it behoueþ alweis be in þis cloude & in þis derknes' (*Cloud* 17/7). It is in this cloud that the contemplative must 'wone [abide] and werke'. The resulting sense of disorientation is further compounded by the need, repeatedly emphasised, to reject all that has hitherto been known or felt: 'As þis cloude of vnknowyng is abouven þee, betwix þee & þi God, ri3t so put a cloude of for3etyng bineþ þee, bitwix þee & alle þe cretures þat euer ben maad' (*Cloud* 24/2ff). The type of meditation which Rolle advocated is not completely rejected but regarded as appropriate only for the beginner. The *Cloud* was not written for a novice, but for a disciple who had already mastered the basics of the **ascetic** life and is now called to attempt 'þat state & degre of leuyng þat is parfite': 'it behoueþ a man or womman, þat haþ longe tyme ben usid in þeese meditacions, algates leue hem, & put hem & holde hem fer doun vnder þe cloude of for3etyng, 3if euer schal he peerse þe cloude of vnknowyng bitwix him & his God' (*Cloud* 27/20). Caught between the cloud above and the cloud below, the **contemplative** may feel panic bordering on despair. He has surrendered all that is known and familiar but has not yet begun to experience the rewards of intimacy with a God who is beyond thought. Human intellect cannot serve him now, the only force which can penetrate the darkness is love: 'By loue may he be getyn & holden; bot bi þou3t neiþer . . . smyte apon þat þicke cloude of vnknowyng wiþ a scharp darte of longing loue, & go not þens for þing þat befalleþ' (*Cloud* 26/3).

The *Cloud*-author is only too well aware of the enormous spiritual, psychological and emotional demands which he is placing upon the 'ȝong goostly prentis [spiritual apprentice]' and the hazards of such a pathway; yet the promised reward is great: 'Þan wil he sumtyme parauenture seend oute a beme of goostly liȝt, peersyng þis cloude of vnknowyng ... Þan schalt þou fele þine affeccion enflamid wiþ þe fiire of his loue, fer more þen I kan telle þee, or may, or wile, at þis tyme' (*Cloud* 62/14). This restraint contrasts strongly with the approach and emphasis of **Richard Rolle**. Though the *Cloud*-author uses Rolle's characteristic phrase 'the fire of love', unlike Rolle, he refuses to enlarge upon these experiences. His reticence stems both from a fear of sacrilege and a conviction that such flashes of illumination should neither be clung to nor depended on. They are not the goal of the mystic's journey, merely brief encouragements along the way: 'ȝif þei come, welcome hem; bot lene not to moche on hem' (*Cloud* 93/15). Over-emphasis on such experiences can lead to many dangers; self-deception, pride, even heresy. He castigates those (presumably misguided followers of Rolle) who seek physical experiences of God's grace and make themselves ridiculous. He bewails the folly of those who are over-literal in their understanding of directions to 'worche inwardes' or 'lift up here hertes vnto God'. His concern to avoid such misunderstandings leads him into a discussion of the problems of mystical language:

> beware þat þou conceyue not bodely þat þat is mente gostly, þof al it be spokyn in bodely wordes, as ben þees: UP or DOUN, IN or OUTE, BEHINDE or BEFORE, ON O SIDE or ON OÞER. For þof al þat a þing be neuer so gostly in it-self, neuerþeles, ȝif it schal be spoken of ... it behoueþ alweis be spoken in bodely wordes. Bot what þerof? Schal it þerfore be taken & conceyuid bodely? Nay, it bot goostly.
>
> (*Cloud* 114/3)

He has already indicated that much contemplative prayer may be of the wordless variety and suggested that where words must be used they should whenever possible be confined to monosyllables, since 'schort preier peersiþ [pierces] heuen' (*Cloud* 75/5).

The *Cloud*-author has also been credited[20] with three other treatises which deal with related aspects of the contemplative life – the *Book of Privy Counseling*, the 'Epistle of Prayer', the 'Epistle of

Discretion in Stirrings' – and three translations – *Denis Hid Divinity* (Dionysius), *Benjamin Minor* (Richard of St Victor) and *Of Discerning of Spirits* (St Bernard of Clairvaux). The *Book of Privy Counselling* is generally regarded as a more mature work than the *Cloud*. In addition to metaphysical arguments in support of the doctrine of the *via negativa*, it also offers guidance for the more advanced stages of contemplation, bringing the **contemplative** to the 'dark night of the soul' and the verge of union with God. Translations attributed to the *Cloud*-author indicate both the chief sources from which he drew his mystical theology and the freedom with which he adapted them to his own time and situation. In the *Prologue to Denis Hid Divinity*, he makes it clear that his chief concern is to communicate with his audience rather than to follow his source (itself a Latin translation of the original Greek) to the letter: 'In translacioun of it, I haue not onliche folowed þe nakid lettre of þe text, bot for to declare [explain] þe hardnes of it' (2/8). The 'hardnes' of his subject matter was undeniable, though he rendered it into prose which has been decribed as 'individual, racy, idiomatic'[21] and 'outstanding for its intellectual subtlety, precision, logical control and not least for its abounding energy.'[22] There were accusations that his writings were 'so harde & so heiȝ, & so curious & so queinte' (*PC*, 137/9) that the 'sotelist clerk' could scarcely understand them, charges against which he defended himself vigorously. His teaching was, he maintained, accessible to the simplest soul, provided that they were truly called to the work of contemplation and not blinded by the 'coryous kunnyng of clergie'. There was, in his view, an inescapable distinction between those called to 'salvacioun' and those called to 'perfeccion', yet he emphasised that there should be no sense of superiority in the latter but a humble desire not to fail in their difficult, even perilous, vocation. Of the ultimate rewards of such a calling he has no doubt whatsoever: '[God] by him-self wiþouten moo, none bot he, is sufficient at þe fulle, & mochel more, to fulfille þe wille and þe desire of oure soule' (*Cloud* 18/15).

WALTER HILTON

In many respects, the writings of Walter Hilton (d. 1396), which include the *Scale of Perfection*, *Mixed Life*, *Eight Chapters on Perfection*, and *Of Angels' Song*, can be said to occupy the central ground of **contemplative** teaching and practice. Described in one manuscript as as 'maister watir hilton hermyte', he seems to have found the solitary life as practised by Rolle unsatisfying and ended his days as a **canon** of the **Augustinian** priory of Thurgarton, near Nottingham. His works contain echoes of both his predecessors, yet their tone and approach cannot be fully aligned with either. 'Less individual than the writings of Rolle, far less esoteric than *The Cloud*',[23] Hilton's writings are concerned with all stages of the spiritual life and with all would-be practitioners of the life of contemplation. Hilton wrote for a wide range of people,[24] showing a remarkable readiness to accommodate his spiritual exhortations to the practical and psychological limitations of his readers. Patient, thorough and systematic in his teaching, he repeatedly stresses the need for steady development in the spiritual life, for both solitaries and lay people. Thus in the *Scale of Perfection*, addressed to an **anchoress**, he writes:

> A soul cannot suddenly jump from the lowest to the highest, any more than someone wanting to climb a high ladder and setting his foot upon the lowest rung can next fly up to the highest. He needs to go gradually, one after another, until he can come to the top. It is just the same spiritually.

> (*Scale*, Book 2, Ch. 17)

Since his anchoress is not able to read the scriptures (Bk 1, Ch. 52), possibly because she has no Latin, Hilton incorporates numerous biblical references (seventy-six to the **Old Testament** and 118 to the **New Testament**) translated into English, which support and illustrate his teaching. Like **Rolle** and the *Cloud*-author he attempts to analyse the different levels of the spiritual life and to relate the **active** life to the **contemplative** life; yet his conclusions are frequently quite different. In a passage reminiscent of Rolle, he describes the stages of contemplation: 'That other part may be called burning love in devotion, but this is burning love in contemplation; that is the lower but this is the higher . . . since it is more inward, more spiritual . . . for this truly [is] a tasting and as it were a sight of heavenly joy (Bk 1, Ch. 9). He is, however, quick to warn that 'visions or revelations of any kind of spirit . . . or else any heat that can be felt like fire glowing and warming the breast . . . or anything that can be felt by bodily sense, however comforting and pleasing it may be – these are not truly contemplation' ((Bk 1, Ch. 10). Elsewhere Hilton is scathing about any would-be mystic who, 'by undiscrete trauellynge turnes þe braynes in his heuede . . . and þane for febilnes of þe brayne, hym thynkes þat he heres wondirful sownes and sanges: and þat is no thynge els bot a fantasie' (*Angels' Song, Yorkshire Writers*, 179). He frequently stresses the need for discretion and moderation and the dangers of striving too hard after spiritual experiences. In contrast to the *Cloud*-author who makes enormous emotional and psychological demands of his disciples, Hilton often shows concern lest his readers should become over-ambitious or be worn out by overwhelming experiences of grace. His goal is long-term spiritual transformation: the soul needs to be re-formed in faith and in feeling, restored to the relationship with God which mankind enjoyed before the **Fall**:

> Reforming in faith is common to all chosen souls . . . but reforming in feeling pertains especially to such souls as can come to the state of perfection – and that cannot be had suddenly: but a soul can come to it after great abundance of grace and great spiritual labor . . . when all bitter passions, carnal pleasures and other feelings are burnt out of the heart with the fire of desire and new gracious feelings are brought in, with burning love and spiritual light.
>
> (*Scale*, Bk 2, Ch. 17)

In Book 1 of the *Scale* he explores the concept of the 'image of sin', which needs to be eradicated and replaced by the 'image of Jesus' (Chapters 52-4, 56). This process will be painful and the would-be **contemplative** will find herself plunged into a spiritual darkness in which she must 'toil and sweat' to wrest her thoughts away from material things. Yet this does not seem to be the darkness of the **Dionysian** cloud so much as the inevitable barrier which **sin** forms between the soul and God: ' "Darkness" for Hilton reflects a condition within mankind itself. It is bound up with the "darkness" of **sin**. So for Hilton, "darkness of unknowing" has a pejorative sense; it is not the same as the "cloud of unknowing".'[25] In Book 2, which may have been addressed to a wider audience, Hilton again uses imagery and vocabulary reminiscent of the *Cloud* yet the thrust of his theological argument and his pastoral advice is quite different.[26] The would-be contemplative is urged to face the darkness with patience and to turn their heart towards Jesus:

> Whoever . . . is ready to forsake [the world] and seek the love of God, cannot at once feel the love of him but has to abide a while in the night. For he cannot suddenly come from the one light to the other, that is, from the love of the world to perfect love of God. This night is nothing but a separation and withdrawal of the thought of the soul from earthly things, by great desire and yearning to love, see and feel

Jesus and the things of the spirit . . . But this is a good night and a luminous darkness, for it is a shutting out of the false love of this world, and it is a drawing near to the true day . . . It is painful at first when someone is very unclean and not accustomed by grace to be often in this darkness . . . for the habit and the familiarity he has had before with sins of the world, carnal affections and earthly things, and his fleshly deeds, so press on him . . . if it should be like this with you, do not be too heavyhearted and do not strive too hard, as if you would put them out of your soul by force, for you cannot do it, but wait for grace . . . And skilfully – if you can – draw your desire and the regard of your spirit towards Jesus.

(Bk 2, Ch. 24)

In Book 2 (Chs 21–32) Hilton compares the spiritual life to a **pilgrimage** to Jerusalem, an image which speakes of perseverance, single-mindedness and the encouragement to be gleaned from glimpses of the goal: 'You are not there yet, but before you come to it you will be able to see it from afar, by the small sudden gleams that shine through little crannies from that city' (Bk 2, Ch. 25).

While his commitment to the **contemplative** way is clear, Hilton's writings breathe a tolerance and flexibility of which neither **Rolle**, nor the *Cloud*-author would have been capable. His instincts seem to have led him towards synthesis and simplicity. Listing the names which other writers have given to true contemplation, he concludes that 'although they all show it in diverse words, nevertheless all are one in the truth they affirm' (Bk 2, Ch. 40). Reluctant to lay down strict rules for meditation, he stresses that God may work in different ways within each individual soul. For heretics and pagans, however, there is no tolerance. Hilton warns his readers to keep strictly within the orthodoxy of the church (Bk I, Ch. 21) and makes acid comments about the false teachings and experiences of heretics (Bk 1, Ch. 58). There is also an essential continuity in Hilton's teaching. Unlike the *Cloud*-author, he does not discard the practice of meditation on scripture or on the character of God, but sees such exercises coming to fulfilment as God's **grace** infuses the contemplative. The encounter with God he describes is not a union beyond thought but an enlightenment *of* thought, as the soul achieves a new knowledge of God, seeing **heaven** and earth, angels and devils, the humanity and divinity of Christ and the purposes of God revealed. His distillation of complex teaching is aided by the use of pithy, everyday images: a **contemplative** must be sure of her calling, for 'A hound that runs after the hare only because he sees other hounds running will rest when he is tired, and turn back' (Bk 1, Ch. 41). To try to deal with **sin** without eradicating self-love is to be 'like a man who had a stinking well in his garden, with many small streams. He went and blocked the streams and left the spring whole thinking that all was safe, but the water sprang up at the bottom of the well and lay there stagnant in such quantity that it corrupted all the beauty of his garden' (Bk 1, Ch. 55). Those who have not yet experienced the fullness of God's love and have only their reason to help them struggle against sin are 'like wrestlers ... sometimes on top and sometimes underneath' (Bk 2, Ch. 36). The flexibility of Hilton's approach is most evident in his attitude towards the spiritual potential of the growing numbers of devout lay people. While maintaining that only solitaries could enjoy to the full the highest degree of contemplation, he also encouraged those with inescapable secular responsibilities to pursue a contemplative life alongside their everyday commitments. It had long been recognised that those holding high office in the Church must necessarily combine the duties of **Martha** and **Mary**. In his *Epistle on Mixed Life*, written 'to a worldli lord', Hilton extended this model to embrace those who were 'bounden to þe world bi children and seruauntes as þou art'. The 'ordre of charite' asks that such men (and women) should combine service to their fellows with an inner life of deep prayer:

> Þow shalt meedele þe werkes of actif liyf wiþ goostli werkes of lif contemplatif, and þanne doost þou weel. For þou schalt oo tyme wiþ Martha be bisi for to rule and gouerne þi houshoold, þi children, þi seruantis, þi neiȝbours, þi tenauntes. . . [Anoþir tyme] þou schal wiþ Maria leue bisinesse of þe world, and sitten doun at þe feet of oure lord bi mekeness in praiers and in hooli þouȝtis and in contemplacioun of him, as he ȝeueþ þee grace.
>
> (*Mixed Life*, 10–11)

Alfred the Great had recognised a king's need for men who worked, men who fought, and men who prayed. The author of *Ancrene Wisse*, **Rolle** and the *Cloud*-author had all stressed the need to choose between the **active life** of charity and the inner life of contemplation. Now Hilton offered hope that men and women could both work and grow in prayer. Again his instinctive feeling for balance and moderation can be discerned: if all who loved God adopted the solitary life, who would care for the sick, the needy and the proper functions of society? This application of the law of love would have pleased Langland:

Þou schalt vndirstonde þat oure lord Ihesu Crist as man, is heed of þe goostli bodi[27] whiche is holi chirche. Þe membres of þis bodi aren alle Cristene men ... Þanne ȝif þat þou be bisi wiþ al þi myȝte for to arraie his heed, þat is for to worschipe hym silf ... and forȝetest his feet þat are þyn childen, þi seruauntes, þi tenauntes, and alle þyn euen-Cristen spille for defaute of kepynge, unaraied, unkeped and not tended to as þei auȝt for to be, þou plesest him not.

*(Mixed Life*, 25–6)

Hilton's writings made the **contemplative** life accessible for everyday Christians who longed for a deeper experience of God. Among those he influenced were two women who in turn offered contributions to the English spiritual tradition: **Julian of Norwich** and **Margery Kempe** of King's Lynn.

## JULIAN OF NORWICH AND MARGERY KEMPE

At first glance the writings of Julian of Norwich (c.1342–c.1416) and Margery Kempe (c.1373–c.1438) seem poles apart: the one disciplined, thoughtful, theologically mature; the other excitable, self-centred, seemingly unbalanced in her excessive sensibility. Yet much as they differed in temperament and circumstances, they shared a common spiritual heritage and approach to piety, and together they illustrate the response of the devout medieval Christian to the call to contemplation. Neither would have set herself up as a teacher of the stature of **Hilton** or the *Cloud*-author; what they had to share was not theory but experience, together with theological insights which grew out of that experience. Their accounts would, they believed, glorify God and benefit their 'even [fellow] Cristen'. Both knew at least some of the works of their English predecessors and Margery especially was strongly influenced by the female mystical writers of other European countries such as **Bridget of Sweden**.[28] Together they illustrate the still ambivalent attitudes of the medieval Church towards women, lay spirituality and the vernacular treatises which encouraged such women to seek direct encounters with God.

Julian of Norwich received her revelations when, in her thirty-first year, she was thought to be on the point of death. It is not known whether she was already an **anchorite** or simply a lay woman at this time, though the likelihood is that she was still living at home since her mother and **parish priest** were at her bedside. What is clear is that she shared with **Rolle**, **Hilton** and **Margery Kempe**, an intense preoccupation with the **Passion of Christ**.

Central to the piety of the later medieval period (and therefore to the world in which both Julian and Margery lived) was the belief that Christ's willingness to endure the pain and horror of the **Crucifixion** provided overwhelming evidence of his love for men and women and His desire to save them from the consequences of their **sins**. Meditation upon the grim details of his sufferings was encouraged among the devout as a means of both awakening **contrition** and reassuring them of God's love. Julian, therefore, was far from unique in her desire to understand, even in some fashion to identify with, the sufferings which Christ had endured on her behalf. Her visions came, she says, in answer to a three-fold request of God that she might have 'mynde of Cryste es passionn', 'bodelye sicknes' (at the age of thirty), and 'of goddys gyfte thre wonndys':

> Me thought I woulde haue ben that time with Magdaleyne . . . that I might haue seen bodilie the passion that our lord suffered for me, that I might haue suffered with him, as other did that loued him. And therfore I desyred a bodely sight, wher in I might haue more knowledge of the bodely paynes of our sauiour, and of the compassion of our lady and of all his true louers that were lyuyng that tyme and saw his paynes; for I would haue be one of them and haue suffered with them.
>
> *(Book of Showings, LT, Ch. 2)*

Julian's record of her 'shewyngs' survives in two forms, the shorter account apparently written not long after the event, the longer version the product of over fifteen years of prayerful reflection and interpretation. Though she describes herself as 'a simple creature that cowde no letter' (*Book of Showings, LT*, Ch. 2), this probably only means that (like most female contemporaries) she was unskilled in Latin. Whether or not, like Margery, she was forced to dictate her account, her words reveal a wide-ranging theological understanding[29] and considerable skill in presentation. She was thoroughly acquainted with the **Vulgate** scriptures, and she may even have provided her own translations. Her visions of Christ's sufferings on the cross, each starkly drawn and interpreted with meticulous care, are central to her understanding. Through Christ's **Passion**, God's love and sovereignty are revealed, the **Devil** defeated and the dark universe made a place of security for those who believe. Interwoven with the visions are moments of joyful union with God and experiences of darkness verging on despair. In time Julian learns to accept that these oscillations of feeling are designed to develop confidence in God both 'in wo and in wele'. Her writings offer experience set in the context of mature theological reflection. Despite the intensity of her own emotional involvement, she was still capable of a remarkable degree of detachment in analysing and evaluating her own responses. A true child of her time, she worked hard at interpreting her experiences, puzzling prayerfully over the more obscure aspects of her visions until satisfied that she had achieved understanding. Thus the account of her visions itself becomes a spiritual quest as she constantly seeks deeper understanding of God and his ways to man. Julian repeatedly affirms her orthodoxy, stating that nothing in her visions is contrary to the teaching of the Church. The only point at which this unquestioning allegiance wavers is when she confronts the problem of **sin** and judgement: 'And me thought yf synne had nott be, we shulde alle haue be clene and lyke to oure lorde as he made us. And thus in my foly before thys tyme often I wondryd why, by the grete forseyng wysdom of God the begynnyng of synne was nott lettyd' (*LT*, Ch. 27). She is answered in words which become a recurring theme: 'Synne is behouely, but alle shal be wele, and alle shall be wele, and alle maner of thynge shal be wele.' Sin, she comes to see, may not easily be understood but it can be overcome. Langland's Active Man lamented that 'synne seweth us evere' (*Piers Plowman*, XIV, 323); Julian has learned to focus not on the sin but on the God whose love offers a way of forgiveness.

Though there are traces of the pseudo-**Dionysius** in her thinking, the tone of Julian's work is closer to that of **Rolle** and **Hilton**. Like Rolle she is conscious of the homeliness of God, whom she describes as 'so reverent and dredfulle . . . so homely and so curteyse' (*LT*, Ch. 7); like Hilton her spirituality is integrated with concern for her fellow Christians. Julian's recurring motifs are her focus on the **Trinity**, her tranquil confidence in God's sovereignty and her emphasis on the centrality of love: 'What, woldest thou wytt thy lordes menyng in this thyng? Wytt it wele, loue was his menyng. Who shewyth it the? Loue. (What shewid he the? Loue.) Wherfore shewyth he it the? For loue' (*LT*, Ch. 86). Her perceptions and images are often startling:

Jhesu Crist, that doth good agaynst evyll, is oure very moder; we haue oure ground of beyng of hym, where the ground of moderhed begynneth, with alle the swete kepyng of loue that endlesly folowyth. As verely as god is oure fader, as verely is god oure moder.[30]

(*LT*, Ch. 59)

And in this he shewed a little thing, the quantitie of a haselnott, lying in the palme of my hand, as me semide, and it was as rounde as a balle. I loked theran with the eye of my vnderstanding, and thought: what may this be? And it was answered generally thus:/ It is all that is made.

(*LT*, Ch. 5)

She repeatedly disclaims special status, stating, 'Alle that I say of me I mene in person of alle my evyn cristen' (*LT*, Ch. 8) and insisting, 'For the shewyng I am nott good, but [unless] I loue god the better' (*LT*, Ch. 9); but her humility does not extend to the suppression of her insights. The widespread developments in lay spirituality and the contributions of women in particular were viewed with mixed feelings by the church hierarchy. There was considerable unease about writing and prayer in the vernacular and Gerson, Chancellor of the University of Paris, probably spoke for many cautious clerics when he declared that 'all women's teaching, particularly formal teaching by word and by writing is to be held suspect unless it has been diligently examined, and much more fully than men's ... Because they are easily seduced and determined seducers; and because it is not proved that they are witnesses to divine grace.'[31] Julian as a respected counsellor was doubtless all too aware of possible excesses, but would not be silenced by such prejudices. She disclaimed the role of teacher, but could not fail to bear witness to what she had seen: 'Botte for I am a woman, schulde I therfore leve that I schulde nouȝt telle ȝowe the goodenes of god?' (*ST* Ch. 6)

It has to be admitted that the *Book of Margery Kempe* would probably have confirmed all Gerson's worst fears about women. Margery's blend of assertiveness, emotion and penetrating spiritual insight polarised her contemporaries and has a similar effect upon modern critics.[32] Her persistent bouts of sobbing caused her expulsion from church; her behaviour on **pilgrimage** to the Holy Land drove her fellow pilgrims to disown her. Yet Margery's outpourings are uniquely valuable; here we see the motivation and experience not of the spiritual director, but of the spiritually ambitious directee; the inner longings not of the nun or anchoress confined within a stone cell but of a business-woman, wife and mother trapped by the expectations of her class and community.[33] Margery's background – proud daughter of one worthy burgess, extravagant and headstrong wife of another – might seem to have fitted her for a place in the *Canterbury Tales*, trotting alongside the Wife of Bath, rather than the pursuit of the mystical life; yet her

*Book* voices a passionate longing for the **contemplative** life. She relates how her dramatic conversion, following a period of mental illness, together with a further period of pursuing disastrous business enterprises, prompted a burning desire to achieve the closeness to God described in the works of Rolle and Hilton. Her spiritual development was strongly influenced by accounts of the lives of the Continental female mystics such as **St Bridget of Sweden** (1303–73) and Mary of Oignes (d. 1213). Here were role-models whose experiences inspired, and in the view of Margery and her supporters validated, Margery's own highly charged and somewhat erratic spiritual journey. Living in an east coast port and travelling extensively in mainland Europe, Margery would also have been aware of the considerable numbers of lay women who had been moved to form communities of *beguines*, taking no formal lasting vows but devoting themselves to service and prayer.

Margery's failures and triumphs are narrated with engaging frankness. Like the Wife of Bath she allowed her eyes to stray; unlike the Wife of Bath she came to repent of her lechery and desire a life of complete chastity. Like **Rolle** she experienced spiritual warmth and heavenly melody. One night, 'as þis creatur lay in hir bedde wyth hir husband, sche herd a sownd of melodye so swet and delectable, hir þowt, as sche had ben in Paradyse. And therwyth sche styrt owt of hir bedde & seyd, "Alas, þat euyr I dede synne, it is ful mery in Hevyn"' (Ch. 3),[34] an experience which echoes a contemporary lyric:

> Think man on thy sinnes sevene,
> Think how merye it is in Hevene.
> Pray to God, with milde stevene
> He be thy help on Domesday.
>
> *voice*
>
> (*Medieval English Lyrics*, 67)

Her repeated prayers for forgiveness and numerous **penances** were eventually rewarded with an encounter with **Christ** during which she was promised 'high meditation and true contemplation' (Ch. 5). Margery's subsequent experiences, during which she entered into the life of Christ in an intensely emotional fashion, led to a blurring of the boundaries of time and space:

> Þis creatur sey a fayr ymage of owr Lady clepyd a pyte. And thorw þe beholdyng of þat pete hir mende was al holy ocupyd in þe Passyon of owr Lord Ihesu Crist & in þe compassyon of owr Lady, Seynt Mary, be whech sche was compellyd to cryyn ful lowde & wepyn ful sor, as þei

sche xulde a deyd. Þan cam to hir þe ladys preste seying, 'Damsel, Ihesu is ded long sithyn.' Whan hir crying was cesyd, sche seyd to þe preste, 'Sir, hys deth is as fresch to me as he had deyd þis same day.'

(Ch. 60)

Everywhere she went she saw intimations of God's presence or was reminded of the **Gospel** narrative. Her prolonged and noisy bouts of weeping prompted accusations of hypocrisy from some but also won her respect amongst others.

as sone as sche parceyved þat sche xulde crye, sche wolde kepyn it in as mech as sche myth þat þe pepyl xulde not an herd it for noying of hem. For summe seyd it was a wikkyd spirit vexid hir; sum seyd it was a sekenes . . . Oþer gostly [spiritual] men louyd hir & fauowred hir þe mor.

(Ch. 28)

Margery usually regarded criticism as a kind of spiritual accolade: the persecution which the **saints** might well expect. She did however seek counsel and verification of her visions from **Julian of Norwich** (Ch. 18) and shared her insights with a vicar of that town who was taken aback by her enthusiasm:

Sche salutyd þe Vycary, preyng hym þat sche myght speke wyth hym an owyr or ellys tweyen owyrs . . . in þe lofe of God. He, lyftyng vp hys handys & blyssyng hym seyd, 'Benedicite. What cowd a woman ocupyn an owyr or tweyn owyrs in þe lofe of owyr Lord?'

(Ch. 17)

Much of Margery's seemingly bizarre behaviour may have derived from her attempts to resolve the tensions which beset the devout medieval lay-person and her determination to assert her identity in defiance of the social and religious structures which hemmed her in.[35] Unable to return to the virgin state so highly prized by the medieval Church, she contrived to persuade her husband (to whom she had already borne fourteen children) to accept a vow of chastity in return for the payment of his debts. She also embarked upon a series of ambitious pilgrimages, visiting Jerusalem, Assisi and Rome. Unfortunately her fellow pilgrims found her intense piety profoundly irritating: 'Þei wer most displesyd for sche wepyd so mech & spak alwey of þe lofe & goodnes of owyr Lord as wel at þe tabyl as in oþer place' (Ch. 26). Margery's meditations usually take the form of conversations with God in which she is commended for her spiritual ambitions and allowed glimpses into the domestic life of the Holy Family. Julian was shown the Virgin Mary and observed 'the wisdom and the truth of her sowle' (*LT*, Ch. 25); Margery on the other hand actually 'takes part' in the story, accompanying Mary to Bethlehem, procuring lodgings for her and assisting at the birth of Christ (Ch. 6). This down–to–earth recital is continued in a later vision, as Margery tries to comfort Mary after the Crucifixion with a hot drink (Ch. 81). Subsequently 'our Lord' thanked her for these services offered 'in contemplation and meditation' (Ch. 83). It is important to recognise that Margery's imaginative entering into the Biblical narrative, like so much of her apparently eccentric behaviour, was not in fact as unorthodox as it might seem. As J. A. W. Bennett points out, she is 'following literally the Bonaventuran *Mediationes*, which in the rendering made by Nicholas Love about the time of Margery's visions, enjoins: "And then also *by devout imagination as though thou were bodily present*, comfort Our Lady and that other fellowship, praying them to eat somewhat." '[36] Elsewhere the pseudo-Bonaventuran *Meditations on the Life of Christ* suggest:

> You too . . . kneel and adore your Lord God, and then His mother, and reverently greet the saintly old Joseph. Kiss the beautiful little feet of the infant Jesus who lies in the manger and beg His mother to offer to let you hold Him a while. Pick Him up and hold Him in your arms . . . Then return Him to the mother . . . and remain to help her if you can.
>
> (*Meditations*, 38–9)

Margery shows the influence of female Continental mystics in several ways: her persistent sobbing[37] and wearing of virginal white clothing is reminiscent of Mary of Oignes (d. 1213); she was allowed to receive weekly Communion (highly unusual for a lay-person) like St Bridget (d. 1373); and, like St Catherine of Siena (d. 1380), believed herself to have gone through a form of mystical marriage with God. Bridget and Catherine were also renowned for their fearless advice to kings and popes. Margery was equally ready to rebuke **monks**, **bishops** and **archbishops** but her comments were not always well received. Indeed her outspokenness, coupled with her claims to special revelations and references to scripture led to recurring charges of heresy against which she defended herself indignantly and ably. A great mystic Margery was not; yet in her we see the mystical tradition filtering down to the ordinary medieval Christian, enmeshed and constantly struggling to escape

from the tensions of marriage, children, financial problems and
sceptical neighbours. The *Cloud*-author would have disowned her
but **Julian** seems to have given her cautious encouragement,
perhaps identifying with the genuine spiritual longings which drove
Margery's somewhat frenetic activities. As **Walter Hilton**, another
wise counsellor, observed: 'As Seynt Gregor seiþ, no man sodeynli
is maad souereyne in grace, but fro litel he bigynneþ, and bi
processe wexeþ, vntil he come to þe moste. And so graunt vs to do
þe fadir and sone and þe holi goost'(*Mixed Life*, 69).

NOTES

1. *Anchoritic Spirituality* (AS). For the Middle English text see *Ancrene Wisse* ed. Tolkien.
2. Walter Hilton, *Scale of Perfection*. An edition of the Middle English text is in preparation for EETS.
3. Warren (1985, 2).
4. Lafarge (1986, 122)
5. See statistics compiled by Warren (1985, 20).
6. On dating see Edwards (1984, 7–23).
7. Warren (1985, 97–100) gives details of these ceremonies.
8. Allen (1918; 1921) and Dobson (1976) suggest identifications for the sisters and author. See also Millett (1992).
9. Cited Warren (1985, 61).
10. See Bennett (1982, Ch. 2) for an account of this shift.
11. Woolf (1962, 111).
12. See Bishop (1979, 198–9).
13. On the English mystics see Knowles (1961); Hodgson (1967); Butler (1967); Riehle (1981); Glasscoe (1993).
14. *Law of Love*, 16.
15. Hodgson (1967, 10).
16. Passages believed to endorse mysticism included Jn 1:14; Jn 14:21, 23; Jn 17: 21–3; II Cor 12:1–4 and the Song of Songs (interpreted by St Bernard as an allegory of the relationship between Christ and the soul).
17. Allen (1927, 267).
18. On Rolle's imagery see Wakelin (1979, 193, 198–9) and Watson (1991).
19. See Hodgson (1955); Clark (1977); Riehle (1977). For the background of the *Cloud*-author see *Cloud*, Intro.
20. See *Cloud*, lxxvi ff.
21. Knowles (1964, 72).
22. Hodgson (1967, 30).
23. Hodgson (1967, 32).
24. Gardner (1937, 103–27) points out the range of people he instructed.
25. Hilton, *Scale*, 177–237.

26. Hodgson (1967, 31) observes: 'when passages seem close in theme or imagery, they are, in fact, quite different in approach'. Clark (1977, 109) comments: 'they use similar language in the interest of diverse theologies.'

27. The image of the Church as the Body of Christ derives from I Corinthians 12: 12–27.

28. See Riehle (1981, Ch. 2).

29. *Book of Showings*, Intro. 45ff; also Allchin (1980, 74); Glasscoe (1990); Beer (1992).

30. This appreciation of the maternal qualities of God stemmed from biblical passages such as Isaiah 49:15, 66:13; Matthew 23:37. It is also seen in the writings of **St Anselm** and in some religious lyrics (see Ch. 7 below).

31. *De examinatione doctrinarum*, i. Cited *Book of Showings*, 151.

32. See Atkinson (1983); McEntire (1992); Staley (1994).

33. Pantin (1955, 256) sees her as 'a kind of spiritual seismograph' who 'records the devout layman's reactions to the spiritual stimuli of the time.'

34. *Book of Margery Kempe*. Eds Meech and Sandford.

35. See Beckwith (1986); Delany (1983); Aers (1988, 73–116).

36. Bennett (1982, 42).

37. Bennett (1982, 41) notes that 'in the Middle Ages tears were accounted a grace not a disgrace.' Watkin (1979, 51) points out that Margery's response echoes Hilton: 'At this sight you feel your heart stirred to such compassion and pity towards your Lord Jesus that you mourn, weep and cry out with every power of body and soul': *Scale*, Bk 1, Ch. 35. See also Medcalf (1980) and Dickman (1980).

# Chapter 7

# The Religious Lyrics

| | |
|---|---|
| Whanne ic se on Rode | *I see; cross* |
| Jesu, my lemman, | *lover* |
| And besiden him stonden | *stand* |
| Marye and Johan, | *John* |
| And his rig iswongen, | *back, scourged* |
| And his side istungen, | *pierced* |
| For the luve of man; | |
| Well ou ic to wepen, | *ought* |
| And sinnes for to leten, | *abandon* |
| Yif ic of luve can. | *know* |
| | *(Medieval English Lyrics,* 30)[1] |

'FOR THE LOVE OF MAN'

Deceptive in its simplicity, profound in its brevity, this fourteenth-century **Passion** lyric states in uncompromising terms the driving motivation of popular contemporary piety. At its starkest, the argument went something like this: **Christ** died for me to show his love, therefore I should love him in return. He demonstrated the depth of his love through the extent of his sufferings; therefore the more I dwell in imagination upon those sufferings, the more profound and rich will be my own response of love. The poem also contains in embryo many of the characteristics of its kind: it visualises the figure of Christ on the cross, with the key figures of the **Virgin Mary** and **John** the beloved **apostle** standing by; it focuses on the details of his wounds and reflects on the tears, repentance and love which the sufferings of such a 'Lover' should evoke. The fact that such poems were written in the first person may be misleading to a modern reader. The flowering of the religious lyric which followed the arrival of the **friars** in England in the 1220s did not simply signify a corresponding growth in devotion amongst individual poets. These lyrics in the main were not vehicles for expressing personal emotion; their purpose was to draw the reader or listener into a religious experience. In fact the very term *lyric* is likely to mislead, since these are not lyrics in the modern sense but poems written to teach, exhort, even coax the audience into a deeper response to God. When the poet says 'I', he usually means 'you and I'.

The medieval religious lyrics, a significant part of the wider body of verse which survives in manuscripts of the thirteenth to the early sixteenth centuries, played an important role in the battle for the souls of men and women. It is clear from the works of Chaucer and Langland that in a period when almost the whole population were baptised members of the Church, there was still an enormous variation in religious conviction and practice. Following the **Fourth Lateran Council** in 1215, which required every Christian to come to confession at least once a year, the Church had adopted a more systematic approach to the practice of confession and **penance** with the production of manuals for **confessors**. The effects were far-reaching. Confessors were required to probe deep; those coming to confession were increasingly expected not only to acknowledge their sins but also to be truly contrite. Chaucer's Parson defined **contrition** as

> the verray sorwe that a man receyveth in his herte for his synnes, with sad purpos to shryve hym, and to do penaunce, and neveremoore to do synne. And this sorwe shal been in this manere, as seith Seint Bernard: 'It shal be hevy and grevous, and ful sharp and poynaunt in herte.' First, for man hath agilt his Lord and his Creatour . . . and yet moore sharp and poynaunt for he hath wrathed and agilt hym that boghte hym, that with his precious blood hath delivered us from the bondes of synne.
>
> (*Parson's Tale*, 128–31)

Ordinary men and women needed to be moved to experience such **contrition** if they were to sincerely confess their **sins** and mend their ways; in this context the lyrics supplied an emotional component, acting both as a stimulus to devotion and as a channel for its expression. The audience for such poems was wide and varied. Lyrics were used by preachers to heighten the impact of their sermons,[2] written and meditated upon by **mystics** such as **Rolle**, and, with the spread of literacy, read by pious laymen and women everywhere. Poets were providing expressions of penitence, petitions for forgiveness and outpourings of thanksgiving, not just for themselves but for Everyman. The writers of religious lyrics aimed at an immediacy of depiction of events and themes as vivid

as the brightly-painted pictures which adorned the walls of **parish**
churches, and as emotive as the images of the suffering **Christ** and
his mourning mother which evoked such a tearful response from
**Margery Kempe** (Ch. 60). Encouraged by writers such as the
pseudo-Bonaventure, both Margery and **Julian of Norwich**
expressed a desire to enter into biblical events, 'to be actually there';
and the lyrics provided a means by which the ordinary lay person
could achieve just that. The audience was invited to stand alongside
the poet as he contemplated the **Nativity** or **Crucifixion** of
Christ, listened to the voice of the suffering Saviour or entered into
the joys and sorrows of the **Virgin Mary**. In their quest for
immediacy and desire to evoke a response it was inevitable that
poets should sometimes overstep the mark, their images becoming
gruesome rather than merely graphic and their sincere appeals to
devotion verging on the sentimental. But amidst the mass of
undistinguished attempts at pious reflection there are masterpieces of
unaffected yet restrained emotion which perfectly embody the
spiritual longings of the age.

> Jesu, swete is the love of thee
> Noon othir thing so swete may be;
> No thing that men may heere and see
> Hath no swetnesse ayens thee . . .
>
> Jesu, my God, Jesu my kyng,
> Thou axist me noon othir thing,
> But trewe love and hert yernying,
> And love-teeris with swete mornyng.

(SRL, 47)

Though the majority of the surviving religious lyrics are
anonymous, research[3] has shown that most were written by clerics,
including the **friars**. During the thirteenth and fourteenth centuries
in England religious and secular lyrics appear to have developed
along separate lines. The English religious lyric owes many of its
forms and much of its inspiration to the Latin tradition of
devotional poetry, which was given new impetus and life in the
early thirteenth century by the infusion of **Franciscan** teachings
and zeal. A sizeable number of English lyrics are translations of
Latin originals, and macaronic lyrics such as 'There is no rose',
which incorporate lines or half lines in Latin or French, are also
common. Many of those sufficiently educated to write such poetry
would have been at home in all three languages. Both Latin and

English lyrics drew on the dominant themes of popular European piety. **Anselm** (d. 1109), **Bernard of Clairvaux** (d. 1153), and **St Francis** (d. 1226) had all in turn encouraged a fervent devotion to Christ and the **Virgin Mary** which, by focusing on the humanity and sufferings of **Christ**, sought to evoke a heartfelt response of love towards God. A thirteenth-century version of a work attributed to Bernard acknowledges this inheritance:

| | |
|---|---|
| Man, folwe seintt Bernardes trace | *track* |
| And loke in ihesu cristes face, | *Jesus Christ's* |
| *How hee lut hys heued to þe,* | *inclines his head* |
| Swetlike for to kessen þe, | *kiss* |
| And sprat hise armes on þe tre, | *tree (cross)* |
| *Senful man, to klippen þe.* | *sinful; embrace* |
| | (CB XIII, 69) |

The coming of the **friars** to England in the 1220s stimulated the spread of these forms of devotion. The **Franciscans** in particular were accustomed to using simple, vernacular songs to attract crowds and enhance their message of penitence and amendment of life; this technique, coupled with their strong affirmation of the humanity of Christ and the emotional power of his death, exercised a profound influence on the English religious lyric.[4] Since the friars wished to communicate with ordinary men and women, they embodied their teachings in simple language and attractive, easily-memorised forms. The value attached to such lyrics in popular piety is illustrated by the comment of Langland's Sloth, who feels it necessary to confess:

| | |
|---|---|
| I kan rymes of Robyn Hood and Randolf Erl of Chestre | *know rhymes about* |
| Ac neither of Oure Lord ne of Oure Lady the leeste that evere was maked. | |
| | (*Piers Plowman*, V, 396) |

The **friars** were active in replacing secular songs, especially *carols* which were associated with the dubious delights of the dance, with religious verses cast in the same attractive idiom but rather more uplifting in content. Their successful exploitation of this form would, in time, be turned against them as this late fourteenth-century lyric demonstrates:

| | |
|---|---|
| Of thes Frer Minoures me thenkes moch wonder, | |
| That waxen are thus hautein that somtime weren under . . . | *grown; haughty* |

Thay preche all of povert bot that love thay noght;          *poverty*
For gode mete to thair mouthe the town is thurgh soght . . .   *through*
With an O, and an I, for sixe pens er thay faile,
Sle thy fadre and jape thy modre and thay will thee assoile!

*slay; seduce; absolve*
(*Medieval English Lyrics*, 59)

Though the religious lyrics were usually simple in tone, it would be wrong to dismiss them as naive. In the well-known lyric *Adam Lay Ibowndyn*, for example, we see theological paradox pared down to its essentials, yet losing none of its force:

Adam lay ibowndyn, bowndyn in a bond,
Fowre thousand wynter thowt he not to long.

And al was for an appil, an appil that he tok,
As clerkes fynden wretyn in here book.

Ne hadde the appil taken ben, the appil taken ben,
Ne hadde never our Lady a ben hevene qwen.

Blyssid be the tyme that appil take was,
Therfore we mown syngen '*Deo gracias!*'

(*SRL*, 2)

The lyric writers used a kind of theological shorthand, drawing on traditional images, familiar from the daily **liturgy** of the Church, and the interpretations given to the scriptures by centuries of preachers and commentators. The brief reference to the taking of the 'appil' in the lyric above stands for the whole saga and consequences of the **Fall of Man**. There was no need for the poet to elaborate what was only too well-known to all; instead he could leap to celebrating the new benefits which came from the need for redemption. Had there been no sin, no *felix culpa* (as it was described in the liturgy for **Holy Saturday**), there would have been no need for a Saviour to rescue Adam from the four thousand years in hell which tradition allotted to him. There would certainly have been no occasion for the example of humble obedience which won **Mary** her place as the glorious but infinitely approachable Queen of Heaven.

'THOU LITEL KING'

Whereas the mystery plays sought to convey the whole sweep of the history of salvation from the **Creation** and the **Fall of Man** to the **Last Judgement**, the lyrics focused chiefly on two crucial scenes in the eternal drama: the **Nativity** and the **Passion of Christ**; in theological terms, the **Incarnation** and the **Atonement**. Naturally, these scenes were dominated by the figures of **Christ** and his mother **Mary**. The figure of Christ was familiar to the medieval churchgoer in three forms: the tiny baby cradled lovingly in his mother's arms, the tormented Saviour on the Cross and the awe-inspiring Judge whom they would have to face on Doomsday. Significantly the lyric writers preferred to concentrate on the first two aspects, those which portray the humanity of Christ. From the eleventh century onward, it is possible to trace in both art and literature a growing emphasis on the human nature of Jesus Christ. This stemmed in part from the teaching of influential figures such as **Anselm** and **Bernard of Clairvaux** that Christ purchased forgiveness for mankind on the cross as a representative man enduring mankind's deserved punishment for sin, rather than as God vanquishing the **Devil**. Anselm among others used extra-biblical material to supplement the **Gospel** accounts of the life of Jesus. The popular thirteenth-century *Meditations on the Life of Christ,* supposedly written by the **Franciscan St Bonaventure**, offered further imaginative elaboration. In this way Jesus the man was provided with a human family, including grandparents, with whom all could identify. **St Bridget of Sweden** (1303–73) was given the details of the Holy Birth in a vision by no less an authority than the Virgin Mary herself and her account shaped subsequent visualisation of the Nativity. St Bridget was shown the Virgin:

and with hir one semeli olde man, and with þame on ox and ane asse . . . And þan saw I in hir wombe a þinge stire; and sodanli sho bare hir son. And þare com so grete a light and brightnes þat it passed þe brightenes of þe son . . . And þe child, wepand and tremeland for colde and hardnes of þe pament, streked him to seke refresheinge. þan his modir tuke him in hir armes, and streined him to hir breste, and with hir cheke ad hire breste scho warmed him with grete ioy . . . And þan rose sho vp, and Joseph helped hir to lai þe child in þe crib, and knelid doune þai bothe and wirshiped him.

(*Liber Celestis*, 486–7)

**St Francis**, himself deeply devoted to the humanity of **Christ**, encouraged veneration of the crib. Artistic portrayal of the babe in his mother's arms slowly changed in character:

In the eleventh century, the West had long been familiar with the Child seated as if enthroned upon his Mother's knee, holding up his right hand as if in benediction and in his left clasping a Book, the symbol of wisdom, or an orb, the symbol of dominion. This conception persisted and was never abandoned but it was joined by many other forms which expressed the more intimate inclinations of later medieval piety, such as the laughing Child, the Child playing with an apple or a ball, the child caressing its Mother, or the Child being fed from its Mother's breast.[5]

It seems to have taken some time for this growing tenderness and homeliness of feeling to manifest itself in the **Nativity** lyrics. Most of the surviving poems which deal with the theme of the **Incarnation** of **Christ**, from the angel's visit to Mary to the stable scene, date from the fourteenth and fifteenth centuries and offer a fascinating mixture of the transcendent and the homely, the otherworldly and the down-to-earth. The finest of all the lyrics which deal with the 'mystery' of Christ's taking flesh, indeed many would say the finest of all the surviving religious lyrics, is the exquisite fifteenth-century poem *I syng of a mayden*.[6] The apparent naivety of its ballad-like structure and diction conceals a wealth of subtle allusions which enhance its beauty without distorting its simple elegance:

> I syng of a mayden that is makeles,                    *without equal*
> Kyng of alle kynges to here son che ches.                    *she chose*
>
> He cam also stylle ther his moder was
> As dew in Aprylle that fallyt on the gras.
>
> He cam also stylle to his moderes bowr
> As dew in Aprille that fallyt on the flour.
>
> He cam also stylle ther his moder lay
> As dew in Aprille that fallyt on the spray.
>
> Moder and maydyn was never non but che
> Wel may swych a lady Godes mother be!
>
> (SRL, 6)

The poem seems to have a distant ancestor in a thirteenth-century lyric which opens:

> Nu this fules singeth and maketh hure blisse,                    *birds*
> And that gres up-thringeth and leveth the ris,     *branches grow leafy*
> Of on I wille singen that is makeles
> The King of alle kinges to moder hire ches.
>
> (CB XIII, 31)

The later poet however chooses to make a quite different theological point. In the earlier poem the emphasis is upon **Christ**'s choice of **Mary** as His mother, but the later version shifts the spotlight to Mary herself, highlighting the importance of her willing cooperation in God's plan. Though we are given none of the Biblical or traditional details of the **Annunciation**, 'to here son che ches' has as its underlying message Mary's words to the Angel Gabriel, 'Behold I am the handmaid of the Lord; let it be to me according to your word' (Luke 1:38). The assertion that Mary is 'makeles' is a typical example of the poet's use of language. Behind the statement that she is without equal (itself something of a paradox since it is her humility which distinguishes her) lie the possible punning connotations that she is 'without a mate' since the child has no human father and *maskeles* (without stain). Stillness was a quality traditionally associated with both Christ's conception and his birth; both events being thereby distanced from human passion and pain. The repetition of the phrase 'He cam also stille' builds up an impression of intimacy and of a joyful secret shared by mother and child. Just as dew falls silently before the dawn, unobserved in its coming yet refreshing and energising where it touches, so Christ's conception in the womb of Mary represents an almost imperceptible demonstration of the power of God intervening in the world. The image of dewfall, which originated in the story of Gideon's fleece (Judges 6:36–40), was one of the most common medieval symbols for the **Incarnation**. A commentary by the twelfth-century theologian, Honorius of Autun, explained how the sign given by God to Gideon prefigured the conception of Christ: 'Gideon, the captain of Israel spread out a fleece on the threshing floor, into which the dew descended from heaven, while the threshing floor remained dry ... The fleece wet with dew is the Holy Virgin, having conceived. The dry threshing floor is her inviolate virginity.'[7] Similarly the *Prymer* stated: 'Whanne he was born wunderfulliche of a maide, þanne was fulfillid holi writ. Þou cam doun as reyn in-tyo a flees, for to make saaf mankynde' (*Prymer*, 21). A fifteenth-century lyric to Mary identified the dew with the **Holy Spirit**:

> Thow ert ek the fleys of Jedeon
>   A-dewyd with the Holy Gost.

(SEC, 50)

The self-sacrifice involved in **Christ**'s descent from the realms of heaven to the cruel rigours of life on earth dominates a number of

the **Nativity** lyrics. Some, like this brief thirteenth-century poem
found in a collection for preachers, content themselves with making
one simple (though theologically profound) devotional point: in this
case the stark contrast between Christ's eternal majesty and the
poverty into which he was born:

> Of one stable was his halle;
> His kenestol on occe stalle,
> Sente Marie his burnes alle.

*royal throne, ox's*
*servants*
(SRL, 8b)

Others make the same point with greater emotional intensity and
tenderness. In this fourteenth-century lyric, **Mary** is pictured
grieving because she can offer so little comfort to her new-born
son. Here practical maternal concern, with which any mother could
identify, is given additional poignance by the unspoken recognition
that the shivering child is in fact the Son of God:

> Jesu, swete sone dere,
> On porful bed list thou here,
>     And that me greveth sore;
> For thi cradel is ase a bere,
> Oxe and asse beth thi fere –
>     Weepe ich mai tharfore.
>
> Jesu, swete, beo not wroth
> Thou ich nabbe clout ne cloth
>     The on for to folde,
> The on for to folde ne to wrappe,
> For ich nabbe clout ne lappe –
> Bote ley tho thi fet to my pappe
>     And wite the from the colde.

*cattle-stall*
*companions*

*breast*

(SRL, 14)

It is hard to know whether the traditional assumption of cold
weather at the **Nativity**, evidenced also in the mystery plays, was
due to the knowledge that Christmas can be cold in Bethlehem or
an instinctive tendency to translate biblical events into a familiar
context. Certainly there can be no doubt about the 'Englishness' or
homeliness of the shepherds who visited the baby in this **carol**:[8]

> The sheperd upon a hill he satt;
> He had on hym his tabard and his hat,
> Hys tarbox, hys pype and hys flagat;

*flask*

Hys name was caled Joly, Joly Wat . . .

Whan Wat to Bedleem cum was,
He swet – he had gon faster than a pace.
He fownd Jesu in a sympyll place
Between an ox and an asse.
    With hoy!
    For in his pipe he mad so mych joy.

(SRL, 11)

The carefree celebration of Wat's visit to the stable contrasts sharply
with the note of the foreboding which creeps into a number of the
**Nativity** lyrics, particularly the lullabies. Secular lullabies of the
period often included an element of foretelling the child's future
and poets used this model to remind their audience that cold and
poverty were only the first installment of this particular child's
sufferings. This fourteenth-century lyric (apparently adapted from a
secular lullaby) draws parallels between the child's present woes and
the pains of the **Passion** to come, concluding:

Lullay, l(ullay) litel child, litel child þin ore
It is al for oure owen gilt þat þu art peined sore;
but wolde we ȝet kinde be, & liuen after þi lore,
& leten senne for þi loue, ne keptst þu no more.
    Lullay, l(ullay) litel child, softe slep & faste.
    In sorwe endet eueri loue but þin at þe laste.

(CB XIV, 65)

In more than one poem the theme is given an interesting twist by
Mary's ignorance of the reason for her son's apprehension and the
opportunity this provides for him to enlighten her.

A baby is borne us blis to bring;
A maidden, I hard, 'Loullay' sing:
'Dere son, now leive thy wepping,
Thy fadere is the King of Blis.'

'Nay! dere modere, for you weppe I noght,
But for thinges that shall be wroght,
Or that I have mankind iboght.          *Before; bought (redeemed)*
Was ther never pain like it, iwis.'                      *indeed*

His exposition of the torments to come evokes the surprised
response:

'A! dere sone, that is a heivy cas.                    *sad plight*
When Gabrell knelled before my face
And said, "Heille! Lady full of grace,"
He never told me noothing of this.'

(*Medieval English Lyrics*, 102)

The feelings of compassion and **contrition** which the association of
future suffering with the vulnerable figure of a new-born child was
intended to evoke are beautifully articulated in a fourteenth-century
lullaby in which the speaker is gradually identified with Eve and
hence with all sinners:

Lullay, lullay, litel child,
Qui wepest thou so sore?

Lullay, lullay, litel child,
Thou that were so sterne and wild
Nou art become meke and mild                          *lost*
    To saven that was forlore.

But *for my senne I wot it is*                         *sin*
That Godis sone suffret this;
Merci, Lord. I have do mis;                            *wrong*
    Iwis, I wile no more . . .                         *indeed*

An appel I tok of a tre;
God it hadde forboden me;
Werfore I sulde dampned be,
    Yef thi weping ne wore.

Lullay for wo, thou litel thing,
Thou litle barun, thou litel king;                     *mourning*
Mankindde is cause of thi murning,                     *long*
    That thou hast loved so yore.

(*SRL*, 15)

## 'JESU, THAT DEYED UPON A TRE'

The **Passion** of Christ stood at the very heart of medieval
spirituality and the Church had no intention of letting anyone,
however simple or ignorant, miss its significance. Ordinary men and
women could hardly have helped being familiar with the image of
the crucified Saviour. Most **parish** churches would have been
dominated by the suffering figure on the cross (with the **Virgin**
and **St John** standing by) which hung on the **rood** screen between
the nave and the chancel. It is clear both from contemporary
accounts and from lists compiled by the iconoclasts of the sixteenth

and seventeenth centuries[9] that medieval churches both great and small were full of visual aids to devotion. Much of the stained glass and many of the statues were smashed and innumerable wall paintings obliterated during the Reformation; yet enough remains to show how vividly the lives of Christ and his **saints** were depicted. The value of such images in encouraging popular devotion was defended stoutly at the beginning of the fifteenth century by John Mirk:

> Herfor ben roodes sett on hey in holy chirch, and so by syght therof have mynd of Cristis passion. And therfor roodes and othyr images ben necessary in holy chirch, whateuer thes Lollardes sayn . . . For ymages and payntours [paintings] ben lewd menys bokys, and I say boldyly th[at] ther ben many thousand of pepul that couth not ymagen in her hert how Crist was don on the rood, but as thai lerne hit be syght of ymages and payntours.

(Festial, 171)

'Ymages and payntours' also shaped the thinking of **mystics** such as **Rolle** and **Julian of Norwich** who wrote: 'I leevyd sadlye all the peynes of Cryste as halye kirke schewys and techys, and also the payntyngs of crucyfexes that er made be the grace of god . . . to the lyknes of Crystes passyonn' (*ST*, 202). They must also have exercised a profound influence upon the lyric writers. It is no accident that lyrics such as 'Whanne ic se on Rode', with which this chapter began, constantly use words such as 'see' and 'behold'. Sight was considered the most powerful of all the senses; the sincere believer being urged to 'biholde' Christ 'wyt ey and herte bo [both]' (*SRL*, 32). The daily **liturgy** of the Church was also designed to bring the **Passion of Christ** constantly to mind. Of supreme importance was the **Mass**, in which Christ's sacrifice on the cross was recalled and which formed the basis for intercession for the spiritual needs of the people. Moreover, by the thirteenth century, each of the eight periods of worship which made up the **Daily Office** (Matins, Lauds, Prime, Terce, Sext, None, Vespers or Evensong and Compline) had become associated with an episode of the Passion. Many lay people were becoming familiar with these patterns of worship through a shortened version, known as ***The Little Office of the Blessed Virgin Mary***, available both in the often exquisitely illuminated **Books of Hours** which became fashionable from the mid-thirteenth century and the **Primers** of the fourteenth and fifteenth centuries.[10] This mid-fourteenth century lyric, a translation of a Latin hymn, typically allots a stanza to each stage of the **Passion**:

| | |
|---|---|
| At the time of Matines, Lord, thu were itake . . . | *Matins (early morning)* |
| At Prime, Lord, thu were ilad Pilat beforn . . . | *Prime (6 a.m.)* |
| At Underne, Lord, they gunnen thee to crucifiye . . . | *Terce (9 a.m.)* |
| At Midday, Lord, thu were nailed to the Rode . . . | *Rood (Cross)* |
| At the heiye Non, Lord, thu toke thy leve . . . | *None (3 p.m.)* |
| Of the Rode he was idon at the time of Evesong . . . | *taken* |
| At Cumplin time he was ibiriyed, and in a ston ipith. | *Compline; buried;* |
| | *tomb; put* |

(*Medieval English Lyrics*, 50)

The constant telling and retelling of the **Passion** story in word and picture was not designed simply to instruct the ignorant in the biblical narrative, but to kindle spiritual devotion. The Latin *Stabat Mater* expresses a desire to enter into the sufferings of Christ and his watching mother:

Sancta Mater, istud agas,
Crucifixi fige plagas
   Corde meo valide.
Tui Nati vulnerati,
Tam dignati pro me pati,
   Poenas mecum divide.

Fec me tecum pie flere
Crucifixo condolere
   Donec ego vixero;
Juxta crucem tecum stare
Et me tibi sociare
   In planctu desidero.

(31–42)

[Holy mother do this for me. Pierce my heart once and for ever with the wounds of your crucified Son. Let me share with you the pain of your Son's wounds, for He thought it right to bear such sufferings for me. Grant that my tears of love may mingle with yours and that, as long as I live, I may feel the pains of my crucified Lord. To stand with you beside the cross and be your companion in grief is my one wish.][11]

The desired reaction was that expressed by the writer of the lyric with which this chapter began: sorrow compounded of compassion and guilt, determination to turn away from the **sin** which made it necessary for Christ to die, and love given in return for love. Thus another fourteenth-century lyric asks:

Jesus, that has me dere iboght
Write thou gostly in my thoght
That I mow with devocion                              *spiritually*
Thinke on thy dere Passion . . .

Jesu, write this *that I might knowe*
*How michel love to thee I owe.*
                                                      *much*
(*Medieval English Lyrics*, 45)

In this cause no holds were barred. The hearts of men and women
were considered to be so hardened by **sin** that it was felt necessary
to dwell in horrific detail upon the sufferings of **Christ** in order to
shock them into genuine repentance and amendment of life. And a
world accustomed to brutality and bloodshed took some shocking.
It is important to keep this perspective in mind when reading some
of the more graphic details of the **Passion** lyrics. Writers dwelt
upon the sufferings of Christ, not out of a morbid fascination with
pain and blood but because those sufferings were part of the logic
of **salvation**. Contemporary theological thought emphasised the
role of Christ as willing sacrifice for the sins of men; therefore each
lash of the whip, each piercing of Christ's flesh, was to the
medieval mind an occasion for both infinite grief and infinite joy.
Hence the growth of popular devotion to the **Five Wounds of
Christ** and the Holy Blood. The extent of Christ's suffering was
evidence of the gravity of mankind's sin and was cause for
repentance; the willing endurance of the victim signalled the
greatness of his love for those he was rescuing from damnation and
was cause for thankfulness. Thus the 'swet passion' to which one
brief fourteenth-century lyric alludes was sweet not in itself but in
its results: the forgiveness of sinners.[12]

The mynde of thy swet passion, Jesu –
  Teres it tolles,                                    *draws*
  Eyene it bolles,                                    *swells*
  My vesage it wetes,                                 *face*
  And my hert it swetes.

(*SRL*, 31)

Poems on the Passion fall into three main categories: those such as
'Folwe St Bernardes trace' in which the reader is exhorted to
meditate; those such as 'Whanne ic se on Rode' which express the
meditator's response; and the dialogues or *complaints* in which Christ
himself speaks directly to the audience. All three are dominated by
the theme of Christ's love for mankind but it is perhaps the

*complaint* which is most highly charged with emotion. Here poets draw both on the **Old Testament** and the **liturgy**. The poem 'Ye that pasen by the weyye' (*SRL*, 26) is based on a reading used in the **Good Friday** services: 'O all ye that pass by the way, attend, and see if there be any sorrow like to my sorrow' (Lamentations 1:12). Also indebted to the **Good Friday** liturgy is this fourteenth-century lyric which recalls God's care for his people throughout the period of the Old Covenant and concludes:

> Ich yaf the croune of kynedom;                    *gave*
> And thou me yſt a croune of thorn . . .
>
> Ich muchel worshype doede to the;
> And thou me hongest on rode tre.
>
> My volk, what habe y do the,                      *people*
> Other in what thyng toened the?                    *injured*
> Gyn nouthe and onswere thou me.                    *begin now*
>                                                    (*SRL*, 29)

Charges of ingratitude and indifference are frequently laid at mankind's door. Sometimes the point is made with gentle irony as in this adaptation of a passage from the *Golden Legend* (de Voragine, i. 72–3):

> Jesus doth him bymene                              *complain*
>   And speketh to synful mon:
> 'Thi garland is of grene,
>   Of floures many on;
> Myn of sharpe thornes,
>   Myn hewe it maketh won.                           *pale*
>
> 'Thyn hondes streite gloved,
>   White and clene kept;
> Myne with nailes thorled                            *pierced*
>   On rode, and eke my feet . . .                    *also*
>
> 'Swete brother, wel myght thou se
> Thes peynes stronge in rode tre
> Have y tholed for love of the . . .                 *suffered*
> Let thi synne and love thou me.'                    *leave*
>                                                    (*SRL*, 30)

An aid to meditation which grew in importance during the fifteenth century and influenced the **Passion** lyrics was the *imago*

*pietatis* (image of pity). These pictures were frequently included in
**Primers** and **Books of Hours**, and prayers before such images
were a popular method of obtaining **indulgences**.[13] In these
drawings and illuminations the **Passion** was presented as an
eternally present reality: Christ was shown as alive and no longer
fastened to the cross, yet clearly displaying the marks of his
sufferings. Thus too in the fifteenth century poem *Wofully araide*,
which is accompanied in the Harley manuscript by a small drawing
of the *imago pietatis*, the events of the **Passion** are spoken of in the
past tense yet Christ's sufferings are presented as an ever-present
occasion for compassion and repentance:

> Wofully araide,                                                  *woefully arrayed*
>   My blode, man,
>   For the ran                                                    *thee*
> Hit may not be naide,                                            *denied*
>   My body blo and wanne,                                         *livid and pale*
> Wofully araide.
>
> Behold me, I pray the, with all thyne whole reson,
> And be not hard hertid, for this encheson . . .                 *reason*
>
> Thus naked am I nailid, O man, for thi sake.
> I love the, thenne love me.

> (*SRL*, 27)

Love is the recurring theme of these lyrics: God's love for men and
women (which **Julian of Norwich** perceived to be the whole
meaning behind her revelations) and the love which should be
offered in return. A number of human models are explored by
poets and **mystics** alike. **Christ** is portrayed as a brother, a friend,
even (startlingly) as a tender mother, but the prevailing image is
that of Christ as the lover of mankind: a great lord stooping to love
and win an unworthy and all-too-often unresponsive lady. The
concept of Christ the lover-knight, expounded also in the *Ancrene
Wisse*, sprang from the fusion of biblical imagery with medieval
social convention. The **Old Testament** Books of Jeremiah, Ezekiel
and Hosea portrayed God as the patient husband of a faithless and
ungrateful bride, willing to pay or fight for her recovery. The **New
Testament** continued the metaphor with Christ redeeming the
Church to be his Bride. Medieval theologians developed this motif,
emphasising love as the overriding motive and message of Christ's
sacrifice and (leaning heavily upon allegorisation of the Song of

Songs)[14] focusing on the individual soul rather than the Church as the object of Christ's wooing. Alongside these theological speculations had evolved the institution of chivalry: a curious blend of high ideals and harsh reality, a world where hard-bitten mercenaries jostled the heroes of courtly romances. It was a natural transition for the Old Testament **types** of the faithful husband, the brave warrior, and the importunate lover to be transmuted into medieval dress and emerge as the composite figure of the faithful knight, willing to fight, suffer and die for the love of his lady. A poem which taps deep into this rich vein of complex imagery and employs traditional images with considerable subtlety is 'In the vaile of restless mind', with its refrain *Quia amore langueo* (Because I languish for love) taken directly from the Song of Songs. The opening is that of a *chanson d'aventure*:

> In the vaile of restles mynde
> I sowght in mownteyn and in mede,
> Trustyng a treulofe for to fynd . . .

but the 'treulofe' whom the narrator discovers is close kin to the *imago pietatis*:

> From hede to fote wowndyd was he,
> Hys hert blode I saw bledyng,
> A semely man to be a king,
> A gracious face to loke unto.
> I asked him how he had paynyng.
> He said, 'Quia amore langueo'.      *because I languish for love*

Christ then describes with moving economy of style his love for his 'sister, mannys soule':

> I left my kyngdome gloriouse.
> I purveyed hyr a paleis preciouse.      *provided*
> She flytt, I folowyd; I luffed her soo.

The audience is reminded of the paradox of a loving God suffering at the hands of ungrateful mankind:

> My faire love, and my spouse bryght,
> I saved hyr fro betyng, and she hath me bett;
> I clothed hyr in grace and hevenly lyght,
> This blody surcote she hath on me sett.

Christ's account of his wooing and suffering interweaves the tone and imagery of the Song of Songs with the terminology of courtly love:

> I crownyd hyr with blysse, and she me with thorne,
>   I led hyr to chambre and she me to dye;
> I browght hyr to worship, and she me to skorne,
>   I dyd hyr reverence, and she me velanye . . .
>
> If she be rechelesse, I will be redy,               *heedless*
>   If she be dawngerouse, I will her pray . . .      *disdainful*
> Myn armes ben spred to clypp her to . . .           *embrace*
>
> My swete spouse, will we goo play?
>   Apples ben rype in my gardine;
> I shall clothe the in new array,
>   Thy mete shall be mylk, honye and wyne.

To these carefully crafted biblical references the poet adds one more image of tenderness, less predictable in its context but no less scriptural.

> My spouse is in hir chambre, hald yowr pease,
>   Make no noyse, but lat hyr slepe.
> My babe shall sofre noo disease,
>   I may not here my dere childe wepe,
>   For with my pappe I shall hyr kepe.
> No wonder though I tend hyr to –
>   Thys hoole in my syde had never ben so depe
> But *quia amore langueo*.

> (*SRL*, 43)

The image of **Christ** as mother, used also by **St Anselm** in his *Prayer to St Paul* and **Julian of Norwich** in her *Revelations* (*LT*, Ch. 59), was derived from several biblical passages (Isaiah 49:15, 66:13; Matt. 23:37).

## 'BLESSED MARY, MODER VIRGINAL'

Like her son, **Mary** was a multi-faceted figure. She was at one and the same time the pure Virgin, example to all, the human mother with whom frail mortals could identify and the glorious yet compassionate Queen of Heaven to whom sinners could plead for mercy. Just as Christ was considered a 'second Adam' born to redeem Adam's **sin**, so Mary was regarded as a 'second Eve' whose obedience opened again the way to **heaven**. This thirteenth-century macaronic lyric uses the common idea that the angel's salutation to Mary reversed the infamous name of Eve:

| | |
|---|---|
| All this world was forlore | *utterly lost* |
| Eva peccatrice | *through Eve the sinner* |
| Till our Lord was ibore | |
| De te genetrice | *of you, the mother* |
| With 'Ave' it went away | |
| Thuster night, and cometh the day. | *dark* |
| Salutis. | *of salvation* |
| | *(Medieval English Lyrics, 5)* |

The cult of the **Virgin** blossomed in the Western Church from the twelfth century onwards, and was extremely popular in England where **Anselm**, **Archbishop** of Canterbury, was one of its chief advocates. In 1215 the **Fourth Lateran Council** added the **Ave Maria** to the **Paternoster** and the **Creed** as essential learning for every lay-person, thus making devotion to Mary a central element of lay piety. Legends of Mary's birth, betrothal and assumption into heaven were absorbed into Western doctrine from the Eastern Church. Collections of stories known as *Miracles of the Virgin* circulated widely and theological recognition of Mary's unique role within the story of salvation grew into a popular perception of her as the 'Mother of Mercy', uniquely approachable and compassionate to sinners. This view was clearly articulated in **Bernard of Clairvaux**'s *Sermon on the Nativity of the Virgin*:

> Perhaps you also fear the divine majesty in Him, for, though it was permitted that He should become man, yet he remained God. Do you want an advocate to plead with Him? Then turn to Mary . . . I tell you certainly that she will be heard because of the reverence due to her. The Son hears the prayer of His mother, and the Father hears the prayer of His Son. My little children, this is the sinners' ladder, this is the firm ground of my confidence, this is the whole reason of my hope.[15]

A number of lyric writers took **St Bernard**'s advice, and adopted his argument:

| | |
|---|---|
| Haill! quene of hevin, and steren of blis; | *star* |
| Sen that thi sone thi fader is, | |
| How suld he ony thing the warn, | *refuse* |
| And thou his mothir, and he thi barne? | |
| | *(SRL, 62)* |

**Mary**'s intercession was particularly valued at the hour of death, when devils stood ready to snatch the sinful soul:

> At myn endyng þou stonde by me,
> When I schal heþen founded and fare,
> When þat I quake and dredful be
> And alle my synnes I rewe hem sare;
> As euer my hope haþ ben in þe,
> Þenke þer-on, leuedi, helpe me þare.

(CB XIV, 93)

The *Liber Celestis* of **St Bridget** showed **Satan** complaining about the souls which the **Virgin** had saved from his clutches (477). According to the *Miracles of the Virgin* her help could be relied upon by devotees of her cult, however great their iniquities.[16] The lyric poets also reflected upon the theme of the **Sorrows of the Virgin**. The biblical narrative simply recorded Mary's presence at the **Crucifixion** (John 19:25) and early tradition held that she bore the ordeal with quiet fortitude. Later writers, however, explored the grief and confusion which she might be supposed to have experienced and there are a number of *complaints* of the Virgin, including this simple yet moving dialogue with her son, in which she is consigned to the care of **St John**:

MARIA:
> Mi suete sone þat art me dere,
> Wat hast þu don, qui art þu here?
> Þi suete bodi þat in me rest,
> Þat loueli mouth þat i haue kist, –
> Nou is on rode mad þi nest.
> Mi dere child, quat is me best?

IHESUS:
> Ion, þis womman for my sake,
> Womman to Ion, I þe betake.
> Alone i am with-oten make,
> On rode i hange for mannis sake,
> Þis gamen alone me must pleyʒe
> For mannis soule þis det to deyʒe.

(CB XIV, 67)

Other laments of the Virgin, designed to invite the remorseful compassion of the audience, derived from the popular image of the *pietà*. An account of this scene (not part of the biblical narrative) occurs in Bridget's revelations: 'þare come of his freendis and tuke him downe of þe crosse, and his modir tuke him in hir armes and sat downe with him, and laide him on hir knee, all torent and wounded' (*Liber Celestis*, 481). Statues and paintings of Christ lying dead in his mother's arms must have been common before the iconoclasts swept them away. **Margery Kempe**'s reaction to one such image is recorded in her book: 'through looking at that *pietà* her mind was wholly occupied with the Passion of our Lord Jesus Christ and with the compassion of our Lady, St Mary, by which she was compelled to cry out very loudly and weep very bitterly, as though she would have died' (Ch. 61). In this fifteenth-century lyric Mary appeals to other mothers for whose children her son died:

> Off alle women þat euer were borne
> þat berys childur, abyde and se
> How my son liggus me beforne                    *lies*
> Upon my kne, takyn fro tre.
> Your childur ȝe dawnse upon your kne
> With laȝyng, kyssyng and mery chere;            *laughing*
> Be-holde my childe, be-holde now me,
> for now liggus ded my dere son, dere.
>
> (CB XV, 7)

In some lyrics the Virgin becomes so identified with her son's sufferings than it is possible to speak of a 'double passion', a concept supported by the influential visions of St Bridget, in which Mary declares:

> Also I was nerere in þe passion and I went noȝt awai. I stode nerrere to his crosse, and right as þat prikkes sarer and sharplier þat is nerest to þe hert, so was my sorowe more greuouse to me þan was ani oþir þat stode beside. When he loked fro þe crosse to me and I to him, þan went þe teres oute of mi eyn as blode oute of vaines . . . And þarefore I sai to þe plainli, þat *his sorowe was mi sorowe for his hert was mi hert*. Right as Adam and Eve sald þe werld for ane appill, *so mi son and I boght againe þe werld as with one hert*.
>
> (*Liber Celestis*, 63)

It is interesting in this connection to compare the two poems which share the refrain *Quia amore langueo*. 'In the vaile of restles mynd', examined above, shows **Christ**, 'a semely man to be a king', complaining of his sufferings and declaring his love for mankind. 'In a tabernacle of a toure', written by a different poet, reveals **Mary**, 'a crouned queen' who appeals to men and women to leave their sin 'for my sake'. The second poem is full of images which were associated with Christ himself and concludes with the invitation:

> 'Nowe, man, have mynde on me forever,
>    Loke on thy love thus languysshyng;
> Late us never fro other dissevere,                    *part*
> Myne helpe is thyne oune, crepe under my wynge
> Thy syster is a quene, thy brother a kynge,
> Thys heritage is tayled – sone, come therto,          *arranged*
> Take me for thy wyfe and lerne to synge,
>    *Quia amore langueo.'*
>
>                                                (*SRL*, 61)

A further example is noted by Owst, who cites a sermon in which Christ's words 'Come to me all who labour and are heavy-laden' (Matthew 11:28) are put instead into the mouth of Mary: 'Ther is . . . no vice in man but ther aȝeyn she hath bote salve and remedie; and therfore she may sey well to all men thise wordes. Mt XI^mo: *Venite ad me omnes qui laboratis* . . . "Commeth to me all ȝe that traveyll or ben charched with synne and I shall refresh you".'[17] A possible explanation of these striking parallels is the fact that the Virgin was also regarded as the symbol of the Church and, as such, empowered to speak Christ's words to the world.

Not all Marian lyrics are characterised by grief and pathos. Mary's life, like that of Christ, illustrated the theme that obedient suffering would in due time lead to glory and honour. The lyrics which celebrate the **Five Joys** of Mary, such as 'O lady, sterre of Jacob' (*SRL*, 64) and 'Ase I me rod this ender day' (*Medieval English Lyrics*, 20), put her sorrows into eternal perspective. With the rise of the secular love lyric at the end of the fourteenth century, poems in praise of Mary also became increasingly expressive and her beauty, purity and mercy were lauded in terms which mirrored the language of courtly love:

> Of alle floures feirest fall on
> And þat is Marie, Moder fre,
> Þat bar þe child of flesh and bon
> Ihesu, Godes sone in Maieste.
> A loue-likyng is come to me
> To serue þat ladi, qwen of blis.
>
>                                                (CB XIV, 111)

Just as theologians had identified people and events in the **Old Testament** as foreshadowing the life and ministry of Christ, so too the figure of **Mary** was surrounded with images and associations. A fourteenth-century lyric, 'Mary, maide, milde and fre' (*Medieval English Lyrics*, 34), attributed to William of Shoreham, lists in somewhat uninspired fashion many of the figures with which Mary was identified. She is 'chambre of the Trinitee' (a somewhat inexact theological concept), 'Quene of paradis', 'colvere of Noe' [Noah's dove], 'the temple [of] Salomon' and all the heroines of the **Old Testament** in one. From the Old Testament came also the tradition of representing Mary as a flower, in particular a lily or a rose (Song of Songs 2:1, Ecclesiasticus 24:18): images carrying connotations of both beauty and chastity.

> Ther is no rose of swych vertu
> As is the rose that bare Jesu;
>   *Alleluya*.
>
> For in this rose conteynyd was
> Heven and erthe in lytyl space,
>   *Res miranda*.

(SRL, 12)

### 'THINK ON DREDFUL DOMESDAY'

The ultimate aim of the religious lyrics was to induce penitence and reformation of life. The tears which many lyrics sought to induce were to be not empty emotionalism but evidence of inner change. The ominous Doomsday scenes which dominated the chancel arches of many parish churches were potent reminders that the loving Saviour would in time return as stern Judge. The devastation wrought by the Black Death in the fourteenth century and the general frailty of human life were reflected both in the visual arts and in poetry. The fear of death, the transience of life's joys and the impotence of the guilty soul facing the wrath of God were themes which undergirded a number of lyrics. A lyric such as this sombre fifteenth-century warning to unheeding merrymakers may well have caused **Margery Kempe** to spring out of bed, crying, 'Alas that ever I sinned! It is full merry in heaven!' (Ch. 3)

> Gay, gay, gay, gay,
> Think on dredful Domesday

Think, man, on thy sinnes sevene,
Think how merye it is in Hevene:
Prey to God, with milde stevene,                              *voice*
He be thine help on Domesday.

(Medieval English Lyrics, 67)

Sudden death was greatly feared because it left no time in which to
make one's peace with God. Hence this plaintive appeal:

Farewell this world! I take my leve for evere;
  I am arested to apere at Goddes face.
O myghtyfull God, thou knowest I had levere
  Than all this world to have oone houre space
To make asythe for all my grete trespace.                   *reparation*

(SRL, 89)

Above all men and women should not be deceived into thinking
this world to be the ultimate reality. This popular translation of a
Latin hymn speaks for many others of its kind:

The joye of this wrechid world is a short feste –
It is likenyd to a shadewe that may not long leste.

And yit it drawith man fro hevene riche blis,
And ofte tyme makith hym to synne and do amys.

Calle no thing thyn owene therfor, that thow maist her lese;
That the lord hath lent the, eft he wole it cese.

Sette thyn herte in heven above, and thynke what joye is there,
And thus to dispise the world I rede that thow lere.     *counsel; learn*

(SRL, 85)

NOTES

1.   Other lyrics quoted in the text are taken from *A Selection of Religious Lyrics*
     (*SRL*) (Gray), *English Lyrics of the Thirteenth Century* (CB XIII), *Religious Lyrics*
     *of the Fourteenth Century* (CB XIV), *Religious Lyrics of the Fifteenth Century* (CB
     XV) and *A Selection of English Carols* (*SEC*) (Greene).
2.   See Wenzel (1986).
3.   Robbins (1940).
4.   See Jeffrey (1975, Chs 1 & 5); Wenzel (1986, 17); *SEC* (1962, 12).
5.   Southern (1953, 227).
6.   See Gray (1972, 102–6) and Raw (1960).

7. *Speculum Ecclesiae*. Cited Raw (1960, 411).

8. See *SEC* (1962) for the *carol*'s history and relationship to the dance.

9. See Gray (1972, 42–6).

10. See Barrett (1975).

11. Connelly (1957, 188).

12. Compare St Paul: 'God forbid that I should glory, save in the cross of our Lord Jesus Christ, by whom the world is crucified to me and I to the world' (Gal. 6:14).

13. Barrett (1975, 269).

14. The Old Testament Song of Songs (Canticles) is an expressive love poem interpreted by commentators such as Bernard of Clairvaux as an allegory of the love between Christ and the Church or Christ and the individual soul.

15. *Patrologia Latina* 183, 441. Cited Woolf (1968, 118).

16. See *Middle English Miracles of the Virgin*, (1964).

17. Owst (1955, 20); see also Graef (1985, 85ff).

# Chapter 8

# The *Pearl*-Poet

Nov ar we sore and synful and sovly vchone;            *unclean; everyone*
How schulde we se, þen may we say, þat Syre vpon throne?    *see; Lord*
3is, þat Mayster is mercyable, þa3 þou be man fenny,        *sinful*
And al tomarred in myre whyle þou on molde lyuyes; *spoiled; mire; earth*
Þou may schyne þur3 schryfte, þa3 þou haf schome serued,
                                        *confession; shame; deserved*
And pure þe with penaunce tyl þou a perle worþe.   *purify; until; become*
                                        (*Cleanness*, 1111–16)[1]

At first glance it may be hard to see what a pair of **homily**-poems,
a vision of **heaven** prompted by the death of a daughter and a
light-hearted, sophisticated Arthurian romance have in common.
Yet a number of factors have led scholars to conclude that *Patience,
Cleanness (Purity), Pearl* and *Sir Gawain and the Green Knight*, which
appear together in a late fourteenth-century manuscript, are the
work of the same poet;[2] not the least of these factors being the
consistent spiritual perspective which they display. The *Pearl*-poet
was clearly a man of considerable artistry and technical flexibility.
His work belongs to a period of transition: English as a literary
medium was blossoming, with both Chaucer and Gower producing
works in English for an audience which included members of the
court. Though the *Pearl*-poet used the native alliterative forms,
which Chaucer's Parson affected to despise (*Parson's Prologue*, 43),
there is nothing naive about his approach. The poems reflect a
considerable range of knowledge and sophistication of thought,
both secular and theological. Spiritually, the *Pearl*-poet was
unmistakably a man of his time. Like Langland and Chaucer he was
well aware of the spiritual perils lurking in the everyday world; like
the **mystics** he wanted to explore spiritual dimensions which the
mind of man could not reach unaided. He shared with the
preachers and lyric-writers a strongly developed sense of drama and
with the creators of the mystery plays an equally strong sense of the
ridiculous. Throughout the poems runs the theme of the difference

between appearance and reality, coupled with an uncompromising assertion of the existence of an unseen world whose priorities mankind would do well to study. His characters are frequently seen facing up to the gulf between their own behaviour and the pearl-like purity which God is shown to require; their penitential progress, however unsteady, is designed to offer both challenge and hope to his audience.

## PEARL

It is ironic that this exquisitely-wrought poem should have become a scholarly battleground. For decades arguments have raged over the meaning of the Pearl, the role of the Dreamer, the doctrinal soundness of the poem[3] and its genre. It has variously been classified as an elegy,[4] an allegory[5] (in part or whole), and most recently (and persuasively) as a *consolatio*:[6] a poem designed not so much to commemorate the dead as to strengthen and sustain the mourner. The stated occasion of the poem is the loss of a precious possession, a 'perle withouten spot', which is gradually identified as the poet's daughter[7] who has died before reaching the age of two. Mourning beside her grave, the narrator falls asleep and experiences an encounter with his lost child (now dazzlingly attired as a Pearl-Maiden), a theological debate and a vision of **heaven** which leaves him resolved to lead a life which will ensure his own **salvation**. The charm of *Pearl* (and the cause of so much critical debate) is the fact that it works on so many levels. The poet's skill ensures that it is never just a poem about a dead child, just a theological debate or just a beautifully constructed series of descriptive passages. The search for truth lends depth and intellectual toughness to a story of human emotion and the poet's careful selection of backgrounds and descriptive details echo and inform each stage of the narrator's journey of discovery. At its simplest *Pearl* presents a tale of human tragedy: a man loses a beloved child and seeks to come to terms with his loss within the context of a Christian world-view. The poet's use of language and images is however anything but simple: fresh layers of meaning and hints of the eventual outcome emerge with each reading of the poem.

The opening stanzas are apparently dominated by human emotion as the narrator outlines the perfection of the loved one (in terms which belong to *fin amour*), the extent to which his happiness depended upon her, and his inconsolable grief at her loss. Yet the poet is in fact already establishing a dual perception of reality within the poem. In the very first line the narrator claims that 'his' pearl is worthy of a prince. In fact he speaks truer than he knows and by the last line of the poem he will have come to acknowledge that her true owner is the indeed the Prince of Peace, Christ himself. His anguish is accentuated by the horror of physical decay which haunted the medieval psyche:

| | |
|---|---|
| O moul, þou marrez a myry juele, | *earth; disfigure; beautiful* |
| My priuy perle withouten spotte. | *special; blemish* |
| | (23–4) |

yet, since even secular wisdom believed that pearls could resist tarnishing, it appears that his vision is clouded by more than tears. Pearls represented purity and incorruptibility and, just as pearls were seen as more enduring than flowers, so the soul was regarded as more enduring than the body. The use of the pearl image reminds the poet's audience of a doctrine which the narrator clearly knows in theory but is equally clearly unable to grasp in practice. He describes the garden in which the pearl is buried in terms which echo **Christ**'s promises of resurrection to his followers ('I say to you, unless the grain of wheat falling into the ground, die, itself remaineth alone. But if it die, it bringeth forth much fruit': Jn 12: 24, 25; 'I am the resurrection and the life: he that believeth in me, although he be dead, shall live': Jn 11:25'):

| | |
|---|---|
| Flor and fryte may not be fede | *flower; fruit; cannot be faded* |
| Þer hit doun drof in moldez dunne, | *sank down into dun (grey-brown) earth* |
| For vch gresse mot grow of graynez dede; | *plant; seeds; dead* |
| No whete were ellez to wonez wonne. | *wheat; harvested* |
| | (29–32) |

The setting of the vision in harvest-time[8] reinforces the biblical imagery, yet the narrator draws no encouragement from the parallel. His grief, though completely understandable, borders on the immoderate, a fault against which the *consolatio* poems of the early Christian era warned. Indeed, the only explicitly Christian reference in this section of the poem merely emphasises that the narrator is failing to draw much-needed comfort from his faith:

| | |
|---|---|
| Þaȝ kynde of Kryst me comfort kenned, | *nature; taught* |
| My wreched wylle in wo ay wraȝte. | *was tormented* |
| | (55–6) |

Since the Dreamer is later rebuked by the Maiden specifically for his discourtesy in disbelieving Christ (301–5), this passage would seem to deserve more attention than it usually receives. P. M. Kean suggests that 'kynde of Kryst' should be translated 'Nature, through Christ,'[9] but the generally accepted rendering, 'nature of Christ', would seem to make much more theological sense. Other contemporary uses of *kynde* to describe Christ's nature include a commentary on Revelation 4:3 (c. 1340–70):

> By þe colours of þe stones bitokened þe two kyndes al miʒtty, þe godhede & þe Manhede.
>
> (*English Fourteenth Century Apocalypse*, 30)

and two references in *Cursor Mundi*:

> Thoru þe kind of his manhede, þat fode of body has of nede.
>
> (1874)

> þe kyng of blis
> Þat coupled þus oure kynde to his.
>
> (18804)

The proffered comfort sprang from the Christian belief that in Christ the divine and human natures were combined: as a man who had experienced both bereavement and the pains of death, he could be relied upon to sympathise with the human condition (Hebrews 4:14, 15); as the Son of God who triumphed over death, he offered the hope of resurrection to all his followers (Jn 6:39, 40). The narrator however does not want comfort; he wants his pearl. There is, therefore, more than a suspicion that neither the narrator's priorities in life nor his spiritual understanding are what they should be and that these factors contribute significantly to his desolation. He has described himself as languishing, grievously wounded by separation from his beloved, a line which evokes not only the terminology of courtly love but phrases from the Song of Songs often applied by theologians and lyric writers to love for Christ. A medieval preacher, commenting on the commandment 'You shall have no other gods before me (Exodus 20:3), states: 'No þinge shuld be more loved þan God; for what þinge þat man or vyman loveþ most, þat þei vorshippe as here god, in as muche as in þam is, be it wiff or childe, golde, siluer or catell' (*Middle English Sermons*, 106–7). If the narrator has allowed love for another human being to displace the priority of love for **Christ** and dependence upon his love, then his problems are greater even than the loss of a child. None of these problems can be resolved, however, by the use of the human mind or reason alone. It is therefore necessary to move into the world of revelation. Exhausted by grief and incapable of further progress on his own, the narrator falls asleep on the grave:

| | |
|---|---|
| Fro spot my spyryt þer sprang in space; | *spirit; ascended* |
| My body on balke þer bod. In sweuen | *remained; mound; dream* |
| My goste is gon in Godez grace, | *spirit; through God's grace* |
| In auenture þer meruaylez meuen. | *on a quest; marvels occur* |
| | (61–4) |

The ensuing vision seems to belong to the type described in the *Chastising of God's Children* as a 'spiritual vision or imagynatif, whan a man is in his sleepe, or whanne a man is rauysshed fulli in spirit in tyme of preier . . . as seint ion þe euangelist . . . say [saw] many figuris and imagis, as we rede in þe apocalips' (169). Instantly the fragile, perishable beauty of the earthly garden is replaced by a dazzling new world, usually identified as the Earthly Paradise,[10] of 'crystal klyffez', leaves which slide over each other 'as bornyst syluer', paths covered with pearls and a river bed glinting with precious stones. Grief is temporarily forgotten in wonder (121–3). The object of this particular exercise, however, is not oblivion but understanding, and thus he is swiftly confronted with the cause of his grief:

| | |
|---|---|
| A mayden of menske, ful debonere; | *courteous; gracious in manner* |
| Blysnande whyt watz hyr bleaunt; | *shining white, mantle* |
| I knew hyr wel, I hade sen hyr ere. | *before* |
| | (162–4) |

Pearls dominate the portrait of the fashionably-dressed Maiden: pearls on her gleaming white garments, pearls in her crown and (most significantly of all) a pearl of supreme beauty and perfection worn at her breast. The appearance of the Pearl-Maiden, like yet strangely unlike his lost love, together with the unearthly unfamiliarity of her setting combine to unnerve the Dreamer and signal that this is not the end of his quest but the beginning of his enlightenment. This is unquestionably the Maiden's own perspective on the situation. Like those familiar female figures of instruction, **Boethius**'s Lady Philosophy, Langland's Holy Church, and Dante's Beatrice, her concern is the imparting of truth. Understandably enough for one who sees life from the perspective

of **heaven**, she has no time to spare for peripheral issues or
emotions; her purpose is to bring her erring parent to a proper
appreciation of eternal verities. Her incisive comments and
corrections may not be what the Dreamer wants but they are what
he needs. Since the loss of the pearl was not the root cause of his
problems, her re-discovery will not in itself meet his needs. Thus
the theological debate which follows relentlessly conducts the
Dreamer through a radical re-evaluation of his spiritual attitudes
until he eventually reaches a point of humility and submission to
God's will. The Maiden's initial points correspond with the basic
tenets of the classical *consolatio*.[11] Firstly she corrects the Dreamer's
error in believing her lost:

> 'Sir, ȝe haf your tale mysetente,            *spoken heedlessly*
> To say your perle is al awaye,              *pearl; entirely lost*
> Þat is in cofer so comly clente       *coffer; beautifully enclosed*
> As in þis garden gracios gaye.'
>
> (257–60)

She rebukes him for fixing his heart on something as transient as a
rose and chides him for his lack of faith in God's promise of
resurrection (301–6). She is scathing in condemnation of his
presumption in hoping to join her immediately and unsympathetic
when he lurches into despair. Excessive grief could lead him into
**sin**; instead she counsels submission to the will of God (341–3).
The opening stanzas of their encounter confirm the Dreamer's
problems: his perceptions and his priorities are in need of
transformation. He relies too heavily on what he 'may with yȝen
se', rejoicing when he should be cautious and despairing when he
should exercise faith. He constantly speaks of 'my' pearl, the *grounde*
(foundation) of all his happiness, and there is an unmistakeable
rebuke in the Maiden's statement that in fact she belongs to **Christ**,
'My Lorde þe Lamb', who is 'þe grounde' of *her* 'blysse' (407–8).
Though it may seem over-long to modern readers, the subsequent
debate between the Dreamer and his re-discovered treasure is deftly
and humorously handled. The doting father who described his child
as 'withouten spot' is disconcerted by the discovery that God
apparently shares his opinion. As an innocent[12] (a child whose
**original sin** had been cleansed by **baptism** and who had not had
time to commit sins on her own account), she has gone straight to
heavenly bliss. Bewilderment at her claim that Christ has 'corounde
me quene' is only partly eased by her explanation of the superior

'courtaysye' which rules in **heaven**. Parental pride continues to strive with a sense of parental justice:

| | |
|---|---|
| That Courtayse is to fre of dede | *liberal* |
| ȝyf hyt be soth þat thou conez saye. | *true; you say* |
| Þou lyfed not two ȝer in oure þede; | *years; land* |
| Þou cowþez neuer God nauþer plese ne pray, | *never knew how to please God or pray* |
| | |
| Ne neuer nawþer Pater ne Cred – | *Paternoster, Creed* |
| And quen mad on þe fyrst day! | *made a queen; first* |
| | (481–6) |

His understandable resentment gives the maiden the opening she requires: armed with a battery of biblical quotations she embarks upon an exposition of the doctrine of **salvation** which is designed not only to meet the Dreamer's emotional and intellectual needs but also to challenge his spiritual condition. Her interpretation of the Parable of the Vineyard (Matthew 20:1-16) claims that length of service is not the deciding factor in the allocation of heavenly rewards. There is no such thing as partial salvation; no one who serves **Christ** could ask for more than entrance to **heaven** and by his grace he will not give less to any of his servants, however brief their allegiance to Him. The orthodoxy of categorising an infant who died before reaching the age of responsibility with the labourers who entered the vineyard an hour before sunset has been questioned but Ian Bishop defends the poet, citing a similar interpretation in the twelfth-century writings of Honorius of Autun.[13] When the Dreamer, probably identifying with those 'Þat swange and swat for long ȝore', still rejects her words as 'vnresounable', she swiftly reminds him that the key question is one not of man's merit but of God's **grace**, her **homily** implying a marked contrast between her own security and the Dreamer's still perilous position. Medieval belief regarded **baptism** as ensuring a clean spiritual slate for the newborn child, erasing the traces of **original sin** inherited from Adam 'oure forme fader'. **St Augustine** had stated that: 'If the child has received the sacrament . . . then even if his life ends at this age . . . not only is he not destined for everlasting pains, but he will not even undergo any purifying torment after death' (*City of God*, XXXI, 16). The longer men and women remained in a fallen world, however, the more numerous the temptations to stray from God's path. Thus Langland's Haukyn complained:

Allas . . . that after my cristendom,                                                 *baptism*
I ne hadde be deed and dolven for Dowelis sake!                    *dead and buried*
                                                         (*Piers Plowman*, XIV, 320–2)

Those wavering in their earthly pilgrimage could be restored to a state of grace through the **sacrament** of **penance**, a point made also in *Cleanness*:

Þou may schyne þurʒ schryfte, þaʒ þou haf schome serued,              *shame;*
                                                                        *deserved*

And pure þe with penaunce tyl þou a perle worþe              *purify; become*
                                                         (*Cleanness*, 1115–16)

This, however, was a costly and, as the Maiden remorselessly observes, a much less certain route than her own assured acceptance in a state of unsullied baptismal innocence:

'Grace innogh þe mon may haue                                          *enough*
Þat synnez þenne new, ʒif hym repente,                                  *anew*
Bot with sorʒ and syt he mot it craue,                         *contrition; grief*
And byde þe payne þerto is bent.                          *endure; pain; attached*
Bot Resoun, of ryʒt þat con not raue,             *Reason; justice; cannot go astray*
Sauez euermore þe innossent.'                                      *always saves*
                                                                      (661–6)

The Dreamer has failed to see the great spiritual advantage of her youth: as a baptised infant, cleansed from sin and below the age of accountability, she inhabited a brief but highly privileged oasis of innocence. Like the Holy Innocents, all also under the age of two, who died in Herod's attempt to slay the infant Christ (Matt. 2:16–18), she was able to bypass the struggles and failures of adult life and enter as of 'ryʒt' into the kingdom of God. Mirk makes the same point in his homily for the Feast of the **Holy Innocents**: 'Þis Innocentes þat holy chyrche syngeþ of, lyueded her wyþout schame, for Þay wer all wiþin two yer of age . . . þes chyldyr lyued not so long forto know þe good from þe euell, but wern jslayne wiþin degre of jnnocentes' (*Festial*, 35). The Maiden warns that the Dreamer and his fellows would be unwise to rely on their own good deeds and service being sufficient to allow them to also enter **heaven** by right, counselling him to seek to be restored to a state of **grace** equivalent to the innocence of childhood. The same parallel is drawn in the commentary on the *Fourteenth-Century English Apocalypse*: 'Þe sterres of Þe cite bitokeneþ þe symple folk in holy chirche þat ben abrode in þe werlde . . . þai shullen ben clere as glas þorouʒ Innocence of baptesme oiþer þorouʒ sooþfast schrift & riʒth bileue' (193–4). Christ, the Maiden points out, taught:

Hys ryche no wyȝ myȝt wynne
Bot he com þyder ryȝt as a chylde . . .
Harmlez, trwe, and vndefylde,
Withouten mote oþer mascle of sulphande synne.

*kingdom; no one could win*
*absolutely like*
*guiltless; undefiled*
*spot; defiling*
(722–3, 725–6)

The role-reversal between parent and child is now complete: she is not only his instructor but also his example in the spiritual life. He has no need to be concerned for her well-being and eternal destiny but he would do well to look to his own. The Maiden's **homily** becomes even more pointed as she retells the Parable of the Pearl of Great Price (Matt. 13:45, 46), making the protagonist not just a merchant, as in the original, but specifically a jeweller, the title which the Dreamer has already claimed for himself (252 ff). The 'makellez perle' for which the jeweller is willing to surrender all that he possesses, is described in terms which echo and yet surpass the lost pearl of the opening stanza of the poem. Here we have side by side two of the three key versions of the pearl image contained within the poem (the third being human souls). The Dreamer's lost human pearl is seen wearing on her breast the 'flawless, pure, bright' pearl which symbolises salvation and admission to heaven. The Dreamer's perceived need and his true need are thus powerfully juxtaposed. The Maiden does not hesitate to drive home the message:

I rede þe forsake þe worlde wode
And porchace þe perle maskelles.

*counsel*
*spotless*
(743–4)

The Dreamer, not yet ready to tackle this direct spiritual challenge, employs diversionary tactics, inevitably revealing his earthbound thought processes. A flattering comment on the Maiden's beauty prompts an account of the grace she has received from the 'makelez Lambe' who has chosen her as his bride:

In Hys blod He wesch my wede on dese,
And coronde clene in vergynté
And pyȝt me in perlez maskellez

*clothing; dais*
*crowned pure in virginity*
*arrayed; spotless*
(766–8)

She is one of the 144,000 pure souls identified in the Book of Revelation as those who 'are not defiled with women; for they are virgins' who 'follow the Lamb whithersoever he goeth' (Rev 14:4).

This verse was used as the Chapter (the one-verse scripture reading) at the Office of Sext on the Feast of the Holy Innocents. Wellek[14] has shown that it was theologically consistent for the Maiden to be included in this company, even though her purity was due to youth rather than to later choice. The particular association between pearls and virginity is examined by Luttrell.[15] In a significant shift of emphasis, the Maiden turns from the cut-and-thrust of theological discussion to focus the Dreamer's attention on Christ the Lamb, sacrificed in the earthly Jerusalem and worshipped in the New Jerusalem revealed to the **Apostle John**. Her account of the death of Christ, which draws on **Old Testament** prophecy (Isaiah 53) as well as the **New Testament** narrative (Matt. 26:67; Mark 14:61; John 19:1), is infused with an emotion reminiscent of the religious lyrics:

| | |
|---|---|
| In Jerusalem watz my Lemman slayn | *was; Love* |
| And rent on rode with boyez bolde, | *torn; Cross; by wicked ruffians* |
| Al oure balez to bere ful bayn | *griefs; bear; readily* |
| He toke on Hymself oure carez colde: | *sorrows; grievous* |
| With boffetez watz Hys face flayn | *blows; scourged* |
| Þat watz so fayr on to byholde. | |

(805–10)

That death, by which Christ took upon himself the sins of mankind, is the source of her present security and joyful relationship with the Lamb (857–61). If the Dreamer could only share her confidence then his grief would be assuaged and his future assured. To this end she employs her final and most powerful means of enlightenment: a direct vision of the heavenly city. She can tell him no more; he must see for himself. It is with the vision of the New Jerusalem that the teaching of the scriptures, the testimony of the Maiden, and the Dreamer's own experience at last fuse and become one.

| | |
|---|---|
| As John þe apostel hit syȝ with syȝt, | *saw in a vision* |
| I syȝe þat city of gret renoun | *saw* |

(985–6)

Sight was regarded as the most powerful of all the senses in the Middle Ages and part of the impact of a vision was that it enabled the recipient to 'see' what had previously only been taught. The Dreamer's somewhat uneven spiritual progress through the poem can be charted in terms of a series of transitions from theoretical acceptance of traditional belief to 'seeing' for himself and believing in earnest. Standing in anguish by his daughter's grave, he finds the concept of life after death unavailing; transported to the riverside, he rejoices to see her alive and well. By the river the Maiden does her best to point him to the Lamb and the Heavenly City; yet it is not till he sees both for himself that his heart is fired with spiritual longing.

The description of the New Jerusalem has been criticised both for its length and for being no more than a ponderous paraphrase of the biblical text. The poet would no doubt have been anxious not to depart from a source of such authority, yet it is also apparent that he is a writer for whom settings are of crucial importance. Each of the three settings in the poem is far more than a mere theatrical backdrop, the garden of loss and the landscape where the Dreamer encounters the Maiden both being built up with meticulous care and charged with significance. The careful depiction of the New Jerusalem is even more vital, for the Dreamer is being prepared for his own vision of Christ. If the Dreamer, and through him the poet's audience, are to be motivated to seek the Lamb and the city where he dwells, then they must see that city vividly and unforgettably. This is the poet's aim. No detail may be omitted yet he can and does add touches of his own.[16] He paints a city resplendent with colour and light; as beautiful as anything earth can offer, yet untarnished by corruption, dirt or despair. Here indeed is a fit setting for the purity of the Lamb and his entourage. This point is underlined by a deliberate and dramatic divergence from the progression of the biblical narrative. The biblical description of the city (Rev. 21) is immediately followed by the exhortations to heed the vision which concludes the book. The *Pearl*-poet chooses instead to re-introduce the vision of the Lamb and the 144,000 pure souls taken from Revelation 14. Attention is focused once more on the Lamb himself and for the first time the Dreamer is moved by feelings of love and compassion which displace his self-preoccupation:

| | |
|---|---|
| Best watz He, blyþest, and moste to pryse, | *most joyful; worthy of praise* |
| Þat euer I herde of speche spent; | *speech uttered* |
| So worþly whyt wern wedez Hys, | *fittingly white; garment* |
| His lokez symple, Hymself so gent. | *expression humble; gentle* |
| Bot a wounde ful wyde and weete con wyse | *wet; was visible* |
| Anende Hys hert, þurȝ hyde torente. | *near; skin; torn* |
| Of Hys quyte syde His blod outsprent. | *from; white side; gushed out* |
| Alas, þoȝt I, who did þat spyt? | *thought; evil deed* |
| | (1131–8) |

Here are the emotions which the religious lyrics sought to evoke and the beginnings of the true **contrition** without which confession and **penance** were held to be invalid. Contemplation of the wounds of **Christ** and his beauty is at last producing in the Dreamer signs of spiritual growth. Full maturity, however, is still some way off. Taking his eyes off the Lamb, he glimpses the Maiden and slips back into his former obsession. Forgetting all he has been told, he rashly attempts to join her – and finds himself back in the garden, thoroughly chastened yet curiously content. The vision has brought both reassurance and challenge: he has seen for himself that his 'pearl' indeed pleases the Prince of Peace; now he must set himself to do likewise.

| | |
|---|---|
| Ouer þis hyul þis lote I laȝte, | *mound; this happened to me* |
| For pyty of my perle enclyin, | *sorrow; lying prostrate* |
| And sythen to God I hit bytaȝte | *which afterwards I committed to God* |
| In Krystez dere blessyng and myn, | *With Christ's; mine* |
| Þat in þe forme of bred and wyn | *in form of bread and wine* |
| Þe preste vus schewez vch a daye. | *shows us every day* |
| He gef vus to be His homly hyne | *granted; humble servants* |
| Ande precious perlez vnto His pay. | *pearls; for; pleasure* |
| | (1205–22) |

So the pearl image comes full circle. Throughout the poem the beauty, purity, and perfection of the pearl have identified it as the most precious of objects, to be prized and sought above all others. On to this core meaning the poet has superimposed a number of interpretations, as the narrator's spiritual understanding develops. Initially it is his daughter who is the pearl, his most precious 'possession', on whom his happiness was built and without whom life seems meaningless. Through her instruction he sees that the most precious thing he can obtain is **salvation**, life with Christ ('my dere Juelle') whose presence signifies the joys of **heaven**. Finally, he recognises the loving perspective of God to whom human souls are pearls for which He paid the ultimate price and which He sets in splendour in the New Jerusalem.


*PATIENCE*

Both *Patience* and *Cleanness* draw on the technique of medieval preachers,[17] who leavened their instruction with a multitude of vividly-told stories or *exempla* designed to make their teaching memorable and drive their points home. Thus the poet states a precept:

Pacience is a poynt, þaʒ hit displese ofte     *virtue; though it often displeases*

(1)

relates it to a biblical text, one of the **Beatitudes** from Christ's **Sermon on the Mount** (9-11), and illustrates his theme with an **Old Testament** *exemplum*, the story of Jonah. In this poet's hands, however, discussion of a seemingly abstract virtue becomes a lively, often comic, exploration of the relationship between mankind and God. Patience, as the poet chooses to interpret it, is active rather than passive; it involves a constructive acceptance of difficulties as part of the will of God. The **Vulgate** version of the Beatitude in question reads 'Beati, qui persecutionem *patiuntur* propter justitiam' (Blessed are those who suffer persecution for righteousness' sake). Railing against suffering is not only futile (as the Pearl-Maiden pointed out to her resentful father (*Pearl*, 341–52)) but potentially dangerous; it may not only deprive man of the blessings of obedience but bring further trials upon his rebellious head. The writer seems to apply this principle to his own poverty and in another passage reminiscent of *Pearl* (497ff) points out that willing obedience is part of the relationship between servant and lord:

ʒif my lege lorde lyst on lyue me to bidde     *liege; wishes; on earth*
Oper to ryde or to renne to Rome in his ernde,     *ride or run; errand*
What grayþed me þe grychchyng bot grame more seche?
    *What would grumbling avail me but to invite more trouble?*
Did not Jonas in Judé suche jape sumwhyle?     *Judah; trick*

(49–51, 57)

It is significant that the poet chooses as his example not Job whose patience was proverbial, but Jonah whose willingness to suffer was non-existent. Jonah needs to learn patience for two reasons: because his lack of it shows a fundamental lack of trust in God and because patience was one of the **Seven Contrary Virtues**, regarded as especially efficacious in combating the anger which is such a clear component of Jonah's character. A treatise entitled *Þe Twelve Frutes of þe Holy Gost* declares: 'What vertu may be founde in þis neccesarie frute of paciens þat þus commendith vs to God and kepith vs from al yvelis: *for it tempereth ire, it refreyneth þe tonge, it gouernyth þe soule, it keepith pees.*'[18] The poet's translation of the **Beatitude**:

Þay ar happen also þat con her hert stere     *blessed; control their hearts*

(27)

changes the original emphasis to one which fits his protagonist's weakness. Jonah does not even pause for thought before reacting to God's command to preach judgement to the sinful people of Ninevah; his rebellious response is compounded of anger, resentment and fear:

| | |
|---|---|
| 'If I bow to His bode and bryng hem þis tale, | obey; command |
| And I be nummen in Nuniue, my nyes begynes: | trapped; trouble |
| He telles me þose traytoures arn typped schrewes; | consummate villains |
| I com wyth þose tyþynges, þay ta me bylyve, | tidings; seize me immediately |
| Pynez me in a prysoun, put me in stokkes, | Confine; prison; stocks |
| Wryþe me in a warlok, wrast out myn yʒen. | torture; fetter, pluck |
| Þis is a meruayl message for a man to preche | marvellous; preach |
| Among enmyes so mony and mansed fendes | cursed sinners |
| Bot if my gaynlych God such gref to me wolde, | gracious; grief; intends |
| For desert of sum sake þat I slayn were . . . | in recompense for some fault |
| I schal tee into Tarce and tary þere a whyle, | go; Tarshish |
| And lyʒtly when I am lest He letes me alone.' | probably; lost |
| | (75–84, 87–8) |

The entire speech is a creation of the poet; the Book of Jonah simply stating that 'Jonah rose to flee to Tarshish from the presence of the Lord' (1:1–3). In order to move his audience the poet must enable them to understand Jonah's psychology and motivation: if they are to learn from him they must both identify with his weakness and perceive the folly of his reasoning. Jonah's ironic description of a *gaynlych* (gracious) God is truer than he yet knows; his childish attempt to evade God's eye would have seemed to a medieval audience ludicrous rather than heroic. Most telling of all is the depiction of God, safely ensconced in **heaven**, as indifferent to Jonah's envisaged stripping and **crucifixion** 'on rode'. God, as poet and audience were well aware, would in the person of **Christ** suffer in fact what Jonah only imagines.

| | |
|---|---|
| 'Oure Syre settes,' he says, 'on sege so hyʒe | Lord; sits; seat |
| In His glowande glorye, and gloumbes ful lyttel | shining glory; frowns |
| Þaʒ I be nummen in Nunniue and naked dispoyled, | Even if; trapped; Ninevah; stripped |
| On rode rwly torent with rybaudes mony.' | cross; pitifully; torn apart; by many villains |
| | (93–6) |

Jonah's subsequent experiences bear out the poet's contention (51ff) that submission is less painful than rebellion. The overwhelming power of the storm summoned by God graphically demonstrates Jonah's folly and the contrasting obedience of the forces of nature. The distinctly unheroic Jonah ('sloberande he routes [snores]', 186) is hauled from his sleep and identified as the culprit. Despite his confession of guilt, the terrified sailors are reluctant to throw him overboard until all other measures have failed; their prayers and sacrifices indicating a responsiveness to the true God which Jonah has ruled out for the Ninevites. The waiting whale is a creature of mixed ancestry. In Christian iconography the whale was associated with **hell**, its jaws representing the mouth of hell in judgement scenes painted on church walls and in performances of the mystery plays. Thus the whale's stomach stinks 'as þe deuel' and Jonah describes it as 'hellen wombe'. Yet this whale has also been called to Jonah's aid by God and he enters its huge jaws:

As mote in at a *munster* dor

*speck; cathedral,*
(268)

Malcolm Andrew has pointed out the propriety of this image, in that the whale's vast interior becomes for Jonah a place of spiritual encounter.[19] God, more patient than Jonah, does not allow him to die but provides the whale to keep him safe (if uncomfortable) until he confesses the error of his ways. Confined in the whale's repulsive stomach, Jonah finally faces God and asks mercy. His lonely vigil brings new knowledge of God, gained, as the poet is swift to note, through the very suffering which Jonah had sought to avoid:

Now he knawez Hym in care þat couþe not in sele. *acknowledges; trouble;*
*did; happiness*
(296)

Jonah's second prayer is derived largely from Psalm 69 (**Vulgate** 68), which in medieval **psalters** was often illustrated with a picture of Jonah and the whale. His appeal to God's mercy and promise of future obedience are rewarded; God commands the whale to deposit him on the shore and Jonah emerges, soiled but safe. Medieval commentators followed the **New Testament** (Matt 12:39–41) in drawing parallels between Jonah's stay inside the whale and the three days which Christ was believed to have spent rescuing souls from **hell** before his **Resurrection**. In the context of *Patience* however, Jonah is to be regarded less a **type** or prefiguring of Christ than as a flawed reflection of what a true messenger of

God should be. An implicit comparison between Jonah and Christ runs throughout the poem.[20] Christ was willing both to preach and to suffer; Jonah had to be coerced. Christ rose to new life and glory; Jonah has been granted a new beginning but has still much to learn. Jonah's continuing limitations are demonstrated by his attitude towards Ninevah as he finally delivers his uncompromising message:

> 'Þe verray vengaunce of God schal voyde þis place!'        *destroy*
> (370)

There is no element of compassion in Jonah's motivation; unlike Christ, he preaches to condemn rather than to convert. The response of the guilt-stricken Ninevites (surpassing anything we have seen from Jonah himself) therefore prompts not joy but rage. Their remorse, expressed in the classic medieval penitential forms of tears, fasting, sackcloth and ashes, is patently genuine and wins them forgiveness from God. The *Pearl*-poet, for whom penance is always an important theme, stresses that their repentance includes a commitment to future obedience (401–5). God is pleased; Jonah is furious:

> 'Watz not þis ilk my worde þat worþen is nouþe,        *This very thing that has come to pass*
>
> Þat I kest in my cuntré . . .        *What I said; country*
> Wel knew I Þi cortaysye, Þy quoynt soffraunce,        *generosity, grace; wise patience*
>
> Þy bounté of debonerté and Þy bene grace . . .        *liberality of graciousness*
> I wyst wel, when I hade worded quatsoeuer I cowþe        *knew; spoken*
> To manace alle pise mody men pat in pis mote
>    dowellez,        *threaten, proud; city; dwell*
> Wyth a prayer and a pyne þay my3t her pese gete,        *penance; peace*
> And þerfore I wolde haf flowen into Tarce.        *fled*
> (414–15, 417–18, 420–4)

This speech is of course short both on accuracy (he did not make any such protestation) and on logic (these are the very qualities to which he owes his own deliverance). Jonah's anger and lack of self-control have warped his judgement. He resents God's *courtaysye*, manifested here as mercy, and bemoans his patience with the Ninevites. His concern is not with God's justice, but his own reputation. God, in Jonah's opinion, has made a fool of him; that being so he would rather be dead. Having retired to a distance, perhaps in the hope that judgement may still fall on the city, Jonah sleeps while God 'of His grace' provides a plant to shade him. Jonah's resulting jubilation shows once more the volatility of his character; he is as unreasoning in his joy as in his sorrows. When God causes the woodbine to wither, Jonah indulges in a third outburst of anger (480–1). God's response draws a sharp contrast between His own reasoned self-control and Jonah's lack of it:

> Why schulde I wrath wyth hem, syþen wyȝez wyl torne,    *be angry;*
> *people; repent*
> And cum and cnawe Me for Kyng and My carpe leue?*acknowledge; words*
> Were I as hastif as þou heere, were harme lumpen;    *hasty; befall*
> Couþe I not þole bot as þou, þer þryued ful fewe.    *suffer; few would*
> *flourish*
> (518–21)

If Jonah cared so passionately for a mere plant which he did not even tend, should not God have compassion upon those he had created and watched over so long? The biblical version is brief: 'Should I not pity Ninevah, that great city, in which there are more than a hundred and twenty thousand persons who do not know their right hand from their left, and also much cattle' (Jonah 4:11). The poet's expansion of the original text suggests an insight into God's response which inevitably humanises his character. He speaks of those whom it would be unjust to judge, such as the stupid, the ignorant or 'lyttel barnez [children] on barme þat neuer bale [harm] wroȝt' (514). This attempt to explain God's reasoning, though at odds with the traditional approach of medieval Biblical commentators, is essential for the poet's purpose. The *exemplum* which he has selected to illustrate his homily is double-sided: Jonah the imperfect human protagonist is a negative example, his responses marred by anger and loss of self-control; yet at every turn Jonah's faults are matched by a demonstration of God's forbearance and moderation. In this poem God Himself is the positive example and Christ, who commanded patience, the model to follow.

## CLEANNESS

In *Cleanness* (also known as *Purity*) the poet selects as his theme another of the virtues commended by Christ in the Sermon on the Mount (Matt. 5:8):

> 'Þe haþel clene of his hert hapenez ful fayre,    *man; pure; is blessed*
> For he schal loke on oure Lorde with a leue chere'.
> (27–8)

In this poem the purity exemplified by the Pearl-Maiden is seen as mandatory for any true follower of God, the pearl image appearing several times as a symbol of true repentance and cleansing (541–56, 1067–8, 1115–32). The reason lies not simply in God's commands but his character (17–22). So 'clene in His courte,' 'so honeste in His householde': such a God clearly cannot tolerate 'fylþe', by which the poet means not just blatant sin but the insidious danger of hypocrisy. Those who come closest to the things of God in their daily service, that is the **priests** who handle Christ's 'aune body' in the **Mass**, must be most careful that their outward appearance and inner lives agree. A pure God demands integrity in his servants; anything less will inevitably bring down His judgement upon them. For the *Pearl*-poet the concepts of *clannesse*, *cortaysye* and *trawþe* are inseparably bound together. *Trawþe,* which has been defined as 'essentially loyalty to God and faith to one's God-given nature and role in the world',[21] requires that men and women live according to God's standards of *clannnesse*; *courtayse* too requires that they honour God in their lives, imitating His character as far as they may.

The structure of *Cleanness*, more complex than that of *Patience*, is usually analysed on the basis of the *exempla*.[22] Important as these (largely negative) illustrations are to the vitality and impact of the poem, this approach has tended to obscure the importance of the poet's *positive* statements about purity, which form the outline of his **homily**. If these statements are highlighted, then the logic of the poem's development becomes clearer:

| | |
|---|---|
| **Introduction:** | |
| **'Cleanness'** | **1–16** |
| **God's Purity** | **17–48** |
| Exemplum: The Wedding Feast | 49–160 |
| **Application: need for baptism and good works** | **161–76** |
| | |
| **God's anger against sin** | **177–204** |
| Exempla: (Lucifer) | 205–34 |
| (Adam) | 235–48 |
| Flood | 249–544 |
| **Application: need for penance/purity** | **545–56** |
| | |
| **Sin cannot be hidden from God** | **557–600** |
| Exemplum: Sodom and Gomorrah | 601–1048 |
| **Application: be pure like Christ** | **1049–68** |

**Christ's Purity: how we must share and maintain it**

|  | 1069–1148 |
| Exemplum: Belshazzar (Nebuchadnezzar) | 1149–1804 |
| **General application/exhortation to purity** | 1805–12 |

Emphasising the teaching content of the poem also makes it evident that just as in *Patience* the negative example of Jonah is balanced by the infinite patience of God, so in *Cleanness* every *exemplum* in fact contains an example of obedience. The key *exemplum* offered by the poet is that of the Wedding Feast, which combines elements from the **Gospels** of Matthew (22:1–14) and Luke (14:16–24). Here the courtesy accepted on earth is translated to the courts of heaven. The original guests (taken by medieval commentators to represent the Jews to whom Christ's message was first declared) refuse the invitation in words which make it clear that they have totally failed to appreciate the honour which they are being offered. They have allowed possessions and relationships to subvert their loyalties and consequently fail in *trawþe* towards their acknowledged lord. Similarly, the serf who makes one of the group invited in their place also reveals by his filthy clothing a lack of proper respect for the lord and his feast. Hosts at such occasions were in the habit of providing suitable garments for guests; in spurning such provision the serf has symbolically rejected the righteousness offered by God. In lines 169-72 the poet makes the equation clear: clothes equal deeds; that is why the serf is rejected. The ruler's swift and terrifying retribution therefore offers a stark warning: it is not enough to be invited; one must also be prepared and fit for the occasion. For the Christian such preparation requires both the cleansing of **baptism** and a life of good works (163–71). As in *Patience* God's character is explored in terms of human reasoning and emotion. He is portrayed as an upright, gracious, earthly lord: approachable to those who respect Him, ruthless with those who reject His authority.

The remainder of the poem is devoted to illustrating how man and woman, like the ill-clad serf, ignore God's standards and to emphasising the inevitability of judgement. The poet provides an amplified list of the **Seven Deadly Sins**, any of which may cause a man or woman to forfeit the bliss of heaven; none of the others however, he warns, call forth such wrath nor rapid retribution as 'fylþe of þe flesch', that is sexual sin. He supports this assertion by a series of examples from the book of Genesis. Both Satan and Adam failed in obedience and were expelled from their homes, yet neither experienced the instant, total destruction visited upon the contemporaries of Noah and the inhabitants of Sodom, who offended against the natural order decreed by God (263–4) and indulged in sexual perversions which He could not tolerate. God's anger is carefully explained in the text and demonstrated by the scale of the natural forces which He unleashes. Noah, whose obedient lifestyle is rewarded by deliverance, is twice told that God's purpose in sending the flood is to 'wasch alle þe worlde of werkez of fylþe' (355). The poet (who clearly does not share Jonah's indifference to the fate of others) describes the resulting calamity with horrified compassion:

> Frendez fellen in fere and faþmed togeder,   *Friends came together; embraced*
> To dryȝ her delful destyné and dyȝen alle samen;   *suffer; sorrowful fate;*
> *together*
>
> Luf lokez to luf and his leue takez,   *Love looks at loved one; takes his leave*
> For to ende alle at onez and for euer twynne.   *at the same time; part*
> *for ever*
> (399–402)

The dignity afforded to the doomed underlines the solemnity of their fate. Their repentance came too late, and the poet is swift to apply the lesson to his audience. They must cleanse themselves completely, while there is still time and attain the purity of a 'margerye-perle' (556), the image so constantly associated in this poet's mind with the concept of **penance**. The poet goes on to warn of the folly of imagining that **sin** can be hidden from an omniscient God. His chosen *exemplum*, the story of Abraham, his nephew Lot and the cities of Sodom and Gomorrah, demonstrates both God's insight into human thoughts and the way in which mankind's actions prove the justice of His judgement. The brief visit to Abraham is enlivened by Sarah's laughing disbelief that she could bear a son in her old age, while the violent attempts of the men of Sodom to molest the angels who have come to warn Lot justifies the judgement which will shortly descend. The poet draws a significant contrast between what he regards as sexual deviation, the 'dedez of schame' which God will not tolerate, and the legitimate pleasures of physical love which God has ordained for humanity. There is no suggestion here, as with some medieval commentators, that 'clannesse' must involve a vow of celibacy; indeed God is given a speech in praise of marital bliss which would have considerably startled such commentators by its enthusiasm:

'Þe play of paramorez I portrayed Myseluen,                    *love; devised*
And made thereto a maner myriest of oÞer:                      *custom*
When two true togeder had tyȝed hemseluen,                     *joined*
Bytwene a male and his make such merÞe schulde come,   *spouse; pleasure*
Welnyȝe pure paradys moȝt preue no better.'    *Hardly would; Paradise*

(700–4)

Indeed it is mankind's rejection of the pleasure which he has planned
for them which intensifies God's anger and revulsion (709–12). Lot
and his daughters are saved, though his disobedient wife is turned into
a pillar of salt. The Cities of the Plains are destroyed, the region which
had been 'as apparaunt [similar] to paradis' (1007) reduced to a barren
wasteland. In his application of this tale, the poet returns once more to
the key image of the heavenly kingdom; if men and women wish to
be known in God's court, then they must become clean, imitating the
purity of Christ himself.

If Þou wyl dele drwrye wyth Dryȝten Þenne,
                                        *wish to exchange love with God*
And lelly loue Þy Lorde and His leef worÞe,   *loyally love; beloved; become*
Þenne confourme Þe to Kryst, and Þe clene make,   *model yourself on Christ*
                                                    *and make  yourself clean*
Þat euer is polyced als playn as Þe perle seluen.   *always polished as smooth*
                                                    *as the pearl itself*

(1065–8)

The poet now turns to Christ's purity as evidenced in his birth and
ministry. Christ's 'clannes' and 'cortayse' are linked; though he
hated evil and filth, he welcomed lepers who were cleansed by his
touch. Examining various nuances of the idea of 'cleanness', the
poet uses a curious image, based on Luke 24:35 and found also in
the N-town play of Christ's appearances to his disciples (285–8).
Medieval society considered it ill-mannered to break bread with the
hands yet Christ, says the poet, could break bread more cleanly
with His hands than the sharpest knife could cut it. Such purity
challenges humankind:

Hov schulde Þou com to His kyth bot if Þou clene were?       *country*

(1110)

The answer, once again, involves confession and penance:

Þou may schyne Þurȝ schryfte, Þaȝ Þou haf schome serued,
                                                    *confession; shame*
And pure Þe with penaunce tyl Þou a perle worÞe.

                                        *purify; penance; become*
(1115–16)

but is followed by a stark warning:

> Bot war þe wel, if þou be waschen wyth water of schyfte,    *be cautious;*
> *confession*
> And polysed als playn as parchmen schauen,    *polished as smooth as scraped*
> *parchment*
> Sulp no more þenne in synne þy saule þerafter,    *Defile; soul*
> For þenne þou Dryȝten dyspleses with dedes ful sore,    *God; grievous*
> And entyses Hem to tene more trayþly þen euer,    *provoke; anger; grievously*
> And wel hatter to hate þen hade þou not waschen.    *hotter; washed*
> (1133–8)

Once a soul is reconciled and consecrated to God, says the poet, it is like any other vessel dedicated to God's service; it must not be polluted again.[23] Thus the transition is made to the story of Belshazzar (Baltazar) and his defilement of the sacred vessels captured from the temple in Jerusalem. Belshazzar's behaviour is contrasted with that of his father Nebuchadnezzar (Nabigodenozar, Nabugo) who was allowed by God to capture Jerusalem because of King Zedekiah's idolatry, yet treated the holy vessels with reverence. Belshazzar, whose kingship is marred by idolatry and lechery, crowns his offences by using the sacred vessels at a drunken feast (1494–1501). God's impending judgement is indicated by the appearance of a disembodied hand which writes a cryptic message on the wall. Daniel, the Jewish prophet summoned to interpret the sign, includes in his explanation an account of Nebuchadnezzar's experience of judgement and his subsequent conversion. When in his pride Nebuchadnezzar claimed equality with God, he was stricken with madness; when he acknowledged God, his sanity and his kingdom were restored to him. His son, however, has ignored this example:

> Bot þou, Baltazar, his barne and his bolde ayre,    *child; heir*
> Seȝ þese syngnes with syȝt and set hem at lyttel.    *See; sign*
> (1709–10)

Still unrepentant, Belshazzar dies that very night at the hands of the invading Medes and Persians. The poet provides a brief epitaph which makes clear the relevance of this *exemplum*:

> And þus watz þat londe lost for þe lordes syne,
> And þe fylþe of þe freke þat defowled hade    *man; defiled*
> Þe ornementes of Goddez hous þat holy were maked.
> *He watz corsed for his vnclannes, and cached þerinne.*
> (1797–1800)

The sermon is complete; all that remains is for the poet to exhort his audience to learn from the examples which he has put before them and to ensure that they are clothed, by God's grace, in apparel fit for his presence:

Þus upon þrynne wyses I haf yow þro schewed                    *three*
Þat vnclannes tocleues in corage dere          *cleaves asunder the noble heart*
Of þat wynnelych Lorde þat wonyes in heuen,          *gracious Lord; dwells*
Entyses Hym to be tene, teldes vp His wrake;
                              *Provokes; angry; stirs up his vengeance*
And clannes is His comfort, and coyntyse He louyes,      *purity; wisdom*
And þose þat seme arn and swete schyn se His face.      *seemly; pure*
Þat we gon gay in oure gere þat grace He vus sende,
              *May He send us that grace that we may go brightly in our apparel*
Þat we may serue in His syȝt, þer solace neuer blynnez. Amen.
                                          *serve; sight; joy never ceases*
                                                          (1805–12)


## SIR GAWAIN AND THE GREEN KNIGHT

It seems a long way from the exploits of the recalcitrant Jonah and the doomed tyrant Belshazzar to the witty, light-hearted tale of Sir Gawain and his uncanny adversary the Green Knight. We have moved from the lands of the Bible to the world of faery; from plain-spoken exhortation to subtle duelling with words. Yet there are similarities of style, language and subject matter which have led critics to conclude that this poem too is the work of the *Pearl*-poet. Once more man faces up to a supernatural encounter; once more the integrity of his beliefs and behaviour are put to the test. The action of *Sir Gawain* begins at Camelot, where Arthur and his court are celebrating the Feast of Christmas. The poet introduces us to the privileged company: the 'gentyle kniȝtes', the 'louelokkest ladies þat euer lif haden' and the king himself, boyish, restless and eager for marvels. The most famous knights in Christendom and their leader sing, dance and play frivolous games: they are relaxed – and off their guard. Into these rather cosy celebrations rides a figure marvellous enough to please even Arthur.

Þer hales in at þe halle dor an aghlich mayster      *hastens; fearsome Lord*
On þe moste on þe molde on mesure hyghe ...   *the very biggest man on*
                                                         *earth in height*
  For wonder of his hwe men hade,                        *complexion*
  Set in his semblaunt sene;                              *appearance*

He ferde as freke were fade,                    *bore himself; bold man*
And oueral enker grene.                          *All over pure green*
                                                                (136–7, 147–50)

This ominous figure, clad in green and gold, bears both a holly
branch, traditionally a sign of peace, and a most efficient-looking
war-axe. The stunned court write him down as an illusion or
supernatural visitant. The visitor's words however are very down to
earth. The Green Knight has, he says, been brought to the court by
its reputation for courage and courtesy; his purpose, it seems, is to
test the reality of such claims. Stung by his taunts, first Arthur, then
his nephew Gawain, respond to his challenge. Thus Gawain steps forth
as the representative of Arthurian chivalry against the unknown powers
of the Green Knight. Under the conditions of the 'Crystemas gomen'
(game) which the Green Knight has proposed, Gawain is to strike
one blow and hold himself ready to receive a return stroke a year
and a day later. The blow is struck, the Green Knight's head falls to
the ground, he retrieves it (seemingly unruffled) and challenges
Gawain to attend him at the Green Chapel on the appointed day.
Thus the scene is apparently set for a typical tale of high romance.
The poet has borrowed elements of his narrative from traditional
material and the inhabitants of Camelot were well known from
other stories. Yet in the hands of the *Pearl*-poet the material takes
on an added dimension. As Gawain eventually sets forth to keep his
appointment, the poet is at pains to demonstrate both the spiritual
and knightly qualities of his hero, summed up in the images
portrayed on his shield. On the outside, displayed to the world, is
the Pentangle, a symbol which the poet suggests is particularly
apppropriate to Gawain, as it represents the five clusters of virtues
which make up his character as a Christian knight:

Forþy hit acordez to þis knyȝt and to his cler armez,        *matches; fair*
For ay faythful in fyue and sere fyue syþez,    *For always trustworthy in five*
                                                            *ways and five times in each way*
Gawan watz for gode knawen and, as golde pured,    *as a virtuous knight*
Voyded of vche vylany, wyth vertuez enourned        *Free from every evil;*
                                                                              *adorned*

    In mote.                                                              *castle*
Forþy þe pentangel nwe                                      *newly-painted*
He ber in schelde and cote,                              *shield; surcoat*
As tulk of tale most trwe                                          *knight*
And gentylest knyȝt of lote.                                       *speech*
                                                                        (631–39)

Guiltless in his behaviour, Gawain was also impeccable in matters of belief:

| | |
|---|---|
| And alle his afyaunce vpon folde watz in þe fyue woundez | *trust; earth;* |
| | *Five Wounds* |
| Þat Cryst kaȝt on þe croys, as þe Crede tellez. | *received; Cross; Creed* |
| And queresoeuer þys mon in melly watz stad, | *wherever; battle* |
| His þro þoȝt watz in þat, þurȝ alle oþer þyngez, | *His earnest intent was* |
| | *this above all else* |
| Þat alle his forsnes he fong at þe fyue joyez | *that he should get all his* |
| | *fortitude from the Five Joys* |
| Þat þe hende Heuen Quene had of hir Chylde. | *gracious* |
| | (642–7) |

The **Five Wounds**, which Christ suffered in dying to save mankind on the cross, were those in his hands, feet and side. There are frequent references to the Five Wounds and to Mary's Five Joys (the **Annunciation**, the **Nativity**, the **Resurrection**, the **Ascension** and Mary's own Assumption into heaven) in the lyrics. Gawain's devotion to the Virgin is evidenced by the presence of her image on the inside of his shield where it inspires him and helps to sustain his courage. The fifth element of the Pentangle is of particular significance for the subsequent development of the plot:

| | |
|---|---|
| Þe fyft fyue þat I finde þat þe freke vsed | *man* |
| Watz fraunchyse and felaȝschyp forbe al þyng, | *liberality; brotherly love* |
| His clannes and cortaysye croked were neuer | *purity; courtesy* |
| And pité, þat passez alle poyntez – þyse pure fyue | *virtues* |
| Were harder happed on þat haþel þen on any oþer. | *more firmly fastened;* |
| | *knight* |
| | (651–5) |

*Clannes* (purity) and *cortaysye*, here set side by side, are of course concepts deeply rooted in the work of the *Pearl*-poet. In *Sir Gawain*, cortaysye is given a somewhat narrower meaning than that which it carries in the other poems. Here it signifies the courtly manners for which Arthur's court, and Gawain in particular, are famed. Yet its presence in the Pentangle suggests that it should not be viewed in isolation. The Pentangle conveys the message that all virtues are interlinked and interdependent;[24] a concept easier to paint on to a shield than to act out in real life. Having endowed his hero with all the virtues, the poet puts those virtues to the test. Gawain is required to leave the comfort and security of the King's court and venture out alone through the wilderness, so that his integrity (and by implication that of the system which produced him) can be examined. His response to the Green Knight's challenge, therefore, takes on the character of a journey of self-discovery. Gawain's action-packed travels through the wilderness are dealt with briefly; yet they are not without significance. His courage and skill are established, together with his dependence on God (718–25). Yet his humanity also emerges, as he endures the loneliness, the bitter cold, the 'peril and payne and plytes ful harde' (733). It is a tired, cold knight who prays to the Virgin Mary for a lodging where he may observe the services of the Christmas festival.

The castle is greeted by Gawain as an answer to his prayers; wearied by the rigours of the journey, apprehensive about the ordeal to come, he is only too glad to relax into the sophisticated comfort of Bertilak's home, so like the court he has left behind. Once again, however, testing comes when least expected: braced to confront the physical threat of the Green Knight, he is surprised by seductive approaches from Bertilak's beautiful wife. Here indeed is a challenge to combine the *cortaysye* for which he is renowned with the *clanness* which Christian morality demands. With each of her three visits, echoing Christ's three temptations in the wilderness (Luke 4), the Lady becomes more insistent and Gawain is not immune to her charms. The threat, the poet assures us, is real:

> Gret perile bitwene hem stod,
> Nif Maré of hir knyȝt mynne.          *Had not Mary been mindful*
> (1768–9)

The cunning of this particular test is that it apparently forces Gawain to choose between his Pentangle virtues. Once Gawain has named the lady's proposal as sin and disloyalty to his absent host, however, it stands revealed as incompatible with the *trawþe* for which the Pentangle stands and therefore incompatible also with any element within it.

> He cared for his cortaysye, lest craþayn he were,          *churl*
> And more for his meschef ȝif he schulde make synne.          *guilt*
> (1773–4)

Even when offered the only excuse admissable in the game of courtly love, the existence of a prior attachment, Gawain is reluctant to offend, yet refuses to lie (1778–91). Having overcome one unexpected test, Gawain could well have been left to relax before facing the final ordeal. The *Pearl*-poet however is not minded to let his hero off the hook so easily. In the real world temptations do not come clearly labelled or neatly spaced. In his poem, therefore, temptation nestles within temptation, each apparently less significant than the one which precedes it yet still a potent threat to Gawain's prized integrity. Thus the Lady moves on from offering her 'cors' to offering gifts of another kind. Gawain refuses the offer of a 'riche rynk'; he is not prey to covetousness (of the straightforward variety). He is swayed, however, by the offer of the girdle, worked in green and gold, colours which should have alerted him to its provenance. In outlining the girdle's ability to protect its wearer (1851–4), the lady is careful not to suggest any particular relevance to Gawain's situation nor does he voice his thoughts. Having yielded once and accepted the gift, Gawain is then snared in a conspiracy of silence, agreeing to break his pact with Bertilak and conceal the transaction. Prudence (or fear) has opened a chink in Gawain's knightly armour. The fact that after this incident he chooses to proceed immediately to confession (1876–84) has provoked uncertainty about his state of mind and sincerity. In itself Gawain's confession need not have been a sign of particular guilt, any more than his mood of penitence earlier in the poem (760). Since he faced the prospect of death the following day it was logical that he should ensure that his soul was clean and prepared to face God's judgement. The problem lies in the omission of any reference to the girdle. Had he regarded and confessed its acceptance and concealment as sinful, he would presumably have been told to restore it; otherwise he could not have been sure of forgiveness.[25] But it does not seem that at this moment Gawain has acknowledged even to himself that taking and concealing the girdle is an act requiring confession and there is no explicit comment from the poet to guide us. Given that the whole area of penitence, forgiveness and restoration to God's grace is of considerable importance to the *Pearl*-poet, it seems unlikely that he would let a deliberate lapse pass unremarked. The immediate impression is that Gawain has, to the best of his current understanding, made complete confession and received absolution. His subsequent gaiety, therefore, is that of a man with a clean conscience.

When Gawain rides out the following morning, the guide Bertilak has supplied tries to persuade him to abandon his tryst. Gawain is not to be deflected and finally confronts his formidable adversary face to face. Twice the Green Knight swings his axe and checks at the last moment; the third time the blade just cuts the skin. His subsequent explanation wounds Gawain far more deeply. With the dawning realisation that the Green Knight is Bertilak himself, comes the uncovering of Gawain's own conduct: his triumphs and his failure.

> For hit is my wede þat þou werez, þat ilke wouen girdel . . .    *garment*
> And þe wowyng of my wyf. I wroȝt hit myseluen;    *my wife's wooing of you*
> I sende hir to asay þe, and sothly me þynkkez    *test; truly it seems to me*
> On þe fautlest freke þat euer on fote ȝede.    *most faultless knight who ever lived*
> As perle bi þe quite pese is of prys more,    *As a pearl compared with white peas is of greater value*
> So is Gawayn, in god fayth, bi oþer gay knyȝtez.
> Bot here yow lakked a lyttel, sir, and lewté yow wonted;    *you fell short a little; good faith*
> Bot þat watz for no wylyde werke, ne wowyng nauþer,    *skilled workmanship; courtship*
> Bot for ȝe lufed your lyf – þe lasse I yow blame.
>
>           (2358, 2361–8)

This is a very different scene from Gawain's brief orderly confession in the castle chapel. Here at the Green Chapel, with his erstwhile enemy acting as '**confessor**', Gawain faces his fault and pours out his chagrin and shame:

> Corsed worth cowarddyse and couetyse boþe!    *covetousness*
> In yow is vylany and vyse, þat vertue disstryez . . .    *vice; destroy*
> For care of þy knokke, cowardyse me taȝt    *concern for; blow; brought*
> To acorde me with couetyse, my kynde to forsake:    *consent; nature*
> Þat is larges and lewté, þat longen to knyȝtez.    *liberality; loyalty; belong*
> Now am I fawty and falce, and ferde haf ben euer    *sinful; dishonorable; who have always feared*
> Of trecherye and vntrawþe.    *dishonesty*
>           (2374–5, 2379–83)

If his conscience seemed a little dulled during his previous confession, the danger now is of over-reaction. Anger fuelled by humiliation is turned first on himself, then, obliquely, against the woman who contrived his downfall. Women after all had been the snare of many a biblical figure (2416–19). For an amateur the Green Knight shows considerable expertise in the confessional. His own judgement is balanced and restrained and he refuses to accept Gawain's extravagant self-denunciation. He points out that Gawain has fulfilled his **penance** through the axe-stroke and offers the girdle as a symbolic reminder. This agreed, the Green Knight resumes his former ambivalent character. He is apparently both victim and tool of Morgan le Fay, Gawain's aunt and Arthur's implacable enemy. She is the malignant power who has devised and directed the whole enterprise. Many critics have found this belated explanation of Morgan's part in the plot unsatisfactory; yet in the final analysis her precise role does not really matter. She may lurk behind the plot to entrap Gawain, but is herself only one of many manifestations of evil in the world. It is Gawain to whom the focus returns; a Gawain grown cautious through experience. However 'courteously' his encounter with the Green Knight and his entourage may have been resolved, he has no intention of trusting himself to their dubious hospitality again. He rides for Camelot wearing the girdle, symbol of his 'failure'. There his third and final 'confession' is greeted not with scorn but with laughter and his 'token of vntrawþe' adopted as a sign of the 'renoun of þe Rounde Table'.

How serious was Gawain's lapse and whose verdict should we accept? Gawain judges himself harshly, the Green Knight judiciously, the court indulgently. Perhaps the ambiguity is deliberate. The various strands of the plot have been woven together precisely to show that life is a complex business and true judgement of ourselves and others hard to achieve. Gawain achieved what the court expected of him: he showed courage, endurance and Christian virtue. His encounter at the Green Chapel was in one sense a personal 'domezday', when his deeds and motives were laid bare. The Green Knight judged him innocent of covetous and lechery (**mortal sins**) and only found him guilty of deception prompted by self-preservation, a **venial sin** at most. Compared to a white pea, he was indeed a pearl (2364). Yet Gawain was aiming higher. It was his own expectations, the perfection which his Pentangle both declared and demanded of him, which he betrayed. His new token, the girdle, was a sign of humility to remind him that no man is perfect in God's sight; all are frail, fallible and constantly in need of repentance. It is therefore fitting that the final lines of the poem point to the suffering Christ, whose sacrifice alone could bring mankind to a certain share in the joys of heaven.

> Now þat bere þe croun of þorne,
> He bryng vus to His blysse!
> > Amen

NOTES

1. All quotations from *Poems of the Pearl Manuscript*. See also *Pearl-Poet: Complete Works*, which has a parallel translation.
2. See Spearing (1970, 32–7); Blanch and Wasserman (1991). For an introduction to the work of the poet as a whole see Putter (1996).
3. See Wellek (1933).
4. *Pearl*, Intro.
5. Symbolic interpretations include virginity (Schofield, 1904), the Eucharist (Garrett, 1918), the soul (Madeleva; 1925, Hamilton, 1955), innocence (Robertson, 1950) and perfection (Kean, 1967).
6. See Conley (1955, 332–47); Watts (1963, 34–6) and especially Bishop (1968).
7. See *Pearl*, Intro, xiii; Davis (1966, 403–5).
8. The 'hyȝ seysoun' or festival (39) may be Lammas (Aug. 1) (corn harvest) or the Assumption of the Virgin into heaven (Aug. 15). Either would be appropriate.
9. Kean (1967, 41).
10. Pearsall and Salter (1973, Ch. 3).
11. See Bishop (1968, 18–21).
12. Bishop (1968, Ch. 7) suggests the liturgy for the Feast of the Holy Innocents (Childermas) as a source for this debate.
13. Bishop (1968, Ch. 9).
14. Wellek (1933, 20, 32)
15. Luttrell (1962).
16. See Field (1986, 10); Stanbury (1991).
17. For techniques of sermon construction see *Middle English Sermons*, xliii.
18. Cited Wilson (1976, 46).
19. Andrew (1996–7, 166).
20. See Andrew (1972).
21. *Poems of the Pearl Manuscript*, 22.
22. Spearing (1970, 43); *Poems of the Pearl Manuscript*, 25; Morse (1978, 132).
23. See Hebrews 6:4–6; II Peter 2:20.
24. See Green (1962); Morgan (1991).
25. See Burrow (1959).

# Chapter 9

# Mysteries, Moralities and Miracles

Lordinges, this significatyon
of this deede of devotyon . . .
may torne you to myche good.

(Chester *Abraham and Isaac*, 460–1, 463)

I pray you all give your audience,
And hear this matter with reverence,
By figure a moral play!
*The Summoning of Everyman* called it is . . .
The story saith: Man, in the beginning
Look well, and take good heed to the ending.

(*Everyman*, 1–4, 10-11)

## THE RELIGIOUS DRAMA

For at least two centuries[1] it was possible to stand in the streets and market-places of medieval cities such as York and Coventry and witness the drama of cosmic conflict, human frailty and eternal destiny played out for all to see – and heed. Scenes familiar from the walls of **parish** churches[2] sprang to life as Adam and Eve were banished from the Garden of Eden, Christ suffered on the cross and the soul of Mankind was wooed by the forces of good and evil. The audience, drawn from every level of medieval society, were vital players in this epic drama, for the mystery cycles, the miracles or **saint**'s plays and the moralities[3] were all designed to warn and win souls. According to views cited in a fourteenth-century treatise,[4] proponents of such plays considered them a powerful means of instruction and conversion:

By siche myraclis pleyinge ben men convertid to gode lyvynge . . . men and wymmen, seinge the passioun of Crist and of his seintis, ben movyd to compassion and devociun, wepynge bitere teris . . . Sithen [since] it is leveful to han the myraclis of God peintid, why is not as wel leveful to han the myraclis of God pleyed, sythen men mowen bettere reden [learn] the wille of God and his mervelous werkis in the pleyinge of hem than in the peintynge? And betere they ben holden in mennes minde and oftere rehersid [repeated] by the pleyinge of hem than by the peintynge, for this is a deed bok [book], the tother a quick [living].

(*A Tretise of Miraclis Pleyinge*, 98)

Such dramatised stories represented not only times past but time present. Cain's rebellion and Herod's pride were still snares into which anyone might fall; Noah's obedience and Abraham's faith were still models for all to imitate. The plays taught, warned, entertained and persuaded, using humour both subtle and crude and stagecraft which was ingenious and naive by turns. Those who constructed and developed the plays did not scruple to use secular material and techniques in presenting Christian truth. It had not always been thus. In the early Christian centuries the immorality associated with the Roman stage had led to the rejection of drama by the **Fathers of the Church** and not until the tenth century did an embryonic form of Christian drama began to emerge within the **liturgy**. The imposition of a standard Latin **Mass** throughout Western Christendom during the seventh and eighth centuries had caused unlettered lay people to become observers rather than participants in the central service of the Church's worship. Churchmen such as Amalarius, **Bishop** of Metz during the reign of Charlemagne, sought to dramatise the ritual of the **liturgy** to bring it to life for the congregation. A parallel development led to the elaboration of the music of the Church and the emergence of *tropes*, brief excerpts from scripture with musical settings, which offered scope for dialogue and simple characterisation. By the tenth century *tropes* associated with the great festivals of **Easter** and **Christmas** were widely used to enhance the impact of the words of scripture.

The Easter *trope*, known as *Quem quaeritis?* from its opening words: 'Quem quaeritis in sepulchro, O Christocolae?' (Whom do you seek in the sepulchre, Christian women?),[5] was the first to emerge, and focused the attention of worshippers upon the message of **Christ**'s **Resurrection**, the central truth of the Christian faith, and upon the **Host**, the consecrated bread and wine which represented Christ's body. The ritual of setting aside the Host in a special chalice on **Good Friday** and 're-discovering' it on **Easter Sunday** became a ceremony which included action and dialogue between the angels who guarded Christ's tomb and the women who came there to anoint his body. The account in the late tenth-century **Regularis Concordia** specifies that there should be one angel and three women, instructs the 'women' (played by three monks) to move 'step by step, as though searching for something' and the angel to sing 'softly and sweetly', and incorporates simple props. Soon there was a *trope* for Christmas, *Quem quaeritis in praesepe, pastores?* (Whom do you seek in the manger, shepherds?); a play about the **Magi**, and two plays which show Herod's encounter with the wise men and the massacre of the Innocents. By the end of the eleventh century a simple dramatisation of the *Ordo Prophetarum* (Procession of Prophets), a collection of prophecies associated with the birth of Christ, had been added to the dramas clustering around the feast of the **Nativity**. Although there was some further development in the liturgical drama,[6] this was limited by the demands of the church's calendar and by ecclesiastical decorum. Liturgical plays existed to enhance the message of the liturgy and increase the devotion of the faithful; they were performed by the clergy reverently and sedately within the walls of the church. No direct link with the vernacular drama can be established, though the very existence of such plays may have encouraged the growth of the more adventurous forms also nurtured by the rich seedbed of Christian worship: the mystery plays, the moralities and the miracle plays.

## THE MYSTERY CYCLES

The mystery cycles, so termed because they were played in the main by craft guilds, later called 'mysteries', illustrate the piety and growing prosperity of the later medieval period. A Beverley ordinance states that the plays were to be performed in perpetuity, 'in order that the honour of God and the repute of the town may be enhanced':[7] a neat blend of religious fervour and burgeoning civic pride. A later Chester Proclamation (1531–2) reviews the reasons for the plays' existence and outlines their dramatic scope:

> For as much as of old tyme, not only for the augmentacion and incres of the holy and Catholick faith of our Savyour Jesu Crist and to exhort the myndes of the common people to good devotion and holsome doctryne therof but also for the commenwelth and prosperitie of this Citie, a play and declaration and diverse storyes of the bible begynnyng with the creacion and fall of Lucifer and endyng with the generall jugement of the world, to be declared and plaied in the Witsonweke . . . at the costes and chargez of the craftes men and occupacons of the said Citie.

> (*REED Chester*, 27–8)

This ambitious programme was essentially carried out by amateurs, though individual guilds would have built up considerable experience and care was taken to ensure the skill of intending performers and the quality of their scripts. A York document of 1476 records the City Council's decree:

> That yerely in the tyme of Lentyn there shall be called afore the Maire for the tyme beyng iiij of the moste connyng, discrete and able playeres within this Citie to serche, here and examen all the plaiers and plaies and pagentes thrughoute all the artificeres belonging to Corpus Christi plaie. And all suche they shall fynde sufficiant in persone and connyng to the honour of the Citie and worship of the saide Craftes for to admitte and able, and all other insufficiant personnes either in connyng, voice or personne to discharge, ammove and avoide.
>
> (*REED York*, 109)

Play texts must have undergone a constant process of adaptation, intentional and unintentional, as material was borrowed from other cycles and parts imperfectly learned or improvised from year to year. Four complete (or nearly complete) cycle texts in English have survived: the York cycle; the Towneley cycle, which was probably performed at Wakefield in Yorkshire and which owes much to the York cycle; the Chester cycle; and the N-town cycle[8] (once known as the *Ludus Coventriae*, from a mistaken attribution to Coventry, and occasionally as the *Hegge* cycle after a manuscript owner), which comes from Lincolnshire or Norfolk. Two pageants survive from Coventry, together with single pageants from Norwich, Newcastle and Brome in Suffolk. A list of pageants performed in Beverley has survived, though the texts have not. Contemporary records sometimes refer to the cycles as 'Corpus Christi plays' because a number of them were performed at least initially on the **Feast** of **Corpus Christi**, instituted in 1311 and well established in England by 1318. This new summer festival fell on a Thursday between 23 May and 24 June (June 4–July 6 in the modern calendar), thus offering the prospect of good weather and maximum hours of daylight, the optimum conditions for outdoor festivities. The feast was designed to celebrate the gift of **salvation** made available by **Christ**'s death and symbolised in the **Host**, the 'body of Christ' or *Corpus Christi*, received by the faithful during **Mass**. The consecrated Host was therefore carried through the streets, accompanied by church and civic leaders with craft and religious guilds carrying their banners. The stated purpose of the feast was to move the hearts of men and women to profound joy:

'This is the glorious act of remembrance, which fills the minds of the faithful with joy at their salvation and brings them tears mingled with a flood of reverent joy.'[9] Such a response could only be expected if lay-people fully appreciated their own need to benefit from Christ's sacrifice. The impact of the feast could be greatly enhanced by setting the death of Christ in context and a suitable theological framework lay ready to hand: the scheme of salvation history laid out in the **Bible** and interpreted and amplified by commentators over the centuries. Christ's representative death for mankind necessarily looked back to the **Nativity**, the moment when God became man. The need for Christ's **Incarnation** and **Passion** was explained by the Creation and the subsequent **Fall of Mankind**. Other **Old Testament** stories were thought to shed particular light on the coming of Christ, either through prophecy or as **types** of sacrifice or deliverance. Finally the need to respond to Christ's offer of forgiveness was brought home by the sobering prospect of Judgement Day when the secrets of all would be revealed and the sheep eternally divided from the goats.

It is impossible to determine the precise relationship between the plays and the Corpus Christi procession but it seems likely that guilds began to carry pictures or models depicting stages in the history of salvation in their processions and that these static representations developed into dramatic scenes, played out along the route or at a single location. The Holy Blood procession enacted by the clergy and townspeople of Bruges in Belgium combines brief dramatic scenes with the carrying of effigies of Christ on the cross and in the tomb in a manner which may reflect the evolution of the mystery cycles. Cycle plays were performed on holy days other than **Corpus Christi** and on occasion different plays, such as the lost **Creed** and **Paternoster** plays,[10] were substituted for cycle plays on the Feast of Corpus Christi itself. It is therefore impossible to establish an exclusive theological link between Corpus Christi and material used in the cycles. The outline of salvation history seen in the plays was well established in art and sermons and would have been appropriate for most Christian festivals. Medieval theologians detected two main patterns in the history of salvation. Firstly, since Christ was the key to **salvation**, the whole of biblical history was interpreted in relation to him and biblical characters and events interpreted as prefiguring or fulfilling his life and ministry. Secondly, the history of the world was divided into 'ages' (usually seven to correspond with the seven days of creation), each associated with a key biblical figure. In England the seven ages were usually linked with Adam, Noah, Abraham, Moses, David and Christ; the last age would be ushered in by Christ's **Second Coming**. Both patterns can be seen to influence the selection of material for the cycles, though the former usually takes precedence.[11] The selection of pageants included in this chapter is designed to indicate the overall scheme of salvation history upon which playwrights drew, while recognising at least some characteristics and preoccupations of individual cycles. While regional variations can be perceived in the extant cycles, all are indebted to a common heritage of spirituality and theological understanding:[12] in them the complex traditions of the Church sprang to life, biblical characters walked the streets and God spoke again to all who would heed Him.

'MYGHTFUL GOD, MAKER OF ALL THAT IS'

Those who shaped the mystery cycles were primarily interested in history not as a record of human activity but as it revealed God's interaction with men and women. Hence the cycles focused upon God's relationship with mankind as Creator, Saviour and Judge. God, it was believed, had intervened in human affairs many times but three great actions gave shape and meaning to all: 'Frendes, for a processe ȝe shull vndirstond þat I fynde in holy writt iij commynges of our Lorde; the first was qwen þat he com to make man; the secound was qwhen he com to bie man; and þe iij shall be qwen he shall com to deme [judge] man' (*Middle English Sermons*, 314). The relationship between these comings or advents of God is constantly explored and signalled as the plays unfold. In the York *Birth of Christ*, Mary greets her son as Creator and Saviour:

> Haile, sovereyne sege all sinnes to sesse!          *man/warrior; end*
> Haile, God and man in erth to wonne!                        *dwell*
> Haile, thrugh whos[e] mi[g]ht
> All this worlde was first begonne.
>
> (York *Birth of Christ*, 59–62)

In the York *Judgement*, God the Father cites the creation of mankind and **Christ**'s sufferings for ungrateful mankind as justification for the condemnation of those who have failed to respond. Other episodes are fitted into the pattern, gaining enhanced significance from their part in the whole. Commentators such as the Chester Expositor are employed to point the links, for example, between Abraham's intended sacrifice of Isaac and the death of Christ:

> This deede yee seene done here in this place,
> in example of Jesus done yt was.
>
> (Chester *Abraham and Isaac*, 464–5)

The interest of the cycle plays lay not in any element of suspense – the stories were too well-known for that – but in these networks of significance which embraced the audience as they watched. The God who spoke to Noah, to Abraham and Moses was also speaking to them. References by Noah to 'Christ's blessing' and Abraham's prayers to the **Trinity** are less naive anachronisms than evidences of a strong sense of identification with the characters portrayed, reinforced by a complex view of time which adds further layers of subtlety to seemingly straightforward texts.

> In the Middle Ages, at least three different visions of time were discussed. At the highest level there is God existing outside time, seeing it all instantaneously and so foreseeing our future without depriving us of free will. Within time, neat divisions of history, **typological** links, fulfilments of signs and prophecies, numerological symbolism, parallel and recreative patterns were enthusiastically stressed by theologians anxious to see time not as a destructive force but as the expression of divine purpose. Only at the lowest level do we have linear time, the time in which, necessarily, one event follows the other; the time within which the audience watch, and the play (as action) progresses.[13]

The mystery cycles function at all three levels of time. God is established as existing beyond time yet intervening in it. The first pageant of the York cycle, scheduled to begin at 4.30 a.m., opens with God declaring

> I am gracyus and grete, God withoutyn begynnyng . . .
> My body in blys ay abydande                 *always abiding*
>
> (York *Fall of the Angels*, 1, 7)

As day dawns, the story of creation unfolds. **Lucifer**, created to be lightbearer, becomes infatuated with his own beauty and for his overweening pride is cast down with his cohorts to **hell**, where they indulge in noisy lamentation and recriminations. This episode does not derive from Genesis but was inferred by theologians from isolated verses in Isaiah (14:12–14), Ezekiel (26:2–19), Luke (10:18) and Revelation (12:7–9). Despite this set-back, God proceeds with

his plan to people the earth. Adam is created from the earth and
Eve from Adam's rib. Together they are enjoined to love their
Creator, who rejoices at the completion of His work:

| | |
|---|---|
| For þis skyl made I ȝow þis day – | *reason* |
| My name to worschip ay-whare. | *everywhere* |
| Louys me, forþi, and louys me ay | *praise/love; therefore* |

| | |
|---|---|
| My warke is endyde now at mane: | *work/man* |
| All lykes me will, but þis is best. | *well* |

(York *Creation of Adam and Eve*, 65–7, 87–8)

This idyllic state of affairs is threatened by the malice of the fallen
**Satan**. In the Chester *Adam* he reveals his determination to ensure
that mankind should share his deprivation:

| | |
|---|---|
| Of yeartly paradice now, as I weene, | *earthly* |
| a man is given masterye. | |
| By Belsabubb, I will never blynne | *stop* |
| till I may make him by some gynne | *trick/device* |
| from that place for to twyne | *depart* |
| and trespasse as did I. | |

(Chester *Adam*, 171–6)

The York pageant shows Satan, 'in a worm's likeness', persuading
Eve to share the ambition which caused his own downfall and eat
the forbidden fruit:

| | |
|---|---|
| Nay, certis, it is no wathe | *danger* |
| Ete it saffely ye maye . . . | |
| right als God yhe shalle be wise . . . | *as* |
| Ay, goddiss shall ye be. | |

(York *Fall of Man*, 65–6, 70–1)

The playwrights took different theological and psychological routes
as they sought to explain the **Fall of Man**. While the York and
N-town pageants show Adam sharing Eve's ambition, the Chester
pageant draws on the tradition that Adam and Eve fell through the
**Deadly Sins** of Covetousness and Gluttony:

EVA:
> A, lord, this tree is fayre and bryght,
> greene and seemely to my sight,
> the fruite sweete and much of myght,
> that godes it may us make.

Adam too is tempted by the sight of the fruit:

> The fruit is sweete and passinge feare . . .
> one morsell I will take.

(Chester *Adam*, 254, 256)

One 'morsell' however, is enough. Overcome by shame, Adam turns upon his mate. As in the *Fall of the Angels*, **sin** is shown bringing discord, recriminations and, most importantly, alienation from God. Following Genesis 3:10, the Chester pageant shows the guilty pair attempting to hide from God because of their newly-realised nakedness; the York and N-town pageants also hint that their very ability to perceive God is beginning to fade:

> GOD:
>   Where art thou? Yhare!                                       *quickly*
> ADAM:
>   I here the[e], Lorde, and seys the[e] noug[h]t.                *see*

(York *Fall of Man*, 138–9)

**Satan**'s goal is achieved: Adam and Eve are expelled from paradise and mankind's wanderings as pilgrims and strangers upon the earth begin. One scene more, however, is required to complete the story of the **Fall** and illustrate the social consequences of separation from God: Cain's murder of his brother Abel. Adam and Eve, despite their disobedience, retained elements of their former glory and achieved dignity in their penitence; Cain's character, however, demonstrates the full effects of sin, displaying many of the characteristics which St Paul attributed to those who refuse to honour God: 'They are full of envy, murder . . . insolent, arrogant, boastful, disobedient to parents' (Romans 1:29). The N-Town pageant offers a straighforward account of the conflict: Abel the shepherd resolves to follow his father's advice to tithe his produce by sacrificing a lamb (*Cain and Abel*, 70-7), an offering which points forward to the death of Christ, the Lamb of God (Jn 1:29). Cain's grudging sacrifice, in contrast, shows his contempt for his father, his brother, and the God they worship:

> Here I tythe þis unthende sheff:                    *poor quality sheaf*
> Lete God take it or ellys lef.                           *leave (it)*

(N-Town *Cain and Abel*, 101–2).

When God signals acceptance of Abel and rejection of Cain's offering, Cain's resentment boils over into violence:

Doth God þe love and hatyht me?      *hate*
þu xalt be ded, I xal þe slo.      *shalt; slay*
(145–6)

In the Towneley pageant, Cain's rebellion is woven into episodes of knockabout comedy, his speeches studded with crude obscenities, yet, as Rosemary Woolf observes, his character 'comes close to being a serious study in damnation, not a state of damnation that is magnificent in its anguish and apprehension of loss, but one that is mean, ugly and churlish.'[14] His efforts to deceive God by 'miscounting' sheaves provided a warning to any who might also try to evade paying the required tenth of their produce to the church, perhaps suspecting like Cain that the priest has kept the **tithe** for himself. Abel dies, like Christ an innocent victim, yet unlike Christ calling for retribution (328–9).[15] Already parallels and contrasts are being established between the disobedient Eve, mother of both murderer and victim, and the obedient **Virgin Mary**, whose Son will bring **salvation**. Cain is banished, an outcast even from his own kind: separated by **sin** from both man and God.

The story of Noah and the Flood offered considerable scope for the drawing of theological parallels. The Chester pageant opens with God recalling his creation of the world and determining to act in judgement upon sinful mankind. Only Noah stands out in contrast to the prevailing wickedness and is therefore offered a way to escape the forthcoming flood. The ark which he is commanded to build was seen as a type of the church through which **salvation** was offered to all who would accept it (I Peter 3:20–1). Noah is characterised by obedience to God (an area in which both Adam and Cain fell short), responding to the apparently illogical command to build a boat, despite the fact that there is as yet no sign of the threatened flood. Noah's obedience is in sharp contrast to his wife's reluctance to comply with God's commands. In the Chester pageant she initally helps by bringing timber for the boat; but later refuses to enter the completed ark until compelled to do so by one of her sons. Her recalcitrance does not derive from the biblical account of the Flood but from an eastern legend which the dramatists adapted for their own purposes.[16] The Towneley pageant exploits the comic possibilities of marital disharmony and the stock figure of the shrewish wife to the full. Stubborn to the last, Noah's wife ignores her husband's pleas and warnings, only seeking safety at the last possible moment:

VXOR:

   Yei, water nighys so nere that I sit not dry!         *approaches*
Into ship with a byr, therfor, will I hy                *rush*
For drede that I drone here. [rushes aboard]       *drown*

                          (Towneley *Noah*, 370–2)

Her wilful disregard of impending doom coupled with her last-minute capitulation made Noah's wife a powerful example of the sinner who was reluctant to repent even as death approached. The parallel would have been driven home by the staging of the pageant, since in all likelihood Noah's wife would have played her part on the same level as the spectators, leaving them behind to be engulfed by the imaginary flood-waters, as she scrambled to safety aboard the ark (set on the stage or pageant-wagon). In the York pageant, Noah further reminded the spectators of their own danger by predicting another judgement hundreds of years hence when the world would be destroyed not by flood but by fire (Matthew 24:35–9; II Peter 3:3–7).

    Most of the extant cycles move directly from the story of the Flood to that of Abraham and Isaac. The Brome pageant opens with Abraham reflecting on his devotion to God and his deep love for Isaac, the son of his old age and the heir through whom God's promise would be fulfilled. With unconscious irony Abraham prays that Isaac may be preserved from harm and fear, unaware that God is about to command him to put the child to death, in order to test the reality of his professed obedience.

I schall asay now his good will,
Whether he lovith better his child or me.
All men schall take exampyll him by
My commawndmentys how they schall fulfill.

                    (Brome *Sacrifice of Isaac*, 43–6)

Though the issue is never seriously in doubt, the pageant still contrives to offer an authentic exploration of the cost of obedience. God knows that Abraham will pass the test, the audience knows that God will provide an alternative victim; they also know that this scene foreshadows the **Crucifixion** of **Christ** when Father and Son went through with the sacrifice for the sake of sinful mankind. Abraham's simple but powerful expressions of emotional struggle would have possessed an added resonance for a medieval audience: through Abraham they are gaining an insight into the heart of God:

ABR:

> For thowgh my heart be hevely sett
> To see the blood of my owyn dere son,
> Yit for all this I will not lett . . .          *desist*
>
> A, Fader of hevyn, so I am woo!          *I am so woeful*
> This child here brekys my harte on sonder . . .          *asunder*
> I am full sory, son, thy blood for to spill
> But truly, my child, I may not chese.          *choose*
>
> (96–8, 151–2, 173–4)

The playwrights reflect the interpretations of the **Fathers of the Church** who saw Isaac less as the passive figure of the Genesis account than as the **antetype** of **Christ**, apprehensive, afraid of death yet unswervingly obedient to his father. The Brome pageant stresses his innocence, his concern for his mother, and the fact that he carries the wood for the sacrificial altar on his back: all foreshadowing Christ and his death. As Abraham nerves himself to deliver the fatal blow, Isaac echoes the words of Christ on the cross: 'Father, into thy hands I commend my spirit' (Luke 23:46). This widely-recognised parallel is also seen in manuscript illustrations, in stained glass (still to be seen in Canterbury Cathedral), and in explanations such as that offered by John Mirk in his book of sermons for **parish priests**:

> Then by Abraham ȝe schull undyrstonde þe Fadyr of Heven, and by Isaac his sonne Ihesu Crist, þe whiche he sparyd not for no love þat he had to hym; but he suffered þe Iewes to lay þe wode on hym, þat was þe crosse apon hys schuldres, and ladden hym to þe mount of Calvary, and þer dydyn him on þe autre of wode, þat was þe crosse.
>
> (Mirk, *Festial*, 77)

The consequence of this interpretation for the drama is that Isaac emerges alongside his father as a character of equal stature; fully human in his fear and relief at escaping death yet standing as a clear pointer to the Saviour to come. The Chester Expositor explains:

> By Abraham I may understand
> the Father of heaven that cann fonde          *try*
> with his Sonnes blood to breake that bonde
> that the dyvell had brought us to.          *Devil*
> By Isaack understande I maye
> Jesus that was obedyent aye.
>
> (Chester *Abraham and Isaac*, 468–73)

Following Abraham, the figure of supreme importance in biblical history was Moses, who led the Israelites out of slavery and through whom God delivered the Ten Commandments. Moses was important to the dramatic and theological structure of the cycles for two main reasons: his role as lawgiver and deliverer meant that he was regarded as inaugurating a new epoch of history, and his life provided a wealth of figurative parallels which could be shown to point forward to the coming of Christ. Some cycles also include elements of the *Procession of the Prophets* from the liturgical drama, in which Old Testament figures, such as Isaiah and Jeremiah, deliver passages believed to foretell the coming of Christ. With the exception of the story of Balaam and his ass (Chester), these episodes are formal, their purpose to point forward to the second 'coming of God': the birth and ministry of Christ.

## 'JOYE IS COME LORD THROUGH THEE'

The principles of selection governing the inclusion of **Old Testament** material in the mystery cycles are mirrored in the choice and organisation of events taken from the **New Testament** and **apocryphal** books. Scant attention is paid to the three-year public ministry of Christ, save for those incidents which have a particular place in the theological pattern of salvation history, such as the Temptation in the Wilderness which mirrors the **Fall of Man**, and the raising of Lazarus which foreshadows Christ's own resurrection. Instead, the plays focus upon the events surrounding Christ's **Nativity** and **Passion**. **Old Testament** events and prophecies provide the framework for this new revelation of God. The prophet Isaiah introduces the Coventry ***Annunciation*** declaring

> Behold, a maiden shall conceive a child
> And get us more grace than ever men had.
>
> (Coventry *Annunciation*, 24–5)

The opening speech of the Towneley *Annunciation* in which God reveals his plan to redeem mankind is full of parallels – and contrasts – with the **Fall**:

> I will that my son manhede take.
> For reson will that ther be thre:
> A man, a maydn, and a tre –
> Man for man, tre for tre,
> Madyn for maydn – thus shal it be . . .
> Angell must to Mary go,
> For the feynd was Eve fo.
>
> (Towneley *Annunciation*, 30–4, 61–2)

Adam, the first man, brought about the downfall of humankind; **Christ**, the second Adam (I Corinthians 15:22, 45), will bring restoration. The tree, whose forbidden fruit brought condemnation, will be replaced by the cross, symbol of **salvation**. Eve, deceived by **Satan** and disobedient to God, will be replaced by **Mary**, instructed by Gabriel and wholehearted in simple obedience. These theological connections, summarised in Gabriel's greeting 'Here þis name, *Eva*, is turnyd *Ave*' (N-Town *Annunciation*, 219), were well established.

> It was well thing reasonable that the angel should come to the glorious Virgin Mary, for like as Eve by the exhorting of the devil gave her consent to do the sin of inobedience to our perdition, right so by the greeting of the angel Gabriel and by exhorting, the glorious Virgin Mary gave her consenting to his message by obedience, to our salvation.
>
> (*de Voragine*, Golden Legend, III, 97)

Lest it should be forgotten that these events are set in the real world, the high tone of Gabriel's visit is rapidly succeeded by **Joseph**'s reaction to Mary's unexpected pregnancy. As in the characterisation of Noah's wife, **apocryphal** material and *fabliaux* are used to embroider the brief biblical account (Matthew 1:19–21). This episode serves both to provide the spectators with some wry amusement and to earth the mystery of the **Incarnation** in a situation charged with recognisable human emotions as Joseph laments Mary's supposed unfaithfulness (170–2). The audience can no doubt identify with his scepticism but they also witness Mary's joyous serenity and hear the angel's words of reassurance. His fears relieved, Joseph begs forgiveness and pledges himself to the task ahead. He and the audience are now ready to move on to the wonder of the birth. In presenting the miracle of the **Incarnation**, the dramatists had a wealth of material on which to draw. Growing fascination with the humanity of Christ had produced the pseudo-Bonaventuran *Meditations on the Life of Christ*, **St Bridget**'s revelations and a host of **legends** associated with the Virgin Mary. The brief accounts in the **Gospels** of Matthew and Luke had been amplified and embroidered with a multitude of details all designed to enhance the emotional impact of the scene and to increase faith. Through their selection of such details, the dramatists sought to convey both the reliability and theological significance of their accounts. The miracles of the cherry-tree and the midwives which feature in the N-Town *Nativity* may seem sensational to modern tastes; to a contemporary audience they offered corroborating evidence of Mary's story. When Joseph demands irritably:

lete hym pluck ȝow cheryes begatt ȝow with childe!

(38)

God's response to Mary's prayer establishes not only her virtue but her child's parentage. Similarly, the *Golden Legend*, following the *Protevangelium* and the *Gospel of the Pseudo-Matthew*, explains why the midwives were required at a birth traditionally held to have been painless and trouble-free:

> We have five witnesses to prove that [Mary] was a virgin ... Bartholomew tells us that when the hour had come in which Mary was to be delivered, Joseph called two midwives, the one being called Zebel and the other Salome ... When Zebel saw that Mary was a virgin, she cried out: 'Truly she is a virgin and she has given birth!' But Salome did not believe this and wished to examine her; thereupon her hand withered and died. Then an angel appeared and bade her touch the child; and immediately she was cured.
>
> (*de Voragine,* Golden Legend, December 25)

The brief York pageant is characterised by a lyrical simplicity which owes much to both the *Meditations* and to St Bridget's vision. As with one of the most successful of the Nativity lyrics, *I sing of a mayden*, this simplicity conceals a skilful blend of theology, artistic skill and tradition.[17] Throughout the scene the dramatist contrives to sustain a blend of realism and tenderness. The setting, a cold, dark, tumbledown stable, evokes the miseries of the fallen, needy world into which the Saviour must come. The cast is restricted to Mary, Joseph and the child who, born swiftly and painlessly to his adoring mother, fills the stable with radiance. This corresponds to Bridget's account which told how Mary, deep in contemplation,

> sodanli ... bare hir son. And þare com so grete a light and brightnes þat it passed þe brightnes of þe son ... And when þe maiden felide þat sho had born hir childe, sho bowed doune hir heed and held vp hir handes and wirschipe[d] þe childe, and said to him: 'Welcom mi God, mi lord, and mi son!'
>
> (*Liber Celestis*, Book VII, Ch. XXII)

Mary's worship is expressed by the York dramatist in very similar terms:

> Haile my Lord God, haile, prince of pees!
> Haile my fadir, and haile my sone!
>
> (*York Birth of Jesus*, 57–8)

Once the birth is over, Joseph returns from his search for light and
fuel to discover that the Light of the World (John 8:12) himself has
been born into the dark stable, and joins Mary in worship:

> Haile, my Lorde, lemer of light!    *source*
>                                       (111)

The presence of the ox and ass is not mentioned in the **canonical**
scriptures but was included in the **apocryphal Gospel of
pseudo-Matthew** which dates from the eighth or ninth century.

> On the third day after the nativity of our Lord Jesus Christ, the most
> blessed Mary went out of the cave, and entering a stable, put her child
> in a manger and the ox and ass adored him. Then was fulfilled that
> which was spoken by Isaiah the prophet, who said, The ox hath known
> his master, and the ass his master's crib [Isaiah 1:3]. The very animals,
> therefore, having him between them, incessantly adored him. Then was
> fulfilled that which was spoken by Habakkuk the prophet, who said,
> Between two animals[18] thou art known [Habakkuk 3:2].
>                                       (*Apocryphal Gospels*)

The crib scene was popularised by **St Francis** and the role
attributed to the animals grew in significance. In the York pageant
**Mary** and **Joseph** note that the animals not only worship the
new-born child but also seek to comfort him:

> MARIA:
>   Ther Lord thay kenne, that wate I wele;    *I know it well*
>   They worshippe him with might and maine.
>   The wedir is colde, as ye may feele;
>   To halde him warme they are full faine    *keep/glad*
>   With thare warme breth.
>                          (York *Birth of Jesus*, 126–33)

The animals' concern for the Child was drawn from the
pseudo-Bonaventuran account of the **Nativity**: 'The ox and the ass
knelt with their mouths above the manger and breathed on the
Infant as though they possessed reason and knew that the Child was
so poorly wrapped that He needed to be warmed, in that cold
season'(*Meditations*, 33–4).

Although, the Towneley *Second Shepherds'* pageant is famous for
its scenes of comic horseplay, it too contains moments of tenderness
and manifests a considerable degree of theological sophistication.
Again the pageant opens with a reminder of the woes of the world,
as the shivering shepherds complain of the weather, high taxes,

oppression by the ruling classes and the trials of marriage. The general air of discontent, together with their petty disputes and the stratagems of the wily Mac, illustrate the disorder characteristic of a fallen world. Mac's theft of a sheep and his attempts to pass it off as a new-born baby, 'swaddled' in a cradle, prefigures the birth of Jesus Christ, 'the Lamb of God' (John 1:29). Ironically it is the shepherds' kindly desire to offer the 'child' a gift which leads to the discovery of the fraud and Mac's unmasking as a thief and cheat. With the appearance of the angel the mood shifts from comedy to joyful solemnity. The true Lamb, the true Good Shepherd (John 10) who will protect his flock, has been born and with his birth comes new hope for the world:

ANGELUS:

| | |
|---|---|
| Rise hyrd-men, heynd, for now is he borne | *gentle* |
| That shall take fro the feynd that Adam had lorne; | *what Adam lost* |
| That warloo to sheynd, this night is he borne. | *To destroy that warlock* |
| God is made youre freynd now at this morne, | |
| He behestys. | *He promises* |
| At Bedlem go se. | *Bethlehem* |

(Towneley *Second Shepherds'*, 638–43)

As they respond to the angel's message, the shepherds' conversation takes on a new tone. Just as the audience could have identified with their problems and disharmony in the early part of the pageant, so now they are invited to share in their united desire to echo the angels' song of praise and to find the Saviour for themselves. The shepherds' surprisingly learned discussion of the prophecies is a mark of their new understanding and the beginning of their new role of proclaiming the good news to others. Their greetings to the child are a lyrical blend of homely tenderness and theological insight:

| | |
|---|---|
| Haill, sufferan Savioure, for thou has us soght! | *suffering* |
| Haill, frely foyde and floure, that all thing has wroght! | |
| | *noble child; flower; made* |
| Haill, ful of favoure, that made all of noght! | |
| Haill! I kneyll and I cowre. A bird I have broght | |
| To my barne. | *child* |
| Haill litill tiné mop! | *tiny baby* |
| Of oure crede thou art crop. | *creed/faith, head* |
| I wold drink on thy cop, | *from your cup* (**Eucharist**) |
| Litill day-starne. | *day-star* |

(719–27)

The shepherds' gifts (not mentioned in the **Gospels** but adopted in medieval tradition to correspond to those brought by the three **Magi**) are both appropriate to the standing of the donors and symbolic of the nature of the Christ Child. The cluster of cherries (a miraculous sign of new life in the depths of winter), the ball (perhaps representing the universe) and the bird (possibly a symbol of the **Holy Spirit**) are all found in association with the Child in medieval religious art.[19] In the pageants which present the coming of the **Magi**, the destructive fury of Herod and the slaughter of the Innocents, the dramatists made it clear that the light and beauty of the stable scene had not banished the surrounding darkness. The reaction of violent opposition to the coming of the Saviour had begun; throughout the scenes of the life and ministry of Christ the audience would be aware that before long the threat would become reality.

The play cycles use only selected highlights of Christ's three-year ministry, which together confirm his identity as Son of God and compassionate Saviour of humankind. Through the pageants runs the undercurrent of **Satan**'s opposition, sometimes overt, sometimes manifested through human tools. The *Temptation of Christ* shows the 'Second Adam' resisting Satan's attempts to lure him into gluttony, vainglory and covetousness (sins traditionally ascribed to Adam and Eve), thus reversing the events of the **Fall**. The Chester Expositor comments:

> syns our forfather overcommen was
> by three thinges to doe evill –
> gluttonye, vaynglorye, there bine two,
> covetous of highnes alsoe –
> by these three poyntes, bowt moe,
> Christ hasse overcommen the devill.

(Chester *Temptation*, 172–6)

*The Woman Taken in Adultery* demonstrates the availability of forgiveness to the contrite,[20] the N-town pageant concluding with Christ's promise:

> What man of sinne be repentaunt,                     *Whatever*
> Of God if he wil mercy crave,
> God of mercy is so habundawnt
> That, what man aske it, he shall it have.        *whatever/ask*
> (285–8)

The York *Raising of Lazarus* not only prefigures Christ's own **Resurrection** but affirms his divinity and his ability to deliver his followers from death (190–4). The Towneley pageant has a more solemn tone, concluding with a sermon on death delivered to the audience by Lazarus, which would not have been out of place in the morality plays:

> Amende the[e], man, whils thou may . . .
> Think thou on the dredefull day
> When God shall deme all mankinde.                                    *judge*
>                                            (Towneley *Raising of Lazarus*, 174, 176–7)

The majority of the remaining pageants focus on the death and resurrection of Jesus Christ, the combined event upon which the whole history of **salvation** hinged. The purpose of Christ's coming was to deal with the problem of **sin** by bearing the punishment which mankind's disobedience had incurred. As in the lyrics therefore, his **Passion** is portrayed in graphic, even brutal detail, designed to draw the audience into the scenes which they witness and to evoke in them a response of contrition and love towards the Saviour who endured such suffering for their well-being. The first of the N-Town Passion plays opens with a speech by Satan in which he complains of Christ's triumphs and vows to raise 'new engines of malicious conspiracy' (50) against him. His plans are swiftly fulfilled in the machinations of the Jewish leaders and the treachery of **Judas**, one of Christ's own disciples. Against this dark backcloth is set the **Last Supper**, when Jesus shared the **Passover** meal with his disciples and instituted the **Eucharist**, the **sacrament** celebrated in the **Feast of Corpus Christi**. In the N-Town play Christ's words and actions reflect not only the biblical text (Matthew 26, Mark 14, Luke 22) but also the familiar ritual of the **Mass**, as the disciples come to Christ one by one to receive the bread and the wine.

> This is my body, flesch and blode,
> Þat for þe xal dey upon þe rode . . .            *shall die; cross*
> Þis is my blood, þat for mannys synne
> Outh of myn herte it xal renne.                        *shall run*
> Takyth hed, now, bretheryn, what I haue do:            *done*
> With my flesch and blood I haue ȝow feð.      (N-Town *Last Supper*,
>                                                 449–50, 490–3)

The arrest in the Garden of Gethsemane is followed by scenes of deliberate brutality as the high priests, Pilate and Herod seek in turn to satisfy their malice or curiosity. Dragged pitilessly from one interrogation to another, **Christ** maintains a still dignity in the face of abuse and mockery. Finally he is led to **Calvary**. The image of the crucified Saviour would have been familiar to every medieval believer, portrayed in paintings, manuscripts, sculptures, sermons and meditations. The cycle plays took the process of bringing this crucial event home[21] to ordinary people one stage further, employing a chilling matter-of-factness in the playing of the **Crucifixion** scenes which is immensely powerful. In the York *Crucifixion*, played by the Pinners (nail-makers), the soldiers who carry out the execution are concerned only with the task in hand and blind to its implications. Mildly surprised that Jesus willingly responds to their rough command to place himself on the cross, they are affronted to find their professionalism threatened by the discovery that the holes bored to receive the nails are too far apart. Their cold-blooded decision to stretch the victim to fit the faulty dimensions and their indifferent comments on the extra suffering this will entail are more macabre in their effect than any wilful sadism. There is also a fine irony in their complaints of the discomfort which their labour brings them (186–94). In this scene Christ speaks only twice, each time to stress his willingness to give his life for mankind. His death is the result neither of Satan's stratagems nor of the antagonism of the authorities; it is taking place in accordance with God's plan as a consequence of the sinfulness of humankind. Christ's second speech blends words from Lamentations 1, also used in the lyrics, with the prayer recorded in Luke 23:34:

| | |
|---|---:|
| Al men that walkis, by waye or strete, | *walk* |
| Take tente ye schall no travaile tine! | *lose* |
| Biholdes min[e] heede, min[e] handis, and my feete, | *Behold* |
| And fully feele now, or ye fine, | *reflect, ere you finish* |
| If any mourning may be meete | *matched* |
| Or mischeve mesured unto mine. [He prays.] | *misfortune compared* |
| My Fadir, that all bales may bete, | *sorrows/remedy* |
| Forgiffis thes men that dois me pine. | *Forgive/cause me pain* |
| What thay wirke wotte they noght. | *They know not what they do* |

(York *Crucifixion of Christ*, 253–61)

The soldiers confirm their incomprehension with accusations that he 'jangelis like a jay' but the power of Christ's appeal would not have been lost on the audience. The original soldiers may not have understood what was happening; those playing and watching this scene had no such excuse. Nicholas Love's translation of the *Meditations* summarises the response which such a visualisation of the death of Christ (imagined or dramatised) could have been expected to evoke:

> Þan also if þou beholde wele þi lorde þou maiht haue here matire ynouh of hye compassion, seynge him so tormentede, þat fro þe sole of þe fote in to þe hiest part of þe hede þer was in him none hole place nor membre without passion. þis is a pitevouse siht & a joyful siht. A pitevous siht in him for þat harde passion þat he suffrede for oure sauacion, bot it is a likyng siht to vs, for þe matire and þe effecte þat we haue þerbye of oure redempcion.
>
> (*The Mirror of the Blessed Life of Jesus Christ*, Ch. XIII)

The first joyful outcome of Christ's death to be shown in the cycles is the rescue of the patriarchs and prophets from hell, which was believed to have happened while Christ's body rested in the tomb. Theologically the **Harrowing of Hell** (drawn chiefly from the **apocryphal Gospel of Nicodemus**) accounted for the destinies of all those righteous souls who had waited in bondage for the coming of the Saviour. Dramatically it provided the decisive encounter between Christ and **Satan** and conclusively demonstrated the effects of the victory which had been won upon the cross. In the Chester pageant, Adam, the first man to **sin**, is also the first to discern the blaze of light which heralds Christ's approach to the gates of **hell**:

> Nowe, by this light that I nowe see,
> joye ys come, lord, through thee;
> and one thy people [thou] hast pity,
> to put them out of payne.
>
> (Chester *Harrowing of Hell*, 17–20)

**Satan** and his followers stand by helpless as their captives are wrested from them and led to **heaven** by the Archangel Michael. The Resurrection pageants record further joyful encounters as the risen Christ appears to his bewildered disciples. The N-Town play is at pains to make sure that the audience grasps the whole purport of the story, as Christ sums up the significance of his death and resurrection and links them to the **sacrament** of the **Mass** which symbolised his provision of forgiveness:

For mannys loue I tholyd dede,                                    *suffered*
And for mannys loue I am rysyn up rede;
For man I haue mad my body in brede,
His sowle for to fede.

(N-Town, *Appearance to Mary*, 81–4)

'THE TYME IS COMEN I WILL MAKE ENDE'

In erthe I see butte synnes seere,
Therfore myne aungellis will I sende
To blawe þer bemys, that all may here
The tyme is comen I will make ende.

(York *Judgement*, 61–4)

Having related the stories of creation and **salvation**, the final task
of the cycle plays was to turn the thoughts of their audiences to the
future; to an event which would involve them all, not as spectators
but as players. Although during the early Christian period, the
prospect of the end of the world had chiefly been a focus of hope
to believers anxious to join **Christ** in **heaven**, later changes in
theological emphasis meant that Judgement Day came to be
regarded with fear and uncertainty.[22] The traditional vision of
Doomsday could have been seen painted over the chancel arches of
many medieval churches: Christ, the wounds of the **Passion** still
visible, seated on a rainbow and below him the small naked figures
of human souls being ushered into heaven or consigned to the
gaping jaws of hell. The records of the Mercers, who played the
York *Judgement*, show that no expense was spared in staging this
momentous scene. The inventory of properties and costumes of
1433 (*REED*, York, 55) includes 'A cloud and ij peces of Rainbow
of tymber', 'ij peces of rede cloudes & sternes (stars) of gold langing
to heuen ij peces of blue cloudes payntid on bothe sydes iiij peces of
red cloudes With sunne bemes of golde & sternes for the hiest of
heuen', 'vij grete Aungels ... iiij smaler Aungels payntid rede to
runne aboute in þe heuene.' At the other end of the spiritual scale,
the Coventry Drapers paid 4d. for 'kepyng of fyer at hell mothe'
in 1557.[23] In the York pageant, Christ, wearing a 'Sirke (shirt),
Wounded', prefaces his judgement with a reminder of all he had
endured for love of mankind:

Here may ʒe see my woundes wide,
Þe whilke I tholed for youre mysdede ...
Man, sore aught þe for to quake,

Þis dredfull day þis sight to see.
All þis I suffered for þi sake –
Say, man, what suffered þou for me?

(York *Judgement*, 245–6; 273–6)

This appeal, so reminiscent of the lyrics, is followed by the division of the resurrected souls into two groups, following the account in Matthew 25. Heaven is for those whose faith in Christ and his teachings has shown itself in action, specifically in performing the **Seven Corporal Works of Mercy**. For them this coming of Christ has brought joy; for the rest, devils in two-faced masks stand ready to drag them into the flames of **hell**. For an audience watching as darkness fell, the scene must have been impressive indeed:[24]

Mi chosen childir, come unto me;
With me to wonne nowe schall ȝe wende;
Þere joie and blisse schall ever be . . .
Ȝe cursed kaitiffs, fro me ȝe flee,
In helle to dwelle with-outen ende.

(365–7, 369–70)

## 'THIS MORALL MEN MAY HAVE IN MINDE'

While the mystery plays employ a large canvas, crowded with people and events, the 'morality' plays or interludes use a technique closer to that of the portrait-painter. The epic narrative of God's interaction with mankind through the centuries is replaced by the story of a representative soul whose life illustrates the practical implications of Christian teaching. The focus falls upon a (usually) solitary figure confronted by their own mortality and facing the prospect of a very personal[25] Judgement Day. Grouped around them, as in many medieval portraits, are figures who influence their lives. As each play progresses it becomes clear that the painting is in fact a mirror, in which the audience are invited to see their lives and prospects reflected. Moral plays cannot be neatly categorised or analysed; they vary in scale from brief interludes such as *Mankind* which could be performed by a small cast to the complex splendours of the *Castle of Perseverance*. They share a common set of dramatic conventions whose immediate antecedents are uncertain[26] but individual authors remained free to voice their own religious, social and political concerns. Moral plays are peopled not by named figures of biblical history but by personifications[27] who make visible the inner conflicts of the the human mind and heart. The audience, however, are not allowed to remain at a safe distance, remote from these moral abstractions. Instead they are wooed by the preaching of Mercy in *Mankind* and enticed to join in the obscene songs of his opponents. They witness Death arriving unheralded in the life of Everyman just as he came all too frequently to their families and communities; they watch the central character in the *Castle of Perseverance* making the moral choices which faced them daily and wait in suspense as his eternal destiny hangs in the balance. The tone of morality plays ranges from high solemnity, sometimes verging on tragedy, to knockabout humour, cruder than anything to be seen in the cycle plays. It is easy therefore to identify differences between the mysteries and the moralities but it is also important to appreciate their complementary roles in the transmission of spiritual truth.[28] Each strand of medieval religious drama both influenced and complemented the others, reflecting their common origin in the content and expression of Christian worship. Liturgical plays enhanced the response of worshippers at key points in the service; the mystery plays brought to life readings from the scriptures; and plays such as *The Castle of Perseverance*, *Mankind* and *Everyman* fulfilled a similar function to that of the sermon: to ensure that individuals not only understood the concepts of sin and forgiveness but would respond. The loss of so much medieval drama makes it hard to trace the development of the morality plays but their aims and content are firmly rooted in the spiritual tradition which shaped so much medieval literature. The three plays which will be examined here are fired by the same concern which motivated the *Pearl*-poet and inspired the religious lyrics: the need to awaken in men and women true **contrition** and lasting repentance, and to warn them of perils which threatened their souls. This concern, focused by the movement to encourage regular confession, also featured regularly in the graphic sermons of the **friars**.[29] Morality plays are hence about practical choices with profound spiritual implications. From birth men and women were seen as poised between **heaven** and **hell**, surrounded by pitfalls and constantly wooed by siren voices eager to tempt them from the straight and narrow way. The point is made repeatedly as the forces of evil conspire to threaten the well-being of humankind, sometimes by deception, sometimes by outright warfare.

*The Castle of Perseverance* (c. 1400–25), the most ambitious of the surviving morality plays, is set, according to a plan included in the *Macro* manuscript, in a large open space, surrounded by five scaffolds or towers (for God, the World, the Flesh, the **Devil** and Covetousness), with the castle of the title in the centre. It opens with the enemies of Mankind drawn up for battle.[30] The World (Mundus), supported by Covetousness, boasts of his destructive power:

| | |
|---|---|
| I do men ravin on a riche rowe | *cause; to behave madly; rich procession* |
| Till they be dyth to dethys dent. | *put to death's blow* |
| | (168–9) |

The Devil (Belial), sharing his scaffold with Pride, Envy, and Wrath, displays the malice which the mystery plays also attributed to Satan:

| | |
|---|---|
| fowle I am anoyed | *foully, grievously* |
| But Mankinde be stroyed | *Unless; destroyed* |
| By dikys and by denne. | *valley (i.e. everywhere)* |
| | (206–8) |

Finally the Flesh, accompanied by Sloth, Gluttony and Lechery, sums up the combined aim of these malevolent forces:

| | |
|---|---|
| Nyth and day, besy we be | *Night* |
| For to distroy Mankende | |
| | (268–9) |

Into this arena step the Good and Bad Angels; between them the frail figure of Mankind, naked and vulnerable, protected only by the mark of **baptism** (276–8). Mankind's journey through life has begun. As the play proceeds, his movements around the playing arena mirror the far from steady progress of his spiritual pilgrimage.[31] His intentions may be good but as soon as he has to exercise his free will and choose between the two angels he becomes confused.

> Whom to folwe, wetyn I ne may . . .
> I wolde be riche in gret aray;
> And fain I wolde my soule save:
> As winde in watyr I wave.
>
> (375, 377–9)

The essential instability of man's resolve is an ongoing theme of the play. Tempted by the prospect of wealth, Mankind ignores the Good Angel's entreaty to 'thinke on thin[e] endinge day' (407).

Wooed by the **Seven Deadly Sins** and their accomplices, he is blind to the conspiracy which threatens his soul.

> Loke he be riche, the sothe to tell.      *See to it; truth*
> Help him, fast he gunne to thrive;    *so that he thrives quickly*
> And whanne he wenith best to live             *thinks*
> Thanne schal he deye, and not be shrive,        *die; shriven*
> And goo with us to hell.
>
> (543–7)

The prospect of sudden death, without time to repent and receive absolution, was a spectre to chill even the most hardened spectator. Unconscious of his danger, Mankind seems lost beyond recall till the Good Angel appeals to God's mercy and Confession and **Penance** appear to awaken the sinner's slumbering conscience. His confession follows models laid down in the manuals used by **parish priests**:

> I have sinnyd many a throwe                    *a time*
> In the Dedly Sinnys sevene . . .
> The ten commaundementys brokyn I have,
> And my five wittys spent hem amis . . .  *And misused my five wits*
> Mercy, God, forgeve me this!
>
> (1474–5, 1481–2, 1484)

His relationship with God restored, Mankind is installed in the Castle of Perseverance ('He that persevere unto the end, he shall be saved:' Matt. 10:22). It was instability of purpose which led to his downfall and only perseverance in his re-discovered allegiance can keep him safe from further assaults. He is welcomed by **Seven Virtues** who are the *remedia* or antidotes to the **Seven Deadly Sins** – Meekness, Patience, Charity, Abstinence, Chastity, Business, and Generosity – but his reformation is short-lived. Enraged by Mankind's defection, the forces of evil lay siege to the castle: trumpets sound, armour is donned, banners are raised on high. According to the stage directions, Belial should have 'gunnepowdyr brennynge [burning] in pypys in hys handys and in hys erys and in hys ars whanne he gothe to batayl.' Six of the Sins direct their hostilities against their counterparts and are successfully repulsed; the seventh, Covetousness, 'the root of all evils' (I Tim: 6:10), tackles Mankind directly and cleverly entices him from his stronghold. The Virtues excuse their failure on the grounds that Mankind must exercise his free will and thus take responsibility for his own sins

(2560-2). Mankind, now old, is consumed by his desire for riches. 'More and more' is his insatiable cry until Death enters unheralded and strikes him with a dart. In his death throes Mankind finds himself rejected by the World to whom he has given his allegiance and sees his much-prized wealth falling into the clutches of an unknown heir. Urging the audience not to fall into his error, Mankind uses his dying breath to call upon God's mercy:

> Now good men, takithe example at me . . .             *take; from*
> To helle I schal both fare and fle                          *go and depart*
> But God graunte me of his grace . . .                        *Unless*
> I putte me in Goddys mercy!
>
> (2995, 3001–2, 3007)

The Bad Angel has apparently achieved his ends and drags Mankind's remorseful Soul to hell. Mankind's last cry, however, prompts a debate before God's throne between the Four Daughters of God;[32] Mercy, Righteousness (Justice), Truth and Peace. Mercy carries the day and God the Father orders Mankind's release. Together the Four Daughters reclaim Mankind from the clutches of the Bad Angel; he is brought across the arena to ascend God's scaffold and to sit in the place of honour at God's right hand. This example of clemency is followed by a warning of the coming general Judgement Day when

> Lityl and mekyl, the more and the les . . .             *Humble and mighty*
> To me schal they geve acompt at my digne des . . . *account; worthy throne*
> And they that wel do in this werld, here welthe schal awake;    *their*
> In hevene they schal heynyd [be] in bounté and [in] blis.    *exalted*
> And they that evil do, they schul to helle-lake             *pit*
> In bitter balys to be brent: my jugement it is . . .     *torments; burned*
> All men example hereat may take
> To maintein the goode and mendyn here mis.         *amend their sins*
>
> (3614, 3616, 3636–9, 3642–3)

The moral of the story is crystal clear: Mankind may have just scraped into heaven at the last moment but the flesh–and–blood members of the audience would be well advised to take a more secure route.

The *Castle of Perseverance* closes with a demonstration of God's mercy; *Mankind*, a moral interlude on a much smaller scale, opens with the figure of Mercy preaching a learned **homily**[33] on **salvation** to the assembled spectators.

Divert not yourself in time of temptation,                    *Do not go astray*
That ye may be acceptable to God at your going hence . . .
In good works I advise you, sovereigns to be perseverant,
To purify your souls that they be not corrupt,
For your ghostly enemy will make his avaunt,               *the devil; boast*
Your good conditions if he may interrupt.

                                        (*Mankind*, 19–20, 25–8)

This solemn advice (which also serves to outline the plot) is rudely
interrupted by Mischief, who lures Mercy into a fruitless argument.
The homily is further disrupted by the boisterous entrance of the
three Vice figures: Newguise, Nowadays and Nought. Together
they torment the unfortunate preacher, tripping him up, mocking
his vocabulary and horrifying him by their casual obscenities. Their
actions may be entertaining but their language signals that in
spiritual terms they are to be taken seriously. Tame as these
representations of contemporary worldliness may seem compared
with the more sinister figures of the **Seven Deadly Sins**, Mercy
regards their flippancy and obscene jests as evidence of real spiritual
degradation. Speech is used as an important spiritual indicator[34] in
*Mankind*, and in this as in other areas the Vices serve as *exempla* or
practical illustrations for Mercy's homilies.

This condition of living, it is prejudicial                       *harmful*
Beware thereof! It is worse than any felony or treason.
How may it be excused before the Justice of all,
When for every idle word we must yield a reason?

                                        (170–3)

The entry of Mankind signals that the real conflict is about to
begin. Once again human good intentions are apparent but
Mankind confesses himself torn by a fundamental inner tension:

My name is Mankind. I have my composition
Of a body and of a soul, of condition contrary.
Betwix them twain is a great division[35] . . .
My body with my soul is ever querulous . . .          *always at war*
I am unsteadfast in living.

                                        (194–6, 211, 214)

Mercy reminds him that he is pledged to fight against the World,
the Flesh and the Devil and departs. With Mercy safely out of the
way, the Vices return, and the complexity of their role in the play
begins to emerge. Their plan to ensnare Mankind is obvious; their

attempted subversion of the audience less so. On stage Mankind struggles with subtle temptations but the audience are also on uncertain moral ground. Led in a 'Christmas song', they find themselves singing an obscene parody, tricked into aligning themselves with the forces of evil. Provoked by the Vices' taunts, Mankind finally beats them off with his spade. They retire, nursing their wounds, but their campaign is far from over. Mischief summons Titivillus, a devil renowned for his invisibility, who treats the audience as co-conspirators, making them privy to his plot and enjoining their silence. Mankind, who has resisted the direct assault of the Vices, falls to the more subtle snares of Titivillus. Frustrated in his digging and distracted from saying his **Paternoster**, he succumbs to sloth and is deceived by a false dream into believing Mercy to be dead. In a parody of the penitential process he begs forgiveness from the Vices and is 'solemnly' charged to embark upon a life of sin. Mercy, grieved by Mankind's fickleness, searches for his wayward charge. Afraid that Mankind may yet be saved, the Vices plot to bring him to despair and suicide (790–2). Saved at the last moment by the entrance of Mercy, Mankind has to be persuaded that forgiveness is still possible (818–21). In his response, Mercy, like all confessors, has to strike a balance between reassurance and challenge. Chaucer's Parson, in the treatise on **sin** and **penance** which forms his tale, cited four factors which were believed to hinder men and women from submitting to the penitential process: 'drede, shame, hope and wanhope, that is desperacion' (*Parson's Tale*, 1056). Mankind must not be allowed to succumb to the last and deadliest of sins, despair; nor must he be allowed to presume upon God's mercy. Mercy is blunt about the hazards of spiritual brinkmanship:

> Sin not in hope of mercy; that is a crime notary . . .     *notorious*
> Ask mercy and have, while the body with the soul hath his
>     annexion;
> If ye tarry till your decease, ye may hap of your desire to miss.
> Be repentant here; trust not the hour of death.
>
> (844, 862–4)

A recurring theme of the moralities is the transience and uncertainty of human life. According to *Jacob's Well*, an early fifteenth-century manual on the spiritual life, 'wrong hope of long lyif' (297) was one of the devil's chief weapons in preventing men and women coming to confession. *Everyman* (c. 1495), described as 'a treatise how the High Father of heaven sendeth death to summon every creature to come and give account of their lives in this world', does not address human life as a whole but focuses solely on the 'hour of death'. The prospect of death and the art of dying well greatly exercised medieval minds. The physical horrors of disease and death were all around and spiritual writers sought to turn this fact to good account:

> What thyng is in eny mannes wit þat sonner meeuyth a man to mekeness, to kepyng of hym-self fro vanytee . . . than doth the consideracioun of a mannes corrupcioun and hys freelte, of his deedlyness, and of the dreedful day of his deeth? For whan a man bigynneth to wex seek . . . the body croketh, the flesch widerith, and alle the beaute is turned into filthe and corrupcioun; whan the body is buried, it falleth into powdir, & is turned alle into wormes. Bihold now, brother, this is a horrible siȝt; but it is a [ful] profitable myrour.
>
> (*Mirror of Sinners, Yorkshire Writers* II, 438–9)

God's opening speech, reminiscent of both the lyrics and the mystery plays, sets out the reason for the impending confrontation: mankind's ingratitude and predilection for the **Seven Deadly Sins** have exhausted divine forbearance:

> Therefore I will, in all the haste,
> Have a reckoning of every man's person.
>
> (45–6)

Death is dispatched to bring Everyman to judgement, the last and unavoidable pilgrimage from which no one will return. The shock experienced by Everyman would no doubt have touched a chord in most of the original audience:

> O, Death, thou comest when I had thee least in mind!
>
> (119)

Everyman's earthly finances may have prospered but his spiritual accounts are woefully in arrears. He begs for time but Death is obdurate:

> Thee availeth not to cry, weep, and pray;
> But haste thee lightly that thou were gone that journey.
> And prove thy friends if you can                                      *test*
> For, wit thou well, the tide abideth no man.
>
> (140–3)

The transience of life is underlined as Everyman's folly is ruthlessly exposed:

DEATH:
> What, weenest thou thy life is given thee?                    *think*
>    And thy worldy goods also?

EVERYMAN:
> I had wend so, verily.

DEATH:
> Nay, nay, it was but lent thee.

(161–4)

Death's temporary withdrawal leaves Everyman to search for friends who will accompany him on his final journey. He turns first to those he has courted during his life: Fellowship, Kindred and Goods. Each in turn is fulsome in their pledges of loyalty but swiftly abandons Everyman when his true plight is revealed. Goods, the worldly wealth in which Everyman has delighted, even turns on his erstwhile admirer with a scathing (if somewhat belated) rebuke.

EVERYMAN:
> Alas, I have thee loved, and have had great pleasure
>    All my life-days on good and treasure.

GOODS:
> That is to thy damnation, without leasing,                   *a lie*
>    For my love is contrary to the love everlasting . . .

GOODS:
> Therefore to thy soul Good is a thief.

(427–30, 447)

Bereft of all other support, Everyman turns belatedly to his Good Deeds. Though willing to help, she is bound by his sin and weakened by his neglect.[36] Before she can be mobilised on his behalf, Everyman must experience true penitence. Guided by Knowledge, he comes to Confession, undergoes **penance** and clothes himself in **Contrition**, a garment 'wet with tears'. Everyman's repentance is the turning point of the play. His fear of eternal punishment removed, he faces the second challenge posed by death: physical decay. With Discretion, Strength, Five Wits, and Beauty by his side, Everyman demonstrates the authenticity of his repentance, making a will which combines gifts to the poor with restitution. This response, which echoes the actions of the reformed tax-collector Zaccheus (Luke 11), was a common feature of medieval wills, as testators sought to safeguard their eternal destiny.

In a will of 1415, Thomas Walwayn set aside money to 'helpe nede men out of pryson', provide for 'pores nedy folk' and make 'restitucion ther eny wronge may be Ifounde be donn, (as I trust to god but litull)' (*The Fifty Earliest English Wills*, 23). The *Book of the Craft of Dying* stated that 'every sikeman and every man in perill' should be urged to make a will and to receive 'spirituall medicins, þat is to seye takynge the sacraments of holy church' (*Yorkshire Writers*, II, 416). This step sets the seal on Everyman's preparation for death. Knowledge and Five Wits explain the **sacraments** and the role of **priests** and dispatch Everyman to receive the Final **Eucharist** and Extreme Unction. Thus prepared, he experiences the onset of physical weakness and finds himself deserted by all except Good Deeds. He dies with the last words of Christ (Luke 23:46) on his lips, words which the *Book of the Craft of Dying* recommended to every Christian as the moment of death drew near:

> Into my hands, Lord, my soul I commend!
> Receive it, Lord, that it be not lost!

> (880–1)

His repentance has ensured his entry into heaven; his reckoning now 'crystal clear'. Like Mankind in the previous two plays, Everyman stands as an example of **grace**, a warning against complacency and encouragement not to despair.

### 'ANOTHER ENSAUMPLE I SHALL SHOW YOU'

The last group[37] of plays considered in this chapter also contain examples designed to promote perseverance by encouraging the faithful, challenging the perverse and reassuring the penitent. Although 'miracle plays' or 'saints' plays' were probably more numerous than either the mysteries or the moralities, few texts have survived. Those that remain vary considerably in content and form, yet are linked by a desire to demonstrate the power of God, whether through miracles or through the conversion of sinners. **Saint** was a term applied to a wide range of figures, some historical, others legendary. Churches and guilds would have encouraged the performance of plays which, in honouring their own patron **saint**, encouraged the faithful to follow their example and seek their intercession. In *Mundus and Infans*, a morality play probably dating from the early sixteenth century, Perseverance cites sinners who have yet found grace:

another ensaumple I shall show you to . . .
For Paul did Christ's people great villainy,
And Peter at the Passion forsook Christ thrice,
And Magdalene lived long in lechery,
And St Thomas believed not in the Resurrection;
And yet these to Christ are darlings dear,
And now be saints in heaven clear.

(865, 869–74)

Two of his examples, **St Paul** and **Mary Magdalene**, feature in surviving texts, both found in the same manuscript. The *Conversion of St Paul*, a 'litell pagent', is a relatively straightforward narrative. Paul (here called by his Jewish name Saul), the avowed enemy of the infant Christian Church, is met by God on the road to Damascus. Convinced by a series of miraculous signs, Saul submits to baptism, a rite carried out on stage with full solemnity. His conversion, the audience is told, is total, his allegiance unswerving:

After his conversion never mutable, but still insue          *striving*
The lawys of God to teche ever more and more.

(350–1)

Saul's new allegiance, however, arouses the fury of Belial, 'Mightee prince of the partes infernall', and his followers:

The conversion of sinner, certaine,
Is more paine to us and persecution
Than all the furies of the infernall dongyon.

(472–4)

Delivered from the machinations of his enemies by an angelic warning, Saul escapes to join the other disciples and continue his new mission, having demonstrated to the audience the power of God both to convert and to protect.

More complex is *Mary Magdalene*, which uses narrative strands similar to those in the mystery plays, together with allegorical figures familiar from the moralities, in an intricate account of its heroine's spiritual adventures. The Mary Magdalene revered by the medieval Church was a composite figure, constructed by **hagiographers** from a range of **New Testament** passages and adorned with a colourful collection of legendary attributes and experiences. The wide scope offered by this multi-faceted biography meant that Mary could be in turn a repentant sinner (the unnamed woman in Luke 7:36-50), a fearless 'apostylesse' to the land of Marcyll (derived from legend), and a solitary contemplative (inferred from Christ's words to Mary, sister of Martha, in Luke 10:38-41). Her life therefore offered multiple examples of **grace** and encouragement to the audience. Mary's spiritual experience is told initially in terms of a morality, as the World, the Flesh, and the **Devil**, with the **Seven Deadly Sins** in attendance, seek to bring about her downfall. Lured from her castle by Lechery, Mary abandons herself to a life of immorality until brought up short by a rebuke on her inconstancy from the Good Angel:

> Woman, woman, why art thou so onstabyll?          *inconstant*
> Ful bitterly this blisse it wol be bowth.     *pleasure; bought, paid for*
> Why art thou agens God so veriabyll?            *against; inconstant*
>                                                              (588–9)

Moved to repentance, Mary seeks out Jesus who offers forgiveness, commending her as an example of **contrition**. Mary's deliverance from the seven devils (or Sins)[38] which have possessed her and the raising of her brother **Lazarus** demonstrate Christ's power over evil and death and prefigure the **Harrowing of Hell** and his own **Resurrection**. The biblically-based account of the death and Resurrection of Christ and the mission of the **Early Church**, carefully structured around Mary's own role, is followed by her adventurous (and wholly **apocryphal**) career as a 'holy apostylesse', during which a pagan temple is struck by fire from heaven, the dead are raised, and the king and queen of Marcyll converted. Her task complete, Mary moves to the desert, 'More gostly [spiritual] strenght to purchase'. Here she becomes the model **contemplative**:

> Of wor[l]dly fodes I will leve all refeccion;     *food; leave off; partaking*
> By the fode that commit[h] from heven on hye,
> Thatt, God will me send, by contemplatiff.
>
>                                                              (2001–3)

The woman chided for inconstancy has now become totally dependent on God's **grace**, her final accolade coming with her assumption into **heaven**.

Although the Croxton *Play of the Conversion of Ser Jonathas the Jewe by Miracle of the Blissed Sacrament* has no **saint** in its cast, it is, as its title indicates, primarily concerned with miracles and conversion. The play is designed to demonstrate the truth of the doctrine of **transubstantiation**, to restore Christians who have strayed and to convert unbelievers. The casting of Jews as the doubters who wish to test the powers of the **Host** has added resonance because their actions mirror the original **Passion of Christ**:

> with our strokys we shall fray him as he was on the rood          *assault*
>                                                                      (455)

Similarly, the role of the Christian merchant bribed to obtain the wafer for them echoes that of Judas. When, however, the **Host** miraculously responds to their ill-treatment and an image of Christ speaks a traditional *complaint*, both parties repent and are reconciled to the Christian community. The audience are warned to avoid 'dowghtys' about doctrine, a growing problem by the time of this play (c. 1461), and to set their minds on eternal life.

EPILOGUE

Sadly, much of the drama which flourished during the fourteenth and fifteenth centuries did not survive the stricter climate of the Reformation.[39] Disquiet about the propriety of presenting sacred subjects in entertainment had already been voiced in a fourteenth-century Wycliffite tract:

> Thanne sithen [since] miraclis of Crist and of hise seintis [saints] weren thus efectuel . . . no man shulde usen in bourde [sport] and pleye the miraclis and werkis that Crist so ernystfully wroughte to oure helthe; for whoevere so doth, he errith in the byleve, reversith [contradicts] Crist, and scornyth God.
>
> (*Middle English Tretise of Miraclis Pleyinge*, 93)

Now the growing influence of Protestantism, coupled with Henry VIII's break with Rome, caused searching questions to be asked about many aspects of Catholic doctrine. The role of the **saints**, the practice of **pilgrimage**, the doctrine of the **Mass**, the feast of **Corpus Christi** itself, all came under scrutiny and were found wanting. Small wonder then that saints' plays and mystery plays were also regarded with increasing suspicion by ecclesiastical and political authorities. Cities such as York and Chester made valiant attempts to retain their plays and revisions were made in order to exclude material considered unscriptural. These however were insufficient to placate the increasingly Protestant authorities. The York cycle was last performed in 1569, and three years later the text of the *Paternoster* play was taken for examination by the

Archbishop and nothing more is heard of it. Instructions issued in 1576 by the Diocesan authorities regarding the Wakefield *Corpus Christi* play are probably an accurate reflection of the concerns which spelled the end of the cycles and the saints' plays:

> This daie upon intelligence geven to the saide Commission that it is meant and purposed that in the towne of Wakefeld shal be plaid this yere in Whitsonweke next or thereaboutes a plaie commonlie called Corpus Christi plaie . . . wherein they are done t'understand that there be many thinges used which tend to the derogation of the Majestie and glorie of God, the prophanation of the sacramentes and the maunteynaunce of superstition and idolatrie, the said Commissioners decreed a lettre to be written and sent . . . that in the said playe no pageant be used or set furthe wherein the Majesty of God the Father, God the Sonne, God the Holie Ghoste or the administration of either the Sacramentes of baptisme or of the Lordes Supper be counterfeyted or represented, or anythinge plaied which tende to the maintenaunce of superstition and idolatrie or which be contrarie to the lawes of God or of the realme.[40]

During this turbulent period, the moralities seem to have fared rather better, proving more adaptable to the changing conditions of the sixteenth century and exerting considerable influence on the emerging drama of the Renaissance.[41] Despite their decline, the mystery cycles and the saints' plays also left their mark on the plays which succeeded them. The authorities might ban performances and suppress texts, but the beliefs which inspired and informed those texts and the images left upon the minds of their audiences were not so easily eradicated.[42] The pendulum would continue to swing between Catholic and Protestant teachings for many years to come and the evolving Church of England would incorporate elements of both into its liturgy and traditions. The drama of the succeeding centuries, like its poetry and prose, would be shaped largely by those to whom Christianity was not merely an acknowledged fact of life but also a matter of passionate debate. For Marlowe and Shakespeare, Raleigh and Donne, Milton and Bunyan, Christianity was a wellspring of controversy and creativity: a cause for which men and women would not only live but were often prepared to die; a faith which left an indelible imprint upon their lives and imaginations.

NOTES

Play texts are taken from *Medieval Drama* with the following exceptions:

*The Chester Mystery Cycle*:
*Adam and Eve*
*Abraham and Isaac*
*Temptation of Christ*
*Harrowing of Hell*

*Everyman and Medieval Miracle Plays*:
*Coventry Annunciation*

*The N-Town Play*:
*Cain and Abel*
*Nativity*
*Last Supper*
*Christ's Appearance to Mary*

*The York Plays*:
*Fall of the Angels*
*Adam and Eve*
*Noah*
*Woman Taken in Adultery/Raising of Lazarus*
*Judgement*

*Three Late Medieval Morality Plays*:
*Mankind*
*Everyman*
*Mundus et Infans*

1. The loss of texts and difficulty of interpreting records make it impossible to be precise about the early history of the religious drama. The earliest definite reference to performance of cycle plays in English comes in a York record of 1394. Most saints', Paternoster, and mystery plays had been suppressed by 1575.
2. See Anderson (1963) for examples of paintings, stained glass and carvings which shed light on the treatment of subjects in the drama.
3. These terms, though not contemporary, are used for convenience. There was in fact considerable overlap in approach and content.
4. The treatise was written by an opponent of the plays but provides indirect evidence for the views of those who defended them.

5. This trope is based on the **Gospel** narratives (e.g. Matt. 28:1–10; Lk 24:1–12) which describe angels announcing the Resurrection of Christ to Mary Magdalene and the other women who had come to anoint his body after the Cricifixion. Harris (1992, 28–31) outlines the development of the trope. See Chapter 4 above for the full text.

6. See Woolf (1972), Chs 1 and 2.

7. Keen (1990, 106).

8. See Meredith (1994).

9. Cited Kolve (1966, 45).

10. Creed plays contained twelve scenes, one for each article of belief and each associated with one of the twelve apostles. See *REED, York*, 757. Paternoster plays may have related each of the seven petitions of the Lord's Prayer to one of the Seven Deadly Sins. See *REED, York*, 693; also Johnston (1975).

11. See Kolve (1966, Ch. 4), Woolf (1972, Ch. 4), Harris (1992, Chs 8 and 9).

12. See Twycross (1983).

13. Jack (1989, 11).

14. Woolf (1972, 128).

15. Kolve (1966, 67) cites a passage from the *Meditations on the Life and Passion of Christ* where the poet makes a similar point:

> But þe ferste Albeles blod
> Cryeþ wreche as it be wod;
> Crystes blod doþ al an oþer:
> It cryeþ mercy for his brother.

16. See Woolf (1972, 136ff).

17. See Robinson (1971) and Cowen (1983).

18. In a misreading of Habuakkuk 3:2 *in medio animalium* was substituted for *in medio annorum* (in the midst of the years).

19. See Ross (1967–8).

20. See Prosser (1961, Ch. 6).

21. See Beadle (1994, 101); Robinson (1963).

22. Sheingorn (1985, 17).

23. Cited Anderson (1963, 128).

24. Twycross (1994, 53) suggests the York *Judgement* had stage lighting.

25. The Church taught that individual souls were judged immediately after death; later all would have to give an account of their deeds at the Last Judgement when they would be despatched to heaven or hell for all eternity.

26. Potter (1975, Ch. 1) suggests that the morality plays, while broadly in the tradition of the *Psychomachia* (Battle for the Soul) of Prudentius (c. AD 400), are more immediately influenced by sermons and the lost Paternoster plays.

27. See Potter (1975, 37–47); King (1994, 241–2).

28. Potter (1975, 8).

29. On friars and the drama see Harris (1992, 88–9); Owst (1966, 526ff).

30. On the origins of the 'Three Enemies of Man' see Wenzel (1967).

31. See Schell (1968).

32 The debate between the Four Daughters of God (also used in the N-Town *Parliament of Heaven* and in *Piers Plowman*) derives from Ps 84:11: 'Mercy and truth have met each other: justice and peave have kissed.'

33. Coogan (1947) identifies Mercy as a priest who guides Mankind (and thus the audience) through the sacrament of penance citing parallels to Mercy's homilies in *Jacob's Well*, a contemporary sermon-collection.

34. Compare Matt 12:36–7; James 3:2–10. On the significance of the language used by Mercy see Dillon (1993b).

35. The conflict between the soul and body was a commonplace of medieval sermons. Compare *Perseverance*, 3012–20.

36. Compare York *Judgement*, 121ff:

    What schall we wrecchis do for drede . . .
    When we may bringe forthe no goode dede
    Before hym þat our juge schall be?

37. So few saints' (miracle) plays have survived that classification is difficult. The plays in this section are linked by subject matter rather than form. See Davidson (1986), Jeffrey (1973) and Grantley (1994).

38. Gregory the Great identified the seven devils said to have been expelled from Mary Magdalene (Luke 8:2) with the Seven Deadly Sins.

39. See Gardiner (1946) and Harris (1992, Ch. 16).

40. Cited Gardiner (1946, 78).

41. See Bevington (1962) and Potter (1975).

42. See Duffy (1992).

# Reference Section

# A. The Early Church

The life of Jesus **Christ**, as recorded in the Four **Gospels**, has two main components: the accounts of his birth and early childhood and the three-year public ministry which ended with his crucifixion around the age of thirty-three. During his ministry he called together a group of twelve disciples: Simon **Peter**, **Andrew**, **James**, **John**, Philip, Bartholomew, Thomas, **Matthew** (Levi), James son of Alphaeus, Thaddeus, Simon the Cananean, and **Judas Iscariot** who betrayed him. After the **Crucifixion** the group went into hiding but was revitalised by the conviction that Jesus had risen from death. The Book of Acts relates that, on the day of **Pentecost**, one hundred and twenty disciples gathered in Jerusalem received power from God in the person of the **Holy Spirit**, and began to preach a message of forgiveness of sins for all who would repent, believe in Jesus and be **baptised**. Despite opposition from the Jewish authorities, the movement continued to grow, led initially by **St Peter** and **St James**. Persecution forced a number of disciples to leave Jerusalem and they travelled through Palestine and beyond, preaching as they went. The conversion of **St Paul** (Acts 9) was followed by the radical (and highly significant) decision by St Peter (Acts 10) to offer the message of **salvation** to the hitherto despised **Gentiles**. Partly in response to the work of St Paul, congregations containing both Jews and Gentiles sprang up in Asia Minor, Greece and Rome.

With the destruction of Jerusalem by the Romans in AD 70, the Church's centre of gravity shifted first to Antioch and then to Rome. Gentile rather than Jewish believers were now in the majority and the church was mainly Greek-speaking. The next two centuries were marked by sporadic intense persecution, during which many suffered martyrdom. The turning point came with the conversion in 312 of the Emperor Constantine and the resulting toleration and favour shown to Christianity. The spread of the church was paralled by developments in both structures and theology. Admission to the church was marked by **baptism** and the chief symbol of belonging was participation in the **Eucharistic** meal of bread and wine. Leadership of each Christian community rested primarily in the hands of a **bishop** assisted by presbyters and deacons. The bishops, regarded as the successors of the **apostles**, exercised authority in matters of pastoral care and doctrine, areas vital to the well-being of the Church, since believers remained vulnerable both to external pressures to conform to the society in which they lived and to the internal threat of heresy. The traffic with the world around was not only one-way. Both Greek and Jewish culture and philosophy needed to be evaluated and related to the message passed down by the apostles. Individuals needed encouragement to remain faithful and the church as a whole required clear guidance and definition of its doctrines. The writings of the **Fathers** reveal the passionate debates which accompanied the Church's attempt to meet such needs.

Following the conversion of Constantine, Christianity gradually emerged as the state religion of the Roman Empire, a change which brought benefits and fresh tensions. During the fourth century Latin-speaking Christian leaders became more prominent and the primacy of the Bishop of Rome was more formally established. As persecution virtually disappeared the church looked back to the heroes of the past and the cult of the **saints** and their **relics** assumed a new importance. Constantine embarked upon an extensive programme of church building and established Palestine as a Holy Land, thus giving additional impetus to the embryonic practice of **pilgrimage**. Alongside the Church's new influence came the dangers of worldliness and materialism as large numbers of sometimes superficial converts were absorbed. Growing numbers of devout believers responded by renouncing the world and joining the **monastic** movement which developed rapidly during the third and fourth centuries. Some fled to become **hermits** in the deserts of Egypt, Palestine or Syria; others, like **Augustine of Hippo**, exercised the role of a **bishop** whilst living in a community and under monastic discipline. Scarcely had the Church achieved relative security within the Roman Empire, when the western portion of that Empire itself began to crumble. Barbarian tribes of Germanic origin began to overrun the western provinces and Rome iself was sacked in AD 410. The eastern, Greek-speaking provinces remained relatively unaffected: a Christian Emperor ruled in Constantinople until it was conquered by the Ottomans in 1453 and the Greek-speaking church (later the Orthodox Church) pursued its own distinctive course. Despite these upheavals the Latin-speaking Church in the West (later the Roman Catholic Church) survived to face the challenge posed by the newly-established barbarian kingdoms. Its contribution was two-fold. Firstly, it preserved major features of Roman civilisation, maintaining Roman systems of organisation to which its own structures had become adapted, continuing to use the Latin language and holding forth a vision of a wider community, now that of Christendom rather than the Empire, which could embrace all the emerging kingdoms. Secondly, it embarked upon missionary outreach to the new barbarian rulers, who were either pagans or Arian Christians whose beliefs differed from those of the Catholic Church. Included in the former category were the new rulers of much of the former province of Britain.

The origins of the church in Britain are unknown but it is recorded that **bishops** attended **councils** in Gaul and Rimini in the fourth century, though some were too poor to pay their own way. With the withdrawal of Roman protection and widespread settlement by Anglo-Saxon tribes during the fifth and sixth centuries, the Church in Britain appears to have survived in the main amongst those Britons who retreated to Wales and Cornwall. These Celtic Christians, like those in Ireland, were for a time largely cut off from Rome and the Continent and hence maintained a distinctive spirituality and church organisation of their own. The conversion of the English was to require the convergence of both Celtic and Roman resources. In AD 597 **St Augustine** arrived in England with a group of monks, sent to the Anglo-Saxon kingdom of Kent by **Gregory I** (c. 540–604), a pope deeply committed to missionary ventures. The same year saw the death of the Irish monk **St Columba**, who had established a centre of Celtic spirituality on the island of Iona, off the west coast of Scotland. Although the English would eventually choose to give their allegiance to Rome, Celtic missionaries from Iona proved indispensable in the conversion of Northumbria and other areas, and their spiritual legacy played a part in shaping the church which emerged in England.

# B. Key Figures

**ABELARD, PETER** (1079–1142). Philosopher and theologian. Taught in Paris where he revived the study of Aristotelian logic as a fundamental academic discipline. Retired to a **monastery** after disastrous relationship with Heloise.

**AELFRIC** (c. 955–c. 1020). **Abbot** of Eynsham. Greatest scholar of the English Benedictine revival. Writings include **homilies** and lives of the **saints**.

**AELRED (Ailred)** (1109–67). **Cistercian abbot** of Rievaulx. Writings include *De Institutione Inclusarum* for **anchoresses**.

**AIDAN, St** (d. 651). **Monk** of Iona, missionary to Northumbria and **Bishop** of Lindisfarne.

**ALCUIN** (c. 735–804). Master of the cathedral school in York. Adviser to Emperor Charlemagne. Wrote on theology, liturgy, grammmar and logic.

**ALDHELM** (d. 709). **Abbot** of Malmesbury c. 675. **Bishop** of Sherborne 705. Wrote poetry in Latin and English.

**AMBROSE, ST** (c. 339–97). **Bishop** of Milan. Famous for sermons. Other writings include commentaries, hymns and letters.

**ANDREW, ST, APOSTLE**. Brother of **St Peter** and one of the Twelve. Later traditions held that he visited Scythia and was martyred in Achaia.

**ANSELM, ST** (c. 1033–1109). **Archbishop** of Canterbury, theologian and philosopher. Writings include *Monologion, Proslogion, Cur Deus Homo*.

**AQUINAS, THOMAS, ST** (c. 1225–74). Enormously influential philosopher and theologian. Joined **Dominican** order 1244, lectured in Paris and Italy. Extensive writings include commentaries on Aristotle and on the scriptures; also produced *Summa contra Gentiles* ('Defence of the Faith against the Pagans') and *Summa Theologica* ('Compendium of Theology').

**AUGUSTINE, ST OF CANTERBURY** (d. 604/5). Sent from Rome by **Gregory the Great** to convert the English. First **Archbishop** of Canterbury.

**AUGUSTINE, ST, OF HIPPO** (354–430). **Bishop** in N. Africa. Author of many influential theological works including *On Christian Doctrine*, *Confessions* and *City of God*.

**BECKET, ST THOMAS** (?1118–70). **Archbishop** of Canterbury from 1162. Dispute with Henry II led to his murder. Miracles soon recorded at his tomb. Canonised 1173, his shrine becoming one of the most popular **pilgrimage** centres in Christendom.

**BEDE, THE VENERABLE** (c. 673–735). Anglo-Saxon historian and biblical scholar. Sent to **monastery** of Wearmouth at seven; later transferred to Jarrow. Renowned in his lifetime for his learning, Bede wrote treatises on poetry, time and cosmography. Historical works include *History of the Abbots*, prose and verse versions of the *Life of St Cuthbert* and *Ecclesiastical History of the English People*.

**BENEDICT BISCOP, ST** (c. 628–689 or 690). Born into noble Northumbrian family. Became **monk** of Lerins (666), **abbot** in Canterbury (669). Founded **monasteries** of **St Peter** at Wearmouth (674) and **St Paul** at Jarrow (682). Made five journeys to Rome; brought back manuscripts, paintings and **relics**.

**BENEDICT, ST, OF NURSIA** (c. 480–c. 550). Educated in Rome, became a **hermit** c. 500. A community grew up round him and twelve **monasteries** were established. c. 525 moved to Monte Cassino where he set out plans for reform of **monasticism** and composed his *Rule* which became the most influential guide to the monastic life in the Western Church.

**BERNARD, ST, OF CLAIRVAUX** (1090–1153). **Abbot** of Clairvaux. Attacked heresy, preached the Second **Crusade**. Writings show a strong **mystical** character and emphasis on God's love and **grace**.

**BOETHIUS** (c. 480–c. 524). Roman statesman and philosopher. His *De Consolatione Philosophiae* (Consolation of Philosophy), written while in prison charged with treason, achieved widespread popularity in succeeding centuries. It was translated into Anglo-Saxon during the reign of Alfred and strongly influenced Chaucer who also made a translation.

**BONAVENTURE, ST, 'Doctor seraphicus'** (c. 1217–74). Minister General of the **Franciscan** Order (1257–74). Theologian and spiritual writer of great influence.

**BONIFACE, ST (Wynfrith)** (680–754). Anglo-Saxon missionary to Germany. **Archbishop** of Mainz c. 747. Martyred in Frisia.

**BRIDGET, ST, OF SWEDEN** (c. 1303–73). Founder of the Brigittine order of **nuns**. The revelations she was believed to have received in visions were highly regarded in the Middle Ages, influencing **Margery Kempe** among others.

**CAEDMON** (d. c. 680). First recorded Anglo-Saxon composer of religious poetry in English.

**CAESARIUS, ST, OF ARLES** (c. 470–542). **Bishop** of Arles 502. Influential figure in the church in Gaul.

**CASSIAN, JOHN** (c. 360–435). Left his **monastery** in Bethlehem to visit the **Desert Fathers** and eventually settled in Gaul. His *Institutes* (one of the earliest collections of instructions for the monastic life to be written in western Europe) and *Conferences* (accounts of conversations with the **anchorite abbots** of the Egyptian desert) profoundly influenced Western **monasticism**.

**COLUMBA, ST** (c. 521–97). Born into noble Irish family. c. 563 established **monastery** on Iona from which he evangelised parts of Scotland and Northern England.

**CUTHBERT, ST** (d. 687). Celtic **monk** and **hermit**. Bishop of Lindisfarne 685.

**DIONYSIUS, THE PSEUDO-AREOPAGITE** (c. 500). **Mystical** theologian whose work was wrongly attributed to the Dionysius mentioned in Acts 17:34. His writings, which combine Neo-Platonism with Christianity, influenced medieval mysticism.

**DOMINIC, ST** (1170–1221). Founded the order of **Friars** Preachers because of his desire to win back the Albigensian heretics to the Church.

**FRANCIS, ST, OF ASSISI** (1181/2–1226). Founder of the **Franciscan** order of **friars**. In 1208, challenged by Christ's words to 'Leave all' (Matt. 10:7–19), embarked upon a life of poverty and was soon joined by others for whom he devised a simple Rule. The order grew rapidly, reaching England in 1224.

**GREGORY I, ST (GREGORY THE GREAT)** (c. 540–604). **Bishop** of Rome from 590. Sent mission to England under **Augustine of Canterbury**. Wrote commentaries on scripture, **homilies**, the *Dialogues* and *Book of Pastoral Care*.

**HILTON, WALTER**. (d. 1396). English **mystic**. After a period as a **hermit** became an **Augustinian canon**. Wrote in English and Latin.

**JAMES, ST, 'THE LORD'S BROTHER'.** See Mark 6:3; Galatians 1:19. Shared leadership of the early Church in Jerusalem with St Peter. The **apocryphal** Infancy **Gospel**, the *Book of James* (also known as the *Protevangelium*), was attributed to him.

**JAMES, ST, 'THE GREAT' (SANTIAGO DE COMPOSTELA), Apostle.** Son of Zebedee, brother of **St John**. Witnessed Transfiguration of **Christ**. First of the Twelve to be martyred (AD 44). Seventh-century tradition claimed he visited Spain. His shrine at Compostela a major medieval **pilgrimage** centre.

**JEROME, ST** (330/347–420). Biblical scholar. Studied in Rome, then adopted **ascetic** life. Eventually settled in Bethlehem. Main translator of the **Vulgate**.

**JOHN, ST, EVANGELIST.** Brother of **St James the Great**. One of the three disciples closest to Christ. Tradition states that he wrote the Fourth **Gospel**, the three Epistles of John and the Book of Revelation. In medieval iconography often stands with the **Virgin Mary** at the foot of the Cross. Symbol an eagle.

**JOHN THE BAPTIST, ST**. Son of Zachariah and Elizabeth (cousin of the **Virgin Mary**). Appeared c. AD 27 by the banks of the Jordan preaching repentance. Baptised Jesus. Later beheaded by Herod Antipas at the instigation of Salome (Matt. 14:1– 12).

**JOSEPH, ST**. Husband of the **Virgin Mary**. According to the **Gospels** a carpenter and descendant of David. The *Protevangelium* describes him as very old at the time of his marriage, a view reflected in the medieval cycle plays.

**JUDAS ISCARIOT**. One of the original twelve disciples of Christ. According to the **Gospels** he betrayed **Christ** to the Jewish authorities and later hanged himself.

**JULIAN OF NORWICH** (c. 1342–after 1413). English **mystic** and **anchoress**. In 1373 during an illness, she received a series of visions of **Christ**'s **Passion** and the **Trinity** which she later recorded.

**KEMPE, MARGERY** (c. 1373–after 1433). Wrote book describing her spiritual experiences and **pilgrimages**.

**LAZARUS**. Brother of **Mary** and **Martha**. According to Jn 11:1– 44, **Christ** raised Lazarus from the dead, an event later held to prefigure his own resurrection.

**LEVI (see MATTHEW)**.

**LOMBARD, PETER** (c. 1100–1160). Taught at Paris, and produced *Four Books of Sentences* (compilation of extracts from the **Bible**, the **Fathers** and other authorities which became a standard theological textbook).

**LUKE, ST, EVANGELIST**. Author of the Third **Gospel** and Acts. New Testament references suggest he was a **Gentile** physician, who accompanied **St Paul** for part of his missionary journeys. His symbol is an ox.

**MARK, ST, EVANGELIST**. Author of the second **Gospel**. His symbol is a lion.

**MARTHA**. Sister of **Mary** of Bethany and **Lazarus**, whose home was visited by Christ. In Luke 10:38–42 she was described as 'busy with much serving'; as a result she became a symbol of the **active** life (practical service and involvement in the world) whilst Mary symbolised the **contemplative** life.

**MARY, THE BLESSED VIRGIN, MOTHER OF JESUS.** See D. ii.

**MARY MAGDALENE, ST**. According to the **Gospels** Mary was delivered by Christ from 'seven devils' (Luke 8:2), stood by the cross (Mark 15:40), discovered the empty tomb, and was the first to encounter the Risen **Christ** (Mark 16, John 20:11–18). Tradition also identified her with the 'sinner' who anointed Christ's feet (Luke 7:37–50) and with **Mary** the sister of **Martha**.

**MARY OF BETHANY, SISTER OF MARTHA AND LAZARUS**. Described in Luke 10:38–42 as sitting at **Christ**'s feet, listening to his word; as a result Mary was held to typify the **contemplative** life of prayer and meditation whilst her sister **Martha** represented the **active** life.

**MATTHEW, ST, APOSTLE AND EVANGELIST (LEVI)**. Author of the First **Gospel**. Also called Levi, son of Alphaeus (Mark 2:14). According to the **Gospels** was a publican (tax-collector) before he was called by **Christ** to become one of the Twelve. His symbol is a man.

**PAUL, ST, 'APOSTLE TO THE GENTILES'** (d. c. AD 65). Born Saul of Tarsus, a Jew and Roman citizen. His initial hostility to the early church was overcome by his conversion on the road to Damascus (Acts 9:1–19). Using the Roman version of his name, Paul travelled through Asia Minor and into Europe preaching to both Jews and **Gentiles**. Eventually arrested and taken to Rome for trial. Tradition holds that he was executed during the persecution under Nero. The **New Testament** letters bearing his name stress that **salvation** is offered as a gift (by God's **grace**) through faith, as a result of the forgiveness won by **Christ**'s death on the cross, and is available to Jews and non-Jews alike (e.g. Eph. 2).

**PETER, ST, APOSTLE**. Originally called Simon, he was given the name Cephas (Aramaic equivalent of the Gk 'Peter', meaning rock) by **Christ**. His profession of faith (Matt. 16:13–20) evoked the promise 'Thou art Peter; and upon this rock I will build my church . . . I will give to thee the keys of the kingdom of heaven', the passage on which the claims of the papacy have rested. His later denial of Christ (Matt 26:69–75) was followed by repentance and a fresh commission to feed Christ's sheep (Jn 21:15–19). In Acts he emerges as the leader of the **early Church**. Early traditions describe him as the first **bishop** of Rome and claim that he was **crucified** head downwards during the reign of Nero. Often portrayed as the gate-keeper of **heaven**, holding the keys promised by Christ.

**ROLLE, RICHARD** (c. 1300–1349). **Hermit** and **mystic**. Wrote in Latin and English.

**WILFRID, ST** (634–709). **Abbot** of Ripon, **Bishop** of York. Influential in moving the Anglo-Saxon church in Northumbria away from its Celtic roots and bringing it into line with the Church of Rome in its **liturgy**, calendar and monastic rule.

**WULFSTAN** (d. 1023). **Bishop** of London (996–1002) and **Archbishop** of York from 1002. Preacher and law-maker.

**WYCLIF, JOHN** (c. 1330–84). English philosopher, theologian and reformer. Unhappy with the state of the medieval Church and believing that the **Bible** should be the sole criterion of doctrine, he called for thorough-going reform, questioning, amongst other issues, the authority of the **Pope**, the validity of the religious life, and the doctrine of **transubstantiation**. A group of his **Lollard** followers translated the **Bible** into English.

# C. The Bible

The Christian Bible (Gk. *Biblia*, books) comprises the Old Testament scriptures inherited from Judaism, together with the New Testament, drawn from writings produced c. AD 40–125.

### i. THE CANON OF SCRIPTURE

(Gk. *kanon*, measuring rod, rule.) The list of books regarded as authoritative by the Christian church.

**The Old Testament.** The Jewish canon was not finally fixed until c. 100 AD, and the Greek **Septuagint** version of the Old Testament primarily used by the church contained a number of books which were eventually relegated to a secondary position by Jewish theologians. The status of these texts, known as the **Apocrypha**, was questioned by **St Jerome** but they were included in the **Vulgate** edition and regarded as **canonical** by **St Augustine** among others. On the whole medieval churchmen were inclined to regard the Septuagint canon as authoritative, because it was this, rather than the Hebrew canon, which had been cited by the authors of the New Testament.

**The New Testament**. The early Church produced a mass of writings, including **gospels**, letters, sermons and treatises, most bearing the name of key leaders such as **apostles** to establish their authority. Inevitably the Church had to decide which of the sometimes contradictory documents were to be regarded as authentic and authoritative. The core of the New Testament canon (the Four Gospels, Acts and the letters of **St Paul**) was decided by c. 200 but final agreement on the rest was not recorded until AD 367.

ii. THE OLD TESTAMENT

**Books of the Law** (The Pentateuch or Five Books of Moses)

**Genesis**: Creation. Adam and Eve. The Fall of Mankind. Cain and Abel. Tower of Babel. Noah and the Flood. The Patriarchs: Abraham, Isaac, Jacob, Joseph.
**Exodus**: Israel's deliverance from Egypt and journey through the desert to the promised Land. Moses and Aaron.
**Leviticus**: Religious laws.
**Numbers**: Life in the wilderness, the Twelve Spies, Balaam and his ass.
**Deuteronomy**: The Ten Commandments.

**Historical books**

**Joshua**: Entry into the Promised Land, Rahab, Fall of Jericho.
**Judges**: Samson and Delilah, Gideon.
**Ruth**: Story of Ruth, Naomi and Boaz.
**I & II Samuel**: Hannah and Samuel, Saul, David.
**I & II Kings**: Solomon, Elijah, Jezebel, Elisha.
**I & II Chronicles**: David, Solomon.
**Ezra**
**Nehemiah**
**Esther**.

**Books of teaching**

**Psalms** (psalter).
**Wisdom literature**: **Job, Proverbs, Ecclesiastes, Song of Solomon (Song of Songs, Canticles).**

**The Prophets**

**Isaiah, Jeremiah (with Lamentations) Ezekiel, Daniel, Hosea, Joel, Amos, Obadiah, Jonah, Micah, Nahum, Habakkuk, Zephaniah, Haggai, Zechariah, Malachi**.

**Old Testament Apocrypha:** Books found in the **Septuagint** text, but not in the Hebrew: **I & II Esdras, Tobit, Judith, the Rest of Esther, the Wisdom of Solomon, Ecclesiasticus, Baruch, the Letter of Jeremiah, the Prayer of Azariah, and the Song of the Three Young Men, Susanna, Bel and the Dragon, the Prayer of Manasses and I & II Maccabees.**

iii. THE NEW TESTAMENT

**The Four Gospels (Matthew, Mark, Luke and John)** which describe the life and ministry of Jesus.

**Acts**. The birth and expansion of the early Church.

**Epistles** (Letters to young church congregations and individuals which outline doctrine and provide practical teaching): **Romans, I & II Corinthians, Galatians, Ephesians, Philippians, Colossians, I & II Thessalonians, I & II Timothy, Titus, Philemon, Hebrews, James, I & II Peter, I, II & III John, Jude.**

**Revelation (Apocalypse).** Description of the Heavenly Jerusalem.

### New Testament Apocrypha

There are various 'Gospels', 'Acts' and 'Epistles', falsely attributed to New Testament authors, which have been excluded from the New Testament Canon. The most influential include the **Gospel of Pseudo-Matthew**, the **Gospel of Thomas**, the **Book of James** (the **Protevangelium**), which all purport to provide additional information about Christ's birth and infancy, and the **Gospel of Nicodemus**, which describes the **Harrowing of Hell**.

iv. TRANSLATIONS

**Septuagint (LXX).** Greek translation of the Hebrew OT. Jewish tradition states that it was made for the Jews of Alexandria in the third century BC by a group of seventy-two scholars (hence LXX). Probably completed by 132 BC. It differs from the Hebrew Bible in the order of biblical books and includes additional books (listed in Old Testament Apocrypha above). LXX was used by the NT writers and by the Greek Church throughout the Middle Ages. In the West it was used chiefly in Latin translations, the most influential of which was the **Vulgate** of **St Jerome**, who, although using the Hebrew text as the basis of his translation, drew on LXX for those books which it alone contained.

**Vulgate**. The Latin version of the Bible most widely used in the West. Translated mostly by **St Jerome** from Greek and Hebrew originals around the end of the fourth-century. The edition produced by the English scholar **Alcuin** (d. 804) became widely accepted although texts were never completely standardised and some mss. continued to include readings from the third-century Old Latin version.

## Vernacular translations and paraphrases

i. Anglo-Saxon. Though no complete Anglo-Saxon version of the Bible remains, portions were translated or paraphrased including Psalms 1–50 and the Four **Gospels**. Inter-linear glosses were produced and poems on biblical themes composed for a population largely ignorant of Latin.

ii. Middle English. Metrical versions of certain books were made and **Richard Rolle** produced a prose version of the **Psalter**. However after 1200 the Church became more cautious about vernacular translations, due to their use by heretical groups. The first complete translation of the Bible into English was made by followers of **Wyclif** (d. 1384). They were condemned as heretics and although their Bible was not rejected in itself, its use was restricted to those who had obtained a **bishop**'s licence.

### COMMENTARIES

Many of the Church **Fathers** wrote commentaries on individual books of the Bible and their interpretations shaped the understanding of subsequent generations. Among the most influential were those produced by **Ambrose**, **Augustine**, **Jerome** and **Gregory the Great**.

### INTERPRETATION

From the **Fathers of the Church** onwards it was believed that the Bible could be understood at more than one level. The predominant method of interpretation offered four levels: the literal or historical, the moral or tropological, the allegorical (which interpreted events in the light of Christ and the Church) and the spiritual or anagogical.

LECTIONARY

A book containing the extracts from scripture to be read at public worship. Since this was the context in which most people encountered the Bible, the way in which passages were juxtaposed and the themes which they were used to illustrate strongly coloured their interpretation in popular thought.

# D. The Faith of the Church

i. ESTABLISHING DOCTRINE

The faith of the Church handed down through the centuries from the days of the apostles was regarded as comprising two elements: the revelation of God given through the life and teachings of Christ and the interpretation of that revelation by succeeding generations under the guidance of the **Holy Spirit**. There was an ongoing process of definition and clarification as the Church faced heresy, disputes and new cultures. Crucial in this process were the summary statements of faith known as creeds and the work of the General Councils of the Church.

**Creeds** (Lat. *credo* I believe). Brief summaries of Christian belief appear in the New Testament and more substantial statements were agreed over the succeeding centuries. Three creeds are used in the Western liturgy: the short Apostles' Creed, the Nicene Creed, which originated at the Council of Constantinople in 381, and the longer 'Athanasian' Creed which probably dates from c. 500 and was used in the instruction of the laity. Of these the most important in the worship of the medieval church was the Nicene Creed, recited at the **Eucharist** on Sundays and feast days.

**Councils**. Although theologians made a contribution to the process of defining doctrine, ultimate responsibility lay with the **bishops** and from the fourth century final decisions were made at a succession of councils.

The seven councils of bishops from East and West recognised by the Catholic Church were Nicea I (325), Constantinople I (381), Ephesus (431), Chalcedon (451), Constantinople II (553), Constantinople III (680–1) and Nicea II (787). After the schism between the churches of East and West the following Councils were recognised as oecumenical by the Western Church alone: Constantinople IV (869–70); Lateran I (1123); Lateran II (1139);

Lateran III (1179); Lateran IV (1215); Lyons I (1245); Lyons II (1274); Vienne (1311–12); Constance (1414–18); Florence (1438–9); Lateran V (1512–17). The Fourth Lateran Council defined the doctrine of **transubstantiation** and required all adults to go to confession and receive Communion every Easter.

**Fathers of the Church**. A collective title given to Christian leaders of the early centuries whose writings (including biblical commentaries, sermons, histories, poetry and biography) were acknowledged to carry particular authority in matters of doctrine. The most influential of the early patristic writers were Tertullian, Origen, **Augustine**, **Ambrose** and **Jerome**.

**Doctors of the Church**. A title given to Christian thinkers of outstanding influence and saintliness. The four great Latin Doctors of the Church were **Augustine**, **Ambrose**, **Jerome** and **Gregory the Great**.

**Scholastic theology**. Following the rediscovery in the late tenth-century of a Latin translation of part of Aristotle's writing on logic, the teaching of dialectic was introduced into higher education and had a considerable influence upon the study of theology in the schools of western Europe. Traditional beliefs were re-examined in the light of human reason and the vast corpus of **patristic** writings re-organised in a more systematic approach to the study of Christian doctrine.

ii. KEY DOCTRINES

**The Trinity**. The Church taught that God was three persons – Father, Son (Jesus **Christ**) and Holy Spirit – who shared one divine nature and together brought about the **Creation** and **Salvation** of the world.

**Creation**. Christian doctrine, based on the first two chapters of the Book of Genesis and amplified by the theologians, stated that God created 'heaven and earth' *ex nihilo*, out of nothing. When the physical world had been formed, Adam and Eve were created 'in the image of God', without sin and able to communicate directly with God. Their mandate was to rule as stewards over the natural world.

**The fall of the angels, Lucifer and Satan**. The visible world was only part of creation. Included in the invisible order were the angels, some of whom, according to an account pieced together by some of the **Fathers of the Church** from scattered biblical allusions, had rebelled against God. Their leader Lucifer (lightbearer) had sought to claim equality with God (Is. 14:12–15) and together with his followers had been cast out of heaven (Rev. 12:7–9) to dwell henceforth in hell. Lucifer became **Satan** (Heb. *satan*, adversary), the **Devil**, and his followers became demons seeking constantly to alienate humankind from God, thus turning the world into a spiritual battlefield.

**The Fall of Man and original sin**. According to Genesis 3, the sojourn of Adam and Eve in the garden of Eden was brought to an abrupt end when Eve was persuaded by the serpent to use her free will to choose to disobey God's command. When first Eve and then Adam ate of the forbidden fruit of the tree of the knowledge of good and evil they lost their innocence and close relationship with God. They were banished from Eden to face hardship, pain, disharmony and death. The state of the world and human society was therefore explained by the belief that humankind inherited not only the consequences of Adam's **sin** but his sinful nature, a situation which could only be remedied by **Christ**'s sacrifice.

**Salvation**. The doctrine of the **Incarnation** taught that, in the person of Jesus **Christ**, God became a human being and willingly offered himself to die on the cross in order to save men and women from their **sins**. There were a variety of interpretations of the doctrine of the **Atonement** (i.e. the reconciliation of mankind to God through the death of Christ). Origen (c. 185–254) viewed Christ's death as a ransom paid to **Satan** who had acquired rights over man through the **Fall**; but this interpretation was later largely superseded by that of **St Anselm** (c. 1033–1109) who taught that Christ died to take the punishment due to human sin, thus paying the debt owed to God and appeasing His righteous anger. The forgiveness offered by God was understood to be mediated through the Church and its **sacraments**. According to the New Testament, the **Crucifixion** and burial of Jesus were followed three days later by the **Resurrection**, after which he met a number of his disciples and convinced them of his victory over sin and death. The account in Acts 1 of Christ's **Ascension** into Heaven includes an assertion that there will be a **Second Coming** when he will return to earth as Judge.

**Heaven**, **Hell**, **Purgatory** and the **Last Judgement**. Upon death human beings faced a personal judgement to determine their immediate destination. It was believed that many would have to endure a period of punishment in Purgatory (a kind of antechamber to heaven) before they would be ready to enter the presence of God. The saints were believed to proceed directly to heaven where they would dwell with God and his angels while those who had rejected salvation would be confined in **hell** with **Satan** to suffer eternal torment. At the **Last Judgement** all human beings who had ever lived would stand before God to have their thoughts and deeds revealed and judged; the blessed would go to be with God, the rest be finally consigned to hell.

**Mary, the Blessed Virgin**. The account of Mary's life in the New Testament was amplified by **apocryphal** documents and a number of doctrines concerning her person and role developed in succeeding centuries. Justin Martyr (d. c. 165) contrasted Mary's obedience with the disobedience of Eve. The Book of James (c. mid-second century) named her parents as Joachim and Anna and asserted her perpetual virginity. The Council of Ephesus (431) confirmed the title of *theotokos*, godbearer. **St Ambrose** held her to be a type of the church. The belief that she did not die but was taken up bodily into heaven was celebrated in **the Feast of the Assumption**. The assertion that Mary, like her son, had been immaculately conceived (i.e. free from **original sin**) was disputed throughout the Middle Ages. Faith in Mary's powers as intercessor on behalf of sinful men and women was given fresh impetus by **St Bernard** (1090–1153) and she was popularly regarded as the Queen of Heaven. Although theologians distinguished between veneration accorded to Mary and the worship due only to her Son, this may not always have been fully understood at a popular level. For festivals see E. i.

**The Joys of Mary**. Usually listed as five: the **Annunciation** (Lk 1:26–38), the **Nativity** (Lk 2:1–7), the **Resurrection** (Lk 24), the **Ascension** (Acts 1:1–9) and Mary's own Assumption into heaven. Sometimes added to the list were the Visitation (Lk 1:39–45), the Presentation of Christ (Lk 2:21ff), the Finding of Christ in the Temple (Lk 2:41–50).

**The Seven Sorrows of Mary**: 1. At the prophecy of Simeon (Lk 2:25–35); 2. At the flight into Egypt (Mt. 2:13–15); 3. At the loss of the Christ Child (Lk 2:41–5); 4. On meeting Christ on the way to Calvary; 5. When standing at the foot of the cross (Jn 19:25–7); 6. At the taking down of Christ from the cross (Jn 19:28–36); 7. At Christ's burial (Lk 23:50–6).

### iii. FORMULATIONS

**Ten Commandments**: Deuteronomy 5:6–21

**Seven Sacraments: Baptism, Confirmation, Eucharist, Absolution, Extreme Unction, Ordination and Matrimony.**

**Seven Deadly Sins**: Pride (Superbia), Covetousness, Lust/Lechery, Envy, Gluttony, Anger, Sloth (Accidie).

**Seven Contrary Virtues**:

i. The Theological Virtues: Faith, Hope, Charity (I Cor. 13:13)
ii. The Cardinal Virtues: Justice, Prudence, Temperance, Fortitude.

**Seven Corporal Works of Mercy**: Feeding the hungry; giving drink to the thirsty; clothing the naked; offering hospitality to the stranger; visiting the sick; ministering to prisoners; burying the dead. See Matthew 25:35–45 and Tobit, Chs 1 and 2.

**Seven Gifts of the Holy Spirit**: Wisdom, Understanding, Counsel, Fortitude, Knowledge, Piety, Fear of the Lord. From Isaiah 11:2 (Vulgate).

### iv. DISSENT

The first seven centuries of the Church saw many struggles over doctrine, some being resolved peacefully, others causing schism. The Church in the West then remained relatively peaceful until small outbreaks of heresy in France and Germany in the eleventh-century. These were followed by the more serious twelfth-century reform movement of the Waldensians, and radical dissenting movement of the Cathars. In England there was little serious challenge to established doctrine until John **Wyclif** (d. 1384) and the **Lollards**. Although the Church absorbed a surprising amount of debate and self-criticism, the deep-rooted conviction that the errors promulgated by dissenters posed a grave threat not only to their own **salvation** but to that of others meant that in extreme cases they were dealt with very severely.

# E. The Worship of the Church

The Christian year evolved gradually around the two feasts of Easter and Christmas which in the fourth-century became fixed on Dec. 25 (coinciding with the pagan winter solstice). The annual pattern of worship which emerged was made up of two overlapping cycles: the *Temporale*, which was based on the life of **Christ** and incorporated some variations in timing according to the date of Easter, and the *Sanctorale*, the feast-days of **saints** which had fixed dates. The following outline is based on the *Temporale* but includes some of the most important additional feast days (marked with an asterix).

**Advent**. From the fourth Sunday before Christmas Day until Christmas Eve. Preparation for the coming of Jesus **Christ** as a baby at Christmas and for his Second Coming as Judge at the end of the world.

**Christmas**. Celebration of the birth of Christ. Festivities lasted for twelve days.

**★St Stephen**. 26 December.

**★St John the Evangelist**. 27 December.

**★The Holy Innocents**. 28 December.

**★St Thomas of Canterbury (Thomas Becket)**. December 29 (after 1173).

**Epiphany**. 6 January. In the West celebrates the manifestation (Gk *epiphaneia*) to the **Magi** and hence to the **Gentiles**.

**★Candlemas**. February 2. The purification of the Virgin **Mary** and Christ's presentation in the Temple (Lk 2:22–38). Candles carried in procession to symbolize Christ, 'a light for revelation to the Gentiles' (Lk 2:32).

**Septuagesima** (seventieth day). The Sunday nine weeks before Easter. The beginning of the penitential season.

**Quinquagesima** (fiftieth day). Sunday before Lent.

**Shrove Tuesday**. Day before Ash Wednesday on which the faithful were expected to go to confession (shriving).

**Lent**. Forty-day season of penitence and **fasting** leading up to Easter. Reflects **Christ**'s forty days in the wilderness (Luke 4:1, 2).

**Ash Wednesday**. First day of Lent. Ashes were placed on the heads of clergy and laity as a sign of penitence.

**Quadragesima** (fortieth day). First Sunday in Lent. Also used of the whole season of Lent.

**Passion Sunday**. Two weeks before Easter.

**Palm Sunday**. The Sunday before Easter, marked by the blessing of palms and a procession commemorating **Christ**'s entry into Jerusalem (Matt 21:1–11).

**Holy Week** (week before Easter Sunday):

> **Maundy Thursday** (Lat. *mandatum*, commandment). Thursday before Easter Sunday. Commemorates the Last Supper (**Christ**'s sharing of the Passover Meal with his disciples) at which he instituted the **Eucharist**, washed the disciples' feet and commanded that that they should love one another as he loved them.

> **Good Friday**. The **Crucifixion** of **Christ**.

> **Holy Saturday**. A vigil was kept in preparation for Easter day. The Paschal candle was lit.

**Easter Sunday**. The Resurrection of **Christ**.

**\*Rogation Days**. Days of prayer and **fasting** in early summer chiefly for the harvest. Major Rogation, April 25. Minor Rogations, Monday, Tuesday and Wednesday before Ascension Day.

**Ascension**. The fortieth day after Easter. Celebrates **Christ**'s return to **heaven** (Acts 1:9).

**Pentecost** (Whit Sunday). Seventh Sunday after Easter. The Jewish feast of Weeks (harvest). Day when the **Holy Spirit** descended upon the disciples (Acts 2).

**Trinity Sunday**. Sunday after Pentecost. Celebrates God the Father, Son and Holy Spirit. Very popular in England.

**Corpus Christi**. Thursday after Trinity Sunday. Feast celebrating the institution of the **Eucharist**, introduced in 1264. Associated with medieval religious drama. See Ch. 9.

★**St Peter** and **St Paul**, **Apostles**. 29 June.

★**St Mary Magdalen**. July 22.

★**Lammas** (loaf-mass). 1 August. Consecration of bread made from first corn harvested.

★**St Michael, Archangel (Michaelmass)**. September 29.

★**All Saints**. November 1 (in West from eighth-century). Celebration of all Christian **saints**, known and unknown.

★**All Souls**. November 2. Commemoration of the souls of the faithful departed.

★ St Andrew, Apostle. November 30.

**Feasts of the Blessed Virgin Mary**:

   **Purification**. February 2

   **Annunciation**. March 25.

   **Assumption**. August 15.

   **Nativity**. September 8.

   **Conception**. December 8.


ii. THE LITURGY

The key elements of medieval worship were the **Divine Office** and the **Mass**.


**The Divine Office**

As outlined in the monastic Rules, the Office consisted of the Night Office (Matins) together with seven hours (times) of prayer during the day: Lauds (at dawn), Prime (first hour of the day), Terce (third hour), Sext (sixth hour), None (ninth hour), Vespers (at dusk), Compline (before bed). This pattern was inspired by the words of the Psalmist: 'I rose at midnight to give praise to thee . . . Seven times a day I have given praise to thee': Ps. 119 (Vul. 118): 62, 164. The major component of these services was the singing of the Psalms.


**The Mass** (also called the **Eucharist,** Holy Communion or Lord's Supper)

The chief **sacramental** service of the Church, incorporating praise, intercession and readings from scripture. The central action is the consecration of the bread and wine by the priest, recalling the words and actions of **Christ** at the Last Supper and commemorating the sacrifice which he offered for the **sins** of mankind on the cross. In the medieval Church the Mass was celebrated daily; it was also offered for the souls of the dead.

iii. KEY LITURGICAL TEXTS

**Psalter**: Containing the 150 Psalms (religious poems) from the Old Testament which were central to Christian worship.

**Canticles**: **Magnificat** (Luke 1:46–55), **Nunc Dimittis**, also called the **Song of Simeon** (Luke 2:29–32), **Benedictus** (Luke 1:68–79), **Te Deum**, **Benedicite**, **Venite** (Ps. 95, Vulgate 94).

**Paternoster** (Our Father): The Lord's Prayer (Matt. 6:9–13; Luke 11:2–4).

**Ave Maria (Hail Mary)**: Based on Luke 1:28, 42.

# F. The Organisation of the Church in England

## i. STRUCTURES

The basic unit of the church's life was the **parish**, an area served by a **priest** who exercised a cure (care) of souls and was thus a **curate**. This priest could be either a **Rector** (who received the tithes) or a **Vicar** who was paid a stipend to serve in his place. **Parishes** were grouped together in **dioceses** under the authority of a **bishop**, who was assisted in his administrative and disciplinary responsibilities by one or more **archdeacons**. In England the dioceses were divided into two provinces, one presided over by the Archbishop of Canterbury, the other by the Archbishop of York. Until the sixteenth-century the church in England was subject to the authority of the **Pope**, who, as Bishop of Rome and hence the successor of **St Peter**, was regarded as head of the Church in the West.

## ii. HOLY ORDERS

There were seven grades of orders in the medieval church:
**Major orders** (of whom celibacy was required): **priests**, deacons and sub-deacons.
**Minor orders**: acolytes (who assisted at Mass), exorcists, lectors (readers), doorkeepers.

## iii. MONASTIC ORDERS

Although the earliest **monks** practised the solitary life, living as **hermits** in the deserts of the East, the majority of those called to the monastic life lived in communities as **coenobites**, taking vows of poverty, chastity and obedience. There were female hermits from the earliest days and communities of women followed similar **Rules** and took the same monastic vows as their male counterparts. In

Anglo-Saxon England there were a number of double monasteries ruled by an **abbess**, and throughout the Middle Ages **convents** acted as important centres of female education.

**Benedictines**. In the medieval West the most influential guide for those following the monastic life was the ***Rule of St Benedict*** (c. 480–550), drawn up for his monks at Monte Cassino and promoted in England by **St Wilfrid** (d. 709). Benedictines (Black Monks) led a highly disciplined life of prayer (the *opus dei* or work of God), study and manual work.

**Cistercians**. The order of White Monks (from their habits of undyed sheep's wool) was founded at Cîteaux in 1098 with the aim of returning to the **Benedictine** ideal. Following the admission of **St Bernard of Clairvaux**, the order spread rapidly, choosing remote locations, such as Rievaulx (c. 1131) in Northern England.

**Carthusians**. A strictly **contemplative** order founded by St Bruno in 1084. First 'Charterhouse' established in England in 1175–6. Each **monk** lived in his own cell under a vow of silence, meeting with his brethren only for the **Daily Office**, **Mass** and occasional meals.

**Canons Regular**. This movement emerged in the mid-eleventh century as part of an attempt to encourage **secular** clergy to move closer to a **monastic** way of life in imitation of that attributed to the Apostles (the *vita apostolica*). Vital in this process was the rediscovery of the ***Rule of St Augustine***. Groups which followed this Rule included the **Augustinian Canons** (Black Canons), the **Premonstratensians** (White Canons) and the **Gilbertines**.

## iv. FRIARS

The friars (*frater*, ME *frere*, brother) or **mendicant** (begging) orders which appeared in the early thirteenth century, represented a radical departure from the monastic tradition in that they rejected the ownership of property and committed themselves to carrying the spiritual life out to lay-people in the everyday world, through preaching and service. Popular due to their sacrificial lifestyle, lively sermons and skill in hearing confessions, they were regarded as a threat by some **parish priests** and were subsequently criticised by many for failing to live up to their ideals.

**Franciscans**. Founded by **St Francis of Assisi** (d. 1226), the Grey Friars reached England in 1224 and spread rapidly.

**Dominicans**. Founded by **St Dominic** (d. 1222), primarily as a preaching order to combat heresy. The Black Friars landed in England in 1221. Very influential in the universities.

**Carmelites**. Originally groups of **hermits**, living on Mount Carmel in the Holy Land, who adopted the **mendicant** pattern of ministry. The White Friars were brought to England c. 1241.

**Augustinians** (Austin Friars). Like the **Carmelites**, moved from being a congregation of **hermits** to an order of **friars**. Came to England in the second half of the thirteenth century. Wore a black habit with white scapular (short cloak).

# G.  Glossary

**Abbess**. Head of community of **nuns**. Some Anglo-Saxon abbesses (e.g. **Hild**) ruled over double **monasteries** containing separate communities of men and women.

**Abbey**. 1. Community of **monks** or **nuns** under rule of **abbot** or **abbess**. 2. Building which they occupy.

**Abbot**. Head of an **abbey** of **monks**.

**Absolution**. Formal declaration of God's forgiveness, pronounced by a **priest**.

**Active life**. Life of practical service and involvement in the everyday world.

**Alb**. Full-length linen garment (usually white) worn by ministers at **Mass**.

**Anchoress** (f). **Anchorite** (m). Person leading a solitary life of prayer.

**Anti-Christ**. Chief enemy of **Christ** (See I and II John). Figure expected to emerge before the end of the world (II Thess. 2:3–10 and Revelation 13).

**Annunciation**. The archangel Gabriel's announcement to the **Virgin Mary** that she would bear the Son of God (Luke 1:26–38). Feast-day March 25.

**Antetype**. Earlier form or symbol. See **type**.

**Antitype**. That which a **type** represents or prefigures.

**Apocalypse**. A revelation or unveiling, e.g. Daniel (OT) and Revelation (NT).

**Apocryphal**. See C.

**Apostle**. One of the twelve men originally chosen by **Christ** and commissioned to preach the **Gospel** to the nations. In Acts 1 Matthias was chosen to replace **Judas Iscariot**. **St Paul** also claimed the status of an apostle.

**Archbishop**. **Bishop** who also presides over a group of **dioceses** or province.

**Archdeacon**. Administrative officer of the **bishop**, responsible for church buildings and the supervision of the morals of clergy and laity in all or part of the diocese. Presided over ecclesiastical courts. Unpopular in the medieval church and often suspected of corruption.

**Ascension**. The withdrawal of **Christ** into **heaven**. See D. ii.

**Asceticism** (Gk. *askesis*, training). Way of life designed to subdue vice and encourage virtue. In Christian thought involves commitment to self-denial in order to follow **Christ** (Mk 8:34). Important in both **monasticism** and **mysticism** as a means to free the soul to love and experience God more fully.

**Atonement**. See D. ii.

**Baptism**. The **Sacrament**/rite of admission into the Christian Church. The candidate is immersed in or sprinkled with water in the name of the **Trinity**.

**Beatitudes** (Lat. *Beatus*, blessed). Promises of blessings given by Christ in Matt 5:3–11.

**Bible**. See C.

**Bishop**. The highest of Holy Orders. Bishops had pastoral care over a diocese and authority to confirm and ordain.

**Book of Hours**. Book for private devotion. Usually contained the **Little Office of the Blessed Virgin Mary**, the Office of the Dead and the seven penitential psalms. Very popular among the laity.

**Breviary**. Contained complete order (psalms, antiphons, hymns and readings) for the daily office (from eleventh century onwards).

**Calvary** (Latin *Calvaria*, Hebrew *Golgotha*, both meaning skull). Place of Christ's execution just outside Jerusalem.

**Canon law**. Collection of ecclesiastical rules governing faith, morals and discipline.

**Canon of the Mass**. Prayer of consecration of the bread and wine in the **Mass**.

**Canon of scripture** (Gk *kanon*, measuring rod, rule). The list of books which were accepted as authoritative by the Church. See **Apocrypha**.

**Canonical**. Included in canon of scripture, authoritative.

**Canonisation**. Formal admission to the list of **saints**.

**Canticle**. Biblical text sung in worship. See E.

**Cardinal** (Lat. *cardo*, hinge). Papal adviser.

**Carol**. Song (originally to accompany a dance).

**Cathedral**. Church which contains the throne (Lat. *cathedra*) of the **bishop** and hence the mother church of the **diocese**.

**Chantry**. Endowment for **priest** to sing **masses** for founder's soul.

Very numerous in fourteenth and fifteenth centuries. Chantry chapels could be separate buildings or a small partitioned area containing an altar within a church or **cathedral**.

**Chrism**. Mixture of oil and balsam used principally in rites associated with **Creed**. See D. i, **Baptism**, Confirmation and Ordination. Chrism (chrysom) cloth was wrapped around a baby's head to prevent the oil from being rubbed off after baptism.

**Christ** (Gk *Christos*, trans. of the Hebrew 'Messiah', the anointed one of Jewish prophecy). Title (eventually used as name) given to Jesus, as fulfilling this prophecy.

**Clerk**. Term used in Middle Ages of those in **Minor Orders**.

**Cloister**. Enclosed space usually in the centre of a religious building. Also used generally of a religious house and the religious life.

**Coenobite** (from Gk *koinos bios*, common life). A member of a **monastic** community (as opposed to a **hermit** or **anchorite**).

**Confessor**. 1. In the early church applied to those who suffered under persecution but were not martyred. Later used of those who demonstrated outstanding holiness. 2. **Priest** who hears confession.

**Convent**. 1. Religious community of either sex. 2. The building in which they live.

**Contemplative life**. Withdrawal from the affairs of the world in order to focus on an inner life of prayer.

**Contrition**. Form of inner repentance, genuine sorrow for **sin**.

**Corpus Christi**. The body of **Christ** believed to be present in the **sacrament** of the **Eucharist**. For the festival see E. i.

**Crucifixion**. Execution by nailing or binding to a cross. Used frequently in Roman Empire. The crucifixion of Jesus, recorded in all four **Gospels**, is believed by Christians to have made **salvation** available to humankind.

**Crusade**. Holy war authorised by the **Pope**. Most were directed towards the liberation of the Holy Land from Muslim control but they were also undertaken against heretics in western Europe.

**Desert Fathers**. Name given to Christian **hermits** who moved to the deserts of Egypt and Palestine from the third century onwards. Some adopted a form of community life which inspired the development of **monastic orders**.

**Devil** (Gk. *diabolos*, accuser). Chief of the fallen angels. See D. ii.

**Diocese**. Group of **parishes** over which a **bishop** has jurisdiction.

**Divine Office**. See E. ii.

**Eucharist** (Gk *eukharistia*, thanksgiving). The central act of the church's worship in which bread and wine are consecrated and consumed. See Mt. 26:26–8, Mk 14:22–4, Lk. 22:17–20, I Cor 11:23–5. Also known as Holy Communion, the Lord's Supper and the **Mass**.

**Evangelist**. Used of the four **Gospel** writers: Matthew, Mark, Luke, and John.

**Excommunication**. Ecclesiastical punishment involving exclusion from the **sacraments**, except the last rites.

**Fast**. Period of abstinence from food. Wednesday and Friday were common fast days, also the penitential season before Easter.

**Fathers of the Church**. Christian leaders and thinkers, living mostly between the end of the first century and the eighth century, whose writings on doctrine were considered to carry particular authority. See D. i.

**Fall**. Adam and Eve's act of disobedience in the Garden of Eden (Genesis 2 and 3) which led to estrangement from God for them and their descendants. See D. ii.

**Feast**. Special **liturgical** celebration to commemorate an event or **saint**. See E. i.

**Five Wounds**. The wounds suffered by **Christ** on the cross, i.e. the piercing of his hands, feet and side. Devotion to the Five Wounds developed in the Middle Ages as interest in the humanity and sufferings of Christ grew.

**Friar** (Lat. *frater*, ME *frere*, brother). Member of one of the mendicant (begging) orders. See F. iv.

**Gentiles**. Biblical name given to non-Jews.

**Glossa Ordinaria**. The standard medieval commentary on the Bible, composed chiefly of extracts from the **Fathers**.

**Golden Legend**. *Legenda Aurea*. Collection of lives of the saints and treatises on Christian festivals compiled between 1255 and 1266 by Jacobus de Voragine (c. 1230–c. 1298).

**Gospel** (Gk *evangelion*, OE *godspel*, good news). 1. The central message of the Christian faith concerning **salvation**. 2. Title given to the four New Testament books which describe the life of **Christ**, i.e. Matthew, Mark, Luke and John. 3. A reading taken from one of the four Gospels which has the place of honour in the **Mass**.

**Grace**. The undeserved favour of God, given to enable an individual to grow spiritually.

**Gradual**. Response sung between the Epistle and **Gospel** readings in the **Mass**.

**Hagiography**. The writing of the lives of the **saints**.

**Harrowing of Hell**. The belief that while Christ's body rested in the Tomb his spirit descended into **hell** to free the souls of the righteous. See I Peter 3:18–20.

**Heaven**. The dwelling-place of God and the angels and eventually all those redeemed by **Christ**. See D. ii.

**Hell**. The abode of devils and the place to which unrepentant souls will pass after the **Last Judgement**. See D. ii.

**Hermit** (Gk *eremos*, desert). Person who has retired from society to follow the spiritual life in solitude. Unlike **anchorites** not confined to one spot.

**Holy Spirit (Ghost)**. Third Person of **Trinity**. See D. ii.

**Homily**. Sermon usually referring to the **Gospel** reading for the day.

**Host** (Lat. *hostia*, victim). Term used of the consecrated wafer in the **Eucharist**, the symbolic sacrifical 'victim'.

**Housel**. Middle English name for the **Eucharist**.

**Incarnation**. See D. ii.

**Indulgence**. The remission by the Church of the time of temporal punishment for **sin**, based on the merits of **Christ** and the **saints**.

**Last Judgement**. The final judgement on mankind when all will have to give account of their lives to Christ as Judge. See D. ii.

**Lectionary**. Arrangement of extracts from Scripture to be read at public worship.

**Legend**. Traditional story popularly regarded as historical.

**Lent**. Period from Ash Wednesday to Holy Saturday which recalls **Christ**'s forty days in the wilderness.

**Limbo**. The abode of souls of those (such as unbaptised babies) who were excluded from the full blessedness of heaven but not condemned to any other punishment.

**Litany** (Gk *litaneia*, supplication). A series of petitions and set responses used in worship.

**Little Office of the Blessed Virgin Mary**. A short form of daily prayer in honour of **Mary**, modelled on the Daily Office. Originated in the tenth century, becoming very popular with clergy and lay-people in the later Middle Ages.

**Liturgy**. The written text of the formal services of the Church.

**Lollard**. Originally a follower of **John Wyclif** but later applied to anyone critical of the Church. Lollards emphasised personal faith and the authority of the Bible; they strongly opposed **indulgences**, **pilgrimages**, clerical celibacy and the doctrine of **transubstantation**.

**Lord's Prayer** (Paternoster). Taught by Jesus to his disciples (Matt. 6:9–13).

**Magi** (Gk *magoi*, sages). The 'wise men from the East' (Matt 2:1) who brought gifts of gold, frankincense and myrrh to the infant Jesus. The NT account says nothing of their rank, number or names. It was Tertullian (c. 160–c. 225) who described them as kings and Origen (b. c. 185) who gave their number as three. A sixth-century work names them as Gaspar, Melchior and Balthasar.

**Major Orders**. See F. ii.

**Martyr** (Gk. *martus*, witness). One who suffers death for their faith.

**Mass**. See E. ii.

**Mendicants** (Lat. *mendicus*, beggar). Member of one of the orders of begging **friars**. See F. iv.

**Minor Orders**. See F. ii.

**Misericord** (Lat. *misericordia*, mercy). The projection on the underside of the hinged seat of a choir stall, designed to support those incapable of standing for long periods during worship. Often carved.

**Missal**. Book containing texts and instructions for the celebration of **Mass** (from ninth century onwards)

**Monastery**. (Minster.) House of a religious community.

**Monasticism**. See F. iii.

**Monk**. Member of male religious community.

**Mortal sin**. **Sin** committed consciously and wilfully, placing the soul in serious jeopardy; could only be forgiven through the **sacrament** of **penance** by confession to a **priest**. Cf. **venial sin**.

**Mysticism**. An immediate, intensely personal, experience of encounter with God, achieved through the practice of contemplation and self-denial.

**Nativity**. Birth of **Christ**.

**Novice**. Prospective member of religious order who has not yet taken full vows.

**Nun**. Member of female religious order.

**Oblate** (Lat. *oblatus*, offered). Used of those placed in **monasteries** as children.

**Original sin**. The state of **sin** which has characterised mankind since the **Fall**. The sacrament of **baptism** was believed to remit original sin.

**Pardoner**. Dispensed **indulgences** in return for contributions of alms. Frequently guilty of promoting abuses of the system.

**Parish**. Area served by a **priest** who has the spiritual care of all those living within it. The system evolved gradually, reaching completion by the thirteenth century.

**Passion of Christ** (Lat. *passio*, suffering). The physical and psychological suffering endured by Jesus on behalf of mankind during the vigil in the Garden of Gethsemane, arrest, trial, scourging and **crucifixion** (Matt. 26–7, Mark 14–15, Luke 22–3, John 18–19).

**Passover**. Jewish spring festival celebrating the deliverance of the people of Israel from slavery in Egypt (see Exodus 12, where the Israelites were told by God to kill a lamb per household and mark the doorway with its blood, so that their homes would be 'passed over' when God struck down the first-born of the Egyptians). According to the **Gospels**, it was at the Passover meal before his death (the Last Supper) that **Christ** instituted the **Eucharist**, comparing himself to a sacrificial lamb whose blood would save sinners (see Matt. 26:26–9).

**Paternoster** (Our Father). See **Lord's Prayer**. E. iii.

**Patristic** (Lat. *pater*, father). Relating to the **Fathers of the Church**, particularly to their writings.

**Penance** (Lat. *poena*, punishment). **Sacrament** involving **contrition**, confession, satisfaction (e.g. prayer, **fasting**, almsgiving or **pilgrimage**) and **absolution**.

**Pentateuch**. The first five books of the Old Testament. See C. ii.

**Pilgrimage**. Journey to holy places (such as biblical sites or shrines of the **saints**) to seek God's help, to give thanks or as an act of **penance**.

**Pope**. Head of Western Church. See F. i.

**Priest**. Cleric in Holy Orders who has authority to celebrate **Mass** and absolve **sins**.

**Primer**. Devotional book, popular among medieval lay-people, containing the **Little Office of the Blessed Virgin Mary**, the seven Penitential and fifteen gradual psalms, the Litany of the **Saints** and the Office for the Dead.

**Prior**. Second-in-command in an **abbey** or head of a small monastic house.

**Prioress**. Second-in-command to an **abbess** or head of a small community of **nuns**.

**Psalter**. The book (sometimes part of the **Breviary**) containing the psalms and canticles.

**Purgatory**. See D. ii.

**Regular clergy**. Those bound by vows to live under a **Rule** (*regula*).

**Regularis Concordia**. Code of monastic rules approved for English **monasteries** in 970.

**Relics**. Remains of a **saint** or articles which have been in contact with a saint and in which some of the saint's power is believed to reside.

**Reliquary**. Receptacle for **relics**.

**Resurrection**. See D. ii.

**Rood**. Cross. Used of the large cross often placed on the screen which divided the sanctuary of a medieval church from the nave.

**Rule**. Code of behaviour for a religious community.

**Sacrament**. Religious rite which symbolises the receipt of an inward spiritual grace. In the fifteenth century the number of sacraments was finally agreed as seven (**Baptism**, **Eucharist**, Confirmation, Ordination, Marriage, **Penance**, Anointing of the Sick) following the list made by Peter Lombard.

**Saint**. In the NT applied to all Christians. Later used of those who were martyred or showed exceptional holiness and whose status was confirmed by the church. The practice of venerating the saints and their **relics** and asking for their intercessions (prayers) can be observed from the second and third centuries onward and played a central role in popular medieval religion.

**Salvation**. See D. ii.

**Satan**. See D. ii.

**Scholastic theology**. The systematic study of the Christian faith using the dialectical method which developed in the twelfth-century theology schools of western Europe, following the re-discovery of the logical works of Aristotle.

**Second Coming of Christ**. The expected return of Christ in glory to judge the living and the dead and to bring to an end the present world order.

**Secular clergy**. Clergy living in the world (i.e. not in a **monastery**), serving as **parish priests**, chaplains, etc.

**Septuagint**. Greek translation of the Old Testament. See C. iv.

**Sermon on the Mount**. Christ's teaching in Matt 5–7.

**Seven Contrary Virtues**. See D. iii.

**Seven Corporal Works of Mercy**. See D. iii.

**Seven Deadly Sins**. See D. iii.

**Simony** (from Simon Magus, Acts 8:18–24). The purchase or sale of spiritual things, e.g. ecclesiastical office.

**Sin**. Disobedience to the known will of God. According to Christian theology human beings have displayed a predisposition to sin since the Fall (see D. ii). The medieval Church taught that there were two categories of sin: **mortal** and **venial**. The Church mediated the forgiveness made available by **Christ**'s sacrificial death through the sacrament of **penance**.

**Summoner**. Summoned offenders to appear at ecclesiastical courts.

**Thurible**. Metal container for the burning of incense during worship.

**Tithe**. A tenth part of all produce paid by parishioners to the **parish** church for the maintenance of the clergy and buildings and the relief of the poor.

**Tonsure**. The shaving of all or part of the head which identified **monks** and clerics.

**Transubstantiation**. The conversion of the bread and wine into the body and blood of **Christ** which was believed to occur in the **Eucharist**.

**Trinity**. See D. ii.

**Trope**. Brief elaboration of passage of scripture or **liturgical** text.

**Type** (Gk *tupos*, example, figure). A person or event (usually in the OT) which while accepted as historical was also held to foreshadow some aspect of **Christ** or the Church; e.g. Abraham's sacrifice of Isaac was seen as a type of God's sacrifice of his only son.

**Typology**. The interpretation of people and events (particularly in the Old Testament) as foreshadowing elements of Christian revelation. See **type**.

**Venial sin**. Relatively trivial **sin** which was not a deliberate act of will; could be confessed privately to God. Cf. **Mortal sin**.

**Vulgate**. Latin version of the Bible most widely used in the West. See C. iii.

# Bibliography

Old English Texts:
Due to limitations of space Old English prose is given in translation only. Old English Poetry, unless stated otherwise, is taken from *Anglo-Saxon Poetic Records*. Ed. Krapp and Dobbie. Translations of poems are from the following sources:

*Beowulf: A Dual-Language Edition*
*The Earliest English Poems*:
*Widsith*
*Anglo-Saxon Poetry*:
*Exodus, Guthlac A and B, Juliana.*
*A Choice of Anglo-Saxon Verse:*
*Battle of Brunanburh, Battle of Maldon, Bede's Death- Song, Caedmon's Hymn, Dream of the Rood, Judith, Ruin, Seafarer, Wanderer.*
*Early English Christian Poetry:*
*Andreas, Genesis A and B, Phoenix.*

PRIMARY SOURCES, USEFUL ANTHOLOGIES AND TRANSLATIONS:

*Adomnan's Life of Columba.* Eds A. O. and M. O. Anderson. London: Thomas Nelson, 1961.

Aelfric, *Catholic Homilies*, Vol. I. Ed. and Trans. B. Thorpe. London: EETS, 1844.

Aelred, *Aelred of Rievaulx's De Institutione Inclusarum: Two Middle English Translations.* Ed. John Ayto and Alexandra Barrett. London, New York: OUP/EETS O.S. 287, 1984.

*Age of Bede (Bede: Life of Cuthbert; Eddius Stephanus: Life of Wilfrid; Bede: Lives of the Abbots of Wearmouth and Jarrow; Voyage of St Brendan).* Trans. J. F. Webb. Ed. D. H. Farmer. Rev. ed. Harmondsworth: Penguin, 1983.

Aldhelm, *Aldhelm: Prose Works*. Eds M. Lapidge and M. Herren. Cambridge: Brewer; Totowa, N.J.: Rowman and Littlefield, 1979.

Aldhelm, *Riddles of Aldhelm*. Trans. J. H. Pitman. New Haven: Yale U.P., 1925.

*Alfred the Great: Asser's Life of King Alfred and other contemporary sources.* Trans. Simon Keynes and Michael Lapidge. Harmondsworth: Penguin, 1983.

*Anchoritic Spirituality: Ancrene Wisse and Associated Works.* Trans. Anne Savage and Nicholas Watson. New York: Paulist Press, 1991.

*Ancrene Wisse*. Ed. J. R. R. Tolkien. London, New York: OUP/EETS 249, 1962.

*Anglo-Saxon Chronicle*. Ed. and trans. G. N. Garmonsway. London and Melbourne: Dent/Everyman, Rev. edn, 1972.

*Anglo-Saxon Missionaries in Germany*. Ed. and trans. C. H. Talbot. London: Sheed and Ward, 1954.

*Anglo-Saxon Poetic Records* (6 volumes). Eds G. P. Krapp and E. V. K. Dobbie. New York: Columbia U.P., 1931–42.

*Anglo-Saxon Poetry*. Ed. and trans. S. A. J. Bradley. London: Dent/Everyman, 1982.

*Anglo-Saxon Prose*. Ed. and trans. Michael Swanton. London: Dent; Totowa, N. J.: Rowman and Littlefield, Rev. edn, 1979.

*Anglo-Saxon World: An Anthology*. Ed. and trans. Kevin Crossley-Holland. Oxford, New York: OUP, 1984.

*Apocryphal New Testament*. Trans. M. R. James. Oxford: Clarendon, 1924.

Augustine of Hippo, *Saint Augustine: On Christian Doctrine and On Catechising*. Trans. D. W. Robertson. Indianapolis: Bobbs-Merrill, 1958.

Augustine of Hippo, *St Augustine: Concerning the City of God against the Pagans*. Trans. H. Bettenson. Harmondsworth: Penguin, 1972. Repr. 1984.

*Battle of Maldon, AD 991*. Ed. D. Scragg. Oxford: Blackwell, 1991.

Bede, *Bede: A History of the English Church and People (HE)*. Trans. Leo Sherley-Price. Rev. R.E. Latham. Harmondsworth: Penguin, 1968.

Bede, *Bede's Ecclesiastical History of the English People*. Eds. Bertram Colgrave and R. A. B. Mynors. Oxford: Clarendon, 1969.

Bede, *De Temporum Ratione*. Ed. C. W. Jones (with *Chronica Maiora*), Corpus Christiariorum Series Latina. (CCSL) CXXIIIB Turnhout, 1978.

Bede, *Homilies on the Gospels, Book I*. Trans. Lawrence T. Martin and David Hurst. Kalamazoo: Cistercian Publications, 1991.

Bede (*Art of Poetry*), *Libri II: De Arte Metrica et De Schematibus et Tropis*. Ed. and trans. Calvin B. Kendall. Saarbrucken: AQ Verlag, 1991.

Bede, *Life of Cuthbert* in *Age of Bede*.

Bede, *Lives of the Abbots* in *Age of Bede*.

*Beowulf: A Dual-Language Edition*. Trans. Howell D. Chickering. New York, London: Doubleday, 1977.

*Beowulf: A Student Edition*. Ed. George Jack. Oxford: Clarendon, 1994.

*Beowulf and the Fight at Finnsburg*. Ed. F. Klaeber. 3rd edn, Boston, 1950.

*Biblia Sacra Vulgata*. Rev. edn, R. Weber. Stuttgart: Deutsche Bibelgesellschaft, 1969.

*Blickling Homilies*. Ed. R. Morris. London: OUP/EETS O.S. 58, 63, 73, 1967.

Boethius, *Boethius: Consolation of Philosophy*. Trans V.E. Watts. Harmondsworth: Penguin, 1969.

Boniface, *Letters of St Boniface*. Trans. E. Emerton. New York: Columbia U.P., 1940.

*Book of Margery Kempe*. Eds Sanford B. Meech and Hope Emily Allen. London: OUP/EETS O.S. 212, 1940.

*Book of Margery Kempe*. Trans. B. A. Windeatt. Harmondsworth: Penguin, 1985.

*Book of Showings to the Anchoress Julian of Norwich*, Vol. I: Short Text (ST) and Introduction; Vol. II: Long Text (LT). Ed. Edmund College and James Walsh. Toronto: Pontifical Institute of Medieval Studies, 1978.

CB: see *English Lyrics, Religious Lyrics*.

*Chastising of God's Children*. Eds J. Bazire and E. College. Oxford: Blackwell, 1957.

Chaucer, *Riverside Chaucer*. Ed. Larry D. Benson. Oxford: OUP, 3rd. edn, 1988.

*Chaucer Sources and Backgrounds*. Ed. Robert P. Miller. New York: OUP, 1977.

*Chester Mystery Cycle*. Eds R. M. Luminasky and David Mills. London, New York: OUP/EETS. S.S. 3,9, 1994

*A Choice of Anglo-Saxon Verse*. Trans. Richard Hamer. London: Faber, 1970.

Chrysostom, St John, *Homilies on the Gospel of John and the Epistle to the Hebrews; A Select Library of the Nicene and Post-Nicene Fathers of the Christian Church*. Vol XIV. Ed. Philip Schaff. New York, 1889. Repr. 1925.

*Cloud of Unknowing and Book of Privy Counselling*. Ed. Phyllis Hodgson. London: OUP/EETS O.S. 218, 1944.

*Cursor Mundi.* Ed. R. Morris. Vol. I. London: EETS O.S. 57, 1884.

*Deonise Hid Divinitie and Other Treatises on Prayer.* Ed. P. Hodgson. London: OUP/EETS O.S. 231, 1955.

de Voragine, Jacobus, *The Golden Legend.* Ed. Alfred Arpland. London: Holbein Society, 1978.

Douay translation, *Holy Bible Translated From The Latin Vulgate.* Old Testament first published at Douay 1609; New Testament first published at Rheims 1582. Dublin: Richard Coyne, 1829.

*Dream of the Rood.* Eds B. Dickins and A. S. C. Ross. 4th edn, London: Methuen, 1954.

*Dream of the Rood.* Ed. Michael Swanton, 1970. Rev. edn, Exeter: University of Exeter Press, 1987.

*Early English Christian Poetry.* Trans. Charles W. Kennedy. New York: OUP, 1963.

*English Fourteenth Century Apocalypse with Prose Commentary, An.* Ed. Elis Fridner. Lund: Gleerup, 1961.

*English Historical Documents (EHD) Vol. I c. 500–1042.* Ed. Dorothy Whitelock. 2nd edn, London: Eyre Methuen, 1979.

*English Lyrics of the Thirteenth Century (CB XIII).* Ed. Carleton Brown. Oxford: Clarendon, 1932.

*English Mystery Plays.* Ed. Peter Happé. Harmondsworth: Penguin, 1975.

*Everyman and Medieval Miracle Plays.* Ed. A. C. Cawley. London, Melbourne, Toronto: Dent/Everyman, 1974.

*EW.* See Rolle, *English Writings.*

*Exodus.* Ed. Peter J. Lucas. Rev. edn, Exeter: University of Exeter Press, 1994.

*Felix's Life of Saint Guthlac.* Ed. B. Colgrave. Cambridge: CUP, 1985.

*Fifteenth Century Prose and Verse.* Ed. A. W. Pollard. Westminster: Constable, 1903.

*Fifty Earliest English Wills, The.* Ed. Frederick J. Furnivall. London: EETS O.S. 78, 1882.

*Four Morality Plays.* Ed. Peter Happé. Harmondsworth: Penguin, 1979.

Hilton, Walter, *Eight Chapters on Perfectioni.* Ed. Fumio Kuriyagawa. Tokyo: University of Keio, 1967.

Hilton, Walter, *Mixed Life.* Ed. S. J. Ogilvie-Thomson. Salzburg: Salzburg English and Renaissance Studies, 1986.

Hilton, Walter, *Scale of Perfection.* Trans. John P. H. Clark and Rosemary Dorward. New York: Paulist Press, 1991.

*Jacob's Well: An English Treatise on the Cleansing of Man's Conscience.* Ed. Arthur Brandeis. EETS O.S. 115, 1900.

*Jerome: Select Letters.* Ed. F. A. Wright. London: Heinemann, 1933.

*Jocelin of Brakelond: Chronicle of the Abbey of St Albans (1173–1202).* Trans. D. Greenaway and J. Sayers. Oxford, New York: OUP, 1989.

*The Law of Love: English Spirituality in the Age of Wyclif.* Ed. and trans. David L. Jeffrey. Grand Rapids, Michigan: Eerdmans, 1988.

*Liber Celestis of Bridget of Sweden.* Vol. I. Ed. Roger Ellis. OUP/EETS O.S. 291, 1987.

Love, Nicholas, *The Mirror of the Blessed Life of Jesus Christ.* Ed. Michael Sargent. New York: Garland, 1992.

*LT*: see *Book of Showings.*

*Medieval Drama.* Ed. and trans. David Bevington. Boston: Houghton Mifflin Company, 1975.

*Medieval English Lyrics: A Critical Anthology.* Ed. R. T. Davies. London: Faber, 1963.

*Medieval English Prose for Women: Selections from the Katherine Group and Ancrene Wisse.* Ed. B. Millett and J. Wogan-Browne. Oxford: OUP, 1990.

*Meditations on the Life of Christ.* Ed. and trans. I. Ragusa and R. B. Green. Princeton: Princeton U.P., 1961.

*Middle English Miracles of the Virgin.* Ed. Beverley Boyd. San Marino, California: Huntingdon Library, 1964.

*Middle English Sermons.* Ed. W. O. Ross, London: EETS O.S. 209, 1940.

Mirk, John, *John Myrc Instructions For Parish Priests.* Ed. Edward Peacock. London: EETS O.S. 31, 1868. Repr. Kraus, 1973.

Mirk, John, *Mirk's Festial.* Ed. T. Erbe. EETS E.S. 96, 1905. Repr. Kraus 1987.

*Non-Cycle Plays and Fragments.* Ed. N. Davis. Oxford: OUP/EETS S.S. 1, 1970.

*N-Town Play, The.* Ed. Stephen Spector. OUP/EETS S.S. 11–12, 1991.

*The Old English Elegies: a Critical Edition and Genre Study.* Ed. Anne Klinck. Montreal: McGill-Queen's U.P., 1992.

*Old English Exodus.* Ed. Edward Burroughs Irving. New Haven: Yale U.P., 1953.

*Old English Exodus.* Ed. J. Turville-Petre. Trans. and commentary J. R. R. Tolkien. Oxford: Clarendon, 1981.

Orderic Vitalis, *Ecclesiastical History of Orderic Vitalis.* Ed. and trans. Marjorie Chibnall. Oxford: Clarendon, 1969–81.

*The Pastons.* Ed. R. Barber. Harmondsworth: Penguin, 1984.

*Patience.* Ed. J. J. Anderson. Manchester and New York: Manchester U.P., 1969.

*Patrologia Latina* (PL) 221 vols. Ed. J. P. Migne. Paris: Garnier, 1844–64.

*Pearl.* Ed. E. V. Gordon. Oxford: Clarendon, 1953.

*Pearl-Poet: Complete Works.* Trans. Casey Finch. Middle English Texts eds Malcolm Andrew, Ronald Waldron, Clifford Peterson. Berkeley, Oxford: California U.P., 1993.

*Piers Plowman by William Langland: An Edition of the C-text.* Eds Derek Pearsall and Elizabeth Salter. London: Edward Arnold, 1978.

*Piers The Ploughman.* Trans. J. F. Goodridge. Harmondsworth: Penguin. Rev. ed., 1966.

*Poems of the Pearl Manuscript: Pearl, Cleanness, Patience, Sir Gawain and the Green Knight.* Ed. Malcolm Andrew and Ronald Waldron. Rev. edn, Exeter: Exeter U.P., 1987.

*Pontifical of Egbert, Archbishop of York.* London: Surtees Society XXVII, 1853.

*Prymer or Lay Folks' Prayer Book.* Ed. H. Littlehales. EETS O.S. 105, 109, 1895-7.

REED, *Records of Early English Drama: Chester.* Ed. Lawrence M. Clopper. Toronto: University of Toronto Press, 1979.

REED, *Records of Early English Drama: Coventry.* Ed. R. W. Ingram. Toronto: University of Toronto Press, 1981.

REED, *Records of Early English Drama: York.* Eds Alexandra F. Johnston and Margaret Rogerson. Toronto: University of Toronto Press, 1979.

*Regularis Concordia Anglicae Nationis.* Ed. Dom Thomas Symons. London: Nelson, 1953.

*Religious Lyrics of the Fifteenth Century* (CB XV). Ed. Carleton Brown. Oxford: Clarendon, 1939.

*Religious Lyrics of the Fourteenth Century* (CB XIV). Ed. Carleton Brown. Rev. G. V. Smithers. Oxford: Clarendon, 1952.

Rolle, Richard, *English Writings.* Ed. and trans. Rosamund S. Allen. New Jersey: Paulist Press; London: SPCK, 1989.

Rolle, Richard, *English Writings of Richard Rolle, Hermit of Hampole (EW)(Commandment, Form of Living, Ego Dormio, Meditations).* Ed. Hope Emily Allen. Oxford: Clarendon, 1931. Repr. OUP, 1963.

Rolle, Richard, *Fire of Love.* Trans. Clifford Wolters. Harmondsworth: Penguin, 1971.

Rolle, Richard, *Prose and Verse.* Ed. S. Ogilvie Thompson. Oxford: OUP/EETS O.S. 293, 1988.

*Rule of St Benedict.* Trans. Justin McCann. London: Sheed and Ward, 1976.

*Sarum Missal in English.* Ed. Vernon Staley. London: Alexander Moring, 1911.

*The Seafarer.* Ed. I. L. Gordon. London: Methuen, 1960.

*Selection of English Carols, A (SEC).* Ed. R. Greene. Oxford, 1962.

*Selection of Religious Lyrics, A (SRL).* Ed. Douglas Gray. Oxford: Clarendon, 1975.

*Song of Songs: Selections from the Sermons of St Bernard of Clairvaux.* Ed. H. Backhouse. London: Hodder and Stoughton, 1990.

*Sources and Analogues of Old English Poetry.* Vol. I. Eds M. J. B. Allen and D. G. Calder. Cambridge: Brewer, 1976.

*ST*: see *Book of Showings.*

*Tacitus: De Origine et Situ Germanorum (Germania).* Ed. J. G. C. Anderson. Oxford: Clarendon, 1938.

*Three Late Medieval Morality Plays: Mankind, Everyman, Mundus and Infans.* Ed. G. A. Lester. London: A. C. Black; New York: W. W. Norton, 1981.

*Travels of Sir John Mandeville.* Trans. C. W. R. D. Moseley. Harmondsworth: Penguin, 1983.

*Tretise of Miraclis Pleyinge.* Ed. Clifford Davidson. Kalamazoo: Medieval Institute, 1993.

*Two Saxon Chronicles Parallel.* Eds J. Earle and C. Plummer. Oxford: Clarendon, 1892–99.

*Vercelli Book Homilies: Translation from the Anglo-Saxon.* Ed. Lewis E. Nicholson. London: U.P. of America, 1991.

*Vercelli Homilies.* Ed. D. S. Scragg. Oxford: OUP/EETS S.S. 300, 1992.

*The Vision of Piers Plowman: A Critical Edition of the B-text.* Ed. A. V. C. Schmidt. Second edn, London: Dent/Everyman, 1995.

*The Wakefield Plays in the Towneley Cycle.* Ed. A. C. Cawley. Manchester: Manchester U.P., 1958.

*Wanderer, The.* Eds T. P. Dunning and A. J. Bliss. Methuen: London, 1969.

*William Langland, Piers Plowman: A Parallel-Text Edition of the A,B,C, and Z versions.* Ed. A. V. C. Schmidt. London and New York: Longman, 1995.

*William of Malmesbury: Gesta Pontificum Anglorum.* Ed. N. Hamilton. London, 1870.

*William of Malmesbury: Gesta Regum Anglorum.* Trans. J. A. Giles. London, 1847.

*Women Defamed and Women Defended: An Anthology of Medieval Texts.* Ed. Alcuin Blamires with Karen Pratt and C. W. Marx. Oxford: Clarendon, 1992.

*Women's Writing in Middle English.* Ed. Alexandra Barratt. London and New York: Longman, 1992.

*York Plays, The.* Ed. Richard Beadle. London: Edward Arnold, 1982.

*Yorkshire Writers.* Ed. C. Horstman. London: Swan Sonnenschein; New York: Macmillan, 1896.


SECONDARY SOURCES

Ackerman, Robert W. (1958) 'Gawain's Shield: Penitential Doctrine in *Gawain*', *Anglia* 76: 254–65.

Aers, David (1986a) *Chaucer.* Brighton: Harvester Press.

Aers, David, ed. (1986b) *Medieval Literature: Criticism, Ideology and History.* Brighton: Harvester.

Aers, David, (1988) *Community, Gender, and Individual Identity: English Writing 1360–1430.* London and New York: Routledge.

Aerten, Henk and Bremner Rolf, eds (1994) *Companion to Old English Poetry.* Amsterdam: V.U. University Press.

Alexander, Michael (1983) *Old English Literature.* London: Macmillan.

Alford, John A., ed. (1988) *A Companion to Piers Plowman.* Berkeley: University of California Press.

Allchin, A. M. (1980) 'Julian of Norwich and the Continuity of Tradition' in Glasscoe (1980): 72–85.

Allen, H. E. (1918) 'The Origin of the *Ancrene Riwle*', *PMLA* 33: 474–546.

Allen, H. E. (1921) 'The *Ancrene Riwle* and Kilburn Priory', *MLR* 14: 209–20.

Allen, H. E. (1927) *Writings Ascribed to Richard Rolle, Hermit of Hampole and Materials for his Biography.* New York: D. Heath and Co.

Anderson, M. D. (1963) *Drama and Imagery in English Medieval Churches.* Cambridge: CUP.

Arngart (Anderson), O. (1937) *The Seafarer: An Interpretation.* Lund: Kungl. Humanistika Vetenskapssamfundets i Lund Arsberattelse 1: 1–30.

Andrew, Malcolm (1976) '*Patience*: the "Munster Door"', *ELN* 14: 164–7.

Andrew, Malcolm (1996–7) 'Jonah and Christ in *Patience*', *MP* 70: 320–33.

Atkinson, Clarissa W. (1983) *Mystic and Pilgrim: The Book and the World of Margery Kempe.* Ithaca and London: Cornell U.P.

Barrett, Alexandra (1975) 'The Prymer and Its Influence on English Passion Lyrics', *MÆ*, 44: 264–79.

Barrett, Alexandra (1980), 'Anchoritic Aspects of *Ancrene Wisse*', *MÆ* 49: 32–56.

Barron, W. J. R. (1980) *'Trawthe' and Treason: The Sin of Gawain Reconsidered.* Manchester: Manchester U.P.

Bately, Janet (1982) 'Lexical Evidence for the Authorship of the Prose Psalms in the Paris Psalter', *ASE* 10: 69–95.

Bately, Janet (1991) 'The Nature of Old English Prose' in Godden and Lapidge (1991): 71–87.

Beadle, Richard, ed. (1994) *Cambridge Companion to Medieval English Theatre*. Cambridge: CUP.

Beckwith, Sarah (1986) 'A Very Material Mysticism: The Medieval Mysticism of Margery Kempe' in Aers (1986b): 34–57.

Beer, Frances (1992) *Women and Mystical Experience in the Middle Ages*. Woodbridge: Boydell and Brewer.

Bennett, J. A. W. (1982) *Poetry of the Passion: Studies in Twelve Centuries of English Verse*. Oxford: Clarendon.

Benson, David C. and Robertson, Elizabeth (1990) *Chaucer's Religious Tales*. Cambridge: Brewer.

Bessinger, J. B. and Creed, R. P., eds (1965) *Franciplagius: Medieval and Linguistic Studies in Honor of Francis Peabody Magoun Jr*. London: Allen and Unwin.

Bethurum, D. (1966) 'Wulfstan' in Stanley (1966): 210–46.

Bevington, David (1962) *From Mankind to Marlowe*. Cambridge, Mass.: Harvard U.P.

Bevington, David, ed. (1985) *Homo, Memento Finis: The Iconography of Just Judgement in Medieval Art and Drama*. Kalamazoo: Medieval Institute Publications.

Binns, Alison (1989) *Dedications of Monastic Houses in England and Wales 1066–1216*. Woodbridge: Boydell and Brewer.

Bishop, Ian (1968) *Pearl in its Setting: A Critical Study of the Structure and Meaning of the Middle English Poem*. Oxford: Blackwell.

Bishop, Ian (1979) 'Greek Fire in *Ancrene Wisse* and Contemporary Texts', *N&Q* 224: 198–9.

Blanch, Robert J., ed. (1966) *'Sir Gawain' and 'Pearl': Critical Essays*. Bloomington: Indiana U.P.

Blanch, Robert and Wasserman, eds (1991) *Text and Matter: New Critical Readings of the Pearl-Poet*. New York: Whitston.

Bloomfield, Morton W. (1952) *The Seven Deadly Sins*. Michigan: Michigan State College Press.

Bloomfield, Morton (1958) '*Piers Plowman* and the Three Grades of Chastity', *Anglia* 76: 227–53.

Bloomfield, Morton (1963) 'Patristics and Old English Literature: Notes on some poems' in Greenfield (1963): 36–43.

Boase, T. S. R. (1972) *Death in the Middle Ages: Mortality, Judgement and Remembrance*. London: Thames and Hudson.

Boitani, Piero and Torti Anna, eds (1990) *Religion in the Poetry and Drama of the Late Middle Ages in England*. Cambridge: Brewer.

Bolton, W. R. (1986) 'How Boethian is Alfred's Boethius?' in Szarmach (1986): 153–68.

Braswell, Mary Flowers (1983) *The Medieval Sinner: Characterisation and Confession in the Literature of the English Middle Ages*. East Brunswick, N. J., London, Toronto: Associated U.P.

Brewer, D. S. (1966) 'Courtesy and the *Gawain*-Poet' in Lawlor (1966): 54–85.

Brooke, C. N. L. (1961) *From Alfred to Henry III 871–1272*. London: Nelson.

Brooke, C. N. L. (1974) *The Monastic World 1100–1500*. London: Elek.

Brooke, Christopher (1989) *The Medieval Idea of Marriage*. Oxford: OUP.

Brooke, Rosalind and Brooke, Christopher (1984) *Popular Religion in the Middle Ages: Western Europe 1000–1300*. London: Thames and Hudson.

Brown, Phyllis, Crampton, Georgia and Robinson, Fred C. eds (1986) Modes of Interpretation in Old English Literature: Essays in Honour of Stanley B. Greenfield. Toronto, London: Toronto U.P.

Bruce-Mitford, R. (1975–83) *The Sutton Hoo Ship Burial*. London: British Museum.

Burrow, John (1959) 'The Two Confession Scenes in *Gawain*', *MP* 57: 73–9.

Burrow, John (1965) *A Reading of Sir Gawain and the Green Knight*. London: Routledge & Kegan Paul.

Butler, Dom Cuthbert (1967) *Western Mysticism*. 3rd edn, London: Constable.

Cabaniss, A. (1955) 'Beowulf and the Liturgy.' *JEGP* 54: 195–20. Repr. in Nicholson (1963): 223–32.

Calder, D. (1981) *Cynewulf*. Boston: G. K. Hall.

Campbell, James, ed. (1982) *The Anglo-Saxons*. Oxford: Phaidon.

Carver, M. O. ed. (1992) *The Age of Sutton Hoo*. Woodbridge: Brewer.

Chase, Colin (1981) *The Dating of Beowulf*. Toronto: Toronto U.P.

Clark, George (1990) *Beowulf*. Boston: G. K. Hall.

Clark, J. P. H. (1977) 'The "Lightsome Darkness": Aspects of Walter Hilton's Theological Background', *Downside Review* 95: 95–109.

Clements, Richard W. (1986) 'The Production of the *Pastoral Care*' in Szarmach (1986): 129–52.

Clemoes, Peter (1966) 'Aelfric', in Stanley (1966): 176–209.

Conley, J. (1955) '*Pearl* and a Lost Tradition', *JEGP* 54: 332–47.

Connelly, Joseph (1957) *Hymns of the Roman Liturgy*. London.

Coogan, Sister Mary Philippa, (1947) *An Interpretation of the Moral Play Mankind*. Washington, D.C.: Catholic University of America Press.

Cooper, Helen (1989) *Oxford Guide to the Canterbury Tales*. 2nd edn Oxford: Clarendon.

Cowen, Janet (1983) 'Heven and erthe in lytyl space' in Neuss (1983).

Cross, J. E. and Tucker S. I. (1960), 'Allegorical Tradition and the Old English *Exodus*', *Neophilologus* 44: 122–7.

Cross, J. E. (1961) 'On the genre of the *Wanderer*', *Neophilogus* 45: 3–75.

Cross, J. E. (1965) 'Oswald and Byrhtnoth: A Christian saint and a Hero who is a Christian', *ES* 46: 93–109.

Damico, Helen and Olsen, Alexandra Hennessy (1990) *New Readings On Women In Old English Literature*. Bloomington: Indiana U.P.

Davidson, Clifford (1975) 'The Realism of the York Realist and the York Passion Play', *Speculum* 50: 270–83.

Davidson, Clifford (1986) *The Saint Play in Medieval Europe*. Kalamazoo: Medieval Institute Publications.

Davis, N. (1966) 'A Note on *Pearl*', *RES* n.s. 7: 403–5 lxviii, 294.

Dean, James (1989) 'Chaucer's Repentance: A Likely Story', *Chaucer Review* 24 No. 1, 64–76.

Deanesley, Margaret (1963) *The Pre-Conquest Church in England*. London: Black.

Delany, Sheila (1983) *Writing Woman: Women Writers and Women in Literature, Medieval to Modern*. New York: Schocken Books.

Delany, Sheila (1990) *Medieval Literary Politics: Shapes of Idolatry*. Manchester: Manchester U.P.

Denny, Neville, ed. (1973) *Medieval Drama*. London: Edward Arnold.

Dickins, B. C. and Fox C., eds (1950) *The Early Cultures of North-West Europe*. Cambridge: CUP.

Dickman, Susan (1980) 'Margery Kempe and the English Devotional Tradition' in Glasscoe (1980): 156–72.

Dillon, Janette (1993a) *Geoffrey Chaucer*. London: Macmillan.

Dillon, Janette (1993b) '*Mankind* and the politics of Englysch Laten', *Medievalia and Humanistica* NS 20: 41–64.

Dobson, E. J. (1976) *The Origins of Ancrene Wisse*. Oxford: Clarendon.

Dodwell, C. R. (1982) *Anglo-Saxon Art: A New Perspective*. Ithaca: Cornell U.P.

Donahue, Charles (1965) '*Beowulf* and Christian Tradition', *Traditio* 7: 263–77.

Du Boulay, F. R. H. (1991) *The England of Piers Plowman: William Langland and His Vision of the Fourteenth Century*. Cambridge: Brewer.

Duffy, E. (1992) *The Stripping of the Altars: Traditional Religion in England 1400–1580*. New Haven: Yale U.P.

Edwards, A. S. G. (1984) *Middle English Prose: A Critical Guide to Major Authors and Genres*. New Brunswick, N.J. Rutgers U.P.

Elkins, Sharon (1988) *Holy Women of Twelfth-Century England*. Chapel Hill, N.C. University of North Carolina Press.

Ellis, Roger (1986) *Patterns of Religious Narrative in the Canterbury Tales*. Totowa, N.J. Barnes and Noble.

Evans, A. C. (1986) *Sutton Hoo Ship Burial*. London: British Museum.

Evans, J. M. (1968) *Paradise Lost and The Genesis Tradition*. Oxford: Clarendon.

Farrar, R. S. (1973) 'Structure and Function in Representative Old English Saints' Lives', *Neophil* 57: 83–9.

Field, Rosalind (1986) 'The Heavenly Jerusalem in *Pearl*', *MLR* 81: 7–17.

Fell, Christine (1984) *Women in Anglo-Saxon England*. London: British Museum.

Fell, Christine (1991) 'Perceptions of Transience' in Godden and Lapidge (1991): 172–205.

Fowler, David C. (1976) *The Bible in Early English Literature*. Seattle: University of Washington Press.

Fowler, David C. (1984) *The Bible in Middle English Literature*. Seattle: University of Washington Press.

Frantzen, Allen (1983) *The Literature of Penance in Anglo-Saxon England*. Brunswick, N.J.: Rutgers U.P.

Frantzen, Allen (1986) *King Alfred*. Boston: G. K. Hall.

Fulk, R. D. ed. (1991) *Interpretations of Beowulf: A Critical Anthology*. Bloomington: Indiana U.P.

Garde, Judith (1991) *Old English Poetry in Christian Perspective*. Cambridge: Brewer.

Gardiner, H. C. (1946) *Mysteries End*. New Haven: Yale U.P.

Gardner, H. L. (1937) 'Walter Hilton and the Mystical Tradition in England', *E&S* 22: 108–13.

Garrett, R. M. (1918) *Pearl: An Interpretation*. Seattle: University of Washington.

Gatch, Milton McC. (1977) *Preaching and Theology in Anglo-Saxon England: Aelfric and Wulfstan*. Toronto: University of Toronto Press.

Georgianna, Linda (1981) *The Solitary Self: Individuality in the Ancrene Wisse*. Cambridge, Mass.: Harvard U.P.

Glasscoe, Marion, ed. (1980) *The Medieval Mystical Tradition in England*. Exeter: University of Exeter.

Glasscoe, Marion (1990) 'Time of Passion: Latent Relationships Between Liturgy and Meditation in Two Middle English Mystics [Rolle and

Julian]' in Phillips (1990): 141–60.

Glasscoe, Marion (1993) *English Medieval Mystics: Games of Faith*. London and New York: Longman.

Gneuss, Helmut (1986) 'King Alfred and the history of Anglo-Saxon libraries, in Brown, Crampton, Robinson (1986): 29–49

Godden, Malcolm and Lapidge, Michael (1991) *Cambridge Companion to Old English Literature*. Cambridge: CUP.

Godfrey, John (1962) *The Church in Anglo-Saxon England*. Cambridge: CUP.

Goldsmith, Margaret (1970) *The Mode and Meaning of 'Beowulf'*. London: Athlone Press.

Gordon, Ian A. (1966) *The Movement of English Prose*. London: Longman.

Graef, H. (1985) *Mary: A History of Doctrine and Devotion. Vol I: From the Beginnings to the Eve of the Reformation*. New York and London: Sheed & Ward.

Grantley, Darryll (1994) 'Saints' Plays' in Beadle (1994): 265–9.

Gray, D. (1972) *Themes and Images in the Medieval English Religious Lyric*. London: Routledge & Kegan Paul.

Gray, D. (1990) 'Popular Religion and Late Medieval Literature', in Boitani and Torti (1990): 1–28.

Gray, Nick (1986) 'The Clemency of Cobblers: A Reading of "Glutton's Confession" in *Piers Plowman*,' *LSE*, n.s.: 61–75.

Grayson, Janet (1974) *Structure and Imagery In Ancrene Wisse*. Hanover: University of New Hampshire.

Green, M., ed. (1983) *The Old English Elegies: New Essays in Criticism and Research*. Rutherford, N.J.: Fairleigh Dickinson U.P.

Green, Richard Hamilton (1962) 'Gawain's Shield and the Quest for Perfection', *ELH* 29: 121–39.

Greenfield, S. B., ed. (1963) *Studies in Old English Literature in Honor of Arthur G. Brodeur*. Eugene: Oregon U.P.

Greenfield, S. B. and Calder, D. G. (1986) *A New Critical History of Old English Literature*. New York: New York U.P.

Grundy, Lynne (1989) *Books and Grace*: Aelfric's Theology. London: King's College.

Hamilton, Bernard (1986) *Religion in the Medieval West*. London: Edward Arnold.

Hamilton, Marie P. (1955) 'The Meaning of the Middle English *Pearl*', *PMLA* 70: 805–24.

Hardison, O. B. (1965) *Christian Rite and Christian Drama in the Middle Ages*. Baltimore: Johns Hopkins.

Harris, John Wesley (1992) *Medieval Theatre in Context: An Introduction*. London and New York: Routledge & Kegan Paul.

Henry, P. L. (1966) *The Early English and Celtic Lyric*. London: Allen and Unwin.

Hill, Thomas (1994) 'Christian Language in *Beowulf*', in Aertsen (1994): 63–77.

Hodgson, Phyllis (1955) 'Walter Hilton and *The Cloud of Unknowing*: A Problem of Authorship Reconsidered', *MLR* 50: 395–406.

Hodgson, Phyllis (1964) 'The Orchard of Syon and the English Mystical Tradition', *Proceedings of the British Academy* 50: 229–250.

Hodgson, Phyllis (1967) *Three Fourteenth Century English Mystics*, London: Longman, Green and Co.

Holton, Frederick (1982) 'Old English Sea Imagery and the Interpretation of *The Seafarer*', *YES* 12: 208–17.

Hughes, Kathleen (1987) *Church and Society in Ireland A.D. 400–1200*. London: Variorum Reprints.

Hunter Blair, Peter (1970) *The World of Bede*. London: Secker and Warburg.

Hunter Blair, Peter (1976) *Northumbria in the Days of Bede*. London: Gollancz.

Huppé, B. (1959) *Doctrine and Poetry, Augustine's Influence on Old English Poetry*. New York: State University of New York Press.

Hussey, S. S., ed. (1969) *Piers Plowman: Critical Approaches*. London: Methuen; New York: Barnes and Noble.

Irving, Edward B. (1989) *Rereading Beowulf*. Philadelphia: University of Pennsylvania Press.

Jack R. D. S. (1989) *Patterns of Divine Comedy: A Study of Medieval Drama*. Cambridge: Brewer.

Jackson, Kenneth (1935) *Studies in Early Celtic Nature Poetry*. Cambridge: CUP.

Jacobs, Nicholas (1977) 'Anglo-Danish Relations, Poetic Archaism, and the Date of *Beowulf*: A Reconsideration of the Evidence', *Poetica* (Tokyo) 8: 23–43.

Jeffrey, David L. (1973) 'English Saints' Plays', in Denny (1973): 69–89.

Jeffrey, David L. (1975) *The Early English Lyric and Franciscan Spirituality*. Lincoln, Neb.: University of Nebraska Press.

Jeffrey, David L., ed. (1984) *Chaucer and Scriptural Tradition*. Ottowa: University of Ottawa Press.

Jeffrey, David L., ed. (1992) *Dictionary of Biblical Tradition in English Literature*. Grand Rapids, Michigan: Eerdmans.

Johnston, Alexandra (1975) 'The Plays of the Religious Guilds of York: The Creed Play and the Paternoster Play', *Speculum* 50: 55–90.

Jones, Glyn (1984) *History of the Vikings*. Oxford, New York: OUP.

Jones, Terry (1980) *Chaucer's Knight: Portrait of a Medieval Mercenary*. London: Weidenfield and Nicholson.

Kahrl, Stanley J. (1974) *Traditions of Medieval English Drama*. London: Hutchinson.

Kane, George (1965) *Piers Plowman: The Evidence for Authorship*. London: Athlone Press.

Kean, P. M. (1967) *Pearl: An Interpretation*. London: Routledge & Kegan Paul.

Keen, Maurice (1990) *English Society in the Later Middle Ages 1348–1500*. Harmondsworth: Penguin.

Kelly, H. A. (1975) *Love and Marriage in the Age of Chaucer*. Ithaca: Cornell U.P.

Kelly, H. A. (1993) 'Sacraments, Sacramentals and Lay Piety in Chaucer's England', *Chaucer Review* 28, No. 1: 5–22.

King, Pamela (1994) 'Morality Plays' in Beadle (1994): 240–64.

Knowles, David (1964) *The English Mystical Tradition*. London: Burns & Oates.

Knowles, D. and Hadcock, R. N. (1971) *Medieval Religious Houses in England and Wales*. 2nd edn, London: Longman.

Kolve, V. A. (1966) *The Play Called Corpus Christi*. London: Edward Arnold.

Lafarge, Margaret Wade (1986) *Women in Medieval Life*. London: Hamish Hamilton.

Laistner, M. L. W. (1957) *The Intellectual Heritage of the Early Middle Ages*. Ed. Chester G. Starr. Ithaca: Cornell U.P.; London: OUP.

Lampe, G. W. H., ed. (1969) *Cambridge History of the Bible Vol 2. The West: From the Fathers to the Reformation*. Cambridge: CUP.

Lawlor, John, ed. (1966) *Patterns of Love and Courtesy: Essays in Memory of C. S. Lewis*. London: Edward Arnold.

Lawrence, C. H. (1984) *Medieval Monasticism*. London and New York: Longman.

Lewis, C. S. (1964) *The Discarded Image*. Cambridge: CUP.

Luttrell, C. A. (1962) 'The Medieval Tradition of the Pearl Virginity', *MÆ* 31: 194–200.

Madeleva, Sister Mary (1925) *Pearl: A Study in Spiritual Dryness*. New York: Appleton.

Mandel, Jerome (1987) *Alternative Readings in Old English Poetry*. New York: Peter Lang.

Mann, Jill (1973) *Medieval Estates Satire*. Cambridge: CUP.

Mann, Jill (1991) *Geoffrey Chaucer*. New York: Harvester Wheatsheaf.

Martin, Priscilla (1990) *Chaucer's Women*. London: Macmillan.

Mayr-Harting, H. (1991) *The Coming of Christianity to Anglo-Saxon England*. 3rd edn, London: Batsford.

McEntire, Sandra J., edn, (1992) *Margery Kempe: A Book of Essays*. New York: Garland.

McNamee, M. B., S. J. (1960) 'Beowulf – An Allegory of Salvation?' *JEGP* 59: 190–207. Repr. in Nicholson (1963): 331–52.

Meade, Dorothy (1988) *The Medieval Church in England*. London: Churchman.

Medcalf, Stephen (1980) 'Medieval Psychology and Medieval Mystics' in Glasscoe (1980): 120–55.

Meredith, Peter (1994) 'The Towneley Cycle' in Beadle (1994): 134–62.

Millett, Bella (1992) 'The Origins of *Ancrene Wisse*: New Answers, New Questions', *MÆ* 61. No 2: 206–28.

Morgan, Gerald (1991) *Sir Gawain and the Green Knight and the Idea of Righteousness*. Co. Down: Irish Academic Press.

Morrish, Jennifer (1986) 'King Alfred's letter as a Source on Learning in the Ninth Century' in Szarmach (1986): 87–107.

Morse, Charlotte, C. (1978) *The Pattern of Judgement in the Quest and Cleanness*. Columbia: University of Missouri Press.

Nelson, Alan H. (1974) *The Medieval English Stage: Corpus Christi Pageants and Plays*. Chicago, London: University of Chicago Press.

Neuss, Paula, ed. (1983) *Aspects of Early English Drama*. Cambridge: Brewer.

Newton, Sam (1993) *The Origins of Beowulf*. Cambridge: Brewer.

Nicholson, Lewis E., ed. (1963) *An Anthology Of Beowulf Criticism*. Notre Dame, Indiana: Notre Dame U.P.

Nicholson, Lewis E. and Frese, Dolores Warwick, eds (1975) Anglo-Saxon Poetry: Essays in appreciation of John C. McGalliard Notre Dame, Indiana: Notre-Dame U.P.

Ogilvy, J. N. D. (1967) *Books Known to the English 597–1066*. Cambridge, Mass: Medieval Academy of America.

Orchard, Andy (1995) *Pride and Prodigies: Studies in the Monsters of the Beowulf MSS*. Cambridge: Brewer.

Owen, Gale R. (1981) *Rites and Religions of the Anglo-Saxons*. Newton Abbot, London: David and Charles; Totowa, N.J.: Barnes and Noble.

Owst, G. R. (1966) *Literature and Pulpit in Medieval England*. Rev. edn, Oxford: Blackwell.

Pantin, W. A. (1955) *The English Church in the Fourteenth Century*. Cambridge: CUP.

Parker, Mary A. (1987) *Beowulf and Christianity*. New York: Peter Lang.

Patterson, F. A. (1966) *The Middle English Penitential Lyric: A Study and Collection of Early Religious Verse*. New York: Columbia U.P., 1911: Repr. AMS Press, 1966.

Pearsall, Derek and Salter, Elizabeth (1973) *Landscapes and Seasons of the Medieval World*. London: Elek.

Phillips, Helen, ed. (1990) *Langland, The Mystics and the Medieval English Religious Tradition: Essays in Honour of S. S. Hussey*. Cambridge: Brewer.

Pope, John (1965) 'Dramatic Voices in the *Wanderer* and the *Seafarer*' in Bessinger and Creed (1965): 164–93.

Potter, Robert (1975) *The English Morality Play*. London: Routledge & Kegan Paul.

Power, Eileen (1975) *Medieval Women*. Ed. M. Poston. Cambridge: CUP.

Pratt, John (1987) 'Was Chaucer's Knight Really a Mercenary?', *Chaucer Review* 22: 8–27.

Proppé, K. (1973) 'King Alfred's *Consolation of Philosophy*', *NM* 74: 635–48.

Prosser, Eleanor (1961) *Drama and Religion in the English Mystery Plays*. Stanford, Conn.: Stanford U.P.

Putter, Ad (1996) *An Introduction to the* Gawain-*Poet*. London and New York: Longman.

Raw, Barbara (1960) 'As Dew in Aprille', *MLR* 55: 411–14.

Raw, B. C. (1970) '*The Dream of the Rood* and its connections with early Christian art', *MÆ*, 39: 239–56.

Raw, Barbara (1990) *Anglo-Saxon Crucifixion Iconography and the Art of the Monastic Revival*. Cambridge, New York, Sydney: CUP.

Raw, Barbara (1992) 'Royal Power and Royal Symbols in *Beowulf*' in Carver (1992): 167–74.

Redmond, James, ed. (1983) *Drama and Religion*. Cambridge, New York: CUP.

Richardson, Christine and Johnston, Jackie (1991) *Medieval Drama*. London: Macmillan.

Riehle, W. (1977) 'The Problem of Walter Hilton's Possible Authorship of the *Cloud of Unknowing*', *NM* 78: 31–45.

Riehle, Wolfgang (1981) *The Middle English Mystics*. London: Routledge & Kegan Paul.

Riley-Smith, Jonathan (1977) *What Were the Crusades?* London: Macmillan.

Riley-Smith, Louise and Riley-Smith, Jonathan (1981) *The Crusades: Idea and Reality 1095–1271*. London: Edward Arnold.

Robbins, R. H. (1940) 'The Authors of the Middle English Religious Lyrics', *JEGP* 39: 230–8.

Robertson, D. W. (1950) 'The Pearl as a Symbol', *MLN* 65: 155–61.

Robertson D. W. and Huppé, Bernard F. (1951) *Piers Plowman and Scriptural Tradition*. Princeton N.J.: Princeton U.P.

Robinson, Fred (1991) 'Beowulf' in Godden and Lapidge (1991): 142–59.

Robinson, J. W. (1963) ' The Art of the York Realist', *MP* 60: 241–51.

Robinson J. W. (1971) 'A Commentary on the York Play of the Birth of Jesus', *JEGP* 70: 241–55.

Rollason, David (1989) *Saints and Relics in Anglo-Saxon England*. Oxford: Blackwell.

Ross, L. (1967–8) 'Structure and Symbol in the *Secunda Pastorum*', *Comparative Drama* 1: 122–43.

Rouse, E. Clive (1980) *Discovering Wall Paintings*. Aylesbury: Shire.

Rubin, Miri (1991) *Corpus Christi: The Eucharist in Late Medieval Culture*. Cambridge, New York, Melbourne: CUP.

Schell, Edgar T. (1968) 'On the Imitation of Life's Pilgrimage in the *Castle of Perseverance*', *JEGP* 67: 235–48.

Schoeck, Richard J. (1960) 'Chaucer's Prioress: Mercy and Tender Heart', in Schoeck and Taylor (1960): 245–58.

Schoeck, Richard J. and Taylor, Jerome (1960) *Chaucer Criticism, Vol. I: The Canterbury Tales*. Notre Dame, Indiana: Notre Dame U.P.

Schofield, W. H. (1904) 'The Nature and Fabric of *The Pearl*', *PMLA* 19: 154–215.

Sheingorn, Pamela (1985) '"For God is Such a Doomsman": Origins and Development of the Theme of the Last Judgement' in Bevington (1985): 15–58.

Shepherd, G. (1966) 'Scriptural Poetry' in Stanley (1966): 1–36.

Shepherd, G. (1969) 'English Versions of the Scriptures before Wyclif' in Lampe (1969): 362–87.

Shippey, T. A. (1972) *Old English Verse*. London: Hutchinson.

Shippey, T. A. (1979) 'Wealth and Wisdom in King Alfred's *Preface to the Old English Pastoral Care*', *English Historical Review* 94: 346–55.

Short, Douglas (1980) *Beowulf Scholarship: An Annotated Bibliography*. New York: Garland.

Simpson, James (1990) *Piers Plowman: An Introduction to the B-text*. London and New York: Longman.

Smalley, Beryl (1983) The Study of the Bible in the Middle Ages. Oxford: Basil Blackwell, 1952. 3rd edn, 1983.

Smith, James (1975) 'The garments that honour the cross in *The Dream of the Rood*', *ASE* 4: 29–35.

Smithers, G. V. (1957, 1959) 'The Meaning of *The Seafarer* and *The Wanderer*', *MÆ* 26: 137–53; 28: 1–22, 99–104.

Smyth, Alfred P. (1995) *Alfred the Great*. Oxford: OUP.

Southern, R. W. (1953) *The Making of the Middle Ages*. London: Hutchinson.

Southern, R. W. (1970) *Western Society and the Church in the Middle Ages*. Harmondsworth: Penguin.

Spearing, A. C. (1970) *The Gawain-Poet: A Critical Study*. Cambridge: CUP.

Staley, Lynn (1994) *Margery Kempe's Dissenting Fictions*. Philadelphia: Pennsylvania U.P.

Stanbury, Sarah (1991) *Seeing the Gawain-Poet: Description and the Act of Perception*. Philadelphia: University of Pennsylvania Press.

Stanley, E. G., ed. (1966) *Continuations and Beginnings: Studies in Old English Literature*. London: Nelson.

Sumption, Jonathan (1975) *Pilgrimage: An Image of Medieval Religion*. London: Faber.

Swanton, Michael (1987) *English Literature before Chaucer*. London and New York: Longman.

Szarmach, Paul E., ed. (1986) *Studies in Earlier Old English Prose*. Albany, N.Y.: State University of New York Press.

Szarmach, Paul E. and Huppé, Bernard F., ed. (1978) *The Old English Homily and Its Backgrounds*. New York: State University of New York Press.

Tentler, T. N. (1977) *Sin and Confession on the Eve of the Reformation*. Princeton, N.J.: Princeton U.P.

Thompson, Sally (1991) *Women Religious*. Oxford: OUP.

Tolkien, J. R. R. (1936) '*Beowulf*: The Monsters and the Critics', *Proceedings of the British Academy* 22: 245–95. Repr. in Nicholson (1963) and Fulk (1991).

Trahern, Joseph B. Jr. (1991) 'Fatalism and the millenium' in Godden and Lapidge (1991).

Turville-Petre, Thorlac (1977) *The Alliterative Revival*. London, Totowa, N.J.: Brewer.

Twycross, Meg (1983) 'Books for the Unlearned' in Redmond (1983): 65–110.

Twycross, Meg (1994) 'The Theatricality of Medieval English Plays' in Beadle (1994): 37–84.

Vickrey, John (1982) 'Some Hypotheses Concerning *The Seafarer*, Lines 1–47', *Archiva* 219: 57–77.

Wakelin, M. (1979) 'Richard Rolle and the Language of Mystical Experience in the Fourteenth Century', *Downside Review* 97: 192–203.

Wakelin, M. (1985) 'A Note on Preaching, "'Roodes and Othyr Images" in Medieval England', *Downside Review* 350: 76–87.

Ward, Benedicta (1987) *Miracles and the Medieval Mind: Theory, Record and Event 1001–1215*. London: Scholar Press, 1982. Rev. edn, Aldershot, Wildwood House.

Ward, Benedicta (1990) *The Venerable Bede*. London: Geoffrey Chapman.

Warren, Ann (1985) *Anchorites and Their Patrons in Medieval England*. Berkeley: University of California Press.

Wasserman, Julian N. and Blanch, Robert J. (1986) *Chaucer in the Eighties*. New York: Syracuse U.P.

Watkin, E. I. (1979) *On Julian of Norwich, and In Defence of Margery Kempe*. Rev. ed. Exeter: University of Exeter Press.

Watson, Nicholas (1991) *Richard Rolle and the Invention of Authority*. Cambridge: CUP.

Watts, V. E. (1963) '*Pearl* as a Consolatio', *MÆ* 32: 34–6.

Weber, Sarah A. (1969) *Theology and Poetry in the Middle English Lyric*. Columbus: Ohio State U.P.

Wellek, Réne (1933) '*Pearl*: An Interpretation of the Middle English Poem', *Studies in English by Members of the English Seminar of the Charles University, Prague* 4: 5–33. Repr. in Blanch (1966).

Wenzel, Siegfried (1967) 'The Three Enemies of Man', *MS* 29: 47–66.

Wenzel, Siegfried (1986) *Preachers, Poets and the Early English Lyric*. Princeton, N.J.: Princeton U.P.

Wenzel, Siegfried (1988) 'Medieval Sermons' in Alford (1988): 155–72.

Whallon, William (1962) 'The Christianity of *Beowulf*', *MP* 60: 81–94.

Whitelock, Dorothy (1950) 'The Interpretation of *The Seafarer*' in Dickins and Fox (1950): 261–72.

Whitelock, Dorothy (1951) *The Audience of Beowulf*. Oxford: Clarendon.

Whitelock, Dorothy (1966) 'The Prose of Alfred's Reign' in Stanley (1966): 67–103.

Whitelock, Dorothy (1972) *The Beginnings of English Society*. Harmondsworth: Penguin, 2nd edn.

Whitelock, Dorothy (1980) *From Bede to Alfred: Studies in Early Anglo-Saxon Literature and History*. London: Variorum Reprints.

Wickham, Glynne (1987) *The Medieval Stage*. Cambridge: CUP. 3rd edn.

Wilson, David (1992) *Anglo-Saxon Paganism*. London and New York: Routledge & Kegan Paul.

Wilson, Edward (1976) *The Gawain-Poet*. Leiden: E. J. Brill.

Wilson, J. H. (1972) *Christian Theology and Old English Poetry*. The Hague: Mouton.

Woolf, Rosemary (1957) 'The Effect of Typology on the English Medieval Plays of Abraham and Isaac', *Speculum* 32: 805–25. Repr. Woolf (1986): 49–76.

Woolf, Rosemary (1958) 'Doctrinal Influences on *The Dream of the Rood*', *MÆ* 27: 137–53. Repr. Woolf (1986): 29–48.

Woolf, Rosemary (1962), 'The Theme of Christ the Lover-Knight in Medieval English Literature', *RES*, n.s. 13: 1–16. Repr. Woolf (1986): 99–118.

Woolf, Rosemary (1966) 'Saints' Lives' in Stanley (1966): 37–65. Repr. Woolf (1986): 219–44.

Woolf, Rosemary (1968) *The English Religious Lyric in the Middle Ages*. Oxford: Clarendon.

Woolf, Rosemary (1969) 'The Tearing of the Pardon' in Hussey (1969): 50–75. Repr. Woolf (1986): 131–56.

Woolf, Rosemary (1972) *The English Mystery Plays*. London: Routledge & Kegan Paul.

Woolf, Rosemary (1975) '*The Wanderer, The Seafarer*, and the Genre of *Planctus*' in Nicholson (1975). Repr. in Woolf (1986): 157–74.

Woolf, Rosemary (1986) *Art and Doctrine: Essays On Medieval Literature*. Ed. Heather O'Donoghue. London: Hambledon Press.

Yorke, Barbara (1990) *Kings and Kingdoms of Early Anglo-Saxon England*. London: Seaby.

Young, Karl (1933) *The Drama of the Medieval Church*. Oxford: Clarendon.

Ziegler, Philip (1969) *The Black Death*. Harmondsworth: Penguin.

# Index

Page numbers in bold type indicate entries in the Reference Section